Born in England, Tracey Cox is a well-known sex and relationships expert. She has a degree in psychology, she's the agony aunt for *Cosmopolitan* (Australia) and hosted her own radio show in Australia before moving back to the UK. She now has her own TV show based on her first book, *Hot Sex: How to do it*. *Hot Sex* became an instant international bestseller and is also published by Corgi.

Don't miss Tracey Cox's worldwide bestseller, *HOT SEX: How to do it*:

'Tracey Cox is stunningly well informed about sex. She can tell a G-spot from an A-spot and could probably find both of them before the rest of us have got the map references'
The Mirror, UK

'A hilarious read with the power to transform your sex life from average to outstanding overnight'
FHM Magazine, Australia

'Frank, forthright and at times hysterically funny . . . the one sex manual you'll want to read cover to cover'
Cosmopolitan, Australia

'I heartily recommend this book and I'll be hanging on to my copy to give to my daughter'
She/More Magazine, New Zealand

'A brilliant book to get hold of if you're planning a night in with the girls. Once you've had a giggle, take it home to your fella and scare the life out of him with everything you've learnt!'
Voted Best Book, *Woman's Own*, UK

Also by Tracey Cox

HOT SEX

and published by Corgi Books

HOT
RELATIONSHIPS
HOW TO HAVE ONE

TRACEY COX

CORGI BOOKS

HOT RELATIONSHIPS
A CORGI BOOK : 0 552 14784 2

First publication in Great Britain

First published in Australia and New Zealand in 1999 by Bantam Australia,
an imprint of Random House Australia.

PRINTING HISTORY
Corgi edition published 2000

1 3 5 7 9 10 8 6 4 2

Set in Galliard and Frutiger by
Phoenix Typesetting, Ilkley, West Yorkshire.

Corgi Books are published by Transworld Publishers,
61–63 Uxbridge Road, London W5 5SA,
a division of The Random House Group Ltd,
in Australia by Random House Australia (Pty) Ltd,
20 Alfred Street, Milsons Point, Sydney, NSW 2061, Australia,
in New Zealand by Random House New Zealand Ltd,
18 Poland Road, Glenfield, Auckland 10, New Zealand
and in South Africa by Random House (Pty) Ltd,
Endulini, 5a Jubilee Road, Parktown 2193, South Africa.

Edited by Jude McGee
Cover and text design by Cheryl Collins Design

Reproduced, printed and bound in Great Britain by
Cox & Wyman Ltd, Reading, Berkshire.

To my family, for their endless love and support

Contents

Acknowledgements

So many people contributed to this book, it would be impossible to name them all. First billing, though, has to go to my family for their constant encouragement. A huge thanks to Mum, Terry, Dad, Mo, Nigel, Deb, Doug, and my niece and nephew, Maddie and Charlie, who make my heart thud with pride and give me supreme faith in the younger generation. Thanks also to all my friends, who put up with me saying no to almost every invitation but still called to say hi and slid chocolate biscuits under the door.

Special thanks go to: Ute Junker, my clever friend, for spending her precious spare time proof-reading and giving 'Seriously – it's great!' pep-talks; Janet Muggivan for to-die-for roast potatoes and girly chats when I needed them most; Pat Ingram and Mia Freedman for their friendship and overwhelming support of all my ventures; the entire team at Transworld, my publishers, but most particularly Shona Martyn, Jude McGee, Louise Thurtell, Nerrilee Weir and Karen Reid (my wonderfully wicked partner in crime) in Australia, Larry Finlay, Diana Beaumont and Emma Dowson in the UK, and Christine Brooks and Jessica Bellucci in the US. You've all worked so hard to make my books a success, I can't thank you enough; thank you also to all the journalists and reviewers who said lovely things about my last book – you helped make this one happen; thanks also go to all the psychologists who contributed via stories I've had previously published, particularly Dr Nicholas Tarrier, Phillip Gorrell, Eric Fleming, the much-adored Gerard Webster, Grant Brecht and my mentor, Dr Janet Hall; and a HUGE thank you to everyone who bared their souls and contributed real-life stories and quotes for the book: Deb, Steve, Leonie Robertson, Mark Watson, Nic McClure, John Graham, Craig

Syphers and others who didn't want to be named for fear of dropping themselves in it.

Thanks also to the various magazines who let me pinch ideas, sentences and small sections from my previously published stories. Small portions of text contained in this book originally appeared in:

Australian Cosmopolitan: 'Jealousy', September 1990; 'Women who love sex and how men tell', August 1995; 'Should you give him an ultimatum?', April 1996; 'He's back but will he stay?', May 1996; 'Relationships in the 90s', May 1996; 'The 20 biggest relationship roadblocks', July 1996; 'Will they ever get on?', January 1997; 'Stop being sensible', February 1997; 'Why he's hurting more than you', February 1997; 'Why your first lover affects you for life', March 1997; 'His Ex – 8 signs he's not over her', June 1997; 'Can Ex-lovers be friends?', October 1997.

She: 'Divorce', August 1996.

marie claire: 'Supermarket sex', June 1996.

Elle: 'Two's a couple, three's counselling', April 1997.

Mode for Brides: 'Is there sex after marriage?'; 'To have or not to have children'.

The quotes from Shirley Glass on pages 353 and 358 are from 'Shattered Vows', *Psychology Today*, August 1998, page 78.

Publisher's Note

This book was originally published in Australia so a few changes have been made to the text in order to make the information as relevant and helpful as possible for readers in the UK.

Introduction

I told my best friend I was writing a book about relationships and she spat wine halfway across the bar.

'You can't!' she said. 'You're, you know, *divorced*!'

'Oh my *God*!' I said. 'I'd completely forgotten.'

Not. Look, I admit it. It doesn't make me feel terribly confident either when I'm described as 'Sex and Relationships Expert. Divorced'. It does sound like a contradiction in terms, so I thought I'd better explain myself up front.

What qualifies me as a relationships 'expert'? Well, I've got a psychology degree for a start. I've also spent close on a decade writing, researching and talking about sex and relationships. I'm *Cosmopolitan*'s agony aunt, I do a talkback radio show on relationships – and I've had, er, lots of practice. I've been married and divorced. I've had six-week flings, several two-year this-must-be-the-one live-in relationships, first-date fizzles, four-year triumphs (and yes, the odd overnighter as well). But if you want reassurance that I met, married and am currently snuggled up on the couch with Mr Bloody Perfect, you're reading the wrong book. I'm just your average 37-year-old who happens to know a lot about relationships on both an academic and personal basis. (And I have to say, out of the two, I've probably learnt more from experience and talking to real people than I have from those psychological studies, however fascinating they are.)

What this book aims to do is answer all the questions people ask me about relationships, over and over and over again. What's wrong with the billion advice books already out there? Personally, I found most of them either mind-numbingly boring, tacky and sexist (how to get a woman in bed within 60 seconds) or a bit too mung-beany and spiritual. Maybe chanting 'ommm' and tinging bells does help, but I've always found rolling up to a great party in a stunning little black dress gets better results, if a date's what you're after.

This book is for singles and couples, men and women, heterosexuals, bisexuals, gays and lesbians. While it's predominantly addressed to straight couples (simply because constantly writing girl, boy or boy, boy or girl, girl all the time would have been confusing), all the advice applies to every couple combination. The book format follows a relationship in logical sequence, so it's a good idea to start at the beginning. There's everything from self-confidence, standing out from the crowd and spotting losers to jealousy, affairs and past influences. There's cute little stats to wow them with at your next dinner party, lots of quotes from real couples and tons of practical advice on where to meet someone, what to do when you've found them and how to skid through those nasty icy patches so you end up in the His'n'Hers towel section rather than on the scrap heap.

I'd love to claim all the ideas are mine but they're not. I've included lots of research and tips from people I admire (like John Gottman, Barbara De Angelis and Dr Maryon Tysoe) as well as information gleaned from psychological studies. I've tried, somewhat heroically, to cover every relationship problem, query and situation I could think of but there are limits (like the number of pages I was allowed to do it in). The book's written in everyday language with lots of humour thrown in, so hopefully you'll have a giggle while you're learning.

Unfortunately, reading the book's the easy bit. You could devour *Hot Relationships* cover to cover, be able to recite extracts off by heart, and still not benefit one iota. Knowledge will only get you so far: you've got to practise what I've preached. That's what people mean when they say, 'You have to work hard at relationships.' You do. But it's not really work, is it? It's more about finding out about each other, exploring each other's minds, hearts and bodies, treating each other nicely and loving each other to death. If that's hard work, I'm volunteering for community service at whatever male model agency Calvin Klein use.

While I was writing this book, lots of people said to me, 'But how can you teach someone how to make a relationship great? It just is or it isn't. You either love each other or you don't.' Alas, love alone doesn't guarantee a happy partnership. You both need good communication skills and relationship skills as well. You need to be able to express your wants, needs and thoughts to each other, to argue without it ending with the door slamming. Both of you need to feel understood, supported and respected. There *are* tried-and-true techniques which can help you achieve all of this. And (I like to think) all the good ones are in this book.

Hot Relationships will never be finished to my satisfaction because, every day, I discover something new about relationships. The temptation to keep on adding bits is enormous but I had to stop somewhere. So this is it. I hope it delivers what you're looking for – and that *your* new relationship is so hot, it *sizzles*!

PS: To all my ex-boyfriends: If you recognize yourself and got a glowing reference, don't mention it, you deserve it. If it's not so fab, ditto.

The Smart Single

Why happy singles who know what they want
end up in happy relationships

••

I'm getting ready to go out. The hit-mix is pumping out of the stereo, I'm in the bathroom plucking, shaving, dyeing, exfoliating, fake tanning, moisturising, blending, hiding and highlighting. I'm also getting drunk – the bottle of white is disappearing fast but I can't help it. I'm over-excited and can't *wait* to get out there. Deep in my bones (and other places), I've got the feeling tonight is IT. THE NIGHT I am going to meet a guy who's gorgeous, interesting, funny, intelligent, ambitious and all-round wonderful. Never mind I've spent the last week moaning to my girlfriends about how there aren't any single men out there. How I feel fat/old/ugly/depressed. Tonight, I'm on a Chardonnay-inspired optimistic high. This guy's going to knock my socks off. All my problems will magically disappear. My mother will never again have to give me ridiculously expensive Christmas gifts because 'You've got no-one darling and the other kids do'. I'm off to a huge party: wall-to-wall men *and* the hostess has promised to lay on at least a dozen single ones along with the tzatziki dip. *Brilliant!*

I jump in the cab, smile beatific-ally at the cab driver and think, '*I'm not desperate, just hopeful*.'

Around 3 am, I'm in another cab, cursing the inconsiderate bastard who appears to have moved my flat. 'Thancshhh,' I say to the cab driver (when I finally find it) and walk sideways up the drive. Alone. Somehow I manage to find the front door. Even more miraculously, I co-ordinate keys and keyhole so it opens. I head straight for the fridge, search for the highest fat-content food I can find, make tea with three sugars (what's the point of being slim, doesn't get you anywhere), take everything to bed, defiantly attempt to read a book, then give up and cry. What's wrong with me? Why can't I find someone to love? Why is everyone attached? I should never have got rid of Brad. He wasn't that bad. Why am I too fussy? I wonder why I feel sick – I've only eaten one packet of Chocolate Digestives. Oh God, my arse will be huge tomorrow. Do I intimidate men? How about that bitch that muscled in on the guy I *know* liked me! Why do I get little lumps on my bikini line after I shave? I wonder why the sky's blue and the grass is green? Should I have fruit salad and muesli for breakfast or bacon and eggs? It's around then I fall asleep.

This is what usually happens to me when I'm in one of those down and depressed single phases and get asked somewhere which sounds full of promise. The reason for revealing straight up how pathetic I can be is twofold. Number one: you, like me, will never meet anyone when you're desperate to meet someone. Number two: before I launch into telling you how

> 'When you're single, you drive yourself more. You force yourself to go out when you'd really rather chill in front of the television. There's always this fear that if you don't make the effort, you'll have missed the one opportunity you had of meeting Mr Wonderful.'
>
> Charlotte, 25, student

fabulous singledom can be, I want to acknowledge that *I know* it's sometimes a very lonely place.

While this chapter is all about *enjoying* being single (and I have to admit it, I'm happy 90 per cent of the time when I am), let's be realistic here. Everyone feels down in the dumps sometimes because they're alone. It's *normal*. We've all done our fair share of pillow drenching after a night out where we'd hoped to meet someone special and didn't. And when you've lost your job, your dad's seriously ill, you've fought with your best friend or just feel blah, being single *sucks*.

But let's look at things from a different perspective. Let's balance it up a little. One thing that never fails to jolt me back to reality when I'm in the midst of single blues is to recall the *other* pillow-drenching sessions of my life: when I've been in a relationship but was desperately unhappy. That felt just as bad – if not worse. When you're down and single, being part of a couple seems *soooo* appealing. When you're attached and miserable, being single seems *soooo* appealing. There are pluses and minuses to both.

For instance, there's one thing no-one can deny singles have all over couples: freedom and variety. While a couple are flopped in front of a video, their single friends are more likely to be popping off to Bali with a group of friends or taking up rock climbing or discovering some fab new restaurant that does *amazing* things with rock-salted snails, balsamic pesto and aged snowpea sprouts. You can't blame married friends for being envious when the most excitement they've had is hanging nappies on the line. Being single *is* fun if you let yourself enjoy it.

The happier you are single, the more chance you have of finding the relationship of your dreams. Sounds like a contradiction, doesn't it? But who do you think would be more interesting to go out with? The girl who does nothing much except wait around for a man to fill the big, empty hole that is her life – or the girl who's so busy getting on with it, she only dates really special guys because she's got far better things to do than hang out with losers? This applies to both sexes. Energy, enthusiasm, sheer love of life: *that's* what people find attractive.

> **Forty-two per cent of twentysomething women say they don't understand men and 27 per cent are cynical and mistrustful of the opposite sex. Despite this, the majority desire and want a man's love and affection. You figure it out . . .**

It's got little to do with looks, money, what car you drive or how big your boobs are. What it *has* got a lot to do with is how much you like yourself. If you look in the mirror and see a nice, attractive person with lots to offer the world, people will see you that way too. If you don't like yourself, no-one else will.

And there's another reason why moping around won't get you anywhere: people who think their life will truly start when they find a mate are usually the ones most disappointed by love. Because even the best relationship won't get you out of a rut, solve your career problems or make your relationship with your mother any better. It won't stop the cat scratching your brand new sofa, make you lose ten kilos or suddenly decide lettuce is as delicious as chocolate. The same old problems you've always had will still be there.

Yet another good reason not to base your happiness entirely on a relationship: love doesn't come with a guarantee. Saying, 'I love you,' doesn't mean your partner will love you for life; saying, 'I do,' doesn't mean either of you will later. Children don't necessarily ensure you're bonded for ever, neither does a mortgage taken out in both names or co-owned share portfolios. It really doesn't matter whether you've pledged lifelong commitment in front of a minister, your mother or while diving out of a plane, hooked up to a parachute and a Buddhist monk. Sometimes, relationships break up. Even a death threat won't stop someone leaving if they're totally and utterly miserable. Cement boots and a trip to the bottom of the harbour can seem pretty appealing compared to spending the rest of your life with someone who gives you heartburn just by looking at them. No I'm not having a bad hair day, I'm simply telling you the facts for a reason. It's dangerous to base your entire happiness on a relationship with a partner.

Having said that, *sharing* your life with someone you love is a pretty wonderful experience – and there are ways to minimize the chances of it all ending in disaster. Like, knowing what you want. Before you can find Mr or Ms Right, you need to know (at least on paper) who they are.

Imagine you're out shopping for something to wear to a party that night. A sales assistant asks, 'What did you have in mind?'

'I don't really know,' you answer vaguely. 'I'm just sort of waiting for something fabulous to grab my eye. I'll know it when I see it.'

Five hours later, you're in a complete frenzy because you've got to buy *something* and suddenly that tartan-print plastic jumpsuit seems like the best option. So you grab it and the minute you get it home, you think, *What the hell was I thinking?* Shopping and dating aren't dissimilar. Go out looking for a smart but sexy suit and chances are that's what you'll come home with: what you wanted. Go out looking for your perfect match, without a clue of what or who that might be, and you'll come home with the human equivalent of the tartan jumpsuit. Hideous.

It's simple really: happy singles are people who feel good about themselves, who don't see a relationship as the source of all happiness and are clear on what they want from one and what kind of person they'd like to have one with. They're also the ones who get all the dates. Here's how to join the club.

SERENELY SOLO

Fall in love with being single and all sorts of doors spring open. Of all the single people I know, it's the people who *like* being single, who *aren't* waiting around for their matching bookend, who get asked out the most. They're not gorgeous, just interesting, fun people to be around. So keep reading at your own risk. If my advice works, you might not just end up being happy solo, you might prefer it (at least for a little while). Besides, you've got no *choice* but to enjoy being single. Moon around, focus on all the bad things about it, put everything on hold until 'they' come along and I guarantee you'll be miserable *for life*. You won't be happy single and you won't be happy in a relationship either because – sorry! – you're never going to attract anyone worth knowing with an attitude like that.

Why it's good for you to be single (at least for a while)

I'm deeply suspicious of people who've never, ever been single. You know the type: they wouldn't dream of leaving someone, no matter how bad their relationship was, unless they had a replacement lined up and waiting in the wings. I know people who find this impressive. They say, 'Wow! They're so fabulous they never have trouble getting a date.' They don't see the fear behind the behaviour, just the end result: a person who's *always* got someone hanging off their arm. But what I think is: *If they've always got someone hanging off their arm, they don't know how to stand on their own two feet.*

If you've never been single as an adult, you've never learnt to survive on your own. You need someone to prop you up because you haven't developed the skills to do it yourself. I'm not suggesting you dump whoever you're presently hooked up with (unless you're *only* with them because you're scared of being alone). But if you suddenly find yourself single – or are single right now – stay that way, at least for a little while. I'm serious. *Deliberately* stay single. Resolve *not* to date anyone seriously for at least six months. I swear, you'll be a different person at the end of it.

Meeting challenges solo, solving your own problems without any back-up, knowing you don't *need* anyone to look after you will not only make you stronger and independent, your next relationship will benefit hugely from it. You won't grab the first person who comes along and cling on for dear life because you're no longer scared of being on your own. You won't go out with losers. We attract people like ourselves: so the more confident and self-sufficient you are, the more likely it is your partner will be too. You'll be together because you *want* to be, not because you *need* to be. Now there's a novel concept!

Being confident and self-sufficient really will help you find Mr or Ms Perfect. Why? Because when you're confident and self-sufficient, you feel good about yourself, which other people notice and find attractive. It's the key to happiness – single *or* in a relationship – but sometimes you need to work at it. Here's how.

Love yourself first

Picture this. You're admiring a painting you think you'll buy, when the artist walks over.

'This is just fabulous!' you say.

'Do you really think so?' they reply. 'Actually, I really stuffed it up there in the corner. Look, see where the proportion's all wrong? I never was very good at painting hands and feet. Oh, it's okay I guess but *way* overpriced. I told the gallery no-one would buy it for that amount.'

Are you going to respond by slapping a credit card on the counter, shouting, 'It's mine'? No way! You'd walk away thinking, *Thank God I didn't spend next week's rent money.*

You're selling a product when you're dating too – yourself. If you don't have high self-esteem and think you've got lots to offer, how the hell are you going to convince someone else?

Think of yourself as an onion (yes, really). The top layers are the tough bits – that's the part you present to the world. All confidence and bravado, nicely packaged in a suit. Keep peeling back those layers until you get to the middle of the onion. This is the part of you that your friends see: slightly softer, a few insecurities and vulnerabilities revealed. Peel off another one or two layers and you get to the intimate you, the part you reserve for your partner: the sexual and loving side. Now keep peeling until you're left with nothing but the onion's tiny core. That's the *real you*: the part of yourself no-one ever gets to see, *except you*.

The core of the onion is where all our true feelings and attitudes toward ourselves are kept protected. We don't often get down to this level but we do panic on occasions. Like when we're lying in bed, terrified about giving that speech tomorrow. *I'll never be able to do this. What if I make a complete fool of myself? Don't they realize I'm a complete idiot? Did they really fall for all that upfront stuff without noticing I've got nothing to back it up with?* If you've got good self-esteem, another little voice will answer, *You're just nervous, that's all. If you really were incompetent, do you think you'd have got this far?* If you *don't* think much of yourself, those negative thoughts keep racing around unchallenged.

When you're at the core of the onion level, it's impossible to lie to yourself. You can try. Say, 'Of course I've got good self-esteem – I'm always the life and soul of the party.' But you know the most insecure people in the world are often the loudest, brashest and most opinionated. They cover up their low self-esteem with noise. The more noise they make, the less likely people are to get close to them. If they don't get close, they can't discover the *real* them, the inner core of the onion which has to be hidden at all costs because they don't really like what's in there. Same goes for people who say things like, 'Of course, I like who I am! I'm successful, I drive a BMW, I own my own flat.' Liking yourself has nothing to do with material possessions.

How's your self-esteem? A quick quiz

To discover how good your self-esteem *really* is, I want you to consciously go down to the inner core before answering these questions. Tap into it, *then* answer yes or no:

1. Do you consider yourself a nice person? Do you think most people who know you reasonably well would agree?
2. Are you reasonably happy with your personality and behaviour? There's nothing major you'd like to change?
3. When you achieve something you've worked hard for, do you secretly congratulate yourself?
4. Do you have lots of goals in life and feel you're working toward achieving them?
5. Do you believe in yourself and know that once you set your mind to something, you usually succeed?
6. Do you stick up for yourself and feel confident expressing your opinion, even if it's different from what other people think?
7. Does what other people think of you seem unimportant compared to what you think of yourself?
8. Do you feel valued by your friends, family and work colleagues?
9. Do you take risks and believe that making mistakes is essential to moving forward?
10. Looking back, are you happy with how far you've come?
11. Do you rarely doubt yourself?
12. Do you accept compliments easily, knowing it's not just people 'being nice'?

How did you score?

If you answered yes to ten or more of these questions, your self-esteem's in good shape. (Just make sure you answered it as the *real* you, rather than the person you'd *like* to be or present to the world.)

A score of six to ten means there's room for improvement or you're in a bit of a down space right now. If you scored six or less on the self-esteem test, you need to put some serious work into building an ego. Forget about a relationship for the time being because you're far too vulnerable to venture into dating land. Put this book down and pick up another, which deals directly and exclusively with building self-esteem. Any good bookshop is crammed with them. Or you could call your local community centre to find out if they run workshops on confidence building, or book in to see a good counsellor to work through any deep-seated issues that may be holding you back. Your doctor can refer you, or contact the British Psychological Society (their number's in the yellow pages). You might find a partner isn't the answer to your problems – learning to love yourself is.

Confidence will get you everywhere

That girl at the gym has it. You know, the cow who's always at the front of the aerobics class, while you're hiding in the back corner. Never mind that you're in size-10 Lycra and she's in a size-14 daggy old T-shirt: she looks great – and obviously knows it. My friend Jamie's also got it. Turn up five minutes late at a café and invariably, someone's standing there chatting to her. All she does is smile and people are drawn to her like ants to sugar.

Don't you just hate those breezy, self-assured, together types that make it all look so easy? Bet you wouldn't if you were one of them. But you can be – it's really just a matter of looking at things differently. Here's why self-confident people have all the fun.

The six secrets of self-confident people

1. **They make decisions (even if they're the wrong ones)**

   Mr Insecure: John's been offered a great job with the competition and is in a complete panic. What if he leaves, gets the sack and then can't get a job back with his old firm? But if he misses this opportunity will he ever get another chance? Tossing back and forth between the two options, John hesitates so long, the offer's withdrawn.

   Mr Confident: Jake's offered a great job. He sits down with a pad and paper and lists the pros and cons of staying where he is or leaving, then sleeps on it. The next day, he decides it's time to move on. He tells his boss he's been offered a job with the competition. His boss comes back with a counter-offer so the new firm up his salary even more.

2. **They step outside their comfort zone**

   Ms Insecure: Jenny's been asked to play in a social tennis game. She loathes tennis because she's hopeless at it. Sure, she'd like to meet new people, but she says no. Why set herself up to look stupid?

   Ms Confident: Jane also hates tennis and says so. 'It doesn't matter,' her friends say. 'It's only a social game.' So she goes along and, with a little encouragement, finds she's not so bad after all. The next week, the same group of friends invite her to play squash. 'Why not?' she says.

3. **They don't let the past dictate the future**

   Mr Insecure: A few years ago, Steven completely embarrassed himself by venturing an opinion on a topic he knew nothing about. A friend ridiculed him and now he keeps his mouth shut during a discussion on any subject he's not an expert in.

Mr Confident: The same thing happened to Simon. For a while he felt a little nervous opening his mouth, so he started prefacing his comments with, 'To tell the truth, I'm not as up on this as you guys, but isn't it a case of ——?' One month later, it wasn't such a big deal any more.

4. **They ignore the voices inside**

Ms Insecure: Trudy doesn't own a pair of jeans because her legs are too fat to wear them. When she was a chubby teenager, her mother told her to stick to long skirts ('They hide your legs better'). She's now a size 10 but whenever she pulls on a pair of trousers, her mother's voice starts playing in her head so she drags on yet another long skirt.

Ms Confident: When Tracy was at school, her maths teacher told her to stick to English because, 'You just don't have a head for figures.' At uni, she enrolled in an accounting subject, ignoring the little voice in her head warning her off. Now she's a chartered accountant.

5. **They let go of emotional baggage**

Mr Insecure: Nick is divorced and he's pretty bitter about it. He still sees his wife because of the kids but he'll never forgive her for what she did. She left him for another man. Can you blame him for not wanting another relationship? His wife scarred him for life.

Mr Confident: Nathan's wife also left him for another man. He was so devastated, he booked himself in for counselling. For a while there, he only saw friends who could put up with him sobbing on their shoulders. Six months later, one of them fixed him up with a girl. At first he found it hard to trust her, but it didn't take long to realize not all women were like his ex-wife. Some were worthy of his trust – like Susan, the woman he's been happily involved with for the last year.

6. **They're in charge of their life**

Ms Insecure: Renee has the worst luck in the world. Her car, which she paid good money for, turned out to be a lemon. Her company downscaled and *her* job turned out to be the one that was axed. The guy she's fancied for ages turned out to be gay. Life's so bloody unfair, but it's just the way things are.

Ms Confident: Rachel has also had her fair share of ups and downs, but she's found even bad things usually happen for a reason. Like when she was crazy about Todd. She asked him out, he told her he was gay and they fell about laughing. He's now her best friend. Life really is what you make it.

But I'm *shy* . . .

My friend Deb was so shy, she had to pluck up courage simply to ask for a stamp at the post office. Strangers frightened the hell out of her. I saw her once, huddled in a corner at a party she absolutely couldn't get out of. Someone came over to talk to her and even from a distance, I could see the telltale bright red flush. She stepped backwards – straight into someone carrying a drink – and I felt her shame. It's pretty hard to grab life with two hands if they're shaking!

I knew Deb because she lived next door to me. Her family was also painfully shy and rarely had visitors. Which is, of course, where Deb's problem originated. People who find it easy to make friends usually grew up in houses that were always full of people – neighbours, friends and family. They learnt the basic social skills of how to interact with strangers, make and keep friends without even trying.

Dealing with strangers does take skill and so does building relationships with other people. You need to know how to start a conversation and keep it going. You need to know what's appropriate to say and what's not. How to turn acquaintances into friends by moving things to a more intimate level: listening as well as talking, sharing your fears and anxieties, revealing what makes you happy and sad. Most of us learn all these things without even realizing – we got lots of practice at home or at school. But shy kids tend to stay in the background and so do shy adults. We forget they're there half the time! If this is you, hopefully this section will help. I got it straight from the horse's mouth: a now-confident Deb. These are her tips on how to stop being shy and start living:

- **Start small**. Every time you go into a shop to buy something, make conversation. Just a simple, 'Hi! Hot isn't it!' is better than nothing. Practise making small talk as often as possible.

- **Mentally rehearse situations you feel nervous in**. Picture yourself at a party. Imagine yourself hovering around the food table until you feel comfortable, then making conversation with whoever joins you. 'Crowded isn't it?' or, 'How do you know so-and-so (the host)?'

- **Approach people like you**. Trying to be best buddies with the girl who's dancing on the table probably won't get you far because you don't have much in common. Look for people who seem a little hesitant, who are standing at the edges rather than the centre stage, entertaining the crowd.

- **Have a few standard lines to fall back on**. 'Where do you work?', 'Do you live around here?' Everyone likes talking about themselves. Try to identify things you have in common. 'You know, I totally agree with you. I love jazz as well.'

- **Listen to what they're saying**. Ask questions to show you're interested. 'How amazing! What happened after that?'

- **Pay them compliments**. 'That's a great shirt, where did you get it?' People like people who like them.

- **Smile a lot**. If you absolutely have nothing to say, just smile and nod. Most people are more than happy babbling on to someone who's willing to listen.
- **Suggest another meeting if you liked them**. 'I've really enjoyed talking to you. Would you like to have a coffee sometime?' Don't be disheartened if they don't seem keen. Maybe they've already got a circle of friends and don't have time for more. Don't take rejections personally.
- **Watch how your behaviour influences others**. As you become more confident, you'll notice that other people seem more open to making friends with you. That's because you're coming across as friendly and approachable – rather than a scared little mouse who'd jump ten feet if they dared to talk to you.
- **Treat your new friends with respect**. Don't bitch about them, share good news as well as bad, support but don't smother.

I know I'm okay on the inside – it's the outside that's the problem

So you think only good-looking people get dates. Oh, *puhleeze*! Of course looks are important. How often have *you* looked across the room at a party and thought, *Gosh! He's sexy!*, when the man in question badly needs dental work, has dandruff all over the shoulders of his lime-green T-shirt, a beer gut and a bowl haircut? Our initial attraction to people is always on appearance so there's an extremely good argument for making the most of what you've got and aiming to be as attractive as possible. Having said that, you *don't* have to be traditionally good-looking to be reeling 'em in.

An average or below-average looking person who makes the most of their looks, is confident and comfortable in their own skin and around the opposite sex might not be the *first* person approached at the party, but they're the ones you end up talking to all night. And the more you talk to them, the more attractive they become. You weren't in the front of the queue when God was handing out good looks? Sure, it might have been easier if you had been. But it's behaviour, personality and presentation that really count.

⑥ FOR HER: IF I WAS THIN OR MY BREASTS WERE BIGGER . . .

While no-one's denying a body like Pamela Anderson will have every guy in the room doing a fair impersonation of Linda Blair in *The Exorcist*, most men aren't as fussy about body shape as we think they are.

It really doesn't matter what your breast size is or what size jeans you can squeeze your bottom into because bodies are another case of horses for courses. Some guys love really small breasts, others like watermelons. Some guys like that starved-and-on-heroin body type, 99.99 per cent hate it. Far more important than your body bits is the person they're attached to and even *more* importantly, *your* attitude to your body.

If you've got little boobs and you like them, he will too. If you're constantly telling him you wish they were bigger, he'll start to agree with you. It's the same with men and their penises. Being comfortable with what you've got is the key.

Ditto for how much you weigh. We all have 'fat days' – even girls who disappear when they stand sideways. Just make sure you keep it in perspective. The truth is – and it's been proven over and over again – most females' idea of a 'perfect body' isn't his. While heavily overweight isn't attractive (or good for your health), a few extra kilos (the world to us) add the curves that men find really sexy. They don't think 'fat' and

> 'My Dad always said, it's all well and good to say, "Accept me for who I am." Just make sure who you are is someone you like.'
>
> Mike, 24, personal trainer

'lumpy'. They think soft, warm, female and voluptuous.

Ask any man in love what he thinks of his partner's body and he'll muster up the best possible interpretation of whatever she's got. If she's overweight, she's got beautiful, big breasts. If she's skinny, she's athletic and lean. In fact, as much as they'll never admit it, most guys aren't as superficial as they like to make out. If you make the effort to take good care of yourself and make the most of what you've got, they're usually pretty satisfied. After all, they're not perfect either.

But there's one area where men and women do differ – there's absolutely NO WAY a man would let any insecurities about his body interfere with his sex life. Yet women do. In a recent US survey, women with a positive body image said they had orgasms 73 per cent of the time. Self-conscious women reached orgasm only 42 per cent of the time. It stands to reason your sex life will suffer if you don't like your body because you're thinking things like: *Will my stomach look flat in this position? I'd better not get on top because my breasts will look funny. Bugger – I'm dying to go to the loo but I daren't because he'll see my fat bottom.*

Sex is all about what's happening inside, not outside. If you're desperately trying to suck your stomach in, you're not mentally tuning in to being turned on. Which means your vaginal walls don't expand, you don't lubricate and you've got no chance of having an orgasm. Good sex is about feeling confident. Feel sexy and you'll be sexy. No-one looks good naked all the time during sex because you have to put yourself in awfully unflattering positions if you're going to make the most of it. Feeling good about your body will improve both your relationships and your sex life.

Get over a bad body image by:

• Looking at yourself naked in a full-length mirror regularly. Instead of focusing on your 'faults', focus on the parts you do like.

- Write down every compliment someone gives you on your body ('I wish I had breasts like yours', 'I wish I had your weight problem – you're skinny compared to me').
- Dress to play up what you perceive to be your 'good bits' but don't hide the 'faulty' areas. Learn to accept them as part of the parcel.
- If anyone (your mother, best friend, boyfriend) makes negative comments about your body, tell them you're not interested in hearing their opinion. If your boyfriend persists in being nasty, get rid of him – not the supposed extra kilos.
- Throw out the scales and instead judge by how your clothes fit. It stops your weight dictating what sort of day you'll have.
- Move your focus to other parts of yourself: your mind, your personality, your relationships – better still, your sex life!

Love your life and you'll love being single

In order to experience this state of relationship nirvana, you need to be happy with your life *right now.* Hate your job, loathe your flat and can't stand your friends? Then *do* something about it! Here's some tips on how.

Surround yourself with happy friends

A friend is someone who makes you feel a million dollars, who gives you the courage and strength to get out there and conquer the world. Friends don't put you down, make snide comments, tell you you're too fat or make you feel bad about yourself. If you've got 'friends' who delight in criticizing you, stop seeing them. They're boosting their egos by stamping on yours. Same goes for the friend who's miserable 365 days of the year. It's hard to stay up and enthusiastic if someone's constantly pointing out the negatives.

Cultivate lots of different friendships with both men and women – and make sure at least some of them are single. Being 'the odd one out' once a week is fine. But always? That's a bore. Give priority to functions that include people you don't know and when you meet someone you click with who's also travelling solo, make an effort. Get their phone number. Suggest you go out for a coffee and take it from there. The more single friends you have the better. It means you won't turn out to be one of those truly pathetic types who gets all narky and depressed when their friend meets someone before they do.

Find a job you love
Even if you're not particularly ambitious, it makes sense to find a career that excites you (unless you *like* being miserable five out of seven days). You're so underchallenged, you use more brain cells watching telly than you do at work? Time for a rethink or a visit to a career counsellor. It's impossible to be happy when you're in a job you hate.

Love where you live
Think about it. Why do we pay exorbitant rates to stay in posh hotels? Because you feel fabulous surrounded by all that luxury. It's pretty hard to be cheerful when your flat's a pigsty, your office looks like a war zone and your car's a portable rubbish bin. A good spring-clean and throw-out will make you feel

much more in control. A coat of paint works wonders: slap some bright yellow over that revolting hospital green and your soul will thank you (not to mention the landlord!).

Accept you'll have down times too

No-one walks around whistling 'Singing in the Rain', day in, day out. Sometimes, you can't help but wallow in misery. Once, I walked out of my flat to buy some milk and had to turn around and go back home again because I'd forgotten it was A Bank Holiday. Bank holidays can be nightmares for singles because the streets are crammed with arm-in-arm couples, licking ice-cream cones and landing kisses on the end of each other's nose. I simply couldn't face it. A permanent blissful state of happiness is unrealistic. But general happiness is attainable – and that's what you should aspire to.

Make yourself happy

Don't expect other people to make you happy, do it yourself. Sure, a few wines with a girlfriend can lift your spirits, but basic happiness comes from within. Start a 'feelgood' folder. Fill it with records of your achievement, cards or messages from friends saying how wonderful you are, and look through it whenever you feel down.

Set goals

Ever felt like you're treading water financially – or worse, sinking lower and lower into debt? Money worries are the biggest robber of happiness, so set yourself a budget and some material goals NOW. Lots of single people say they feel in limbo financially and left behind when they compare their assets to those of married friends. But while two pooled incomes can buy a lot more than one can, that doesn't mean you can't build a nice little nest egg on your own.

Think of all the time and energy you devote to a

relationship (or trying to get one). Channel that into doing up a modest flat you've just bought and you'll be amazed at what you can accomplish. The days when single people (particularly women) couldn't get housing loans are thankfully over. And buying your own one-bedroom flat isn't accepting defeat, it's smart. If your future partner has done the same, you'll be nicely set up for your future together. If you end up opting to stay single or don't meet them for the next couple of years, you'll kick yourself for missing out on all that lovely profit.

Don't forget emotional goals and intellectual goals as well. Like resolving to see your friends and family more, enrolling in self-help courses, reading more, taking an evening course.

Make the most of every second
Corny, I know, but true: live every day as though it were your last. If you're as accident-prone as I am, it might be.

Stop listening to other people
To be happy single you have to stop listening to people who tell you you shouldn't be, that it's 'unnatural' to be single, that life can only be good when you're part of a couple, people who insist your entire life purpose is to find a mate.

Bollocks! People mean well but those boring, repetitive, silly things others assume just because you're (*Gosh! How tragic!*) On Your Own, can be soul-destroying. Even when you're feeling on top of the world, a well-placed barb can have you feeling sorry for yourself quicker than they can say, 'Poor you!' Here's how to stop those depressing conversations before they even start.

F FOR HER: YOU'RE A SINGLE GIRL? AHH! WELL, YOU MUST BE . . .
It's different for him – he's playing the field. Sowing those wild oats while he can. But no girl in her right mind would *choose* to

be single, would she? What a shame you can't find someone. You must be . . .

Desperate
They say: 'You'll never guess what. A single man's just moved in next door. Now, he's a little older than you and quite podgy. But nothing a good woman can't sort out. Can you believe it? Single! When shall I set something up?'

What you want to say: 'Jesus – do I look *that* hard up?'

What you should say: 'Actually, I'm seeing someone right now. Nothing serious but it's probably not the right time to meet your neighbour.'

Fatally flawed
They say: 'I really can't understand why you're still single after all this time. I mean, you're attractive, funny, talented. Why hasn't someone snapped you up?'

What you want to say: 'I ask myself the same question every night.'

What you should say: 'Thanks for the compliment and, hey, they try! I'm asked out all the time. But, right now, I'm really enjoying being single.'

Still heartbroken over your ex
They say: 'Poor dear! Not only did that guy break your heart but you're still getting over him. I know how totally humiliating being dumped is. Remember how long it took me to get over Stephen? Years!'

What you want to say: 'Misery must love company otherwise I wouldn't be hanging around with you.'

What you should say: 'Actually (lean forward conspiratorially), can I tell you a secret? I was upset for a little while but now I've decided I quite like being single. Weird isn't it? I wouldn't have Mike back if he came around in a wedding car.'

Lonely

They say: 'You should get a cat to keep you company. Being on your own isn't good for you. You know George and I are more than happy if you want to pop over when you're lonely one Saturday night. We're always home, aren't we George?'

What you want to say: 'If I ever get that desperate, I'll throw myself over the nearest cliff.'

What you should say: 'That's so sweet. You know, I've thought about getting a cat but I think it would starve since I'm out six nights out of seven. And I promise I will find time one Saturday night to see you but I'm booked out until May. Sorry guys.'

Sex-starved

They say: 'Pete and I had the *best* oral sex last night. Oops! I forget you're not getting any. Hope I didn't make you jealous.'

What you want to say: 'Good for you! Nice to know Pete's finally progressed past wham-bam-thank-you-mam.'

What you should say: 'Not at all. I just don't kiss and tell.' (Smile mysteriously.)

Too fussy

They say: 'What *was* wrong with Peter? I know he had that unfortunate incident with the bank and went to jail that time, but he wasn't *that* bad, surely? You're just too fussy, that's all.'

What you want to say: 'Actually Mum, I lied. It wasn't embezzlement, it was robbery.'

What you should say: 'Don't *you* think I deserve the very best, Mum?'

Trying to bonk your way through the entire male population
They say: 'You can't play the field for ever, you know. I mean, a different guy every week? At some point you really have to settle down, get married and all that.'

What you want to say: 'Why?'

What you should say: 'Why?'

Deafened by the sound of that biological clock ticking
They say: 'You'd better hurry up and meet someone if you want to have babies.'

What you want to say: 'Why don't you just plunge a stake through my heart? Of course I'm worried sick about it.'

What you should say: 'Don't you just hate being female sometimes?'

Now, this is the one criticism I can't argue with. Or can I? Let's start with how old you are. If you're under 30, I don't think they have a leg to stand on. And neither do you, if you're stressing unnecessarily. Sure, you might prefer to have children young but if you're healthy and haven't got any gynaecological problems, you've got another ten years or more before you have to move into panic mode. Even if you *are* approaching 40, you've still got options. Plenty of women have IVF babies on their own, plenty

Mr Right is No 13 – or so say researchers. They claim once you've experienced 12 relationships, you'll know what you want and who's best suited to give it to you. With No 13, you'll finally get it right!

of others get sperm donated by supportive male friends. Not the ideal situation, I admit, but if it's really important to you, it's worth looking into. You still have options.

The doubting Thomases still aren't convinced? Dazzle them with statistics because these are the facts

- Single guys cop it far worse than you do. The myth of the happy bachelor is just that: a myth. Choose any poll you want and the message is clear: men are lonelier single than women are.
- Single women are healthier, happier and wealthier than their shackled sisters. Single women travel more, are more likely to drink champagne, own a sports car, eat in expensive restaurants, buy French perfume and designer clothes than girls who've got guys. (Why? You get to spend all your money on yourself – and don't have to justify your purchases.)
- Single women go out more, have more friends, meet more new people and have more sex than people who are married.

Sounds dreadful, doesn't it? You can see why everyone's so sorry for you.

Ⓜ FOR HIM: YOU'RE A SINGLE GUY? AHH! WELL, YOU MUST BE . . .

It's different for her – she doesn't *choose* to be single, she's waiting for some guy to *pick* her. So why aren't you out there chasing the cream of the crop? I mean, as a single man, you must be . . .

Starving
They say: 'I bet you haven't had a good meal in ages. What you need is a nice girl to fatten you up. You're looking awfully scrawny – come over for dinner tonight.'

What you want to say: 'I'd rather eat pizza every night than suffer through Sarah's cooking again.'

What you should say: 'Thanks for the compliment. I've been trying to get rid of that beer gut for ages.'

Gay
They say: 'Darling, you know we love you, don't you? You know that we'd support you whatever (lots of throat clearing) . . . whatever, well . . . (more throat clearing). What I mean to say is, is there anything you want to tell us, son?'

What you want to say: 'I'm never, ever wearing these trousers again.'

What you should say: 'No Mum, Dad, I'm not gay. But it's wonderful to know you'd love me just as much no matter who I chose as a partner.'

Hard up
They say: 'Bet the old wrist's getting a bit of a workout. If you don't use it on a woman soon, mate, it'll drop off.'

What you want to say: 'At least I need to use my whole hand.'

What you should say: 'Don't you worry about me, John. I just don't tell you all my conquests in case you get jealous. You know, being married and all that . . .'

Still hanging out for a supermodel
They say: 'Mate, maybe you're not going to pull a 24-year-old. What's wrong with Susan's friend, Beryl? I know she's no stunner but she's a nice girl and you could do worse.'

What you want to say: 'That old cow! Are you serious?'

What you should say: 'I agree, Beryl's a nice person. But she's 53. Thanks for the offer, but I think I'll give it a little bit longer and see if someone my own age comes along.'

Commitment phobic
They say: 'Have you read *Men Are from Mars, Women Are from Venus?* There's a whole section in there on commitment phobia. Now, don't shake your head. You've *obviously* got a problem or you'd be settled down by now.'

What you want to say: 'Rebecca, I love you as a friend but no matter what you say or do, I still won't fancy you.'

What you should say: 'If I'm commitment phobic, how come I was married for five years and with Ellen for seven?'

Trying to bonk your way through the entire female population
They say: 'You can't play the field for ever, you know. I mean, a different woman every week? At some point you really have to find a nice girl, settle down, get married and all that.'

What you want to say: 'Why?'

What you should say: 'Why?'

Solo and sorry for yourself? Turn around that bad attitude
Pick up an old gossip magazine and flick through the celebrity pages. Yes, there they are. That fabulously in-love couple you envied. He's gazing adoringly at her, she's snuggling in with that smug I'm-in-love-and-you're-not expression all over her face. 'If only I had a love like that,' you sighed at the time. And the lifestyle! There they are skiing in Aspen, sipping champagne

onboard a yacht, hobnobbing it with the hotshots. Remember how depressed they used to make you feel? Funny how you don't envy them now, isn't it? Now they're suing each other over who gets the house in Malibu.

There's a simple point to this sad little tale: not everyone's life is as wonderful as it looks. And pots of money, cellulite-free bottoms, concave stomachs and a drop-dead gorgeous partner don't necessarily make you happy (even if they would help). Remind yourself of this the next time you feel yourself sliding into the single blues – or try any or all of the following.

Remember, 95 per cent of people end up in relationships
Do you honestly believe you're going to be one of that 5 per cent who stay single *for ever*? (And most of that 5 per cent *choose* to be.) Single is usually a temporary state. If you could look up a computer, which said you'd be married with kids in two years, you'd be out that door in a millisecond, sprinting to the nearest nightclub. In other words, make the most of being single while you can. I can't *guarantee* this will happen to you in two years, but I'll bet money that you'll be fighting someone for the remote control. So get out there and enjoy it while it lasts!

People don't feel sorry for you, so why should you?
I've got married-with-kids girlfriends who'd cheerfully hand over their first-born to trade places with me for one weekend. Eating a leisurely breakfast in a café while reading the papers, collapsing on the bed for an afternoon kip after too many wines at lunch – I take all this for granted. They don't. Their lives aren't as spontaneous because they have to check in with their partners or take the kids to football practice. Feel sorry for you? If your attached friends are honest, they'll admit to envying you 50 per cent of the time!

Stop thinking that all couples have perfect relationships

Couples don't all treat each other like royalty or never, ever get bored. Really good relationships are rare; they're not as common as colds.

Remind yourself why you're single

Because you *choose* to be. Imagine hooking up with someone, just for the sake of it, and how dreadful your life would be. A bad relationship would make things worse, not better.

Make the most of your friends

Got some great news and feel down because there's no 'special someone' to celebrate with? Call your best friend, grab a bottle of champers (actually, make that two) and get over there to spread the news. A good friend loves you just as much as *they* would (if not more!).

Ask your happily attached friends to tell you all the bad things about being a couple

Like her hogging the bathroom, him forgetting their anniversary, her mind-bogglingly revolting habit of picking her toenails while they're watching TV, his tendency to shove snotty hankies down the side of the sofa and all those other charming I-swear-if-they-do-it-one-more-time-I'll-leave things couples do to annoy the hell out of each other. (Be a little bit careful with this one. You might be envious but you don't want to split them up, do you?)

Turn the tape off

No, not the CD player, the one that's whirling around in your head saying, 'Life would be so much better if I had someone to share it with.' The next time someone says the same to you – 'Why do I feel so empty when I've got a great job, lots of friends and a terrific flat?' – ignore the insinuation ('All this is great – but it would be better if I could share it with someone') and say instead, 'I have no idea! Why do you feel empty when your life is pretty wonderful?'

Indulge yourself
A frothy, yummy, fat-packed hot chocolate, reading a book in bed when it's raining outside, turning the first page of a magazine. Life's simpler pleasures are often the best. You don't need someone else to indulge you – do it yourself!

Smile so much your face aches
If you like and respect yourself, it shows. Bound out the door happy, smile at everyone you pass and you'll notice a rather pleasant domino effect: you make them happy, they make you even happier by smiling back. Look for the best in people and you'll find it. Love life and it'll love you back. Believe all men are bastards, the system rips you off and everything worth having is out of your budget and it will seem true.

Swap the glass-is-half-empty attitude for the glass is half full
Of course there are times when being single is truly horrible, but when everything's cruising along nicely, it's criminal not to be happy just because you're not attached. Single isn't a life-threatening disease, you know!

WHAT DO YOU WANT FROM A RELATIONSHIP?
It's quite simple: you have to know what you want in order to get it. Most of us *think* we know what we're looking for, but few have actually made the effort to reduce those airy-fairy ideas to specific needs and wants. The fact is, you've got a much better chance of finding someone who'll make you happy if you're

TEN GREAT THINGS ABOUT BEING SINGLE
For him
1. You don't have to answer to *anyone*.
2. No-one rolls their eyes when the remote accidentally sticks on the sports channel.
3. You can clip your toenails without someone vomiting in the background.
4. *Playboy* gets pride of place on the coffee table – and no-one lectures you about how much porn degrades women.
5. You can dress up in your old football shirt and criticize the hell out of the players without someone saying, 'You're kidding yourself. With that beer gut you'd be flat out catching the ball, so don't give him a hard time!'
6. You don't have to tell her she doesn't look fat/her bottom's not big/more than a handful's a waste.
7. You can masturbate in the middle of the lounge room without fear of her walking in and saying, 'Ohmigod! This must mean you don't want to have sex with *me*.'
8. You can put tomato sauce on *everything* without 'tut-tut's and 'Honestly, Harry, you're such a pig with food!'
9. No-one tells you you're driving too fast.
10. You don't have to be nice to her stuck-up, snotty friends.

For her
1. You don't have to answer to *anyone*.
2. You can walk in the door after a *horrible* day's work, throw your clothes in a pile, flop down in front of the telly in a disgusting, food-splattered dressing gown, and eat rubbish while watching rubbish – without anyone surfing the channels just when it's at the good bit.
3. Fat days seem less important. So long as your stomach's flat by Friday night, who cares if you're bloated on Tuesday? ➢

4. You can talk on the phone all night about absolutely nothing and lie outrageously about how wonderful Susan looked in her new outfit without someone saying afterward, 'But you told me she looked like mutton dressed up as lamb.'
5. You can change your mind every five minutes, just for the hell of it.
6. You can masturbate to fantasies of the gorgeous workman you passed on the way to the office, without feeling guilty.
7. Everything smells clean and fresh. There are no lingering boy smells (the obvious mixed with cheesy socks, all vainly disguised with bad aftershave).
8. You can make your own smells – without feeling 'unladylike'.
9. You don't have to explain why it's essential to own 25 pairs of black shoes.
10. You can get drunk and sob over your hated-when-sober ex – without feeling totally silly the next day.

crystal clear about what you're looking for. This is what this section aims to do:

- **Sort out what's really important from what's not.** In other words, what you really need to make you happy rather than what you *think* will make you happy.
- **Pinpoint the differences between what you wish for and what you could live without.** You need to know what to compromise on (external things like looks) and what you shouldn't budge on (values like trust and honesty).
- **Discover whether your wish list is realistic** or destined to keep you single for life.

Give it a go – you can't help but benefit from it!

The relationship wish list

It stands to reason that you've got to know what you want from a relationship before you can decide on the type of person who'll give it to you. Some things are pretty universal – like love, companionship, someone to look after you when you're sick – but there are drastic variations in other areas. For me, a relationship is important but it's got to fit in *around* my career or I wouldn't be happy. My friend Simon wants the opposite: total and utter devotion – the classic moulded-to-each-other's-side partnership. The question is: what do *you* want from a partner long term?

> **❶** *Sick of trying to find your perfect match? In the year 2005, technology may do it for you. Hot Badges, tiny electronic devices that store and transmit info about your likes and dislikes, are set to become as popular as mobile phones. When you meet someone with a badge storing similar information, they both glow. The ultimate ice breaker!*

How to do it

Divide the page into two before you start: write 'wish for' on one side and 'must have' on the other. You're going to write down what you'd like and what you insist on, in the relevant columns.

The questions

1. How long do I want it to last? Do you honestly believe you can meet someone at 20 *and* be sitting side by side in rocking chairs at 90? *Or* do you think ten years is a pretty good innings? Perhaps you'd actually like two or three semi-serious relationships before settling down for life.

2. What's your idea of commitment? Do you want to get married or would you be happy living together? What about when you have children – how would that alter it? Does it matter if your partner has been married before?

3. Do you want children? Are they essential to your happiness or are you a little ambivalent? What if they've got children from a previous marriage?

4. Do you want to be joined at the hip or independent? Do you want the sort of relationship where you do *everything* together or are you a bit of a free spirit and need the odd separate holiday and lots of time alone?

5. Do you want a monogamous relationship? Ninety per cent of us automatically tick 'yes' but some of you might opt for, 'What I don't know won't hurt me – so long as it's not flaunted in my face'.

6. What level of intimacy are you looking for? A completely open, share-everything sort of relationship or are you happier cruising along on surface level?

7. How important is sex to you? A crucial ingredient in a good relationship or a bonus if it turns out to be good?

8. How secure do you need to be? Is being able to trust someone important to you? (If it isn't, it should be!) What about honesty? Do you believe in laying everything out on the table, or are there some things you think you shouldn't be too honest on?

9. How much support do you want from your partner? Do you need to know they're totally, 100 per cent behind you?

10. Do you want them to be your best friend? Most of us would answer 'yes', some people don't mind if their partner doesn't share their life passions. They're happy to satisfy those needs with friends.

The partner wish list

I have a type. Just picturing him makes my toes curl in antici- pated bliss. He's tall, gloriously muscled. He's got olive skin and a permanent three-day growth. Chiselled cheekbones. Long, lean legs. Dark hair, cut short. He's successful but he's not ruthlessly ambitious. Gen- erous but not clingy. Sensitive but manly. He doesn't exist.

I've been out with bits of him: I got the muscles, height, olive skin and chiselled cheekbones all in one parcel. But he wasn't terribly intelligent or sensitive (thick as two planks and a complete prick actually). I've been out with manly (substitute semi-evolved) and generous (with his money but not his affec- tion). Which probably explains why the men I've actually fallen for in real life have absolutely nothing in common with my fantasy man. The first step to finding your perfect partner? Accept they aren't out there.

It's actually far more sensible to choose a mate the same way you choose your friends. Like, even if they do look so delicious you'd give up *ER* for them, you've really got to talk sometimes (though there are exceptions – see Fancy a fling, page 110). All that stuff your mother harped on about – common interests, similar backgrounds, age and intelligence levels – they are important. But lovers need something extra that friendships don't – chemistry. They have to do 'it' for you. Anyway, enough of me telling you what's important. The point of this exercise is to work out *your* individual needs and wants.

> 'When I was 18, I remember thinking, *Now I know who I am.* When I was 26, I thought, *I didn't know anything back then – now I know who I am.* At 42, I realize I'll never really know because I change constantly, depending on what's happening in my life.'
>
> Craig, 42, lawyer

For this exercise, I want you to write down all the things you want from a partner under the following headings: 'wish for' and 'must haves'. In other words, what you'd like and what you won't compromise on. Be as specific as possible and do it over a few days, not all in one sitting.

The questions
Physical: Stop right now! Forget the blond hair and stomach of steel, instead, concentrate on physical lifestyle habits. For instance, if you're a gym junkie and think of exercise as a pleasure, you're probably not going to find joy with a slobby couch potato. So you might write down 'must exercise regularly and enjoy sport'. Are you an avid anti-smoker? 'Non-smoker' is a perfectly acceptable thing to ask for. What about your alcohol consumption? Are you the type that adores sitting around chatting over more than a few wines? Someone who's anti-drinking would drive you nuts. If going out to dinner is your absolute favourite activity, a fellow gourmet would work well (probably make you fat, but hey!).

> **Example:** *Non-smoker. Likes exercise. Enjoys the odd glass of wine. Vegetarian.*

Chemistry: Automatically write 'must fancy and lust after' under the 'must have' side. There's only one stipulation: I want you to allot a time period. If the chemistry's not there immediately, how long are you prepared to wait and see? Two dates? Three weeks? Six months?

> **Example:** *Prepared to give it two months for chemistry to develop* or *Must be instant or it'll never work for me.*

Relationship attitudes and skills: If you're a sentimental, soppy person who gets dewy-eyed during the Kleenex ads and thinks they should bottle puppy breath because it smells so divine, your ideal match isn't the person who didn't bother going to their mother's funeral and thinks nothing of flushing kittens down the loo. So think about what your attitude to relationships is: romantic, realistic, pragmatic, cynical? Ideally, your partner should share the same views. Is marriage the logical (and highly desired) climax of a long-term relationship – or is it a worthless piece of paper?

Think about their relationship skills. Do you want someone who's easily able – and willing – to wax lyrical about how much they love you? Who shares their feelings openly and intimately? How much relationship experience do you require? Personally, I'd expect any man I dated to have had at least three or four serious relationships under his belt. That means he's had plenty of experience developing the relationship skills you need to make something work.

Example: *Romantic, gives relationships highest priority, wants to marry eventually.*

Social: What sort of person do they need to be to fit into your life? If you're a social butterfly and constantly entertaining, it helps if they enjoy it too – and are good at making small talk. Is it essential they're able to mix it with the best so you can take them to work functions?

Example: *Outgoing, socially skilled – can get on with anyone.*

Intellectual: What level of education did you complete? Are you an academic or more street smart? What are your other achievements? For a blissful blending of brains, it helps if they're on the same level as you. How important is it to you to be able to talk on the same level?

Example: *University educated, creative, able to think outside the square.*

Sex: Do me a *huge* favour: decide what level your libido's on and *please* at least try to match up with someone on the same level. A high-libido/low-libido couple truly is a recipe for disaster. One of you is always left feeling unsatisfied; the other's constantly feeling pressured. There are things you can do to even the score (see page 222) but if you can avoid it, do. It also helps if you share the same attitudes to sex. The adventurous, try-anything-once types should stick together. Ditto the 'I'd really rather have a cup of tea' people. The icing on the cake would be to match in experience and skills as well.

Example: *High libido, adventurous, uninhibited, experienced.*

Communication skills: Are you a talker or a listener? Do you want someone who'll babble on as much as you do or would a listener suit you more? Someone who's easy to talk to – and who finds it easy to talk back – is crucial for most of us. But remember communication skills can be learnt. If they're shy, there's plenty you can do to help them open up.

Example: *A good communicator, likes having a chat, a good listener.*

Finances: It's not the amount someone earns that's important, but more their attitudes to money. Are you a spender or a saver? How important are material possessions to you? If your idea of an essential expense is a daily massage and theirs is No-Frills tea bags and milk, saving for that house deposit is going to be one argument after the next. Same applies if you've built up a nice little bank balance and they've frittered their money away. A hell of a lot of resentment comes from unbalanced finances.

Example: *A saver, appreciates luxuries but doesn't waste money.*

Career: Again, it's not important what profession they're in but more your attitudes to work. If you work simply to live, someone who lives and breathes their job will bore you silly. If you give 200 per cent to your career, you'll be more compatible with someone who's also ambitious.

Example: *Career-orientated, ambitious, supportive of my career.*

Aspirations: Make sure you're both treading the same path at the same pace. If you're a stroll rather than pace person, someone whose energy level's on go-go-go won't suit you. If you're constantly trying to improve yourself, your ideal partner is someone who's equally as aspirational.

Example: *Lives life in the fast lane, aims high.*

Interests and hobbies: You're not going to be joined at the hip so it doesn't really matter if they're into cricket and you prefer soccer. But a stamp collector and a rock climber? The sort of hobbies and interests you have usually reflect your general personality. And it would be rather nice to do some things together that both of you enjoy, wouldn't it?

Example: *Loves reading, into outdoor activities, likes sport.*

Religion: If you're not at all religious, it's probably not import-ant to you what religion your partner is. Unless, of course, they're very religious and it's important to *them*. If you're a devout Christian, it's sensible to look for someone who shares your beliefs. One word of warning though: check it's important to *you*, not your parents before you write this one down. This is all about who *you* want, not who other people want you to be with.

Getting rid of the silly stuff

The moment of truth! Now's the time to go through your relationship and partner lists and check they're realistic and achievable.

Check the two lists match up

Q: What's number one on most people's prospective partner list?
A: Being able to make each other laugh.

Look at your relationship list and compare it to the partner list. Can the sort of person you're describing fulfil the needs on the relationship list? Go through it painstakingly – if the two lists are asking for two different things, you'll never be satisfied.

Is it the right kind of wish list?

If you've got money, fancy cars, a man who's cashed up to take you to the right restaurants on the 'must have' side, transfer them to the 'wish for'. Better still cross them off completely. The ideal list doesn't have any qualities that don't relate to values or behaviour. External things like looks and money aren't important; things like honesty, faithfulness, kindness are. Make it a shopping list of values instead.

Check that everything you've asked for, you can give in return

Your partner's got to be witty, creative, intellectual and a fab entertainer? Good luck finding them if you've got none of these qualities. You have no right demanding things you can't deliver yourself. Ideally, your wish list should be pretty close to a list of your own good qualities. The more like you are to the person you want to attract, the more likely you are to attract them.

How flexible is it?

If the 'must have' side's got reams written on it and the 'wish for' side hardly any, go through again and even them up a little. Near enough might be as close to ideal as you're going to get.

Check the physical heading

Cross off anything that relates to appearance. It's pointless writing things like 'must have long legs' because most of the time the person we fall for is packaged differently than we expected. My friend Cathy *despised* redheads. If she'd done this exercise, it would have been the first thing she'd listed – 'must not have red hair'. One year ago, she introduced me to the man who had 'everything I've been searching for' and he had bright orange hair. 'He's a redhead! You hate redheads,' I told her in the loo. 'He's got red hair? I've never noticed,' she said. True love, mother nature, the X-factor, chemistry, charisma – call it what you like but it has an astonishing knack of completely ignoring the more ridiculous things on our list. Try to fight primitive instincts like these at your own peril!

How long are your lists?

Now cut back to ten points on each side on each list. Yes, you must.

Is it realistic?

Look at the sort of person you've described by looking through *all* your wants and wish fors. Check you haven't fallen into the difficult-to-find-in-one-person trap. (Macho but likes cooking/ A nice girl who likes taking party drugs.)

Use when applicable

These lists are for long-term partnerships, not when you're happily out there dating for the sheer fun of it.

How to use your lists

Keep them. Update them as you change. Look at them whenever you meet someone new. Check the lists again three dates on and three months on. How close is this person to what you really want? Are they lacking something in the wish-for department or the must-have department? Are there things you're now willing to forgo because they've got positives you hadn't listed? Or is this

person way off target and you're kidding yourself? It doesn't matter if they're not a keen horse rider and you are. Small things like that don't affect the base of the relationship. But if they're a womanizer and you want security and honesty, you're heading for guaranteed heartache.

Are you too picky?

Who you? Never! Hmmm. My friend Trish says she isn't either – yet she wins the dubious honour of being the pickiest girl I've ever met. I asked her to write down the last ten times she'd been asked out (she's stunning, it happens often) and the reasons why she refused or didn't progress to date two. Here they are:

- too short (five feet ten)
- funny feet
- didn't use knife and fork properly
- hairline receding
- burped out loud in posh restaurant
- didn't like his friends
- didn't earn enough money
- appalling dress sense (a checked shirt)
- didn't ring when supposed to (called at 6 pm instead of 5 pm)
- too soppy.

Now, I'm with her on the burping bit but *hello!* The rest of those poor bastards didn't stand a chance. I've just asked you to make a wish list to refer to when choosing a partner – and I'm not taking it back. Insisting on some standards shows you've got high self-esteem and a sense of your own self-worth. But if you're ditching partners because their left toenail's not quite straight, you've got zero chance of ever finding someone.

As much as I hate to say this, it's a bit of a female thing. Ask a man what he's looking for in a woman and he'll say something like, 'Big tits.' Ask a woman and she'll start counting off on her fingers. 'Well, he's got to be taller than me. And have great teeth, I can't *stand* guys with bad teeth. I could never date a guy who had those awful patches of hair on his fingers – and he's got to be blond and make me laugh and . . .' Psychologists say it's because women expect more from relationships than men do. We don't just want a boyfriend, we want a lover, friend, playmate, career adviser, confidant, handyman, accountant, masseur, dishwasher and shrink. That's an awful lot of skills to find in one person. Most of us drop a few (hundred) things off our wish lists when it becomes painfully clear we'd need to date a football team to fulfil all of them – but not all women are willing to let go. Their wants remain etched in stone and they cling stubbornly to the belief that Mr Perfect is out there, they just haven't met him yet.

Is this you? Count up the number of dates you've been asked out on in the last year. How many did you accept? A coffee with one guy out of seven? Sorry, but you just made it onto the picky list and I have a question for you: if you don't go out with very many men, how have you got the experience to know what sort of guy really would suit you? Don't you think it's a bit hard to know what you want unless you've been out with enough people to know what's out there to choose from? Loosen up and live a little. Make exceptions for casual, short-term relationships.

Saving yourself for Mr or Ms Perfect isn't just boring, it's actually stopping you meeting them. Most of us pick up relationship skills from every relationship we have, so the more people you date, the better at relationships you are. Plus, you need to be out there. Your perfect match is going to turn up when you least expect it, in the least likely place, looking not at all like you expected. But they're not going to come knocking on your front door (though I *do* know a girl who ended up marrying the man who came to fix her ceiling fan – true story!).

If you're a picky person, humour me for six months and give the following suggestions a try:

- Give people you find appealing a chance. So what if you decide you don't fancy them after all? You might have found yourself a great friend.

- Go out with lots of different types of people. The more diverse your dates, the more tolerant you'll become. You'll realise no-one's perfect – not even you.

- Be nice. The nicer you are to people, the nicer they'll be to you and you'll get to see good qualities where before you only saw bad.

- Focus on dates as people, not packages. Concentrate on individual good features rather than lumping them into one category.

YOU'RE TOO PICKY IF . . .

- **Dates accuse you of asking too many questions, too early.** It's a date, not a job interview, and they're well aware you're fishing. Asking where they went to school is fine. Asking what their father does for a living and what sort of car they drive isn't.

- **You've only ever seen your perfect partner on a movie screen.** The chances of meeting Cameron Diaz or Leonardo DiCaprio are slim. The chances of them falling in love with you if you do, pathetic. ➤

- **Your friends roll about in hysterical laughter when you tell them the type of person you're hanging out for.** Ask friends of both sexes to check out your relationship and partner lists and read between the lines. 'Bernard, perhaps "size 38DD breast and waist no bigger than two hands span" might restrict your choices,' means, 'Bernard, a girl built like that isn't going to even look at you.'
- **Your friend, who rates similarly on the attractiveness scale, goes out on ten dates to your one.** The point here's rather obvious, don't you think?
- **You wipe people after the first date.** Give them at least three before you make up your mind. First impressions are often wrong.
- **You won't go out with someone because they're not your type physically**. A wit as sharp as a razor blade, the ability to really listen to you, make you laugh your knickers off (literally) – all can change your perception of how someone looks if you give them a chance.
- **You refuse dates because of where someone lives, the car they drive, their salary or their clothes.** You're not just being picky, you're a snob. Does the word superficial ring a bell?

WHEN IT'S SENSIBLE TO BE A FUSSPOT

- **If you were abused**, you may subconsciously pick potential abusers. It's wise to be cautious and screen new partners.
- **If you've just come out of a long-term relationship and are feeling raw and vulnerable.** Why cause yourself more pain by diving into another bad relationship?
- **If you can't say no to anyone.** You've been on 25 dates in the last two weeks and didn't really like or fancy any of them? Reverse all the suggestions I've made: you need to be *more* choosy, not less!

YOU'RE READY FOR A RELATIONSHIP WHEN . . .

Answer me one simple question: Do you *want* a relationship or do you *need* one? Score ten out of ten if you answered 'want'. If you don't quite understand the difference between the two, here it is in a nutshell. You're ready for a relationship when you're able to stand on your own two feet. Needing someone means you can't survive on your own. Wanting someone means you can, you're just looking to enrich your life further.

'Will it last?' is the most common question couples ask during premarital counselling – and just about all think love is the crucial ingredient. Wrong. Liking each other – sharing feelings, talking and feeling supported – is the most essential quality. Researchers rate passion as number two and being 'good friends', the third. Interestingly, passion decreases over time for women, but not for men.

See how you score on the following. Answer 'yes' to at least 13 of the following and you're officially approved to move on to the next chapter!

1. You're getting on with your own life. It would be nice if you met someone but in the meantime, it's not stopping you moving forward.
2. You've got lots of friends – both male and female.
3. You're happy at work (or at least making plans to get to the point where you will be).
4. You've accepted responsibility for your own happiness.
5. You've set financial, emotional and intellectual goals.
6. You're pretty happy with who you are.
7. Your self-esteem's in good shape.
8. You're not afraid to take risks, make decisions – and live with the consequences.
9. You're well and truly over your exes. You've sorted

through all the emotional baggage and left it behind.

10. You feel in charge of your life.

11. You listen to the advice others give you, but ultimately make up your own mind.

12. You've discovered lots of positive things about being single.

13. You aren't in any great hurry to find Mr or Ms Right. A relationship isn't the goal of your life but an added bonus.

> 'This is the first time I've been single for any period of time. At first, it took a bit of getting used to and I was desperate to meet someone but I'm just starting to enjoy it. I met a really nice guy the other night and it was like, "Oh no! I hope I don't like you because I don't want to give up all this freedom just yet."'
>
> Lynda, 34, journalist

14. You don't just want a partner, you want the *right* partner for the *real* you.

15. You don't just want them to love you, you want them to love you for who you really are.

16. You're confident enough to be yourself. If being you doesn't appeal to someone, you're intelligent enough to know it wouldn't have worked anyway.

Finding Mr or Ms Right-for-You

Likely hang-outs, how to spot a loser, plus tips on flirting, flings and breezing through the first few dates

● ●

Finding a partner isn't easy for most people. Others pop out for a loaf of bread and come back with flowers and six phone numbers. One of my best friends found love in a phone box. She sauntered down the street to make a call, leaving her husband at home. The marriage wasn't going fabulously well, he was sick, she was bored and their phone was out of order.

There was a guy inside the phone box, all done up in fancy dress. He took one look at my friend, threw open the door with a flourish and dramatically bowed in front of her. 'Come live with me and be my love,' he said, quoting John Donne, the 16th-century poet.

'And we will some new pleasures prove,' she replied, delivering the next line.

They both laughed. 'Want to come to a party?' he asked.

Why not? she thought. *I'll only be gone a few hours.* It turned out to be a little longer than that. She didn't go home at all. Like, never. Ended up living with the guy for close on a year.

If anyone else had told me that story, I'd be sceptical.

Knowing her, it seems perfectly plausible. She's one of those women who's got 'it'. Lucky her. And lucky *you* because, while some people seem to be born knowing how to attract the opposite sex, it is a skill you can learn.

Standing out from the crowd, sending out the right signals, flirting and finding someone who'll make you happy – there's an art to 'it'. 'It' has got a lot to do with good judgement: knowing the right thing to say and when to say it. Knowing who to steer clear of and who deserves a second try. That's what this chapter's all about: how to flirt your way into the arms and heart of someone amazingly special.

So how will *you* know when you've met *the one*? The sky will rumble and an angel will fall from heaven, hover mysteriously in front of you and mouth, 'You have chosen wisely.' Oh, and a lightning bolt will strike you on the head. Not. 'I knew the minute I met them.' 'I felt suddenly complete.' Excuse me while I vomit. I'm sorry, but there's nothing magical about it at all.

Funny how people always meet their 'soulmate' when they're ready to settle down, isn't it? Funny how they never meet them when they're barging out the door, suitcase packed and ready to hit Club Med for a whoop-it-up bonkarama holiday. Timing is everything.

We all mumble on about finding our soulmate – but what *is* a soulmate exactly? I think they're someone who brings out the best in us, who we click with. Someone who has the same goals and wants the same things out of life as we do. In other words, 'soulmate' is simply a romantic way of describing the person who's *the right choice for us right now*.

Sorry to dash those illusions but there's actually quite a few 'soulmates' out there for everyone. (And so there should be. What if we all only got one shot and yours was locked away chanting in a Buddhist monastery?) But to find even one of them, you have to be open to finding them. For all you know, your soulmate sits right in front of you on the bus every day but you've never noticed because you were too busy dreaming about Mr or Ms Wrong and how they removed your underpants with their teeth. Or you've had so *many* Mr and Ms Wrongs you're worn out and more than happy coming home to your cat.

My point here is this: if you're still waiting around for that lightning bolt, you've been watching too much telly. Throw out that soppy romance novel because you probably *won't* know instantly when you've met 'the one'. But you will have a pretty good idea a few months in. Just as important as finding your soulmate is recognizing when you haven't, hence the spot-the-loser and keep-your-eyes-wide-open tips at the start. There are lots of warnings in the first section of this chapter designed to get your bitch/bastard radar turned on. Once that light's blinking furiously, it's safe to move on to the fun bit. And have fun you will . . .

CHOOSING WISELY: PICK A PARTNER WITH YOUR HEART *AND* HEAD

No-one likes getting hurt, and one way to protect your heart is to be careful who you give it to. I'm all for giving in to chemistry, but don't turn off your brain while you're at it. I don't care how strong the attraction is, if the person you're feeling it for is looking at you through bars, forget it. On those first few dates, be sensible, look for warning signs and get out early if you see them. Watch yourself as well – we're all cheery little optimists at heart and *want* to think we've found true love.

Spot the loser

People often say to me, 'I always end up dating losers. But how can you tell in the beginning? Everyone looks good at the start.' They're wrong. Most losers give themselves away within three dates. People look good at the start because you *want* them to.

Meeting someone when you've been single for a while is a buzz. You've finally got 'and partner' functions all sewn up. Regular sex is blissful and you don't have to stress about what you're doing on the weekend because, when you're a couple, well, you can do *nothing* and still have fun and not get lonely. It's so easy to get carried away with the great feeling of having a relationship, people forget to have a good look at the person they're having the relationship with.

Next time, pay attention. Most of the time, the signs that someone's a total loser are right there in front of you, you're just not noticing them. It's great to be optimistic, but you're wiser to take off the rose-coloured Raybans and pick up a magnifying glass in the beginning. *Don't see what you want to see, see what's really there.* And don't be gullible.

For a start, you're asking for trouble if you date people who are unavailable. Just for the record, unavailable includes: married people and people who are already involved with someone else (living together, dating someone or bonking the same person once a week). Also unavailable are people who are getting over someone else or about to get involved with someone else. In other words, anyone who has *any* type of romantic involvement with another person.

These are some of the excuses unavailables will give you to make themselves appear available (translation – so they can have you on the side): 'I'm going to leave soon'; 'I don't really love them but I feel awful about hurting them'; 'I'm just staying until the kids reach 15'; 'It's an open relationship'; 'I'm not *really* with them because it's all very casual'; 'It's definitely over but I haven't found somewhere else to live'.

Lies! All lies! And even if

> 'I rush to the phone each time it rings, hoping it will be her. I walk around smiling at everyone. I look at flowers growing and can't stop thinking about her. I now make tentative arrangements with the boys to leave myself open if she's available. If she dumps me now, I'm going to be devastated.'
>
> Phillip, 31, technician

they're not, wait until they've *done* whatever it is they're promising *before* you get involved with them. That's your first step to spotting a loser: check their availability.

We did partner and relationship lists in Chapter 1 so you'll have a good idea of what sort of person suits you. Now we're going a little deeper into character.

Barbara De Angelis, America's relationship guru, believes character is all-important. Personality is the icing on the cake, she says, character is the cake itself. Don't ask yourself, 'Do I love this person and will they love me?', says Barbara. Ask, 'Are they *capable* of loving me the way I want to be loved?'

It's a very highbrow, intellectual way of looking at love, but it's a damn good way of avoiding heartache. When you next meet someone, ask yourself that question. If you're constantly getting hurt, reduce the risk by putting things down on paper. Score a new date on the following *before* getting in too deep, so you're aware of what you're taking on. No-one's perfect and we all have our foibles, but while some troubled souls are worth saving, others are just trouble.

How 'in touch' with themselves are they?

Are they aware of their character and personality faults? Do they know their strengths? They don't have to have spent the last decade on a therapist's couch to have done some soul-searching. Have they sorted out the emotional baggage from childhood and past relationships or are they trailing it along behind them?

To find out, ask: What are your family like? Are you close to them? Are you friends with your exes? Why did you split up? Did it hurt? How do you stay positive?

Are they affectionate and able to express their feelings?

In *Men Are from Mars, Women Are from Venus* John Gray is all for letting men go into their cave and respecting the right for people to remain silent. I say, if someone behaves like a caveman, let them be eaten by wild animals. The person who knows what they're feeling and shares their feelings with you is going to be a lot easier to share a bathroom with than the person who locks themselves in it.

To find out, ask: Anything which will get them to open up. You seem a bit distant tonight, anything bothering you? What did you think of the movie – wouldn't it be awful to feel like that? Also, do they grab your arm, kiss you spontaneously, say nice things – or does hugging them feel like you're cuddling an ironing board?

Are they honest? Are they a 'good' person?

Can you count on them to do the right thing by you *and* others? Do they treat their friends and family well? Do the right thing in business? Whatever your partner does to other people, they're more than capable of doing to you. That's why bits-on-the-side get really paranoid when their married lover finally leaves their spouse to be with them. They think, *They did it to them, what's to stop them doing it to me?* (Nothing.)

To find out, watch: Do they have lots of friends, or have much contact with their family? Are they generally popular, or do people seem a little distrustful of them and standoffish? Are they well liked at work?

Are they an adult?

A girlfriend of mine is 28 and acts 16. She's a scream as a friend but God help the guy who has a relationship with her. Does this person know how to cook, clean, look after themselves, pay bills on time and manage their money? Are they mature enough to know they can't afford a Lamborghini when they're barely covering the rent? Are they responsible?

To find out, watch: Check out their home. Does it look like a bomb's hit it? Check the fridge: any way-overdue bills tacked up there? Do they seem to be living beyond their means for the job they have? Do they ever ask you to lend them cash or bail them out?

Want to find out if he's the faithful type? Take a long, hard look at his genitals. Scientists claim men with larger than average testicles and wide penises are the most likely to cheat. A case of if you've got it, flaunt it?

Do they love themselves?

The more they like who they are, the healthier your relationship will be. The more hang-ups they have, the more you'll be used as their therapist. Needy, clingy, scared-little-mice people suck all your energy and confidence until you feel like a balled-up, soggy teatowel.

To find out, watch and listen: Do all your conversations centre around them? Do you spend a great deal of time solving their problems and boosting their self-confidence? Do you feel exhausted after you've seen them?

Are they positive and happy most of the time?

Do they look for problems or solutions? Are they a doer or a procrastinator? I once went out with a guy who was constantly depressed because of all the starving children in Bosnia. He thought he was holier-than-thou because they were never far from his mind. I thought he was a hypocritical son of a bitch. His fretting didn't help one iota – but a big fat cheque from his very healthy bank account might have.

To find out, watch: If they're unhappy or depressed, do they have a good reason for it? Do they often seem overwhelmed by life itself? Are they moody – up one minute, down the next?

SIGNS YOU'VE HOOKED UP WITH A HEART BREAKER

Don't believe all you hear. When your (not so) hot date says the following, they might well mean something totally different:

- *Don't let's talk about me – you're far more interesting.*
  You are. Or they're hiding something.
- *I like to live for the moment.*
  They're there for a fun time, not a long time.
- *I don't see my family.*
  Extreme danger sign. Unresolved family baggage makes for a very troubled adult.
- *I want to spend every second with you.*
  At first it's flattering, not so when the jealousy and possessiveness kick in. Smothered, controlled – yuk!
- *I need space.*
  You're smothering them or you care more than they do. They're either not interested in you or a bit of a commitment phobic.
- *I don't think it's appropriate for you to meet John/Jane* [*an ex who they're still friends with*].
  It's more than friendship. They can't commit to you until it's over with them.
- *But you can't drink there.*
  Excessive use of alcohol and drugs means, at best, you're in for mood swings, at worst, seeing them through rehab.
- *But I was only being friendly!*
  They're a flirt. The grass is always going to be greener on the other side – and they might well sneak a few mouthfuls while you're not looking.
- *I hate all my exes.*
  You'll be next on the hate list.
- *Can you lend me some money? I'm a bit short this week.*
  If it happens more than once, you'll soon be taking on a weekend job to support them. ➢

- *On Friday we're doing this, on Saturday we're going there, on Sunday we're . . .*

  The supreme organizer suits some but no-one wants to be controlled or dictated to *all* the time.

- *Let me do that for you.*

  They want to wrap you up in cotton wool and take care of you. The motherly/fatherly protective thing is great but not if you're constantly treated like a two-year-old.

- *I know we've had it six times already. But just once more?*

  Fab if your libidos match but if all they *ever* want to do is have sex, they're addicted or using it as a replacement for true intimacy.

- *No-one understands me but you.*

  Pretend you're sad and need rescuing and caring-sharing types home in like flies to a cow-pat. The old little-boy/girl lost act is often exactly that – an act.

- [Him] *I'm all for women's rights. Why don't you pick up this one?*

  He's a freeloader.

- [Him] *Great bag, great shoes, great outfit.*

  Great to go shopping with – not so great to marry someone who's more interested in the best man.

Little white lies and big, bad black ones

We've all done it. Reinvented ourselves a little (well, a lot) when we first meet someone. In nightclubs, I've been a ski instructor, taxidermist, midwife, vet, restaurant reviewer and Freudian psychotherapist with Jungian leanings (that one stumped them). The temptation to paint a vividly fascinating picture on a blank canvas is just too tempting sometimes. Why do we do it? Quite apart from being a good laugh, we think it makes us more intriguing. Let's be honest here: which guy would you be most attracted to? A nine-to-five bank teller or a private detective who's currently trailing a well-known personality for an incredibly sordid reason but, unfortunately, they can't tell you what it is.

Most of the time (300 drinks later) we shoot ourselves in the foot anyway ('You don't know where Aspen is? But I thought you were a ski instructor?'). If we don't slip up (we're on antibiotics and can't drink), most of us 'fess up when we find someone we really like.

> 'I used to have a thing going with my friends where we'd rate each woman by her CPI – cost per insertion – how much money you had to spend on her before she'd put out. The average was two dinners and one bunch of flowers.'
>
> Simon, 34,
> nightclub owner

Then we swap that set of lies for another. Roughly one-third of what we say to each other on the first three dates is either a straight-out lie or heavily exaggerated, especially if it concerns past lovers or recent indiscretions. According to psychologists, the average person lies at least once or twice a day, but dating couples are the biggest fibbers of all.

We all roll out the 'I want you to like me because I like you' lies in the beginning. 'Your apartment is charming!' we squeal, when it's really a dump. Those sorts of lies are pretty harmless and, most of the time, meant with the best intentions (protecting people's feelings while simultaneously painting ourselves in the best possible light).

Men lie for one basic reason: they want to bonk you but not necessarily have breakfast with you (ever). Women lie for more complex reasons. Sometimes, it's for the same reason – we want no-strings sex. Other times, it's because we not only want to have breakfast, but dinner, and another breakfast and another dinner as well – but we don't want you to know that yet. But more often, it's because we're not really *sure* if we want to bonk you *or* have breakfast *or* marry you and have your children, and until we've decided, we'll play it safe and paint a Ms Pure-and-Perfect picture just in case.

Of course, not everyone just lies about little, inconsequential things, like the car they drive. Some people tell fibs about things that do matter – like the fact that they're married. So while some lies should be mentally filed for a good ribbing later on ('My last girlfriend was a model'), others are downright dangerous. Learn how to spot the difference.

Harmless female fibs
- 'Of course you're the best lover I've ever had.'
- 'No, I don't fancy your friend Tony at all.'
- 'Oh my God, that's the biggest I've ever seen.'
- 'I've got my period.'
- 'You're the third guy I've ever slept with.'
- 'This old thing? I've had it for years.'
- 'I used to drive an MG.'
- 'You're an hour late? I hadn't noticed.'
- 'I hate expensive restaurants. I much prefer places like this.'
- 'Flowers are totally overrated.'
- 'I think your clothes are great.'
- 'Your tummy's not fat, it's cute.'

And the not-so-harmless: pay attention when –
- She says to call her at work – she's got a full-time boyfriend or living with someone.
- She says she's too busy for a relationship – she doesn't want one with you.
- She says she just wants to be friends – she likes you but doesn't fancy you or you're already a friend and she doesn't want to lose the friendship.
- She says her husband doesn't appreciate her – she's the equivalent to the guy whose wife doesn't understand him.
- She says she wants to leave him but can't afford it – she's looking for a meal ticket.

Harmless male fibs

- 'I love you (I want to sleep with you).'
- 'I'll call you.'
- 'I've been looking for someone like you all my life.'
- 'If you could only see how beautiful you look right now.'
- 'I really want to settle down.'
- 'If only it were summer we could walk hand-in-hand along the beach.'
- 'Your flatmate's kind of cute.' [If I hadn't met you, I'd want to have sex with her till I am blue.]
- 'Isn't that funny? I hadn't noticed how good-looking my flatmate Jane was until you pointed it out.' [She knocked me back.]
- 'My car's in for repairs. A mate loaned me this old thing.'
- 'It's just orange juice, try it.' [Three more drinks and she'll have her legs wrapped around my head.]

And the not-so-harmless: pay attention when –

- He says he's too good for you – he is.
- He says he needs space – he doesn't want to go out with you.
- He says he doesn't want a relationship – he doesn't.
- He says his wife doesn't understand him – he's not just a sleaze but totally unoriginal.
- He says he's about to leave her – why would he when he can have you on the side?
- There's a pale band of skin on his left finger – he's married.
- He won't give you his phone number – he's married.

'He'd be just perfect, if only . . . '

Ahh, we're so good at it, aren't we girls? We can walk into a dingy, run-down dog of an apartment and visualize exactly what it'll look like once we've made a few trips to Ikea. Unfortunately, flats aren't the only thing we see potential in. We think,

With a bit of work, I could change him into someone fabulous!

Men don't think like this. They don't see a girl in a baggy jumper with coke bottle-bottom glasses and spots and mentally transform her with contacts, make-up and a Little Black Dress. They just see a girl in a baggy jumper with coke bottle-bottom glasses and spots. Call them unimaginative but at least they're realists. We look at the guy sitting in the corner with greasy hair, ripped jeans and smoking a joint and think, *If he was with me, he wouldn't want drugs.*

Be honest. How many times have you said to a girlfriend, 'He'd be perfect if only . . .' ? The biggest mistake most women make is to fall in love with a man's potential. The quickest way you can up your chances of being happy long term is to fall in love with someone as they are now. Not who they could be. Not who you hope they'll be later. Not even what they'd look like with their hair cut, new clothes, if their car had new seat covers on it or their flat was painted ice-blue with a really interesting yellow around the skirting board. What you see now is what you'll get.

Another form of this is always going out with the bird with the wounded wing: the poor old underdog. Unless you're with the RSPCA, you don't have to pick up every stray or wounded animal or human being and heal them. Sometimes damaged goods can be restored and if it pays off, fabulous. But if you're always playing shrink and rescuer, you're deliberately seeking out uneven relationships. You're *always* the parent, they're the child. You've got power, they don't. You're independent, they're dependent. In other words, they won't reject you. There are lots of reasons why we do this (see Chapter 8), but at this stage, it's simply enough to be aware of it. Become a Darwinian. Seek out the strongest in the pack, not the weakest. Even they'll have more than enough problems to keep you busy for years.

THE MEET MARKET: WHERE TO FIND MR OR MS PERFECT-FOR-YOU

You see them. You want them. You get them. It's a simple equation that somehow doesn't always add up in the real world. For a start, most of us tend to get stuck on the first bit – actually meeting someone we'd like to go out with.

> 'Once you've had your heart broken a few times, you're much more careful. I tend to break up with men pretty early unless I can see a lifelong future together. I don't want all that pain again.'
>
> Nikki, 22, sales rep

Someone once said to me, 'If you're not meeting the right person, you're mixing in the wrong social scene.' There's probably a grain of truth in that. After all, if you're looking for a conservative academic with family values you probably won't find them snorting coke down the back of a seedy nightclub. But you might well bump into them outside because, truly, you can meet someone anywhere at any time. Not just on the nights when you 'go out'.

'Where are all the single men?' women wail.

'Where are all the single women?' men moan.

Now, unless all singles are agoraphobics and refuse to budge from their own living rooms, it's obvious you're crossing paths at least some of the time. Nightclubs and bars aren't the only places singles hang out. Why not try . . .

Parties

When you're feeling fab and looking terrific meeting people at parties is a cinch. Not so when you're frumpy, frazzled or the competition is hot. But it's worth making an effort because parties force people to spend at least a few hours in one place out of sheer politeness. So you've got time to sit back and study your target, watch who they're talking to and for how long.

They're being chatted up by a girl with legs as long as a giraffe or a guy who's so bloody good-looking he must be gay? They could be brain-dead boring for all you know. (You, on the other hand, have personality and lashings of style.) So find whoever organized the party and do some sleuthing. Single or attached? Nice person or steer-clear material? Find something you both have in common, then get them to introduce you.

'X, you must meet Sarah/Simon. They're as addicted to the movies as you are.'

The host/ess is snogging someone they've just met in the corner? Find an excuse to do something near your target – change the CD, grab some nibbles or enlist a friend's help and just go and stand over there. Next, simply catch their eye and smile a few times. If they seem friendly, close the gap and introduce yourself. Once there, flirt like mad, completely monopolize them and don't even think about going to the bathroom if the competition is hovering like vultures. (If you must, offer to get them a drink so you can come back to claim them.)

Top tactics

- Smile. Happy people attract people to them.
- Start a conversation. How do they know the host or hostess? What do they do for a living?
- Give them a compliment. Your friends have just voted them best-looking guy/girl at the party.
- Drop lots of clues on how to find you again in case you get separated. Where you work, the suburb you live in, the fact that you know so-and-so.

No-nos

- Don't give up if you smile and they don't smile back. They might not have seen you (were too vain to wear their glasses) or simply drifted off in la-la land.

- Don't get drunk before meeting them.
- Don't muscle in when they're obviously already chatting up someone else or attached.

Nightclubs

In all the years I've been single, I estimate I've been to at least 50 different nightclubs around ten times each. Out of those 520 attendances, I've spoken to and flirted with hundreds of men. But you know what? I've only ever had a relationship with one that lasted past two dates.

'You're kidding!' said my girlfriends, when I revealed this astonishing fact. *Silence*. 'But dead right – I've never ended up having a relationship with someone I've met in a club either.'

The stats back me up on this one: less than four per cent of people who meet in a nightclub, on holiday, or through the personals end up marrying. Subtract the other two and it evens out to one out of one hundred.

But there are nightclubs and nightclubs. I'm talking the dimly lit, music blaring, dance floor, can't-talk-unless-you-shout type. Clubs with cosy little bars off to one side and fabulous fresh-air outdoor drinking areas are a little different. For a start, you can actually see each other – and you can talk without all the veins in your neck popping out (most unattractive). So unless it's casual sex you're after, avoid the dark spots. Like your mother said, stick to the well-lit areas if you want to play it safe.

Top tactics

The dark bit: Anyone you meet after 12 drinks will seem wonderful. Don't give your home phone number to anyone you meet after three stiff spirits, work number only after you've downed up to five. (Get theirs if you're still able to talk after this and be sure to write a description to jog your memory the next day: 'girll who waz druk with fizzy hare' or 'blok wat tried to kizz me'). Whoever you meet, assume they're half as attractive as they appear under dim light. Don't expect anyone to call when they say they will and it'll seem a nice surprise if they do.

The lit bit: Be 50 per cent more suspicious than you would normally (the vibes from the dark bit leak out under doors). Use the flirting techniques described later in this chapter, especially the ones that make you stand out from the crowd. Don't wear black. Nightclub gear is more uniform than McDonald's.

Pubs and bars (minus the dance floor)

Now we're talking – especially if it's a pub. The combination of a packed crowd, plenty of chance to take the long way round and accidentally rub your way through the best-looking group in the place, a few ales to take the edge off, not too noisy so you can talk but noisy enough where silences don't seem uncomfortable . . . The only thing that could possibly make it better is a pool table. Personally, I would rather eat 12 hot chillies than pick up a pool cue, but I have to admire people who work the table: the old 'lean forward to show off the cleavage' if you're a girl; the 'push the cue really hard with your shirt sleeves pushed up so your biceps flex' if you're a bloke. We know what you're playing at guys (and it isn't pool) but the floor show works anyway!

Top tactics

Use the same formula as you do for parties. Move closer to whoever you've got your eye on. Smile a lot, make eye contact, make sure you're standing at the bar when they are. 'A bit crowded, isn't it!' or, 'Phew! Hot in here!' is all you need to get the conversation rolling.

No-nos

It's very easy to get carried away when you're drinking in 'shouts'. If you find you're singing 'Twelve Green Bottles' at the top of your lungs, you've had too many. Tip for male pool players: a bulging erection pushed into our back as you're 'helping' us is taking things too far, too soon. Doing that aggressive macho sulk thing when you lose isn't attractive either.

Think twice before hitting the clubs in that mini and plunge top: it's nature's way of trying to get you pregnant. One bar and club survey showed single women's hemlines got shorter and necklines dropped during ovulation, your most fertile time of the month.

The friend-of-a-friend

This is how most people meet the love of their life – they're introduced through a third party (most often your family or a friend). A cinch when it's someone you know well – not so easy when you've seen them over at your neighbour's or at a distance at a sort-of-friend's party but never got to meet. You're too shy to ask them to set you up but if you don't act soon, you fear they'll be snapped up by someone else. Take a deep breath! There's nothing desperate about calling your friend or neighbour and saying, 'X looked cute. Are they single? What are they like?' A gracious friend will immediately offer to set you up (assuming they're worth being set up with!). If they don't suggest it, you do – and remind them often until they're so sick of you hassling them, they finally do arrange that drinks party.

Don't play it coy once you finally do meet face to face. Sure, they might have figured out it isn't a chance meeting, but so what? If they're not flattered, they're not interested. Talk to them, pay them lots of attention and make it blatantly obvious you're interested, but leave the ball in their court to arrange another meeting. You've done the hard work – if they don't pick it up from there, the attraction's one-way (yours).

Top tactics

- Flirt but don't be *so* easy-to-get you remove all challenge. Once you're convinced they've got the green light to ask you out, cool it a little. You're interested – but not desperate.
- Call to thank the person who set up the meeting, but go easy on the 'What did you think X thought of me?' questions. You'll put them in an awkward position if the answer's, 'Not much.'
- Make sure the person who organized the meeting has your phone number (better still, give it to them at the end with a simple, 'Call me if you'd like to').

No-nos

- Friendly doesn't mean frothing at the mouth. Resist giving thumbs-up signs to involved parties when they're not looking (they'll catch you for sure). Pretend you're talking to your best friend and keep it light.
- Don't ignore everyone else in the room. You don't need to superglue yourself to their side.
- Don't hassle the person who got you together if they don't call you afterward. And don't bag them either. It's not their fault they didn't fancy you.

A class

Someone once told me to sign up for a course that usually only attracts men. Brilliant idea, I thought, and trotted along in heels and a mini to 'Basic Mechanical Skills Part I' at the local college. There, sitting around in their woollies and (where did they find them?) polyester slacks with permanent creases down the front, were all the nerds that lived in my area. Because let's face it: any *real* man who doesn't know how to check the oil and water isn't going to completely humiliate himself by admitting it in front of a bunch of strangers.

I was unlucky but that doesn't mean you will be. Night courses, especially, are a great idea. Two friends have 100 per cent success ratings: one did a Thai cooking course, licking more than the spoon after school. Another signed up for an 'Internet for People Who Still Use Pencils' course and landed herself a cuddly, bald but totally adorable uni lecturer.

Top tactics
Everything from 'I didn't quite hear that last point, what did they say?' to 'Can you come over to help me with my homework?'

No-nos
Loudly chatting someone up so the rest of the class can't hear the lecturer. Some people actually enrol to learn.

The office
Not surprisingly, around two-thirds of people meet their partners through work, because this is the one situation you know exactly what you're letting yourself in for. Not only do you spend most of your time at work, you get to check out how people perform under pressure (that is, you see the *real* them rather than a dressed-up, well-behaved version). Plus, there's a million opportunities to chat them up.

Top tactics
How to find out if they're single? Meet them first. It's easy. Just say, 'Hi, I'm Jo/John and I work in ——.' After a few smiles

exchanged down the corridor ('How's your day going?' etc.) it's time to move in for the kill. Corner them in the lift or the coffee room or whatever, sigh, and say, 'What a week! I'm really looking forward to the weekend. How's your week been?' They'll answer, then you can drop in the all-revealing question: 'What have you got planned for the weekend?' If their answer starts with 'we', forget them immediately. 'We' never means their mother, dog or best friend, it means a lover/partner/ spouse. Even if they don't drop the royal 'we', you'll get a big clue from what they do have planned. A few parties or clubs? They're probably single or not dating seriously. Renovating the house? Almost certainly attached.

Got the green light? It's easy to follow it up with something like, 'I'm going to check out X (a bar or restaurant). Have you been there? Why don't you come along if you're not doing anything?'

If you don't want to be that forward and they work in your area of the office, ask them if they want coffee while you're passing their desk. Do they want to take ten minutes out to go *out* for a coffee? If they seem snowed under, offer to pick them up a sandwich while you're out. Next time, ask them if they want to have lunch at that great new lunch place.

No-nos
- Anyone who's married or in a serious relationship or your boss.
- Following them around, sending lovey-dovey e-mails, staring at them like a love-sick puppy dog.
- Flirting heavily (that is, snogging beside the photocopier). Save it for outside work hours.
- Discussing the ins and outs (particularly the ins and outs) of your relationship with colleagues.

Your flat

You just can't believe it. For six months, you've shared the dishes, toothpaste and coffee. People keep assuming you're a couple because you do the shopping together, but it's a strictly flatmate/friend thing – at least it was until now. Now you can't imagine why you didn't realize how stunning they were. Now you lie in your bed wishing you were in theirs across the hall. A gift from heaven – or the beginning of a nightmare?

Personally, I'd think twice before sharing a bed with a flatmate. For a start, you become instant de factos – the relationship's serious before it's even started. If you split up, one usually ends up moving out (leaving one of you with the problem of finding a replacement); if they don't move out, bringing home a new partner is never going to feel comfortable again. Having said all that, more than one married couple met when one answered a 'room for let' ad.

Top tactics

Don't act on impulse. Wait until you're absolutely certain you want to take the relationship further, then sit down and talk about it. Say how you feel and ask if they feel the same. If they don't, drop it (if you can't, move out). If you do decide to start dating, create your own 'space' for each other. Don't automatically sleep together every night. Keep going out separately with friends, in fact, go out *more*. In other words, don't live in each other's pockets even though you actually are.

No-nos

- Don't do it because you've just had an awful night where no-one chatted you up and you want reassurance that you're attractive.
- Don't do it because you're both drunk, you've just been dumped or your vibrator just died.

Introduction agencies

Oh no, has it really come to this? Hold on one second. You might be surprised who's using introduction agencies these days. Busy people. Career people. *Intelligent* people who realize they're unlikely to meet someone at a bar or a nightclub or don't have the time or energy. Isn't it logical to have a computer (because that's how it's done) match you up with someone with similar interests and aspirations? Sure, they can't predict chemistry but you never know your luck in a big introduction agency. Your 'how we met' story possibly won't thrill the grandkids but, truly, is it more dignified to say you met in a bar? Introduction agencies do the legwork so they're especially useful for people who are in their late thirties or forties when your options or avenues may have decreased. They can't promise miracles but a good, professional dating agency is well worth a try.

'I went to a Desperate and Dateless Ball and got matched up with this complete moron. He started by banging his bread roll on his side plate, shouting, "Where's the food?" and got worse from there. I escaped to my girlfriend's table and spent the night looking nervously over my shoulder, expecting my "date" to materialize at any moment. Despite being matched to someone so awful though, I've always found D & D and Bachelor and Spinsters' Balls heaps of fun. Everyone's out to have a good time, you all walk around the room and it's like, "Gosh! They're cute!" No wonder they're so popular.'

Alison, 25, photographer's assistant

Top tactics

- Talk on the phone for at least an hour or so to make sure you're compatible. Don't be afraid to ask lots of questions: you both know you're after a long-term relationship so there's no need to pretend you aren't.

- Arrange to meet for coffee rather than lunch or dinner so you don't waste time if it doesn't work. Be polite always but don't lead people on. If you don't like them, say, 'You're a great person, X, but unfortunately, not quite what I was looking for.'

No-nos
- Don't invite strangers to your home and don't go to theirs until you know them very well.
- If it's just sex you're after, spell it out. If you think that's all they're after, ask them.
- Trust your gut instinct and listen carefully to their relationship history. Are they using the service for the right reasons or because they really are such a no-hoper this is a last resort?

Dinner for Six (and other organizations like it)
These deserve special mention. They don't bill themselves as introduction agencies but provide a way of 'supplementing people's social lives', in other words, a way to meet new people. They work because it's a big enough group not to feel obliged to be nice to one person in particular and small enough to get to know everyone reasonably well. A friend of mine went to a couple, and while he didn't meet the woman of his dreams, he made some great friends (who, I might add, were responsible for introducing him to his current two-year love). The more single people you meet, the more you up your chances of finding someone who's available that suits you.

Top tactics
By all means shine but don't dominate the conversation. If you see the person you're keen on being chatted up by someone

else, don't panic, just move to sit next to them at the first avail-able opportunity. It's totally acceptable in this situation to give your (work) phone number to more than one person in the group, even if they have obviously hooked up with someone else. You're there to make friends as well as possibly meet someone. In other words, even if you are hoping like mad they'll take it as a come-on, it's still considered polite.

No-nos
* Leaving after the entree because there's no-one there you fancy or particularly want to be friends with. Unless it's truly ghastly, it's polite to hang around until after the main course. Amuse yourself: try out a few funny dinner party stories to see if they get a laugh.
* Being openly critical: of the food, venue or the people. Just because you're not having a fab time, doesn't mean others aren't.

The personals
They used to be for men who couldn't go near a girl without tripping over their shoelaces and girls called Beryl and Marge who wore twinsets before they became fashionable again. Now people use them because there's no need for corny chat-up lines, nasty rebuttals and red, bleary eyes from smoke-filled bars. You can spell out exactly what you want from a partner, screen them over the phone and get to know them via the earpiece without ever having to press flesh.

But there are drawbacks. Be careful what you write in your ad and learn how to interpret other people's. It may come as a shocking surprise but not everyone uses the personals to meet lifelong partners: about 70 per cent are after sex. So keep it simple and steer clear of adjectives that could be misinterpreted (like 'fun-loving' – keen for casual sex). Give the basics of your appearance (tall, slim or short and petite) and that's it. Don't say 'lonely' or 'open minded'. 'Sexy' will only attract sleazes. If you're a professional person, say so, but don't advertise your income unless you want someone who wants a free ride.

Top tactics
As per introduction agencies, spend as long on the phone as possible.

No-nos
- If you decide to meet them, meet in a public place where you're known so that the person you're with can be identified.
- Take a friend with you first time around. Ask for identification.
- Stick to an area that's well lit with lots of people around.
- Give the details to several friends – where you'll be, the time you'll meet, the person's name, phone number and address.
- Never invite them to your home or go to theirs.

The Internet
If I had my way, I'd still be typing on my beloved typewriter with the dodgy 'h' key. But there's got to be something in it or else 50,000 Americans would not be engaging in cybersex every day. This is when you go into a private 'chat room' and type sentences like, 'Ummmm,' and, 'That feels great, baby,' very fast, using one hand. Not all Net nutters are after an intergalactic orgasm, however – plenty use their computer as a dating agency. All you do is call up a local dating site (or an overseas destination that appeals) and choose from the options available. There's everything from singles chat rooms to cybervow weddings on offer as well as an Internet version of

the personals. Fill in a form on the computer, describe yourself, attach a picture if you like, then sit back and wait for the e-mails.

It's safe (no-one can track down where you live by your e-mail address) and, even I have to admit, bloody convenient. Once you've connected to someone you like, use the same rules that apply to personal ads and introduction agencies. In other words, chat on screen until you feel you've got a sense of the person. There are as many loonies (possibly more) on the Net as in your average nightclub so meet in a public place and tell people the details beforehand.

> '**I live in the country and have a child so I find it difficult to meet people. One day, I was flicking through the paper and stopped at the personals. I thought,** *Why not?*, **then a little voice said,** *Jesus! I must be a bit of a loser if I'm stooping to this.* **But I gave it a go and I ended up meeting a really nice guy who I went out with for eight months. Another I went out with for two years. Pretty good innings really.'**
>
> Judy, 35, single mum

Top tactics

- Talk on the phone as well as through the computer. You can tell a lot about someone by their voice and phone manner.
- Buy a book about the Internet if you're a beginner. There are all sorts of strange codes you'll need to know: (:-) means smile). If you want to come across as hip and happening in the chat rooms (and avoid saying yes to something you don't understand!), brush up on your Netiquette beforehand.

No-nos

- Don't lie about your appearance unless you never intend meeting in the flesh.

- Don't type in capital letters. Apparently, this is the equivalent of shouting. (I told you, this is weird stuff!)
- Also remember a lot of people use the Internet to shield shyness (the girl who's a scream on screen might get tongue-tied without her keyboard).

The chance meeting

They're in the queue at the deli, sitting alone in the next row at the movies, across the aisle on a plane, snivelling into a tissue at the doctor's surgery. It takes guts and confidence to front up to a complete stranger and the rejection factor is about 90 per cent (they're gay, married or just met the love of their life). But what have you got to lose? If they turn out to be the new lover of your best friend, get out of it by saying, 'I knew we'd end up friends!'

No time calls for drastic measures – especially if they're only going to be around for a few minutes. Swallow all pride (there's no way to get around this one without putting yourself on the line), walk up to them and say, 'Hi. I know this is ridiculous, but I've got the weirdest feeling we're meant to meet.' This will prompt either a warm, intrigued smile or a cold, 'Sod off, loony.' If it's a smile, follow it up with, 'Have you got time for a coffee or drink just so I can satisfy my curiosity?' Now, good looks and a tingly feeling in your tummy won't guarantee they'll turn out to be what you desperately want them to be, but at least you won't spend the next six weeks dreaming about a total stranger!

If they're trapped on a plane, train or bus, ask a question. Do they know which stop to get off at if you want to get to X? Where are the loos? Could you borrow their paper? While you're doing it, make it obvious you're looking for an excuse to talk to them. Smile every single time they look in your direction and look them straight in the eye. Bar writing 'Come and talk to me' in black felt pen across your forehead, give them a definite green light (and I wouldn't rule out the former if it's an emergency). You think they're interested but shy? Use the old 'haven't we met?' trick. 'Sorry I keep staring at you but you really remind me of my friend X. I don't suppose you're a relation?'

Places you just might get lucky include:

- **The supermarket**: Those new, wide aisles aren't for easy trolley access, they're for flirting in. That seemingly innocent jingle slipped in between Seal and Marvin Gaye? They're not talking about the food when they say, 'You can't get fresher than that' at Tesco's. Admittedly, you feel more confident date-hunting with a few stiff drinks under your belt than hovering around the loo rolls in your tracksuit, but don't underestimate the supermarket as a potential hunting ground. Whether people add 'one blonde with big knockers' to their shopping lists is one thing but more than a few singles have connected while reaching for the same loo paper. Besides, you can tell a lot about someone by what's in their shopping trolley. Like, it's a pretty safe bet the man stocking up on nappies and tampons is married with child; the guy with chocolate biscuits and 25 frozen pizzas is most definitely single. Just one word of warning: couples frequently split up while shopping.

> *Ever noticed how the talent looks better at closing time? It's not just the alcohol, say psychologists. We unconsciously inflate our opinions of others late at night to make ourselves feel better about the dwindling options. At 10 pm, singles judged the average attractiveness of opposite-sex club patrons as 2.3 on a scale of 1–5. Ratings soared to 3.8 an hour before the club shut. Unfortunately, the effect evaporates in the harsh light of the morning after.*

Just as you're chatting nicely about Colgate versus Macleans, the other half comes thundering down the aisle clutching bread rolls.

- **The beach**: To be avoided at all cost unless you have a similar body type to Elle MacPherson or the new Levi's guy. On the other hand, if someone shows interest when you've got sand up your bottom, zinc cream up your nose and sweat dripping from every pore, they've got to be genuine. One word of warning though: never go underwater while on the hunt. Stuff from your nose smeared across your face is not a good look.
- **The laundromat**: A terrific chance to check out their underwear without having to peel it off. Pick one which has a coffee shop just around the corner to satisfy both your caffeine cravings while your clothes are swishing around in the dryer.

Top tactics

- Don't be put off if they stare at you blankly when you deliver your come-on line. Simply repeat it. After all, their mind's not really in pick-up mode if they're in the deli tossing up between pastrami or the shaved turkey.
- Don't think too much. First, there's no time. Secondly, you'll never do it if you start worrying about making a fool of yourself.
- Can't think of one thing to say? Ask them *anything* to stall: the time, directions.

No-nos

- If they've got a wedding ring on, it's not on to approach them.

- Following them is also out – unless you intend catching up and saying something. They'll think they're either on *Candid Camera* or see scenes from *Fatal Attraction* flashing before their eyes.

HOW TO FLIRT THEIR KNICKERS OFF (WELL, ALMOST)

It's a fact: confidence and a great sense of humour will score you more dates than good looks (though, I will admit, you're laughing if you've got all three). Chatting people up really is quite easy: all it takes is the right attitude and the willingness to take a few risks and make things happen.

Getting noticed

There are ways to stand out from the crowd *and* retain a sense of dignity. Attract his or her attention by using any (or all) of the following tricks.

Have a good time

Look around any crowded singles venue and you'll see groups of two (sorry girls, but it's usually us), their chairs facing outward, faces peering hopefully into the crowd, waiting for someone to come and talk to them. This sends two signals: 'I'm bored, come and entertain me' (hard work); or 'I'm desperate' (the supreme no-no). If you're smiling, laughing and thoroughly enjoying yourself, people notice. They think, 'I wish I could be with them. They're having fun.'

Attract attention

Pull out a Filofax or start writing intensely on the serviettes at a café and people have something to talk to you about. 'Is this going to be your first novel? What are you writing?'

DIAL-AN-ORGASM (BUT NOT A DATE)

I did a radio show on phone-meeting lines and figured I'd better give it a go first. They're supposed to be 'the Nineties way to meet someone' but, quite honestly, I wasn't convinced. You'll find them in the back section of any tabloid paper. I, rather predictably, chose the one with the biggest ad.

Most meeting lines work on the same system: you leave a message to say you're on the line, then you're allowed to scan through the other messages. If you like the sound of someone, you send them a message saying you'd like to talk. If they agree, you're put through. If someone wants to speak to you, a voice tells you to check your mailbox.

Despite leaving a deliberately provocative message ('Hi, I'm Susan. I'm five feet nine, rich, slim and people tell me I look like Julia Roberts' (who said I was going to be honest?)) not one person called me. Humiliating. But I soon found out why. Ninety per cent of people who use phone lines are after something a little more than just a coffee.

Like Rolly. 'Hi. I'm Rolly. I'm six feet two, blond, athletic, intelligent, rich and want to make you feel good right now.' I couldn't resist and, funnily enough, Rolly was free when I requested a live chat with him. This is how it went.

'Hi, I'm Rolly.'

'Hi, I'm Susan.'

Then Rolly cut straight to the chase. 'What are you wearing, Susan?' (Who was this guy? Head of the fashion police?)

'Er, just old track pants,' I answered rather lamely.

'Susan, I want you to pull those track pants down, pull your knickers to the side and put your fingers ——'

I hung up. Holy moly! Now, I might be a little naive sometimes (especially before I've had a few coffees), but wasn't this an *introduction* line rather than live phone sex? Seems not. The verdict from the regular users: phone-meeting lines aren't fab for finding a long-time soulmate but as Dial-an-Orgasm, they're terrific!

Use the old 'look-then-look-away' trick

It's the best way to let someone know you fancy them without feeling like a twit if they don't fancy you. Look at them until they look back, then drop your eyes and smile to yourself. This says, 'I think you're cute but I'm too shy to come over.'

If you're with friends of the opposite sex, make it obvious you're not lovers

My brother and I are best friends. Which is fabulous – but not so great when you're out hunting. We're around the same age and everyone assumes we're a couple. Bar wearing 'I'm her brother' and 'I'm his sister' badges (which we did consider), the only other thing that seems to work is very definitely saying, 'This is my *brother*, Nigel,' whenever we are introduced to, or introduce, anyone.

Smile at them

If they pick up on it and smile back, great. If they look straight through you, move your glance ever-so-slightly over their shoulder and they'll think you were smiling at someone else. A smile can say, 'Come over and talk to me,' 'Ask me to dance,' or simply, 'I like you and find you attractive.'

Make eye contact

Like the smile, this one's fairly foolproof and incredibly versatile. It doesn't matter where you are – in a café, on the beach (ditch the sunglasses) or buying sausages in the butcher's. All you do is catch their eye, hold it for a second longer than usual, then look away again. The more often you do it, the more likely they are to get the hint.

Don't worry too much about your opening line

People clam up when they see someone they fancy because they think the first thing out of their mouth has to be witty, charming or dead funny. It doesn't. A short 'Hot isn't it' or 'Great pub!' will do the job. Keep it simple and keep it logical. The best lines are often the obvious. 'Have you tried the chicken salad?' while you're standing in line at a sandwich shop. 'Do you know how to work this machine?' while you're at the gym.

Be impulsive and unpredictable

Most people aren't terribly creative so they're awfully impressed when they meet someone who is. It's not hard to be seen as unpredictable and wildly interesting. Thrusting a cold, frosty beer into an unsuspecting male hand while saying, 'Hi. My name's Lucy,' will be seen as highly impulsive and wonderfully eccentric. Telling a girl you love her earlobes will guarantee you a smile.

If you're not getting anywhere, take drastic measures

I'd fancied this guy for ages, but every time we met (he was a friend of a friend), he'd look straight through me. After trying every single ploy I could think of, I decided I didn't really care that he didn't fancy me, I just wanted to bloody well find out *why*. I plonked myself down beside him and said, 'So – why don't you fancy me? Are you gay, hate brunettes or just don't find me attractive?'

He burst out laughing and his flatmate piped up with, 'He *does* fancy you – he just didn't think you fancied him.'

We ended up going out for eight months. The point is, sometimes you really do have to take the bull by the horns.

If all else fails, blame it on a friend

'My friend and I have got a bet. She thinks you're a merchant banker, I think you're a surfer.'

'My mate told me I wouldn't have the guts to come over and ask you if you've ever been on telly. Aren't you the girl in the toothpaste ad?' (Come on, we'd all love it!)

While you're watching them, they're watching you

The way you walk, what you're wearing, how you hold your drink (in all senses): make no mistake about it, you'll be judged instantly on all of them.

Make sure your clothes reflect the real you

A white mini teamed with thigh-high boots will brand you a party girl (and that's putting it nicely). A shirt undone to your waist, hairy chest and a gold medallion means womanizer (add crotch-hugging pants and women will start wearing garlic around their necks and making cross signs with their fingers when you approach them).

Not sure what to wear when you're out on the hunt? Two rules: wear something you feel comfortable in and make sure it suits the occasion. If in doubt, dress down rather than up. The girl who shows up at a barbecue, picking her way across the lawn in heels and stockings, instantly earns the label of 'pretentious snob'. A girl in jeans and a T-shirt is seen as carefree and down-to-earth when she's surrounded by standard black.

Feel desperate and you'll look it

Your biological clock is ticking like a bomb, you're dying to get over an ex, haven't had a date in ten years or simply having a fat day: those 'I'm desperate for attention' vibes send out waves that spread over a ten-kilometre radius. If you're walking out the front door praying to God this is the night, stay home. Murphy's Law guarantees not even the bar staff (and they're *paid* to be nice to you) will give you a smile when you most need one.

The better looking you are, the more work you have to do

This is what people automatically assume when they spot someone drop-dead divine. He thinks: *She'd never be interested in me/Bet her boyfriend's rich, powerful and built like a gorilla/What could I say that she hasn't heard a thousand times before?* She thinks: *Anyone that good-looking has to be vacant between the ears/Bet he's a bastard and really up himself/Bet he only dates models, he'd never go out with someone like me.*

The good-looking person is thinking: *Why doesn't anyone ever talk to me?/Why doesn't anyone ever ask me out?/What's wrong with me?* If you're above average in looks or have something particularly spectacular (a great set of knockers for instance), no-one will come near you unless you make it incredibly obvious you want them to.

If you're a confident female, some men will find you scarier than Godzilla

'Confident' in boy talk translates to any female who earns more than he does, has a more prestigious job, is more articulate, has a better sense of humour, is more attractive – and I'm really not kidding. A woman who knows what she wants and is confident of who she is, is as attractive as hell but requires a lot more courage to approach than your average girl (that is, six beers as opposed to two). If you're getting lots of looks but no action, this is probably what's happening. The solution? Smile a lot and look friendly. Or approach guys yourself.

Now you're talking . . .

OHMIGOD! They've taken the hint and on their way over. Relax, take a deep breath then:

Pretend you're talking to your best friend

Skip the small talk and clichéd 'do you come here often?' stuff and talk about what you normally would. Adopt a relaxed, friendly attitude even when you're screaming inside, 'God, they're *gorgeous*!' When you're both a bit more relaxed, then you can move into full-on flirting mode.

Don't leave your brain in the back seat of the cab

That LBD will be appreciated but you need more than a Wonderbra and great legs to keep someone's attention. Same for men. A jaw that looks like it's been carved with a chisel is what dragged us over but you need to open your mouth for us to hang around. A male friend of mine put it perfectly. Men are looking for a best friend with breasts. Someone they can share the good and bad times with – and bonk afterward. Women are also looking for a best friend with benefits.

Say their name three times in the first conversation

Repeating the name of someone you haven't met before not only shows you're interested, it makes them feel noticed and important. An added bonus: you'll actually remember it.

Give a compliment

But only if you mean it. Sincere flattery will get you everywhere. Insincere flattery sounds like a line (because it is).

Tease but not too much

Some people love a challenge and adore it when someone instantly takes up a contrary position to whatever it is they're talking about. If you're clever and articulate, go for it. Just make sure it doesn't turn into a slanging match where you're both trying to score points. Trading insults isn't sexy.

Make them laugh – but only if you've got a good sense of humour

Body language experts believe women should use more humour while flirting, men less. Why? Because men like to keep things on a more superficial level (and what better way than with a joke?), while women like deep conversations. Similarly, men laugh more among their own sex, women talk more and laugh less. It's something to think about, but if humour's not your strong point, don't push it. There's nothing worse than delivering the punchline and seeing a sea of expectant faces still waiting for it.

Be reasonably easy to please

The drink they bought hasn't got enough ice in it. It's too cold/too hot/too crowded/not crowded enough. Someone keeps bumping you. You can't hear them properly. Honestly, if it's that difficult, suggest going somewhere else.

Always leave when it's going well

Ahh, here she goes, sounding like those dreadful people who wrote *The Rules*. I don't mean to, but any performer will tell you you should always leave your audience wanting more. Flirting requires energy and 100 per cent undivided attention. Even the best flirt can only keep it up for a few hours – leave before you run out of steam.

Girl talk, boy talk and why it's often double Dutch

Men and women speak the same language but the words have different meanings. Men are more literal, women figurative. It's because, usually, women have much more training in communication skills than men do. We quickly learn to read between the lines because, biologically, we need this skill. When a baby cries, a mother needs to be able to tell the difference between a hungry cry, a bored cry and a sick cry. We're naturally more in touch with the right side of our brain (the touchy-feely bit) so pick up on feelings even when we're not conscious of doing it.

We talk a different language too. For a start, we're rather fond of overstating things. 'I feel like an elephant' means 'I've put on 0.000005 of a kilo.' 'Everyone hates me' means 'The man in the newsagency didn't smile at me as warmly as he usually does.' We do this because it sounds wonderfully dramatic, and since most women spend most of their lives talking, we naturally have better vocabularies and are adept at expressing ourselves (we read more which also helps). Needless to say, some men are often bamboozled by the words that come out of our mouths.

Men are much more literal. They use language in a

straightforward way, and they don't manipulate as much as women do. A woman will say, 'God! That movie's so romantic. I wish someone would feel that way about me,' because she's fishing to find out how he feels about her. (The correct answer, guys, is, 'I do,' or, 'I bet a billion guys have.') A man will say, 'That was a great movie.' It wouldn't occur to him to think, *Hey, this is a great opportunity to find out if she really does like me.* If he wants to know that, he'll say, 'Do you like me?'

> 'I find women incredibly confusing – I don't think they even know what they want. Sometimes, she wants me to act like a man – open doors and stuff – other times she wants me to be her girfriend and sit there and listen to all the stuff girls talk about. She wants me to be both male and female, but doesn't give me any hint as to which role I'm supposed to play when.'
>
> Jeremy, 28, small-business owner

With very different styles and ways of communicating, it's not surprising words are the cause of umpteen problems. She hints, he takes it literally. 'I'd love to wake up beside you,' to women, means, 'Play your cards right and it'll happen sometime soon.' 'I'd love to wake up beside you,' to men means it's time to settle the bill, call the cab and do just that.

Most men aren't blabbermouths either. They mull over what the correct response to something is, toss up whether or not they want to say it, then speak. Women answer just about any question after a one-second pause (they're drawing breath). Some (women) might say it's because our brains work faster. Others (men) think it's because we've had a lot more practice at talking (that is, we do it too much). Our lives are based around talk, his, action. Girl-friends go out for coffee to chat; guys do things together. If you feel your message isn't getting across, this could be why.

The bottom line? Be aware of how he or she may be interpreting your language and you'll have more chance of getting across what you're *really* trying to say. (If you want to learn how to communicate more effectively, read Chapter 4.)

The ins and outs of body talk

Sometimes, sexual signals get more tangled than phone lines. The reason? Men and women often interpret body language and behaviour differently.

Actually, let me simplify that: it's *men* who get it wrong most of the time. What you think is a direct come-on is often experimental flirting on our part – or sheer politeness.

'Girls dance too confidently and sexually,' says Mike, a friend of mine. 'All that hip wiggling and shaking their boobies – can you blame me for thinking it means you want to come home and have sex?'

Er, yes! For all the Mikes out there, listen up. Girls just happen to like dancing, so we often do it well. Quite frankly, if we've accepted a dance with you just to be nice, we often forget you're even on the dance floor. We're carried away by the beat, not you (sorry).

Ditto for kissing. Women *like* kissing. For us, it's not necessarily a prelude to sex, even if we are aiming for your tonsils with our tongue.

'If you're adults, a long, deep kiss definitely means you're about to have sex. Why would you bother otherwise?' says Rob.

For lots of reasons. It's intimate but not risky. While

Twenty-six – that's the number of strategies men and women use to say 'I'm not interested' when being chatted up. A US study catalogued all of them, ranging from the subtle (avoiding meeting their eyes) to the more devious (slipping them a false phone number). Women use more elaborate tactics but that doesn't mean we're more manipulative – we're just careful to let guys down gently.

some of us do get carried away in the heat of the moment, others use kissing as a litmus test (theory being, if he's good at it, he'll also be good in bed. The jury's still out on that one).

Yet another classic crossed-wire situation: if we leave with you, we must be intending to have sex. Wrong again. Letting you walk us to our car probably does mean we'll hand over our phone number, but it's not a cue to fumble around in your wallet for the condom. So be careful when interpreting 'she wants me, I know it' signals: instead of scoring, you might just score a slap across the face.

Now the lecture's over (sorry guys, but it was necessary), I can safely move onto the next bit: how to let someone know you *are* interested by letting your body do the talking. Use the following body language tips to attract attention yourself – and to discover the messages someone's trying to send you:

- **Push your fingers through your hair.** Pulling your hair back away from your face lets them have a good look. It's a confident gesture that means, 'I'm happy with how I look.'
- **While they're watching you, look around the room, then let your gaze settle back on them.** It's the equivalent of saying, 'You're my pick of everyone who's here.'
- **Deliberately walk past someone.** Especially if it's obvious you're taking the long way round.
- **Move closer.** Make it look like there's a reason for it (a better seat, away from the crowd or moving into where the action is – there's always something!) but the message is still 'I'm here, come and get me.'
- **Touch them.** Grab onto her arm to explain a point, pick a bit of fluff off his jumper, gently remove a hair that's falling across her eye – any excuse to touch, take it. If you like someone, you touch them more often; the more you touch someone, the more they like you.

- **Mirror their behaviour.** Anthropologists claim that 'mirroring' – imitating each other's body movements and gestures – is the best indicator of all of sexual and romantic interest.
- **Put your shoulders back.** Both sexes instinctively lift their shoulders (probably to pull in their stomach muscles and mentally 'square' themselves to perform at their best) when they meet someone attractive. We also uncross our arms. If you're talking with someone who crosses their arms across their chest, you're delving too deep. It's a protective gesture which, in essence, means, 'Don't intrude'.
- **Rapid blinking.** When we're sexually attracted to someone we blink more than usual.
- **Hold eye contact for more than two seconds.** Strangers usually glance at each other for no more than two seconds. Repetitive three-second-or-more looks is a pretty certain indicator that it's more than just curiosity.
- **Lean forward.** Moving your upper body toward someone means you're interested. If they also lean forward, they are too. If they lean back, forget it.

GETTING THROUGH THE FIRST TWO DATES

While first dates are stressful for women (like, who can ever decide which black dress?), I have to say men have it tougher. Approaching a woman, risking rejection by asking her out – it's not easy. If you're overconfident, she thinks you're cocky. If you're a shoe shuffler, she thinks you're a twit. And when's the right time to do it? If she's told you her ex dumped her last week, she might think you're insensitive if you rush in too soon. But wait too long and some other guy will get there first.

No matter how ordinary a girl looks, she becomes super-woman if you want to ask her out. For every woman who has waited by the phone, there's a man, sitting by one, trying to pluck up the courage to dial that number. So girls, unless the guy who's asking *you* out is drunk, rude, sexist or outrageously egotistical, be nice. Don't go out with him out of pity, but *do* be polite.

Moral lecture over, let's move onto the nitty-gritty.

That desired but dreaded first date

I'd rather tell a wedding congregation the groom's buggered off with the chief bridesmaid than repeat some of my first dates. There you are, trying to give this fabulous first impression and you end up doing quite the opposite. You never have trouble reverse parking but when *they're* in the car, you muck it up. You're so jumpy you become clumsy, you're so worried about saying the wrong thing you get tongue-tied. You're both trying to be sexy but not *too* sexy, intelligent but not boring and the pressure's just too much. And some things really are out of our control – like the restaurant's awful or you can't get a parking space or you run into your ex.

First dates make us nervous for good reason. They *are* a test. What we're really asking each other is, 'Am I likeable/attractive/rich enough/thin enough/successful enough for you?' Even if we don't like them, it's a blow to the ego if they don't like us. So be a little sensitive from that very first phone call. If you're the one being asked out and you don't want to go, a white lie is called for. 'I'm flattered but I'm involved with someone else,' is a polite way of saying, 'You've got to be joking.' If you'd like to go, say so. 'I'm really looking forward to it. Thanks for asking me!' It takes courage to ask someone out, so make it easy for them whichever response you give.

THE SIX SECRETS OF WOMEN WHO GET MEN (AND MEN WHO GET WOMEN)

There are certain qualities that make *anyone* appear attractive and all reduce to this simple equation. If you love sex and love people, you're probably sexy. All of us have a subconscious 'sexy' radar which automatically tunes in to people who've got 'it'. Our looks radar sets off first – instantly scanning for the best-looking person in the crowd – then the sexy radar clicks in, looking for more subtle (and surer) indicators that someone's worth talking to. Men have exceptional sexy radars. The average guy can spot the sexiest woman in the room before she's finished her first G & T, even when she's *not* wearing neck-to-thigh lycra. How? They know the other giveaway signs:

1. **They're enthusiastic.** It's infectious – you can't help but smile and respond to someone who's full of life. It doesn't really matter what it is you're passionate about (though plankton and grey-speckled tree frogs are pushing it), so long as you're throwing your arms around and getting excited about something. As one guy put it, 'The girl in the corner whose facial expression doesn't change and talks in a monotone isn't appealing, even if she is discussing how to give a great head job. It's the girl who's gesturing madly and talking a million miles an hour who you want. Even if *she's* discussing what colour to paint her bathroom.'

2. **They make you feel like you're the only person in the room.** Jerry Seinfeld's just walked in, the girl at the next table has just taken off her clothes and the waiter just dropped a £100 bill at his feet but his eyes haven't moved from your face. The person who looks you directly in the eye, really listens, calls you by name and focuses on what you're saying wins every time.

3. **They know who they are and are proud of it.** A person who isn't scared to express an opinion even if it's the ➤

opposite to everyone else's, might be called opinionated, stroppy or even rude, but there's one thing they'll never be branded – boring. Stick up for your beliefs and believe in yourself. We all respect and admire people who hold their head up and fight their own battles.

4. **They touch a lot.** Never, ever underestimate the power of touch. The person who really hugs hello, who puts a concerned hand on your arm if you're upset, gives a firm handshake to say, 'Congratulations!' is making warm, sexy gestures that make them seem approachable.

    Don't forget to touch yourself too. Smoothing your stockings, pushing back your hair, hugging yourself if you're a bit cold – it's all very sensual and inviting and draws attention to whatever body part you're touching. If you're stingy with your affection, others assume you're cold, hard to get to know, uptight. None of which are adjectives you want applied to you, right?

5. **They're aware of their body language – and their body.** The more you like your body, the better you'll present it to the world. Sit with your arms crossed, clutching a pillow across your stomach and the message is obvious: I feel fat and I'm trying to hide my stomach. A woman who does a big, lazy stretch, lifting her arms up, sends a very different message: I'm proud of my body. Ditto for men. Grimace and roll a shoulder and she'll notice how broad they are.

6. **They aren't looks-obsessed.** 'My girlfriend is sexiest when she's got lipstick smeared everywhere from kissing me.' 'I love Brad first thing in the morning when his hair's sticking up all over the place, he's got sleep in his eyes and morning breath. He looks so gorgeous and vulnerable.' It's hard to accept someone will find you sexy when you've got a red wine stain on the inside of your lips, but it really is true. That's why the just-got-out-of-bed tussled look never, ever goes out of fashion.

What to wear?

Wear something you feel good in, that suits you and the venue. If you've forgotten to ask, call back to find out what the dress code is. While dressing down is cool in most situations, first dates are one occasion where I'd dress one notch up from what's expected. Their definition of casual might be your smart casual and you're better to be slightly overdressed than under (especially if the venue has dress rules). More importantly, looking like you've made an effort makes them feel the date means something to you. It's a compliment. (A word of warning if you're female: keep in mind that if you overemphasize the outside, he'll never get past it. Wear that tight, black mini and plunging neckline and you can't blame him if he doesn't hear a word you say.)

Where to go

There's a reason why dinner nearly always wins. Parties are a nightmare (you end up fancying someone else or they do), movies are pointless (two hours of sitting in silence doesn't tell you a thing about them) and anything creative is destined for disaster (your parachute doesn't open, for instance).

Dinner gives you the chance to talk, but there's enough going on to cover up those awful silences. Choose a mid-range restaurant or a cheap eats with pots of atmosphere rather than that expensive place with the starched linen tablecloths. You feel nervous enough without snotty waiters frowning when you pick up the wrong fork.

What to talk about

Anything. Babbling on about how the beavers in Canada build dams with their teeth is still preferable to sitting there, gazing at the floor. As a basic rule, it's always good to ask lots of questions: where did they grow up, how many kids in their family, what's their job like, how did they get into it. After all, you're curious, most people like talking about themselves and even the socially inept can take the lead from questions like that and ask you the same questions back.

Don't censor your conversations (there's no use pretending to be something you're not – they'll find out soon enough anyway) but there are three danger zones.

> **Dish up desire . . .**
> Fresh figs followed by sausages? Baby potatoes artfully arranged around a whole baked courgette? Not exactly a gourmet's delight but if it's *after*-dinner activity you're after, these are the meals to serve. According to 'the law of similarities', foods that resemble sexual organs give us a subconscious jolt in all the right places. Banana Split anyone?

Ripping shreds off your ex (or anyone for that matter) will make you seem mean and bitchy, launching into your sexual fantasies (especially the one about honey and the football team) isn't appropriate when you've only known each other an hour and telling your entire life history in under three hours is not on either. At the end of the night, you want to have a sense of what someone's like, not know every single thing that's happened to them. Who needs a second date if you do?

Who pays?
When it comes time to pay, both of you should fish for your wallets. But the general rule is whoever asked the other out picks up the bill. (After that, split the bill, take turns or pay according to your respective salary levels.) Him paying for you doesn't mean you owe him anything (sex or a second date). Ditto for her.

Guaranteeing a second date
Just when you think all the hard bits are over – you're getting along famously and finally relaxed – comes the

hardest part of the first date: the end of it. If you can't wait to get out of there, you're frantically thinking of how to say, 'Had a great time but let's not do it again.' If you really like them, it's tempting to take it through to a different level (that is, sex).

Let's deal with the first scenario first. You've had a pleasant time but were ready to go home at 9 pm. This is all you need to say: 'Thanks X, that was great. It's always nice meeting new people. Maybe we'll run into each other again sometime. Bye!' If they try to pin you down to another date say, 'Look, I'm frantic at work right now but give me your number and I'll give you a call sometime.' That way no-one's waiting by the phone but you haven't been rude.

For the couple who've already moved on to the intimate bar to have 'one for the road', thighs touching and lips itching to mesh, sometimes it's the right thing to give in, snog passionately, desperately hail a cab and take each other's clothes off the minute the front door shuts. But you're taking a huge risk. Apart from the obvious safety issues (rape, assault, passing on sexually transmitted diseases [STDs] if you don't wear a condom), there are emotional implications. Will he think you're easy? Will she think you were only out for a bit? Sex moves things rapidly into intimacy mode, and in the bright light of day, when the alcohol's worn off, you might not feel like you know each other quite as well as you thought.

If your attraction to each other is strong, saying, 'Goodnight,' and sealing it with a promise-of-things-to-come kiss is by far the better bet. Plenty of people regret sleeping with someone too soon. I don't know one person who wishes they'd done it earlier. When you sleep with each other depends on how well you're getting on, the circumstances, your individual morals and what you want from the relationship. Forced to put some sort of time frame on it, I'd say the consensus is at least three dates. If you're hoping for a long-term relationship, I'd *strongly* recommend waiting longer, until *both* of you feel comfortable and reasonably secure that you both want the same things from the relationship. That might take three dates, three weeks, or six months. By all means put your best knickers on for the first night out (it'll make you feel sexier), but you don't have to take them off. (See 'Between the sheets', page 106, if you're still not convinced.)

> 'One girl took me to an ice-skating rink for a first date. She was a great skater and very impressive but it didn't do much for my confidence. I felt like a complete fool flailing along behind her like a novice. It gave her way too much power.'
>
> Nick, 27, barman

In short: be yourself, have a sense of humour, don't drink too much and don't make snap judgements – first impressions are often wrong. Instincts, on the other hand, rarely are, so trust your gut feeling.

Ⓕ FOR HER: CLASSIC FIRST-DATE MISTAKES

- **Sleeping with him**: It might be the only time you've ever done it but he thinks you do it every time.
- **Spilling all your secrets**: Revealing too much, too soon moves him into a space he's not comfortable with. He suspects you must really like him to trust him that much and feels trapped already.

Ⓜ FOR HIM: CLASSIC FIRST-DATE MISTAKES

- **Getting drunk**: You're nervous and keep downing drinks to gain confidence. Slurring isn't attractive. Neither is offering to drive her home when you're well over the limit.
- **Clamming up**: You're so keen to make the right impression, nothing seems witty or intelligent enough so you sit there in silence.

- **Talking about yourself too much**: You think you're impressing her by showing off all your expertise. She thinks you're a bighead.

The acid test: date two!

The better the first date, the more nervous you'll be for the second. He's thinking, *She's far too pretty/intelligent/cool/classy to bother with the likes of me. Especially after I dribbled soup down my shirt.* She's thinking, *He's far too good-looking/ intelligent/cool/sophisticated to ask me out again. Especially after I babbled on like an idiot.* If there's to be a second date, both of you will spend the next day analysing every word and gesture to convince yourselves the other person enjoyed the first as much as you did.

Who calls who?

Usually, one of you (often the guy) will say, 'I'll call you,' at the end of the first date. If that's how it was left, leave it a few days to see if they do. You swapped phone numbers but it was left up in the air as to who'd call who (or you were too drunk to remember)? If *they* called *you* for the first date, it's perfectly acceptable for *you* to call *them* for the second (assuming it all went swimmingly well).

But don't say I didn't warn you if you're a girl calling the guy. Some of my girlfriends don't think twice about calling men – with terrific results. The guy's knocked out to find a girl confident enough to put herself on the line. But every single time I've done that, it's backfired. Miserably. I convince myself that they're just too shy, that I didn't give enough green lights, there's been something wrong with my phone or they've lost the number,

Forty-three per cent of men and forty per cent of women have hidden incriminating evidence before a date.

and call them. The minute I say, 'Hi. Just wanted to say thanks for such a great night,' I *know* I've done the wrong thing.

I ended up friends with a guy I did this to (we met later through mutual friends) and asked him why it freaked him out so much. 'You were too eager,' he said. 'You removed the challenge. Men like the chase most of all.'

So there – you're warned, but good for you if you decide to do it anyway!

If you're a coward like me and opt for the waiting game, give up if the person who said they'd call hasn't after three days. If you had sex on the first night, give up after one.

What to wear, where to go

The pressure of what to wear and where to go eases a little on date two. Most couples still opt for dinner or drinks out, though it's usually at a more casual venue than the first. Don't be surprised if you find yourself acting like shy schoolchildren when you first link up again. You probably won't snap straight back to the same level of intimacy you last left on. Give it an hour or so, because if you thought the first date was loaded with expectations, the second's even worse. After all, here you both are again which means you've admitted you like each other and want more!

What to expect

Date two, if you're still both keen, usually turns into a talka-thon, the old 'let's stay up and tell each other all the stuff you never tell anyone' scenario. You part (reluctantly) and, despite having had half an hour's sleep, float into work having hitched a ride on cloud nine. Either that or it's been a total disaster. You both realize date one was a fluke, the best behaviour starts to slip and you get a glimpse of what you're both really like. Brave couples will struggle on to date three to make sure it wasn't just a case of clashing bio-rhythms or the moon rising in Scorpio.

Sensible couples give it a miss when date three's equally as bad.

In short: don't panic if you get tongue-tied, don't reveal *all* your secrets, no matter how tempted you are. Remember that date two is the 'heavy infatuation' date: take everything they say as a compliment but don't treat it as gospel.

Ⓕ FOR HER: CLASSIC SECOND-DATE MISTAKES

- **Assuming you're now an item**. Don't launch into, 'My parents will love you,' and, 'What are you doing at Christmas?' It's acceptable to suggest date three – but that's it.
- **Planning the next three dates**. Same deal as above but for different reasons. Women are natural social organizers so we think nothing of organizing him. You want to know when you're next going out so you can plan your week; he interprets it as being overeager.

Ⓜ FOR HIM: CLASSIC SECOND-DATE MISTAKES

- **Backing off big-time because you're embarrassed about how intimate you got by the end of date one**. She'll take it as a sign you're not interested and also take ten steps back, leaving you both nowhere.
- **Relaxing too much, too soon**. You know she likes you or she wouldn't have agreed to date two. But believe me – she's still not quite ready for that really funny party trick you do with the match.

THE TREAT 'EM MEAN, KEEP 'EM KEEN THEORY

While playing serious mind games with people isn't on, there's absolutely nothing wrong with playing your cards right. I totally and utterly admit that using the treat 'em mean, keep 'em keen (TEMKEK) trick is emotionally manipulative. It's underhand and thoroughly sneaky. But hell, all's fair in love and war, and besides, the pay-off for getting this right is well worth sitting

HIS IDEA OF A GREAT DATE

A girl who holds her own – and holds her drink. Who greets him with a huge smile, enjoys her food, is spontaneous and goes with the flow. Who says, 'I know exactly how you feel,' and means it. Who relaxes and is herself. Who laughs at his jokes, offers to split the bill and makes him forget he's 'dating' because he's having such a great time. She leaves him wanting more.

HIS IDEA OF A DISASTER DATE

A woman who is indecisive. Who drinks too much or takes party drugs. Who is overeager, clingy and starts planning the wedding reception after the first five minutes. Who doesn't let him get a word in edgeways. Who sleeps with him then calls every day afterward, even though he's fobbed her off. Who is stuck up and criticizes the venue and him.

HER IDEA OF A GREAT DATE

A guy who arrives with flowers – and arrives on time. Who makes her feel special without feeling patronized. Who really listens and gets past the small talk. Who treats her as an equal but still makes her feel feminine. Who's willing to talk about his feelings. Who laughs when things don't quite go as planned. Who doesn't pressure her to sleep with him – but makes it clear he fancies her like mad.

HER IDEA OF A DISASTER DATE

A man who arrives late without calling. Who dominates the conversation. Who is rude to the waiter and throws money around in an attempt to impress. Who gets drunk and punch-happy. Who expects her to do all the talking. Who hasn't got a sense of humour. Who demands she put out because he paid for dinner.

through a dozen talking-tos from your more puritan friends. Besides, it's a win–win situation. The person you practise TEMKEK on thinks you're more wonderful than perhaps you really are, so they're happy. You get the person you want, so you're happy. What's the problem here?

TEMKEK works on a simple psychological formula that can be applied to any situation, not just romance. *We always want what we think we can't have and if something is 100 per cent guaranteed, it loses its appeal.* In other words: play hard to get and even when they've got you, leave them wondering, just a little. I don't mean turn your partner into a nervous wreck, causing ulcers, hair loss and chronic diarrhoea. But I do think it's unhealthy if either of you *know*, without a single doubt, that your partner will stick by you *no matter how you treat them*.

The best thing about this game is that two can play at the same time with a terrific spin-off: you're both kept on your toes and never, ever take each other for granted. Here's how it's done.

An experienced TEMKEKer works their magic from the very beginning of the relationship. They spot the best-looking person at the party and watch others panting, like eager little puppy dogs, for their attention. *They* might have their tongues hanging out and paws up in begging position but a TEMKEKer wouldn't dream of lowering themselves! Instead, they sit back and watch, an intriguing (or is it cynical?) half-smile on their face.

'My boyfriend and I went out for two months before we had sex. In the beginning, I thought he deliberately didn't put the hard word on me out of respect and I appreciated it. But after six weeks or so, I started thinking, *What's wrong with me, why doesn't he want to sleep with me?* I felt really unsexy and determined I wasn't going to be the one to make the first move. In the end, I dumped him.'
Karyn, 28, consultant

The female TEMKEKer sends cool (but lingering) glances his way, but they're cut short by a swish of hair which obscures her face and has him *straining* for a better look. Within five minutes, he's deserted the pack and is by her side.

The male TEMKEKer openly watches his target until she notices him. Then he smiles once, lets his eyes travel appreciatively up her body, then finishes his drink (always in one gulp) before striding toward the kitchen for a top-up (target scurrying along behind, of course). Yes, they do sound like characters out of a Mills and Boon novel, but I think you get my drift. Overeager is out, cool and confident is in.

My mother's got TEMKEK down to a fine art. 'Don't you think you should think about settling down again soon, Mum?' I asked on her 50th birthday. 'After all, you split from Dad years ago.'

She gave me one of her 'haven't I taught you anything?' looks. 'There'll always be men, darling – what's the rush?'

Just one word of warning with the TEMKEK theory: don't take it *too* far. It works best to reel someone in. Once you've got their attention, drop back to using it 20 per cent of the time. Once the relationship's established, to 10 per cent. Because no-one's going to hanker after someone who never, ever lets them get close. The secret is to leave them guessing (they *think* they've got you, but have they?), but not leave them feeling utterly paranoid and insecure.

The TEMKEK rules
- Don't always be available.
- Let the answering machine pick up occasionally, even when you're standing next to the phone. Psychologists call this intermittent reinforcement – the most effective of all. If every time they call you, you're on the end of the line, it's pleasant but it doesn't really get the heart racing. You're a

sure thing. If you're *never* there, they give up. But if you answer one out of two calls, the excitement level's sustained. Will you answer this time or won't you? A mild desire to speak to you suddenly becomes a desperate need. Manipulative? You bet. But it works.

> 'The problem with having great sex with someone you've just met is that it stops you getting to know each other. All you do from then on is bonk. You stop talking.'
>
> Katie, 34, customer service

- Have a life that doesn't include them. Don't relegate your friends to week nights only, and occasionally make your own plans for weekends that don't include your partner. (Though don't be rude – give them lots of notice.)

- Make it very clear you're used to being treated with respect and won't put up with anything less.

- Don't jump straight in when they give you a compliment by giving them one back. Just say, 'Thank you.' When you give a compliment, immediately change the subject to show you don't need one in return.

- Be brave enough to let them see all your different sides. The tough, business person. The little kid, all sweetness and light. Mr or Ms Independence but also Mr or Ms Vulnerable. Same goes for emotions. Let them see you when you're angry and sad as well as on top of the world. All of us have different sides and different moods yet we try to be cheerful and happy all the time when we've first met someone. Why? Because we think we should be on our best behaviour or they won't like us. Rubbish. Act predictable (and boring) and they'll think you are predictable (and boring). I'm not saying they'll love all sides of you but you're sure as hell going to stand out from the crowd. (And if they can't cope with the real you, they don't deserve you anyway!)

BETWEEN THE SHEETS

When should you sleep together, and how do you make it fabulous when you do? Don't rush it. (There, I got it out before you could skip to the good bit.) I *know* you're just dying to rip each other's clothes off and you're both adults and what's the big deal and all that, but the fact is, sex with someone you think you might just fall in love with *is* a big deal. Even in these liberated days.

Sleeping together too soon is the most common mistake most couples make. It truly can destroy a relationship before it's even started. Why? Because despite the fact that, these days, we recognize that we can have good sex (fabulous sex) with someone we don't love, when it comes to someone we *do* – or *think* we could – sex gets thrown straight back into the 'special' box.

That 'old-fashioned' gene starts tapping us on the shoulder, saying, 'Wait. Save it. Make it special.' And usually, it's good advice. As I said earlier: make no mistake about it, if you're a girl and you 'put out' too quickly, men will judge you. They really will think 'less' of you. Why, then, do men try to sleep with us if they don't really want us to say yes? Maybe he thinks *you'll* think he doesn't fancy you if he doesn't give it the old college try. Maybe you're being tested. Whatever it is, even if he is hyperventilating with lust as he's pushing that bra strap off your shoulder, take it from me, he's secretly wanting you to say, 'No, not yet.' That is, if you're someone he wants to see long term. If it's a fling he's after, he's praying for the opposite.

I'm not saying I condone this attitude or necessarily think you should put up with it *or* agree with it, but it is a fact. I know plenty of 'liberated' men who hate themselves for thinking like this, but they still do. I know three times as many liberated women who also detest it. But they also admit the attitude's out there. So, at this point it's something you need to factor into the relationship equation.

Sixty-eight per cent of men like the way they look naked – compared to 22 per cent of women. Which may explain why we cry five times more often than he does.

There's another reason for not jumping between the sheets until you know the name of each other's childhood pets. Once you sleep with someone, there's no excuse for not doing it again. You're instantly thrust into a far more intimate space than you were. Ideally, you should date each other (minus sex) until you're reasonably sure you're compatible, want the same thing out of the relationship and, most importantly, think you might make each other happy. This requires logical thinking and objectivity. Good sex rather effectively robs us of both instantly. It's extremely difficult to look at your new partner sensibly and objectively while their tongue is working their way up your inner thigh.

The experts call it 'lust blindness'. You get so involved with your partner's body, you forget to look closely at the person inside it. This is how people end up emotionally involved with people they later find out are bad for them. That 'I know he's a bastard, but I love him' thing. No-one falls in love with a bastard when they're thinking straight. But if you put your brain on hold and get involved with their body, you stumble out of that glorious, lust-infused haze, rub your eyes and find you've made all sorts of promises and commitments to someone who wasn't worth getting intimate with in the first place.

Look, I'm a huge fan of sex. I know I sound like a boring old fuddy-duddy by telling you to wait but I see so many people getting hurt by committing themselves to the wrong people. There's no magic way of guaranteeing this won't happen to you, but you can reduce the risk by putting off sex until you're confident you've got a handle on the type of person your partner is. The more confident you are of your judgement in people and the less you've been burned in the past, the sooner you'll know when it's safe to have sex. If you *haven't* made great choices in the past, force yourself to wait another six dates *after* you're convinced you're ready.

Eight steps to orgasmic first-night sex

Tonight's the night and you both know it. Here's how to turn that butterfly in your tummy to a tingle in your toes.

1. Pick the time

Wait until you're both reasonably relaxed with each other – and the idea of having sex.

2. Get the condom(s) ready

The minute it's obvious you're going to have sex, say, 'I'll get the condoms now because I know we're not going to want to stop later.' Thinking each other's special isn't protection against HIV or other sexually transmitted infections.

3. Create a mood

Lighting is crucial. Dim them but don't make it so dark you're bashing into furniture on the way to top up the drinks. Music helps enormously but make sure it's not going to stop suddenly at a crucial point. (Load as many CDs in as your player takes.)

4. Spend ages on foreplay

Kiss lots, take it slow and take your time exploring each other's bodies. Don't panic too much about your underwear: if the time's unexpectedly right, it's better to go with the flow than squirm your way out of it because you've got once-white-now-grey baggy, unflattering knickers on (actually, if they're that awful, encourage them to take them off while they're hidden by your top or skirt). I wouldn't suggest going without underwear on the first night. If he's a little nervous, his erection will disappear faster than he can think, *Oh God. This one really expects me to perform.* Help him remove your clothes if he's having trouble (and feeling like an idiot). Besides, it shows you want sex as much as he does.

Q: How do you tell if your new relationship is headed for happiness or disaster?
A: Ask your flatmate. Researchers asked one member of a dating couple, one of their parents and their flatmate if they thought the couple would last. Six months and one year later, flatmates proved uncannily cluey at getting it right. The least correct? The couples themselves.

5. Don't expect too much

Ideally, you'll have joked about your first time beforehand to relieve the pressure. It's really not make or break time: if you really like each other, you won't split up over one bad sex session (though you will find out if the chemistry is there). If you lose your erection or orgasm too soon, just say light-heartedly, 'Sorry! I'm a bit nervous.' Don't panic if you can't make her orgasm – lots of women are too shy to tell you what they need to make it happen the first time you're in bed.

6. Relax about your body

There's nothing you can do about it now anyway! If she really likes you, she's not going to run from the room when she sees that sock tan line – and he's not on cellulite patrol. You're the only naked woman in the room and he'll think you're gorgeous.

7. Guide each other but not too much

You're both under enough pressure first time round: wait until the second run before you start directing.

8. Don't worry if you feel embarrassed afterward

You've both exposed yourselves – literally and emotionally – and the relationship's now on a new level. Men, especially, go into a strange space after they've 'done it' for the first time. He's uneasy, *you're* uneasy. She thinks, *Is this it? After all, he got what he really wanted.* He thinks, *I bet she thought I was awful.* Some guys do take the nearest exit ramp (the front door) after sex – no matter how long you've waited. But most – God love them – seem miserable because they're waiting for some kind of thumbs-up sign. He's not thinking of leaving you, he's self-conscious. Like, did you notice his love handles, that his penis was a tad undersize, that he lasted all of four seconds.

MR AND MS RIGHT-FOR-NOW: FANCY A FLING?

Not all relationships last for ever – and neither should we want them to. A lusty three-week fling with a brain-dead but body-beautiful might be just what you need to get over that ex-obsession for good. The person who's cute and clever but about to be transferred to another city in three months? So what if the only aisle you'll walk down together is at the movies.

There are lots of different types of relationships and each has their own appeal. But you wouldn't know it. Most of us tend to divide relationships into two, mutually exclusive categories – serious (will end in marriage) or not serious (bonking and that's about all). There's also a perception that somehow you're 'wasting time' or 'being cruel' by dating someone when you know it's not going to be long term. Silly. Really silly. As long as you're honest (and not pretending to think white picket fences), there's absolutely no reason to refuse a date on Saturday night just because you know it won't last past a week. In fact, I thoroughly recommend it. Not just because first impressions are often wrong (and that one date can turn into a lifelong love) but because relationships are like everything else in life. Practice makes perfect.

The more people you go out with, the more you get to hone those relationship skills. The more diverse the people you date, the more likely you are to know exactly what type of personality suits you best. A just-for-the-hell-of-it fling is good for the heart, soul and spirit!

Date outside the square

I once went out with a man who was dead-set perfect 'marriage material'. Nick was tall, good-looking and earned enough money to single-handedly rescue all Ethiopian orphans. He was polite, stopped to pat dogs and children and wouldn't *dream* of parking in the disabled spot even if he was ('There's always someone worse off than you'). I dutifully ditched my miniskirts for the sort of clothes Nick preferred (conservative co-ordinates), spent my money on facials and manicures instead of wine and ciggies and hosted terribly proper dinner parties without ever forgetting to scoop my soup from the opposite side of the bowl. A few months later, as I reluctantly pulled on yet another blah beige ensemble, I suddenly thought, *What the hell am I doing here?* I was going out with a guy who did zilch for me, pretending to be someone I wasn't, simply because he was Good Marriage Material. And guess what? I didn't even want to get married! I dumped him quick smart and ended up going out with a totally unmarriageable (and rather nutty) psychology student. He made me laugh more in one week than Nick had in three months.

Like every other female I knew then, I'd fallen prey to the only-date-men-who-could-be-prospective-husbands trap. I wised up quickly after that. Long-term relationships and marriage aren't just about salaries and stability; they're about liking someone, chemistry and 'clicking'. What's right is what feels right for you *right now*.

I'm not suggesting we date everyone who asks us, but I am suggesting you open your mind and your Filofax to someone you probably don't want to share your room with at the old people's home. Date outside the square. Don't stick to the same type over and over. They seem a little out there? Give them a chance – you're going for a drink, not about to bear their children. The more motley your collection of exes the better – it shows you're adventurous and open enough to step outside your personal square.

> 'When you're in your thirties and date women the same age or older, there's definite pressure. Both of you are well aware that if she wants children, she can't just date for fun.'
>
> John, 36, stockbroker

Great reasons to play the field

- **You build a rather useful network.** Need your car fixed? Call the mechanic you once dated. Your computer's playing up again? That nerdy tech-head comes in very handy.
- **You can't have a serious relationship right now.** You're not ready for (or don't want) one but you do want someone to have fun (and sex) with? So long as you make this perfectly clear to your partner, there's no need to feel guilty.
- **You've just recovered from a long-term split-up and are easing back into dating again.** Resisting the urge to replace one long-term partner with another immediately means you'll give yourself time to work through the fall-out properly.

- **You aren't sure what sort of person would suit you long term so you're dating as many different types as possible.** Bravo! The best reason of all!
- **You haven't kissed (let alone had sex) for six months.** Assuming you're not grieving for a past relationship or person, haven't been in intensive therapy or intensive care or haven't just been made managing director of your company, that's way too long without erotic contact. It's fling time – get out there!

Good reasons not to even consider it
- **To boost your self-esteem.** Even the word 'fling' sounds jaunty – and it's meant to be. You're there for fun and games, not deep psychological stroking.
- **To get back at someone.** Sleeping with your ex's friends won't show the arrogant so-and-so a thing or two – it'll just convince them you're still heartbroken.
- **Because you feel pressured into it.** Don't listen to your friends, your family (or me for that matter): if you're not ready or don't want to date someone, don't do it.
- **To ease the pain of loneliness.** A stranger in your bed, who doesn't really care about you and you'll never see again, isn't the person to pour out your troubles to.
- **You don't honestly agree with no-strings sex.** If your morals or religion mean you'll wake up feeling 'dirty' and 'used' after sex that doesn't have a could-develop-into-something tag on it, stick to sex within serious relationships.

I Think I've Met Them – Now What?

Getting from the bonking-each-other-senseless bit
to couplesville (without losing the urge)

●●●

You're intoxicated. You can't stop thinking about them.
Images of them smiling/laughing/sleeping, flash up out
of nowhere to dance in front of your eyes. A Mariah Carey
song comes on the radio and *you don't switch it off*! Either
you're 'in love' or you're experimenting heavily with party
drugs.

Assuming it's the former, good for you! If you think you've
found someone worth hanging on to, hold on hard. But there's
something else you should also hold on to: objectivity. Sorry to
squash that soaring-above-the-clouds feeling but there's a long
way to go before you're shopping for queen-size sheets and his
'n' her bathrobes.

This chapter shows you how to make it last when you've
hooked up with the *right* person – and how to know when you
haven't, so you can stop it right there. I know you don't want
to even *think* about the second option right now because it's
like all your Christmases have come at once (or, more accurately,
you've come so often it feels like Christmas). But it's not a

real relationship yet. You're still in that goofy, 'You like me? Aww shucks!' first stage, and there are plenty of obstacles to dodge, jump or squeeze through before you're officially a couple.

Even worse, there's another influence on your relationship you have absolutely no control over: other people. Sometimes, you'll meet the person you've been waiting for all your life and be buggered if someone *else* stuffs it up for you: an interfering friend who spreads rumours; an overprotective parent who insists on knowing your partner's 'intentions' when the only one they have at this point is to lick the inside of your thigh the minute you get home; a sibling who thinks they're not good enough for you.

We can't control other people's reactions to our new partner – and don't I know it. I met my husband-to-be about one month before Christmas. So besotted were we, I invited him interstate to stay with my family when I found out he had no family here. All went swimmingly well, until the traditional Christmas Eve get-together. My mother ushered us into the lounge room, packed with people. 'This,' she said proudly, 'is Tracey's latest boyfriend.' Chris, my now ex-husband (did I ever have a chance?), was rather put out.

'*Latest* boyfriend? What does that mean? Do you upgrade them like cars?' he hissed at me.

'Perhaps it's easier if you just give me a number,' he said to Mum.

'What darling?' she answered, blissfully unaware of her faux pas.

During our stay, she called Chris by the name of every significant ex I'd ever had. Lucky for me, Mum just happens to be one of those totally adorable types who get away with complete murder, so it all turned into a massive joke. But I have to admit it, I was holding my breath for a little while there (not a very good idea when you smoke as much as I do).

The only way to completely avoid things like this happening to you is never to introduce your partner to anyone (tempting but unrealistic). Like the rest of us, you're going to have to risk it – but you can minimize the other pitfalls. We're now going to talk about how to build a healthy relationship – right from the tentative, both-on-best-behaviour beginning. I warn you – there's a lot in here that isn't terribly romantic, and I've included some exercises that require you to put your heart on hold and use your head instead. But would you parachute out of an aeroplane without checking your equipment first? Bungee jump without a cord? That's exactly what you are doing if you let yourself fall in love and turn your brain off while you're doing it.

It's fine to doodle their name and bore your friends stupid with 'Brad said/Judy said' stories but keep a little part of yourself – just 30 per cent – objective. While the rest of you is walking hand-in-hand along that beach, let that 30 per cent watch, analyse and form accurate conclusions about this person. You wouldn't go to a doctor unless he was qualified. Why commit to spending your life with someone without checking out *their* credentials?

Let's start by looking at how a typical relationship usually runs, so you can see where (hopefully) you're going, and what you'll need to do to get there.

THE SIX STAGES OF A RELATIONSHIP

While each and every relationship is unique, most move through the same love stages. If you're a typical couple, you'll probably experience them in the order I've listed; other couples may skip a stage and go straight onto the next. Or the opposite. If you've just found out your partner's cheated or work pressures keep you apart more than usual, you might slip *back* one or two stages before moving forward again. Whoever said the path to true love is never smooth was spot on!

Right now, you're in stage one: the gooey part. Arguably the best bit of all because you're both so idealistically optimistic, anything seems possible. Unfortunately, it's virtually impossible to stay in stage one for ever. Real life has an annoying habit of tapping you on the shoulder and saying, 'Excuse me, but don't you have friends, family and a job as well as a lover? How about some attention.' So you both emerge, blinking in the sunlight (having spent the last few weeks in the bedroom with the blinds down), and the *real* relationship begins.

As with anything, knowledge is power. The idea of this section is for you to see how the average relationship progresses so you can get an idea of potential trouble spots you may be headed for, what's normal, what's not. But before you dive in, eager to see what's awaiting you, a word on the time frames I've used. They're estimates, that's all. We're all individuals and I'm generalizing horribly. You'll also notice a section at the end of each stage called 'Keep it going' with references to things like 'pace', 'compatibility' and 'common goals'. I've expanded on these in the section following this one.

Stage 1: *yahoo!*
Timing: anywhere from date one up to three months
They're available and interested, so are you. There's chemistry both above and below the waist. You go out, you like each other. Euphoria! Stage one is that lovey-dovey, soppy stage. You're reacting to primal instincts from your heart and your groin. You give each other those goofy grins. She spends a fortune on sexy new lingerie, he buys four new shirts. Where and how you met is a constant topic of conversation.

'I can't believe I didn't want to go to the dinner party,' he says. 'Imagine if I hadn't.'

'I nearly didn't go because my Mum was sick,' you say.

The thought of not having met fills you with dread. Life before them now seems dull and boring. The future is deliriously, ridiculously bright.

Sex
The only time you stop having it is when you lie back, snuggled in each other's arms, to talk about 'us'.

Keep it going
Treat them the way you'd like to be treated. Be yourself as much as possible. Don't push for intimacy too soon.

Check for
Chemistry: Does it *feel* right – do you fancy as well as like them?

Stage 2: fairytale fantasies
Timing: around two to six months into the relationship
In stage two, you still haven't found one thing wrong with each other; in fact, everything's just perfect. This is the heavy idealizing stage. You know enough about them to feel you know them well but you haven't been together long enough to see their faults, so there don't appear to be any. If a friend points out a glaring incompatibility (you're a brain surgeon, they're the cleaner; you want ten kids, they want none), you tell them, 'Have faith! True love conquers everything!' You lie to each other constantly. You force down hot curries because they love Indian; you sit through each other's favourite films and pretend you adore them. You hate spending even a

> First impressions do count. Scientists claim it takes between 90 seconds and four minutes to decide if we fancy someone.

night apart, and if you do, call each other three hundred times just to say, 'I miss you.'

Sex
It's still fun, fresh and exciting but a little less frenetic. Instead of having it twice a night, once is enough. Sometimes you even manage to eat first.

Keep it going
Let your heart rule your head but don't do anything rash (like get married or toss in your job to live in Saudi Arabia). Don't make long-term promises. It's okay to say, 'Wouldn't it be nice if this lasted for ever,' but not, 'Let's get married so it does last for ever.'

Check for
Compatibility: Do you share lots of similar interests, look at life the same way?

Stage 3: you officially emerge as 'a couple'
Timing: three to six months in
This is the bit where things start going wrong. The just-you-and-I-alone video nights are starting to wear thin – or your friends have threated to disown you if you don't come out with them – so you and your love venture out to be judged by others. You've met each other's friends before, but they now realize it's more than just a fling so look harder. And so do you. You start to see each other through other people's eyes. You watch your mum lift an eyebrow at his rattly old car and realize he earns a quarter of what you do. Your best friend says, 'She's great – but I wouldn't have picked her as your type,' and you realize she's blonde and you only ever go out with brunettes. The lies start to be exposed: his childhood home's not quite the mansion he'd

described, her ex couldn't possibly have been a model. You meet them at work and see a different side.

What's happening is this: you're both reconciling your glorified images of each other with a realistic idea of who you or they really are. Plenty of couples take the exit at this point when they realize the person isn't all they'd hoped for or find out they don't want the same things out of life. If you decide you do want to continue, you both drop the best behaviour act and feel safe enough to expose not-so-loveable sides, like a bad temper, insecurity, possessiveness and impatience. You start having a few arguments and question each other's judgement and opinions on things that really matter.

Sex
If you like the 'real them', sex shifts from the lusty, 'forget the bed, let's just do it right here' variety to a more loving, intensely romantic stage.

Keep it going
Don't panic when you discover your perfect lover's not so perfect after all. Give each other time to get used to the 'real' version, and you might just slide through. If it is obvious you've made a bad choice, however, now's the time to cool it. Split or agree to be friends.

Check for
Timing: Are you both ready for, and want, a long-term relationship? Because that's where it's heading.

Stage 4: why are you acting funny?
Timing: six to twelve months in
You're starting to think long term, so you start examining them with a microscope. In stages one and two you focus only on the

good points; in stage four you focus only on the bad. 'You've changed,' you say accusingly. They haven't changed – you're just looking at them from a different perspective. Sometimes this is the end of what you thought was going to be 'the relationship': you can't move past the nit-picking or don't think it's worth it. Even committed couples feel a let-down. You're not as spontaneous. It's starting to feel familiar; maybe you're a little bored in their company sometimes. The arguments intensify as you both struggle for power and control. You drop almost all pretences: if you really are going to be together, there's no way you're eating sushi for the rest of your life. If you survive this stage, your faith in the relationship zooms higher. You know a major row doesn't mean you'll split up and you start to believe your partner actually loves *you*, warts and all.

'A very old, very wise lady once said to me: you don't know if you love someone until you've seen through each season, twice over. This literally translates to two years but it also means going through the bad times as well as the good.'
Jeff, 26, chef

Sex
You may be arguing more, which reduces the frequency, and differing libidos become apparent. It's around now you'll realize if one of you wants sex much more or less than the other.

Keep it going
Because you're arguing more frequently, planning a few good times is essential. Now's the time for a few relaxing, pampering weekends away from it all. Be honest with each other about what you're not happy with, but be tactful as well. Try to balance any criticisms with compliments.

Check for

Pace: Are you both 'fast' people and do things a million miles an hour or both stop-and-smell-the-roses people? The fights could be caused by mismatched energy and intensity levels.

Stage 5: the readjustment

Timing: around one to two years after you met

You both know exactly what you're letting yourself in for. You see each other as 'wholes' – good points and bad – and if the commitment's still there, start compromising on things you don't agree on. When people like me say you need to 'work on' your relationship, this is the stage at which you'll usually do it. Because it seems likely you will stay together long term, you both take a careful look at the relationship to decide if it really is what you want for ever. You'll both need advanced communication skills to move further (see Chapter 4). You need to 'think for two', come up with win–win solutions to keep both of you happy, listen properly and be open about your needs.

Sex

You've established a pattern by now and settled into some sort of routine. If you've sensibly worked on your sex life as well as your relationship, you'll have reached some compromise on frequency and be able to let go of inhibitions without fear of being judged. If you haven't, sexual tension is starting to build. The low-libido person is feeling pressured; the high-libido person is frustrated.

Keep it going

You need to instigate *serious* discussion on what both of you want from life and relationships. Listen carefully and don't kid each other or yourselves. It's around now friends, family and perhaps your partner expect a deeper commitment like moving in or marriage. Make sure you're doing it for the right reasons, and not because it seems like 'the right thing to do'.

Check for

Common goals: Have you planned mutual goals for the future and are equally excited about reaching them together?

Dating couples want to be adored; married couples want to be understood. Why the shift? Being uncritically adored feels great at the start but it's far more flattering to be loved warts and all when someone knows you well. Married people feel most intimate when partners see them as they see themselves.

Stage 6: true commitment
Timing: three to five years from your first date

Whether you marry, move in or build a duplex, you make some sort of public statement that you intend staying together permanently. If it's a healthy match, you'll start to focus less on your relationship and more on your lives. You feel a deep, secure sense of satisfaction when you're with your partner but are equally as secure when flying solo. You hone your relationship skills to perfection. You can tell from across the room she's unhappy, simply by the way she's standing. She knows you're bored when you do that hand-through-the-hair thing. You feel comfortable sharing the most humiliating, embarrassing fears and don't criticize unless it's really important. You're kind to each other and there for each other. The bonds are strongest now: external events like the death of a parent, shattered career dreams, the realization that you won't ever earn a million/get your waist back may cause friction but it won't shake your faith in each other.

Each couple is unique in what true commitment and intimacy means to them. Some marry and never spend a night apart for the rest of their lives. Friends of mine say it's given

LOVE REALLY IS A DRUG

Why can't we stay in the really good 'in love' stage for ever? Some experts claim it's biologically impossible: our natural 'love chemicals' dry up after 18 months.

When we're infatuated, our brain produces a range of intoxicating chemicals, says UK sexpert Sarah Litvinoff. Great sex (and lots of it) keeps the hormone surge fizzing. But in 18 months – around the time a Saturday night in's definitely lost appeal – the 'love buzz' chemicals run out and the 'in love' feeling disappears.

The most potent love chemical is phenylethylamine (PEA). There's also a snuggle-up chemical called oxytocin, which scientists believe is responsible for the urge to hug your partner so much at the start. As with any drug, the longer you have it, the more of it you need to get 'high' and the newer the love, the more chemicals produced. This could explain why love junkies swap partners: they're addicted to the chemical rush which is strongest at the start.

But if you do make it past 18 months, your body rewards you with another drug dose. This time it's endorphins: soothing substances that make us feel warm, content and peaceful. This is the stage when you can most trust your feelings, both biologically and psychologically (couples who get engaged around the two-year point have the best chance of avoiding divorce). In fact, the longer we stay with a partner and the happier we are, the more endorphins we release.

them the freedom to separate for up to six months of the year, pursuing work projects on different sides of the world. Another very happy match have decided living together doesn't work. They rent apartments next to each other.

Sex

Your sex life reflects what else is happening in your life. If you have children, sex may be put on the backburner for a while (maybe even years). Ditto if something major happens – one of you gets a promotion or loses a job or a parent. Most couples drift in and out of great-sex and no-sex stages but if you've both given sex a high priority, especially since stage four, you're happy. You might occasionally yearn for new flesh but certainly aren't dissatisfied with what you're getting at home.

Keep it going
Love, respect and treat each other as the most important person in your life. Never take each other for granted. Remind each other constantly how lucky you feel spending your lives together.

Check for
You should be well and truly connected in all areas of life by this stage. All you need to do now is keep the communication lines open so you *stay* that way – for ever.

ARE THEY RIGHT FOR YOU?
THE FIVE CRUCIAL CONNECTION POINTS
Through decades of intense study of all sorts of relationships, most psychologists agree on five key areas that appear to make or break a relationship:
1. chemistry
2. compatibility
3. common goals
4. pace
5. timing.

Couples who remain blissfully bonded for life tend to connect on all five. Those who match on three or four still enjoy very happy, satisfying relationships, but the couples who struggle to hit two inevitably find they are barking up the wrong trouser legs and split. How soon will you know how you and your lover score? Pretty much instantly on one (chemistry). As for the others, only time will truly tell – and *that's* essentially what dating is all about. It's also the reason why those whirlwind meet-then-marry relationships rarely work: you *can't* tell immediately whether you'll click on all these levels. Jump in boots and all and you could be forced to walk the same path through life with someone who's desperate to turn left, while you want to go right.

To find out how well you connect, you need to start initiating open, honest discussion about your feelings and relationship, the sooner the better. Practice makes perfect. After three months of heavy dating, it's sensible to talk honestly about where you're headed and to make it clear what you want from the relationship and what the rules are. (If they're out the door and down at the local singles bar after you say you'd like a future, better to find out now.) During the discussion, check you both agree what words like 'serious' and 'monogamy' mean. Some people interpret monogamy as no physical contact at all with anyone but their partner. Others think it means no penetrative sex. Everyone's different and we all put our own interpretations on things. (If you want to know more about communicating effectively, see Chapter 4.)

Dating is – and should be – a try-before-you-buy exercise. Unless you're just in it for a good time not a long time, it's sensible to keep an objective eye focused on your long-term compatibility. Knowing what to look for along the way obviously helps, and this is what this section is all about. It's not a bad idea to check how many areas you're connecting on (and how well) at one month, three months and one year into a relationship. Keep reading so you know what to watch for, then drag this book out and read this section again at various points.

I know, I know, you're starting to think a computer would have a better chance at finding you the perfect mate. The truth is, it probably could predict a fairly accurate survival score if fed all the relevant information. But there's no way it'll ever be able to predict the most mysterious connection point of all: chemistry. Ain't love grand?

> **Researchers now claim they can tell the tasks women are best at just by looking at their breasts. Women who are good at right-brain tasks (creative) generally have bigger right breasts; women who are good at left-brain tasks (logical) have bigger left breasts. Guess those who are evenly matched are good at both. (Bet scientists were lining up for that one!)**

Chemistry: does it *feel* right?

Finally, the good-looking guy Kate had been eyeing up all night took the hint and came over to chat to her.

'Hi, I'm Pete,' he said. 'Oh – and this is my friend Dave.'

Pete looked like all he had to do was pull on a G-string and he'd be 'Manpower'. Dave was short, balding and looked as though he'd dressed for a bad-taste party, but Kate was besotted within minutes. 'It was so *weird*,' she says. 'Here was this gorgeous hunk paying me attention and all I could think of was how much I wanted to kiss his unattractive friend.'

Lust at first sight. Instant attraction. Feeling really comfortable around someone after exchanging two words. Suddenly feeling awfully hot and restricted by having to wear clothes. Wishing you hadn't scoffed that dessert after all. *That's* chemistry. And there's a simple way to tell if you've got it with your partner: if you have to think too hard about it, you haven't.

Chemistry is instant: it's either there right from the start or it develops rapidly.

Apart from being none-too-subtle, chemistry is illogical, irrational and out of our conscious control – which is why it can land us our perfect match *or* in scalding hot water. Chemistry doesn't care if this person will dump you after three nights, taking the family heirloom with them, or whether they'd make a fabulous parent for future children. It works on a primitive level – like whether your body wants to get close to theirs. It's involuntary and feels delicious, which is why it's so frustrating when we find chemistry with people we know we shouldn't (your best friend's husband, for instance).

Find it with the *right* person, however, and you're streets ahead in the relationship stakes. While chemistry alone won't guarantee you a great relationship, it's essential for a long-term happy liaison. If it's not there in the beginning, it's likely you're not going to be aroused by your partner in the future. Lose the chemistry – or never find it – and you've lost the relationship.

Which begs the question: is it a bad sign if you're not ripping each other's clothes off in the beginning? In a word – yes! If you've only made love once or twice and a deep, tonsil-touching kiss doesn't end with both of you ripping your gear off in the lounge room, it is *not* a good sign. Burning loins, frantic under-wear removal, snogging in inappropriate places – if you're not doing it in the beginning, you sure as hell won't be six months down the track (let alone 20 years on, when every couple goes through that 'I'd rather eat slugs than sleep with you' stage). Love without lust is friendship. Some experts disagree with me, but I honestly don't believe it's possible to have a passionate relationship for life unless the passion's there in the beginning.

Can chemistry develop over time? If you're both emotionally healthy and don't have any hang-ups, my honest answer is, not usually. But there are exceptions. If you've had bad sexual experiences that have made you afraid of sex, you might be too scared to feel passion. You probably won't have 'chemistry' with any partner, not just this one. Or perhaps you've been hurt one too many times and fear that if you give all of yourself (commit your heart, mind *and* body) you'll never survive if it happens again. In those situations, it's worth getting some therapy and seeing how you feel afterward. Otherwise, think about whether this person should really be a friend rather than a lover.

The other question, which people often ask me, is: what if it's the opposite and there's nothing *but* chemistry? Can a good relationship develop when all you have in common at the start is the frantic urge to shred the sheets together? You bet it can! Sexual attraction is incredibly powerful. If you're shooting off the Richter scale for chemistry, it's well worth hanging around to see if there's any other areas you click on. Besides, what have you got to lose? If it does turn out to be just sex and both of you didn't expect more, you've lost nothing except a few dozen weekends locked in each other's bedrooms.

How long before you'll know? If you're working through the Kama Sutra for the sixth time and still don't know the names of their brother and sister (or even if they have any), it's a pretty safe bet it's lust. If you're still spending *most* of your time having sex but have at least emerged long enough to meet each other's significant friends and family, hang in there.

You've got chemistry if:
- You find them very, very attractive. They definitely do it for you.
- You feel a little intoxicated when you're with them. Even in a crowded room, it still feels like you're alone because you only have eyes (and ears) for each other.
- You feel like you 'click': your initial gut instinct on meeting them was a very definite 'Yes please!'

- You're either having lots of sex or you can't bloody well wait to start.

Compatibility: how much do you have in common?

When your mother told you to 'go out and find a nice boy or girl', what she really meant was, 'Go out and find someone who's like us.' My friend Nathan did quite the opposite. He's a 25-year-old medical student from a privileged Australian background. His girlfriend was 32, came from a poor, religious Italian family and worked in the family business, a laundrette. The chemistry was there – they couldn't keep their hands off each other – but compatible they weren't.

'The sex was great,' says Nathan. 'But on almost every other level we disagreed. The age made a difference, but it was our backgrounds that caused the squabbles.'

Most of us have cultural beliefs and values, even if we aren't conscious of them, and we tend to match up with someone whose views correspond with ours. Compatibility is about past experiences and future expectations – it's an identification that makes us feel comfortable with someone. Without it, relationships flounder – unless one person consciously adopts the other person's values, which can lead to a *different* set of problems.

If you're ridiculously incompatible, you'll find out early in the relationship (when you can't even agree on which restaurant to eat in and what night to do it on). Most couples discover whether they're basically compatible within a month or so, but it obviously take years to discover if you're compatible enough to last a lifetime together.

Rolled up in the compatibility package are our secret expectations of life and what we want out of the relationship. One of the biggest causes of break-ups is when expectations don't match. It's like a holiday fling. You love them when you're lounging around on an island but when you see their *real* life – working at the bank, dinner with Mum on Wednesday, football every Saturday – you may start thinking, *There's no way I'll fit into this lifestyle!*

HOW COMPATIBLE ARE YOU?

Okay, so you've been dating a few months, done a few Cosmo quizzes together and talked enough to decide you think pretty much along the same lines. Now put your relationship to the real test by rating it and giving honest answers to some of those 'big' questions you've been avoiding.

Each of you should answer the questions separately on a sheet of paper. Rate each question on a satisfaction scale of 1–6, 1 being very unsatisfied, 6 being extremely satisfied. For the second section, use the same scale to rate how important the named issues are for you. When you've finished, prepare for a few home truths as you compare scores and answers, then talk about any major discrepancies. Can you fix them or come to some sort of compromise?

How satisfied am I with:

- my partner's appearance
- the way my partner manages their moods
- the routine that we follow
- the split of household chores
- my partner's attitude to life in general
- my partner's commitment to telling the truth
- my partner's commitment to fidelity
- how often we have sex
- the quality of our sex life
- the common goals and interests that we share
- how we handle money issues
- the amount of time we spend separately
- the amount of time we spend together
- the amount of independence we give each other
- my partner's family and friends ➢

- the level of communication we share
- the way we solve problems and resolve arguments
- the amount of affection we give each other – both physical and verbal

How important is:
- having a child at some point in our relationship
- having several children
- having children immediately
- my career
- my career versus the relationship (which has first priority?)
- a satisfying sex life
- a partner who understands me
- being in love
- loving someone deeply for the rest of my life
- being surrounded by friends and family

Common goals: how many do you share?

When people think of common goals, they think of things like buying houses and children. But while agreeing on where to live and how many children to have is very important and can keep you both focused and moving in the same direction, it doesn't do much for the excitement factor. There's a difference between keeping busy and having fun together.

You need to make sure that the only common goals you share aren't just the big, boring ones. Saving for a house deposit isn't much fun, even if buying the house is. It needs to be balanced with things like wanting to travel together, because planning an overseas trip *will* keep the fun factor high. Throwing parties, doing a course together – these are the things that keep partners motivated and interested. The more common goals you have, the better. Set another goal the minute you complete the first one. It doesn't take long for a relationship to get very flat, very quickly. Obviously, this connection point applies more to long-term relationships, but there are early clues to watch for.

You're progressing nicely if:

- You work well as a team. One of you picks up the video and takeway, the other's in charge of the wine and nibblies.
- You both place the same importance on planning 'special' nights or weekends away. Anniversaries or birthdays hold the same significance for both of you.
- You both make an effort to make the other feel special with impromptu presents or phone calls out of the blue.
- You both put effort into keeping the relationship fresh and exciting by suggesting new things to do.

Pace: are you moving at the same speed through life?

The chemistry's there, you're compatible, have lots of common goals but still having problems? Chances are, it's a pace problem that's causing it. We all live our lives at a different pace – how fast we think or move or the rate at which we want the future to move. If you're a 'fast' person – juggle a dozen projects at once, talk on the phone while you're typing on your computer, rarely sit down for five minutes and plan to be Managing Director within five years – it's not a good idea to choose a partner whose idea of excitement is watching 'Cheers' reruns on a Saturday night. Eventually, you'll either both decide you're not matched or the fast person will move on. Fast people are the ones who constantly crave excitement and, if they aren't getting it, they'll create it (that is, through an affair). Pace is also about ambition. If you're aiming for a six-figure salary, you'll need to devote a great deal of time to your career. If your partner doesn't share or understand your drive to succeed and rates their leisure time above their job, you're definitely headed for some rough spots.

You're travelling at the same speed if:

WHAT IF WE AREN'T 'MATCHING BOOKENDS'?

The most successful relationships are usually those that are balanced: both of you rate pretty much the same on the scale of attractiveness, wealth, intelligence and background. But there is an argument for hooking up with someone who's not quite as fabulous as you are. Experts call it 'down-dating'.

Sometimes oddly matched couples find their own balance. If you're an ambitious career woman, a guy who's less ambitious and domesticated could be perfect. You've got yourself a 'wife', and simply trading places in an age-old formula: one goes out to earn the bacon, the other stays home to butter the bread. Most oddly matched couples are getting some sort of trade-off. The gotta-have-him looking guy who chooses Ms Plain Jane? She could have more personality in her thumbnail than all the bimbette beauties he's ever dated combined. The Harvard graduate who married someone from the wrong side of the tracks could be getting a much-needed grass-roots perspective on life.

Down-dating only works, however, when both parties are secure in themselves. Society (that is, 'friends') will constantly point out to one of you that 'you could have done better'. The other will be told, 'You're very lucky someone like X has chosen you.' The 'lucky one' needs to know they're not going to be thrown over for someone 'better'; the person who could have done 'better' has to watch they don't become resentful. You both need to be in the relationship for the right reasons so that comments like this don't destroy you.

Also make sure you're not *deliberately* choosing someone who doesn't measure up to your own standard out of insecurity. *Always* having to be the one that's richer, more attractive, more intelligent and articulate means you're picking people who make you look good by comparison. Is it fear of rejection that's got you here or a geniune love and respect for someone who just happens not to measure up in society's eyes?

- Your energy levels seem matched. You either both want to slob in front of the telly or both want to get out there and *do* something.
- Your attitude to work is similar. You both place the same importance on career.
- You think and talk at a similar pace.
- You seem to need and want similar proportions of quiet time and excitement.

Timing: are you at the same stage in your lives?

You can have all the four previous connection points – chemistry, common goals, compatibility and pace – but if your timing's wrong, forget it. What stage in life are each of you at? There are certain times in anyone's life when a long-term, serious relationship is the *last* thing you want – or need.

The timing's not great if either of you:

- Have just come out of another long-term, serious relationship. Lurching straight from one relationship to another isn't sensible.
- Are at crucial stages in your careers. It's less of a problem but you need time to make a relationship work.
- Have unfinished business. You haven't quite got that ex out of your system or got over a trauma.
- Just aren't ready to settle down yet. You still feel there's lots you want and need to do on your own before sharing your life with someone else.

Sometimes, you'll meet the right person at not quite the right time and think, *Bugger it! I'm doing it anyway.* Your feelings are so powerful, they override whatever it was that stopped you wanting to commit. Other times, you'll meet the right person at not quite the right time and think, *I wish I could stick you in the deep freeze for five years while I traipse around Europe.* Even if they do seem perfect for you, your need to be solo is greater.

One point I want to make crystal clear here: timing doesn't always relate to age. What you want at 18 is different to what you're looking for at 28 or 38, but being around the same age doesn't guarantee synchronization. You could easily be ready at 25 for what they want at 35 – or vice versa.

The number of marriages between older women and younger men has nearly doubled in the past two decades. According to an extensive Australian study, the most common 'acceptable' age gap is five years but there are plenty prepared to push the limits considerably further.

When you're ready to 'settle down' depends very much on what you've accomplished, your personality, expectations and morals. So while age is a rough predictor, there are numerous exceptions. Check your maturity levels rather than birth dates, and don't get too hung up on the age thing. If you're both over 25 and your age difference is 5 years or under, I wouldn't give it a second thought. Even if there's a ten-year gap between you, it can work – especially if you're older. The older you are, the less important age differences become. (There's less of a generation gap if you're 40 and he's 30 than if you went out when he was 16 and you were 26!)

Having said that, you do need to prepare for some problems if the difference *is* ten years or more. There's the issue of kids for a start. If he's 25 and you're 35 and you both want children, will he be ready to change nappies before your biological clock ticks out? If you're the younger partner, you're in the 'pupil' position. Your partner's lived longer so they probably (hopefully) know more. The power's automatically on their side and there's a tendency for you to view them as a teacher or parent: someone to hide things from if you've been 'naughty'. You may feel like you can't have fun for fear of being thought immature. Plenty of younger partners say no to boozy all-nighters or weekends away with the girls or boys (you know, the *fun* stuff), then regret missing out later in life.

If you're the older partner, your lover's lack of experience and wisdom can be frustrating. You've been through all the experiences they're about to and some people don't *want* to go back for round two. You probably earn more, so once again, the power is skewed in your favour. Major decisions will probably be left up to you and sometimes it would be rather nice if you didn't have to carry all the burden. Just as they'll try to act older, you'll feel obliged to act younger. Instead of going out to dinner, you'll drag yourself along to the hottest nightclub and feel like a geriatric up on the dance floor.

Another common timing question is: what if I'm ready to settle down and my partner isn't? Should I wait for them?

It depends very much on why they're not ready and when they will be. If you've just met and they're about to go travelling for a year, I wouldn't spend the next 12 months hanging around the postbox and looking longingly at planes flying over. (Though I would get or give the phone number of their or your parents so you can contact each other when they come back.)

It's a different scenario if they're not ready because they've just split from someone else. Play it cool, don't pressure them, give them lots and lots and *lots* of space and in six months or so, they might change their mind. Ditto if it's a time problem rather than tim*ing*. If they need to concentrate on their career for a year or two and you're happy being slotted in whenever they can, again, it's worth a try.

The one I'd be most wary of is the guy or girl who says they're just 'not ready' to settle down yet. It's not a concrete reason so there's no end in sight. Besides, 'not ready' often means 'not bonked around enough yet', so unless it's just (safe) sex you're after, personally I'd run for the hills.

WELCOME BACK TO THE REAL WORLD

Sorry, but you have to come out sometime. When friends and family ask, 'When are we going to meet them?' quit the vague promises and instead set a date. After all, if you are to be joined at the hip, it's got to happen at some point!

Meeting the family

It's the moment you've been simultaneously dreading but desperate for. After all, if your partner takes you home to meet good old Mum, Dad and the rest of the clan, they *must* like you! Keen for it all to run smoothly? Here's some tips for that first meeting:

- **Smile like you're in a Macleans ad:** Smile until your face hurts and you'll be forgiven a multitude of sins (bar wearing a bottom-skimming mini and thigh-high boots).
- **Be polite but try to act naturally:** 'I found myself saying things like, "Would you care to pass the sugar?" and, "I'm just going to powder my nose",' said my friend Anabel, who was desperate to impress her new lover's parents. 'After a glass of much-needed wine, I stopped behaving like I was visiting the Queen and started being myself. They visibly relaxed and did the same.'
- **Be nice and show interest:** Even if his Mum's a frump, she might have beautiful skin. If his Dad collects something, ask him to tell you about it and he'll be on your side instantly.
- **Stick to safe topics:** Now's not the time to tell them your university thesis is about female ejaculation. Politics, religion, sex, anything remotely controversial is out until you know them better. It should go without saying that swear words and slang won't get you invited for a roast next Sunday.
- **If you don't think they like you, don't panic:** Sure, your last boyfriend's folks treated you like a daughter, but some people find it easy to express emotion and ➤

affection while others don't. Give them time to get used to you and warm to you.

- **Don't bitch in the car on the way home:** Let's be honest here, it's a lot easier to go out with someone if they like your family and your family likes them. If you're complaining before you've even pulled your seatbelt on, it's obvious any future family get-togethers are going to be a free-for-all.

Meeting their friends

Meeting their mother is nerve-racking but friends probably have more influence. Here's how to survive and win them over.

- **Dress for success:** Think about what image you'd like their friends to have of you. Want to be one of the crowd? Wear jeans and a big smile. If it's respect you're after, arrange to meet after work while you're still in a suit.
- **Don't get huffy if your partner acts weird:** They're anxious for both parties to get on because it'll make life a lot easier if you do. If their friends are protective, they're nervous you're being scrutinized and judged. If they're the type to give them a hard time, they'll avoid being affectionate for fear of being ribbed later.
- **Ask questions:** Where did they meet your partner, how long have they known each other, where do they work, what did they do on the weekend? Ignoring them and insisting on playing footsies with your partner won't score points with either.
- **Don't flirt:** Even if their best friend is supermodel material, flirting is bad form, humiliating for them and you'll end up on the scrap heap (along with all the other exes who couldn't resist).

EARLY WARNING SIGNS YOU'VE FOUND MR OR MS *WRONG*

Not all of you will be patting yourself on the back, thinking, *Wow! I chose well!* at this point. If you've absorbed most of what I've been talking about and know, deep in your heart, that somehow your relationship's not measuring up to the standards I'm suggesting, it's time to face reality. Even if you have invested a great deal of time and energy (and possibly cash) into making it work, you're still better off cutting your losses and getting out NOW if it's got all the signs it's not going to last. See if you recognize your relationship in any of the following.

Too many ups and downs

We tend to equate stormy, tempestuous relationships with grand, passionate love. Cathy and Heathcliff. Romeo and Juliet. Most of us are suckers for up-and-down relationships when we're younger (we've got the time and energy). When we're older (and have work commitments and other pressures), they're usually not worth the effort. Relationships of this type usually mean you've got pots of chemistry and passion but are hopelessly incompatible in every other area, hence the constant arguments and miscommunication. The highs are addictively delicious but they'll wear you out eventually.

Get out now if:

- You're having as many bad times (or more) as good. The first five dates at least should be fun; preferably you should hit ten before having a bad time or a major row.
- You constantly misread each other: you say tom*ar*to, he says tom*ay*to. You're saying things like, 'No, I didn't mean that at all,' every second sentence.
- They're moody, defensive and overreact to situations.
- They seem to *like* arguing and deliberately pick fights.

- The only time you really seem happy together is when you're making up after an argument.

Too many stops and starts

Instead of, 'How's Richard?' people are asking, 'Are you seeing Richard at the moment?' because one week it's on, the next it's over, only to be kick-started afresh the following week. You're long-suffering; they're unreliable. They're awful; then they're nice. Just when you think you've had enough, they turn up with flowers, apologies and a smile that melts your heart.

Why are you sticking around? Because of the poker machine effect, officially known as 'variable-ratio reinforcement'. Just as addictive as gambling, you're hooked on the if-only principle. If, every time you put your hands on a hot stove to warm them, they burn, you'll leave. But if it's intermittent – sometimes they burn, sometimes they feel deliciously toasty – you'll keep going back for more. It's the same with relationships. If occasionally, they come through *just* when you're at the point of giving up, all that effort was worth it after all. The 'if only' has been realized – until the next time. The longer you stay in a relationship like this, the more trapped you are. If you've worked hard to fix unsolvable problems, you're even more vulnerable to the poker machine effect. After all, you've put all the hard work in, why should their next partner reap all the benefits?

Get out now if:
- In the three months you've been 'going out', you've broken up twice.
- They're not consistent in how they treat you. One minute you're treated like royalty, the next like dirt.

- They try to buy you back after an argument. Instead of talking through the issue, they'll bring champagne and say, 'Let's not rehash the whole thing.'

Sixty-two per cent of men and 73 per cent of women say they find their partners more sexually attractive now than when they first met.

- One minute you feel secure and cosy about the two of you, one phone call later you're convinced it'll never last.

Your partner treats you badly

We've all seen it. The couple standing next to us at the bar. She's picking hairs from his coat jacket, he's brushing her off in more ways than one. Even from ten paces away, it's obvious he's flirting with the barmaid. Your heart goes out to her as she slinks off to the loo for the hundredth time that night to have a cry or to look at herself in the mirror and ask, 'Why am I putting up with this?'

It's a good question. Nothing makes me angrier when I meet attractive, intelligent people, bursting with personality and love of life, only to find out they've hooked up with Ms Bitch or Mr Bastard who walks all over them like a well-worn doormat.

I was at a wedding recently where there were two different entrees, which were plonked down in front of you without a choice as to which you preferred.

'Yum!' said the girl opposite me. 'I scored the seafood. I love seafood and hate tortellini.'

'I want the seafood,' said her boyfriend, and swapped, putting the hated pasta in front of her.

She smiled brightly at me. 'Never mind,' she said.

Later, she confessed she was 'dreaming of her wedding'.

'When is it?' I asked.

'Whenever I can get Jason to ask me,' she said.

Jason smirked and said charmingly, 'Keep dreaming, babe.'

She shrugged, smiled at me again and said, 'One day.'

I would have handled the situation somewhat differently. First, the tortellini would be dumped over his head and mashed in with two fists. Next, an oyster (in the shell) shoved up his nose. Had someone slipped something into her drink? Was she a masochist? Who in their right mind would be dreaming of marrying such an arrogant, rude person who treated them so badly?

I'd really love to say it's rare to see this sort of thing, but it's not. I've often met women matched up with men who, quite frankly, aren't worthy of kissing their feet let alone smugly sitting beside them. And it's not just females who put up with bad treatment: men do it too.

'Yes I know it's her 30th and I'm not invited,' says Phil. 'But the numbers were restricted and she's promised she'll make it up to me tomorrow.' Where's his brain? He'd been dating this girl for six months!

If you're staying with someone who, even this early on, is already treating you badly, you're quite possibly codependent. Codependent was the buzzword in psychology a few years back. The textbook definition is a pattern of behaviour and/or personality which causes people to stay in relationships or situations which are unhealthy and bad for them. In other words, a codependant thinks their partner is God when they're behaving like the Devil. (See Chapter 8 for a more in-depth look at bad relationships.)

Psychologists aren't sure what makes people codependent, but there are theories. The first says if you've been treated badly by your parents and/or previous lovers, you're so used to being put down, it feels odd if someone is nice to you. You subconsciously choose nasty over nice because it feels familiar, it's what you're used to. On the opposite end of the scale are people who've had such idyllic childhoods and past relationships, it doesn't occur to them that people might be mean. You'll excuse atrocious behaviour because you honestly don't believe it's directed at *you*.

Get out now if:

- You suspect you're a codependent person (see the quiz opposite) and have made yet another bad choice.
- Your friends are saying things like, 'I can't believe you're putting up with being treated like this.' No-one seems to like your partner but you.
- They put you down or criticize you. At this early stage, they should be showering you with compliments, not pointing out your faults.
- They're emotionally abusive: they shout at you, call you names and make disparaging remarks about your appearance, personality or abilities.
- They're showing violent tendencies (like hitting walls during arguments). If you feel even slightly physically threatened, leave immediately. (See Chapter 8 if you feel unable to.)

How to avoid bad relationships in the future:

- Try this trick if you're unsure of your judgement in a situation. Imagine your best friend describing their partner treating them the same way, then see if you agree it's acceptable or not. It's ironic, but we'll put up with far worse personally than we will for other people we care about.
- Absorb and believe this: insist on being treated well and you will be. Lie down and people will walk all over you. Make a pact with yourself right now that you will only go out with people who treat you with respect, admiration and

- Six months into your relationship, friends, family and career are still on the backburner.
- Images of your partner constantly preoccupy you months or years in. You drive past their house on the one night you've agreed to stay apart. You vomit in the toilet when they tell you a new person's started at work and they're – nightmare! – of the opposite sex.
- You feel addicted to the relationship the way others are to drugs or alcohol. You don't feel you could survive without them. Them trying to get a night out with the boys or girls is like wrestling a bone off a Rottweiler.
- You take on other people's problems as your own. You're always knocking yourself out to do things for them.
- You want everyone to like you: you're a 'people pleaser'.
- You don't trust your own judgement: others can easily talk you into thinking their way.
- You've been accused of being a martyr several times in the past.
- You feel out of touch with your true feelings, unsure of what you really want.
- Even though you have lots of objective evidence that your relationship isn't good for you, you've still made no attempt to leave or make it better. The thought of leaving makes you scared so you cling on even harder.
- You try to change but feel so anxious, you fall back into your old patterns simply to stop feeling frightened.

Answered yes more than six times? It's time to call the rescue team. Try:

- Going cold turkey. It takes one phone call to break off a relationship with someone who treats you badly – that's all they deserve. Do it, don't see them again, don't ➤

try to be friends (why the hell would you want to anyway?). Force yourself to dry out.

- Sit down with a friend and record the way past lovers have treated you. No excuses, no justifications, just the cold, hard facts. This is black and white evidence of your codependency. Stick the list somewhere obvious and look at it daily until you've analysed *why* you're putting up with bad treatment.

- Redirect the energy you put into relationships back to yourself. Why is your self-esteem so low? Is there a problem in your past you need help to work through? What are you really searching for? What did you hope to achieve?

- If you haven't come up with answers or see improvement after two months, read Chapter 8 and/or take yourself off to a good therapist.

affection. You're a nice person. You're warm, loving and adore making other people feel good. These are great qualities but don't let that natural urge to *give*, *give*, *give* be taken advantage of. Set high standards for how you expect to be treated. And don't drop them for *anyone*.

- Try adopting the following six points as your own personal commandments for your next, or current, relationship. I promise your confidence and dignity will return if you do – and you'll be pleasantly surprised how much better you'll be treated.

  1. I will never give up my own interests, friends or anything that is important to me for a partner.
  2. I will not stop seeing people I like just because they don't get on.
  3. I will not put my dreams on hold to help them achieve theirs.
  4. I will be the same strong, confident person I am around

my friends and family when I am with my partner. I will not change anything about myself to suit them.
5. I demand the same level of respect, love, attention and admiration that I give back.
6. If my partner starts treating me badly, I will end the relationship no matter what stage it's at.

ARE YOU READY TO COMMIT?

Congratulations! If you've got this far (and been paying attention), you're reasonably confident you've chosen well and can see a future together. The next step is commitment: making a pact with each other that you're ready, willing and able to move the relationship onto a more serious stage.

The first commitment most couples make to each other is monogamy: promising you won't play footsies under the sheets with anyone else. 'I love you,' tends to follow fast. (While not technically a commitment, most of us translate 'I love you' to mean 'I intend to stick around – at least for a little while.') Moving in together is usually the next stage, followed by marriage and (the most serious commitment of all) deciding to have children together. (More about those in Chapter 6.)

If you're travelling along like two peas in a pod, you'll both want the same level of commitment at the same time. Others (like, most couples) wouldn't qualify for the synchronized swimming relationship team. One's ready to move forward, the other wants to wait. Or you're both ready but too scared to suggest commitment just in case the other isn't. Think you're ready to take the plunge? Hopefully the following will make the transition from casual to committed a little easier.

The first commitment: monogamy

Few people can love someone and still happily share their partner with others. Rightly or wrongly (and there are plenty of people who'll argue that humans aren't designed to be monogamous), it's a basic human instinct to want our lovers all to ourselves. A few brave souls try 'open' relationships, but even they have rules (you're allowed to bonk other people but only if the other person knows/it's not a mutual friend/you do it between 5 pm and 6 pm on Mondays/it's a supermodel). In my experience, most open relationships don't work. Usually one partner secretly wants monogamy but goes along with the free-for-all idea because they'd rather have part of their lover than none at all. In exceptional cases, however, it does work for both. Whether this means the people involved are truly exceptional individuals or were abducted by aliens as young children and tampered with, who knows. But this book's aimed at the majority of couples, and because most of us want and need monogamy, I'll assume you do too.

> 'She broke it off because she said I wouldn't open up to her. What she didn't know was that I'd told her stuff I'd never told anyone else. She knew all my secrets. That was as open as I can be.'
> Evan, 25, apprentice

How to bring the subject up? If you're convinced you've given it enough time, you're ready to commit to one person and pretty sure they are too, simply say to your partner, 'X, are you happy with our relationship? Do you want to continue going out together?' If they say yes all you need to follow it up with is, 'That's great because I'm really happy. Does this mean we won't be seeing other people?'

You'll get one of two responses to this. Either, 'Yeah. I guess it does. But I thought that was pretty obvious anyway.' (Mission accomplished!) Or, 'Look, I'm really enjoying this but I want freedom to see other people.' It's up to you how you react to that answer. You can decide it's not worth it (the correct answer then is 'Get knotted') or ask when they would be ready. Don't kid yourself though. If they say, 'Look I'm not interested in a serious relationship and I don't want a commitment,' believe them. They're not playing hard to get, they're telling the truth. Accept this or find someone else.

Saying (gulp!), 'I love you'

They're the three most significant words in the English language. Deliver them at the right time to the right person and the first time they're said out loud calls for champagne. Blurt them out at the wrong time to the wrong person and you need a stiff drink for totally different reasons. It's the ultimate embarrassment.

Most of us have a justifiable phobia about being the first to say the 'L' word. Why? Because we don't know what the hell we'd do if our partner doesn't say it back. There is only one correct response to 'I love you' and that's 'I love you too.'

So, what if they say, 'That's nice. Anyway, as I was saying . . .'? Or look at you with pity and say, 'Sharon, you're awfully sweet but . . .'?

Timing is everything. Say 'I love you' too soon and you not only look desperate, you instantly lose power and dignity. Leave it too late and you risk missing that magic moment which could launch you both onto the next relationship stage. One couple I know have been in love for at least six months. I know it. They know it – but neither of them can get up the courage to say it to each other. They say things like, 'I really miss you. I really, really, *really* miss you,' and, 'God, I love being with you,' but you can see the frustration mounting. Sometimes, often, no other words but 'I love you' can express how you're feeling. (In fact, if they don't say it soon, I'll betray both their confidences and tell them what each other has said, in front of the other.)

So how do you judge when it's appropriate to let the cat

out of the bag? Only you can truly answer that one, but these are some things you might like to think about:

Make sure you both speak the same language

Your 'I love you,' might mean, 'I think this is special, let's give it a go.' His interpretation might be, 'When's the wedding?' If you think your partner will overreact, tack something on the end like, 'Don't panic – I'm not about to propose. I'm just telling you how I feel.'

Wait until you're absolutely bursting

Like, you'll explode if you don't say it right now. Wait until you're 150 per cent convinced you mean it. And no, you can't possibly mean it after three dates.

When I was 12, a kid at my school came up to me and delivered a message. 'See that guy over there?' he said, pointing to a kid from my English class. 'Well, that's Brad and he sent me over here to tell you he loves you and wants to go steady.'

'Okay,' I said.

Brad and I went steady for a whole week. We didn't speak once though we did sit together outside E-block for a full five minutes and look at our feet. True love? You betcha! Telling someone you love them on the second date or second week is just as ridiculous. It's daft – and that's what they'll think you are if you do it.

The fact is, the first time anyone says, 'I love you,' they usually don't. Not really. True love takes years to develop and if you're lucky, it's always growing. You look back and think, *I really thought I loved them when I said it back then but it's nothing compared to how I feel now.* That's not to say you can't feel 'in love' after three months of heavy dating, and it probably is acceptable to trot it out then. For absolute maximum impact, I'd wait six. If someone says, 'I love you,' after you've dated for six months, they've thought long and hard about it. They truly do think there's long-term potential because it's often harder to say it later than it is earlier. Saying, 'I love you,' when you're in the infatuated part of the relationship is easy: you aren't aware of any faults. Saying it when you've got a pretty good idea of what you're letting yourself in for is far more of a compliment.

I just called to say –

- *'I love you': 70 per cent of lovers have rung simply to say those three words.*
- *'It's over': 12 per cent have taken the coward's way out and ended it with a phone call.*
- *'Marry me': 2 per cent have proposed, or been proposed to, over the phone.*

A much-loved ex of mine told me he loved me when I stumbled back to bed after throwing up for the sixtieth time that night because of food poisoning. Call me strange but I was far more complimented than if he'd said it across the candlelit dinner table earlier that evening, when both of us were tarted up and looking fabulous, totally unaware I was about to swallow a dodgy oyster.

If you're saying it first, sneak it into conversation

Who says it first? Whoever's bravest I guess. The coward's way out is to say, 'I *think* I'm falling in love with you.' If they look at you in horror, you can always say, 'Don't panic, I know it's just casual with us. I was only *kidding* . . .' or, 'That's why I've decided to break it off – you don't feel the same way.' Another less traumatic option is to pop it at the very, very end of a conversation when you can disappear immediately after saying it. Like just before you walk through the doors to catch a plane or at the end of a phone call. 'Love you,' then clunk. Dropping the 'I' off it also makes it less heavy. 'Love you' is what you say to your mum. Again, if they look uncomfortable, you can always add, 'As a friend, of course.'

If you're unsure of whether it's reciprocated, try putting something on the end of the sentence. 'I love it when you do that', 'I love it when we spend time together.' If they look wide-eyed and gaze at you hopefully, it's safe to say the big three words solo.

Don't ask them
Never ever follow up, 'I love you,' with, 'Do you love me?' If they do, they'll tell you immediately. If they don't, they're forced to say something like, 'Gee. Uhhh. I guess so.' Dignity demolished.

Don't do it with sex
Don't say it just before (especially before) or after sex – you won't be able to trust their reply. Some people will say anything to get laid, and if it's afterward, feel forced to say, 'I do too,' because they've just had sex with you, for God's sake. Few of us are courageous enough to ravage someone then say, 'Actually, it was just the sex I wanted.' Even if it was, they'll mumble something appropriate just to be polite.

Getting more serious: moving in together
Think it's time to move in? DON'T think about it without doing a reality check first. I'll discuss the emotional ramifications of moving in and marriage in Chapter 6, but if you insist on rushing things (and you are if you're only in the early stages of a relationship and considering living together), it's time to put on your objective hat and see how many of the following you can honestly answer yes to. If you can't answer yes to the majority, give it a bit more time.

Essentials
1. They make you feel good about yourself, you're happier since you met them and you're able to be yourself.

SECRET TESTS

You're so keen you froth at the mouth if you're apart for two days, but there's no way you're letting *them* know that until you're damn sure they feel the same. So instead of asking (too humiliating), you set up little 'tests' and see how they perform.

'I went round to see Steve last night,' your boyfriend will say casually, 'and a girl called Natasha was there.'

If you instantly launch into, 'Who's she? Did you fancy her? What did she look like? Did you talk to her all night?' he'll get the info he needed: she likes me as much as I like her. Never mind that Natasha was Steve's six-year-old niece. If you're not sure what priority you are in his life, you'll invite him to a romantic dinner for two on a planned boys' night. He's forced to choose between you or them, and God help him if he chooses the boys.

We all test our partners to a point, but there's a huge risk in deliberately setting up scenarios like these. Why? Because the person who's doing the testing is usually the one who's more committed to the relationship. If that's the case, your partner will probably fail every test you set them and you could walk out on what could have been a great relationship. People don't always fall in love at exactly the same rate. Some people fall fast and hard, others take time. You might not be in the slightest bit interested in who Natasha is because you're not as into him as he is you *right now*. Six months down the track might be a different story. And while most of us *think* our tests are a foolproof way to work out where their heart is, we forget about other circumstances. He might choose the boys' night out simply because his friends are giving him heaps for not being so available since he's met you. So quit testing. Save the creativity for your sex life instead – it'll get you a lot further!

2. You've seen how they behave in all sorts of different situations: day-to-day, happy events, under pressure at work, with their family and friends. In other words, you've seen them survive a few crises.
3. You're similiar in most things: tastes, views, what you like doing.
4. You connect on at least three, preferably four, of the crucial points: chemistry, compatibility, common goals, pace and timing.
5. You communicate well (or at least think you'll learn to in time).
6. You trust them to be faithful. How do they handle temptation? If they go out alone, do they reassure you with details of who they saw, where they went, who they ran into? In other words, do they make it clear they're not straying from the rules?
7. You get on with each other's friends and families. If neither of you can bear each other's significant people, it's not a great sign. The old saying 'we are the company we keep' has a grain of truth to it.
8. You both want the same things out of life at around the same time. You have similiar career aspirations, thoughts on marriage, kids and the future.
9. Your gut instinct tells you it's right.
10. You like as well as love them.

Important
1. They're reliable; you share decisions.
2. You've had a few fights and learnt how to resolve them. Arguments are healthy and the amount of arguments you're having isn't as relevant as how well you solve them. Your partner should be able to rationally explain their side without getting overtly angry, say they're sorry when it is

their mistake, and talk things through so the issue is solved.

3. They've done some work on themselves. There aren't any major battles to win. They're not excessively jealous, overprotective or addicted to illegal drugs.

4. You're both on the same level of intimacy. The sharing secrets, feelings, desires and anxieties isn't lopsided. There's been serious soul-sharing on both sides.

> *Who's got time to fall in love? When Harlequin, publishers of Mills & Boon romance novels, questioned 6,200 women from 21 countries, the overwhelming majority said time restraints interfered with their relationships. More than 60 per cent of Australian women said work stopped their partners spending enough time with them. (Funny, he always seems to find time to watch sport!)*

5. You laugh together. You share the same sense of humour and can laugh at each other and yourselves, without anyone getting huffy.

6. You're compatible sexually. If your libidos don't match, you've worked out a compromise you're both happy with.

7. You agree on time spent together. Both are happy with the amount you spend together and apart: there's a nice balance between 'us' and 'me'.

8. You trust each other to keep promises. Not just to be faithful, but to stick by you through the rough times.

9. You can live with each other's faults. Everyone has the odd annoying habit but if it really, really irritates you now, it's only going to get worse.

10. You're with each other because you want to be not because you think it's time to settle down.

Lost in space: commitment phobia

'I need *space*.' Anyone over the age of 14 knows what *that* really means. It means, 'It's over and I don't quite know how to tell you yet, so I'm going to start seeing you less and less in the hope that you won't notice when I finally don't show up at all.' That's what most of us mean when we trot out those three not-so-magic words. But not everyone.

There's a certain type of person who means exactly what they say when they say they need space. If they can't have space, they can't be happy in a relationship. In a sense, that's all of us, because we all need time apart as well as together. Space and intimacy are on opposite ends of the relationship spectrum, and healthy couples settle a little right of centre. They give each other freedom and time alone but the need for intimacy is stronger, so they end up spending two-thirds of their time together. That's normal. It's normal even if you prefer to settle a little left of centre – so long as you *both* agree. What's not so normal is needing so much space, if your lover lived in the next country it wouldn't be far enough away. This is what psychologists call commitment phobia: fear of commitment and intimacy.

We're all a little bit commitment-phobic these days. But while we'll certainly weigh up the pros and cons before commit-ting ('Jane and John didn't make it – but then again, Sarah and Mark did'), most of us do end up closing our eyes and taking that leap of faith. Giving it a go anyway. Better to have loved and lost and all that stuff.

But not the commitment phobe. They find it incredibly difficult, if not impossible, to take relationships onto that 'sign here' stage. Whether it's a mortgage, marriage certificate or a six-month shared lease on a stereo, they just can't bring them-selves to say, 'I do.' Some people take it even further: they won't commit to a date next Saturday night, let alone make plans for Christmas.

If you're going out with someone like this, it's not much fun. But neither, by the way, is being a commitment phobe. Pretty well all of us would like to find someone to share our lives with. Commitment phobes are just big scaredy-cats – often for good reason. Look at the past of most commitment phobes and you'll usually find the reason why they've ended up that way. They've been married or in a long-term relationship that ended badly. Their parents divorced and they saw the fall-out. Even worse, their parents are together but utterly and completely miserable or venomous. In other words, their experience of relationships isn't fab. If all *you'd* seen was people hurting each other, you wouldn't be too keen to put yourself in that situation either.

A lot of commitment phobes get over their fears once they find someone who gives them time to get used to being part of a couple. But I'll be honest here: think twice before you let yourself fall in love with a long-term sufferer. If they're over 40 and have never, ever settled down for more than a few months, it's going to take a lot of hard work to overcome their disillusionment. Unless you particularly like people who want more space than NASA, beware.

How to spot a commitment phobe

- **They've had a bad experience in the past.** Find out if they've experienced any of the situations above.
- **They like to be in control.** If your partner hates being told what to do, watch out. Commitment phobes often become really defensive and argumentative if you take control of a situation because they like being the ones in control. If they're in control, they can control their emotions and they can't get hurt. That, of course, is ultimately what they're scared of.
- **They're irresponsible.** Often, commitment phobes have problems committing to *anything*, not just relationships.

They're the people who are always late because they resent having to be somewhere at a certain time. It's the same with money. They don't pay bills until they're stamped red with 'overdue'.

- **They don't like making plans.** If your partner hates tying themselves down to things even a few days in advance, be afraid. Be very afraid if they cover up their feelings and don't show affection. Again, it's the control thing. If they tell you intimate things about themselves, they've given you the power to hurt them.

- **The absolute giveaway – they panic when you mention the 'c' word**. C-o-m-m-i-t-m-e-n-t. Spell it out nice and slow for them as you mention the other two no-nos – the 'l' word and the 'm' word (moving in *or* marriage) – and watch for terror. There's no need to put yourself on the line – simply say something like, 'My friends Jane and Brad have decided to move in. How sweet!' or, 'My best friend's getting married this weekend. Would you like to come to the wedding with me?' The true commitment phobe will a) be out that door so fast, your head will spin; b) look as though they have an intense diarrhoea pain; or c) change the topic immediately.

One word of warning! Don't tar everyone with the same brush. People who need time to make big decisions – like marriage or moving in – aren't commitment phobes. Not being 100 per cent sure of something doesn't make you one either. Like all western countries, the UK has a high divorce rate: anyone with half a brain cell looks around and realizes no relationship is guaranteed. What's even more frightening is we *know* most of those couples floating up the aisle really do think it's for ever at the time, yet only a little over half will make it. That's a sobering thought. Even people who are happily married still have those moments after an argument when the doubts creep in ('Yup. I bloody well knew it! I've made a mistake').

We live in a very uncertain world, we're never 100 per cent sure of anything 100 per cent of the time. So if your partner's waiting for God to come down and say, 'Look. Let me reassure you this person's definitely the one for you,' it ain't going to happen. None of us knows what the future holds; all you can do is make a sensible choice and put all you've got into making it work.

Having said all this, it also depends on what their doubts are. If it's just 'what if, in 20 years' time, they stop loving me' stuff, that's natural. But if they're serious doubts – like they truly aren't sure you're compatible or want the same things out of life – that's a different story. That's not being commitment phobic, it's being sensible.

What to do if you want a commitment and your partner's not sure

You've been going out for what seems like ages and while all your friends are buying houses, having babies and painting the white picket fence, you're still struggling to get them to commit to Christmas with your family. What to do? Try the following.

Check you've got the diagnosis right

Are they really commitment phobic or are you asking for a commitment too soon? Some people have the opposite problem to commitment phobia – they're commitment junkies. So desperate to be wanted, they find someone who's equally as desperate then they latch onto each other like they're drowning and have just discovered a plank of wood floating in the ocean. It's not the person they want, but the relationship.

All relationships need to grow and move forward in order to last. That's why people move in, get married, renovate houses and have kids – you need to do things together to keep it interesting. But don't be in such a rush to get to the finish line. If you're both young – 25 or under – I'd be very careful about making lifelong commitments until you've been together at least five years. I know that's an awfully long time but most of us are still maturing right up to the grand old age of 30 or so. If you really do want to have the best possible chance at making it, you'll wait until after that to make sure you're still compatible. If you meet when you're older, say in your late twenties or early thirties, you're in a better position because at least then you've got experience and hopefully some wisdom behind you (like, you can both change the duvet cover without ending up inside it). So the first thing to ask yourself is: am I asking for a commitment too soon?

Find out why they're not ready

If you're absolutely convinced that what you're asking is reasonable and your partner comes back with, 'I'm not ready to make a commitment,' the obvious questions to ask are, 'Why aren't you ready? What are you waiting for?' You'd be amazed how many people don't ask those two very obvious questions.

You'll get one of two responses to this. The true commitment phobe will say something like, 'I don't know but that's all there is to it.' In other words, end of discussion. If that's the answer you get, bail out, because there is no solution if they don't know what the problem is.

If they say something like, 'Look, I'm not ready now but I might be in the future,' that's more promising. Again, ask what it is they're waiting for. Do they have doubts about how they feel about you? Or is it because their parents broke up and they're scared they'll be hurt if you two split? If they'll open up and tell you the reasons why, I'd stick around. Maybe they're frightened of commitment because they've been in a relationship where they did commit and it all ended in tears. If that's the case, they probably just need time before they truly trust you.

Something else to keep in mind: although we all say we're terribly liberated these days, those old stereotypes still hang on. If your guy doesn't want to get married just yet, he might be waiting until he's more financially secure. It seems silly because you both work, but he might feel he's still got to be the bread-winner and take care of you. Same goes for women. If your girlfriend's crossing the street to avoid bridal boutiques, it might be because she's terrified she'll turn into Mum and lose her independence – have to stay at home with floury fingers and make biscuits all day. The way to get around all this is to spell out, very clearly, what marriage, moving in, monogamy or whatever it is you're discussing means to each of you.

Reassure them

Is it a simple case of lacking courage? It takes guts to say to someone, 'Okay, I'm choosing you and only you as the person I'm going to spend the rest of my life with, regardless of who I might meet.' That's a big call! Let them know it's normal for everyone to have doubts. Some commitment phobes are simply too idealistic. They think they should have a solid-gold guarantee the relationship will work for ever. If your partner thinks like that, point out, ever so gently, that relationships don't come with warranties like the telly does. They're being a tad unrealistic.

Follow your instinct

What's your gut instinct on it? Are you sure you're not pushing for commitment out of panic because they're pulling away? If they're seeing you less often, going out with the girls or boys more and muttering about needing time alone, they're headed for a nightclub, not the jeweller's. You asking for a commitment will only push them out the door sooner rather than later. Force someone to think about whether they want to be with you long term and you run the risk of them using it as the ideal time to say, 'Actually. I've been meaning to talk to you about this – I think it's time we broke up.'

Compromise

If you want a commitment from them to spend more time with you, aim for a compromise. Draw a straight line with zero at one end and ten at the other. Zero means time alone ('space'); ten means time together ('intimacy'). Put a cross where you are on the scale, then do the same for your partner. Then show them and talk it through. If you move back a point or two, will they move forward a point or two?

Work out your bottom line. What's the minimum level of commitment you'll accept? Spell this out to them very clearly and give them a week to think about it. If they can't oblige, move on.

Drop your *level of commitment*

If you want more commitment from your partner, try dropping *your* level of commitment to *them*. Don't return phone calls immediately, go out on your own with friends and don't rush to reassure them it wasn't a date. Let them know they're not *so* special you'll hang around for ever, by taking the 'specialness' out of it. Take a friend to 'your' restaurant, invite a friend of the opposite sex home to meet your parents. In other words, do something they know was 'yours' with someone else.

Make it clear your life will go on quite happily without them. Say you're considering applying for a job overseas, travelling for a few months (solo), buying a flat (solo). This usually has one of two effects: a) they suddenly realize you'll move on if they don't get their act together (and they do); or b) they don't even notice. Either way, you've got nothing to lose except someone you haven't got anyway.

Why men have more trouble committing than women do

Most women know a serious relationship *doesn't* have to mean all of the things I'm about to list. Either that or they're not as important to us. Again, we're a lot more advanced in the intimacy game. But he's still secretly paranoid that:

He'll have to 'give up' things

He notices you've stopped going to the gym on Wednesday nights to see him instead and thinks, *Does that mean I have to give up my Thursday night squash game?* Relationships involve sacrifice, and he hates the word. Just because she wants to stay home and watch videos, why should he give up a night out drinking with the boys? Committing to someone is like saying, 'Here's a big chunk of my life – it's yours.' He takes it one step further and imagines a life with *only* you and him in it.

He's worried about sex

There are lots of horror stories out there. Like the girlfriend who gave a hell of a head job right up until the wedding day and hasn't given one since. Men worry women will stop putting out once that ring's on the finger because they don't truly believe we enjoy sex as much as he does (silly boys).

He's worried he'll rate a poor second

He thinks: *She could pull much better than me. Some guy who earns more, is funnier, wears better clothes, drives a better car.* Rolled up into the magnificent men she's bound to meet in the future, is a fear of the past. That ex who 'went on all night' – what if he turns up again? What about the rich one – could he lure her away? If he commits and it all falls apart, he knows how devastated he'll feel.

He'll miss out on meeting the perfect woman
He can't help but wonder if there's someone better out there, and the more you boost his ego by telling him how fabulous he is, the more he thinks, *Maybe I could pull a babe from Baywatch.*

He doesn't like criticism
Before, you'd tease him in a nice way about his addiction to TV. Now it's delivered through tight lips. Which leads straight into his top fear—

He doesn't want to be tamed
My friend Pete put it wonderfully. He said he caught himself putting dirty clothes in the basket instead of on the floor and was horrified. 'The next night I said no to drinks with the boys – not because she wouldn't let me go but because I'd rather stay home with her. The realization that I was becoming domesticated scared the hell out of me.'

He doesn't have to commit as early as women do
A man can decide to have kids at 50. So long as he marries someone younger, he can play Daddy much later.

He's worried he won't measure up to what women want from men these days
This is the biggie. It's true – women *do* want different things. Instead of someone to look up to and look after us, we want companionship, good sex, emotional support, a partner who'll stand by our side, not over us. He felt comfortable with the breadwinner bit (his dad taught him that one very early on). But that other stuff? Phew! That's hard. He hasn't been trained in it and honestly doesn't know *how* to deliver things like 'emotional support'. That's why you have to teach him.

Women are asking men to take more of a female role in relationships because we've taken on lots of male characteristics. We're more assertive, independent and financially secure, and that has to be a good thing, right? He doesn't have to worry about making enough money for the whole family. He doesn't have to worry about *us* because we can take care of ourselves. In return, we figure he can even the score by becoming more tolerant, expressive and understanding. Many perceptive men are working hard on delivering the goods – and doing it. Others feel like relationships have changed and no-one's given *them* the rule book. (Want some hints on what the rules really are? See Chapter 4.)

> Remember the so-called man shortage which made headlines in the 1980s? Australia supposedly had too many single women for the single men available. It's not just officially over, it has been for some time. In 1996, there were 101 available, slightly older men for every 100 women aged 35–39 and 94 such men for every 100 women aged 40–43.

DON'T BREAK THE SPEED LIMIT (EVEN IF YOU *ARE* OVER 30)

When we're deep in the infatuation stage, all of us want to click our heels three times and whisk ourselves forward to the nice, safe, *really* committed bit. You adore them, want to believe they'll be by your side for ever and the temptation is to race toward the finish line. Don't. First, you'll miss out on all the nice parts of the relationship (you don't quite know if they feel the same way about you and then they confess they do and you touch noses and smile stupidly and life's wonderful). Secondly, it's ridiculous to commit for life when you've only known them for a second of yours. Third, if you push for intimacy before *they're* ready, they may well run away.

Sometimes it's both of you speeding ahead. You meet at a party on Saturday night, stay up talking till dawn, end up sharing breakfast, then watch the Sunday night movie snuggled in each other's arms. The only thing that stops the marathon date is having to go to work on Monday morning. It just has to be the start of something wonderful, right? Not necessarily. Therapists say long-lasting first dates send our expectations soaring ridiculously high – and few relationships live up to them. When the 'magic' wears off and real life creeps in, the affair fizzles out faster and leaves you feeling even more disillusioned than normal.

> 'Jane was the third of my friends to marry that year. I remember standing in the church, alone as always, thinking, *What's wrong with me? Why aren't I ever the one that's up there?* I met Alex about two months later and grabbed on like he was a lifeline. One year later, we got married. Two years later, we're divorced. I wasn't in love with him, I just wanted someone.'
> Katherine, 30, painter

Women are often the ones who push for intimacy too quickly, probably because we're so comfortable with it. Some women go out with their victim (yep, victim) once, then call him three times the next day, drag him around to meet Mum three dates in, book next year's Valentine's Day dinner on the fourth date and then wonder why the guy ran away so fast he left burn marks on the hallway carpet.

Here's why: he figures if you're this full-on in the beginning, you'll *strangle* him with intimacy within a few months. An astute guy also realizes wanting to be instantly committed isn't a compliment. Some women want a relationship and don't really care who it's with. You've also removed the mystery. He doesn't have to lie in bed wondering if he's really worthy of a girl like you because you've practically proposed already.

Relationships expert Dr Maryon Tysoe cites several studies which show the longer the courtship, the more likely it is a couple who marry will stay together. In one study of couples who lived together before marriage, those who were now divorced had dated for around seven and a half months and lived together for 14 months before marrying. The couples who were still married had dated for 20 months then lived together for 16 months before marrying.

Put the brakes on if:

- You're *desperate* for them to like you because you're over 30 and feeling panicky. All your friends are getting married (or worse: they're having kids and on their second mortgage) and you're sick of not even having someone to spend next Saturday night with.
- You're thinking about them constantly. It's normal to emerge blinking from that delirious state of infatuation to find the budgie half dead from starvation, but while it's okay to fantasise about a new partner for the first few months, some people get permanently stuck in the 'what are they doing now . . . now . . . now?' stage.
- You're tempted to ask, 'Do you think we'll ever get married?' within the first three months.
- You're saying things like, 'I plan to be utterly faithful to you. Will you to me?' or, 'You mean more to me than anyone ever has. Do you think I'm special?'

Guilty of any of the above? Calm down, take a few deep breaths and think logically. If you're planning on spending the rest of your life with this person, you've got the rest of your life to move in, get married and/or have babies. What's the rush?

Keeping Each Other Happy

Want their dentures soaking next to yours when you're 80? The essential ingredients in the recipe for lifelong love

• •

It's not just your imagination: it *is* harder to find and keep a good long-term relationship than it was in our parents' day. The divorce rate is soaring, infidelity has reached an all-time high, single-parent families are commonplace and almost everyone over 30 has seen friends swap wedding vows for a divorce contract. Given such gloomy statistics, it's surprising we're still dating at all! But despite the break-ups, the friends with half a dinner service and one of two matching sofas, there *are* couples out there who give the rest of us hope.

My sister Deb and her husband Doug are one such couple. They're coming up for their 20-year anniversary and *still* call each other about six times a day. I watch them at parties. Deb's at one end of the room, Doug's at the other yet, while they're rarely by each other's side, there's no doubt whatsoever they're connected. Every few minutes (average five, I've timed them), one will look up and check on the other. Not out of jealousy but to make sure they're still okay, still smiling, that they don't need saving or a fresh drink.

They've achieved an enviable balance of independence and intimacy, and God knows they deserve to enjoy it and each other because they've worked damn hard to get to that point. Like other couples, rare as they might be, that we look at and think, *Aren't they lucky!*, luck has little to do with it. It's hard work, communication and compromise that gets them to the state of relationship bliss.

Couples who survive the distance today are there for different reasons than before. You no longer need to be married to be accepted by society. There's no stigma attached to 'living in sin' and you're not an 'old maid' if you're not married at 30. Even having a child on our own is okay. Rather than being taboo, it's accepted, even advised, to sleep with several different partners before settling down. Women might want a husband, but they don't *need* one. We're more independent financially, emotionally and sexually: we enjoy successful careers and casual relationships, earn substantial incomes, buy our own homes. We don't require a partner to provide or care for us, we do it ourselves.

This equality has bred a new respect between the sexes but also problems. On the up side, many men are happy to relinquish the burden of being the breadwinner: they enjoy playing second fiddle to wives or girlfriends in more prestigious, higher-paying jobs so they can pursue *their* dreams without financial pressures. Other, more conservative, traditional men find it threatening. They've been brought up to believe the man is 'boss' and are confused by the fact that today's couples function more as a team, with both partners sharing equal importance and responsibility.

Some women, as well as men, yearn for the old style of relationships. They were certainly simpler! Each sex knew exactly what was expected of them (not much). Most of us, though, have embraced the new style of relating to the point where we find it hard to understand the old. 'My accountant, who's in his late fifties, sent me a questionnaire recently that included the question, "Do you talk to your wife about your finances?"' said Andrew, a 27-year-old businessman. 'I laughed out loud. What a ridiculous question: my wife manages the money, not me! Then I thought about it and realized that, in his generation, that didn't happen. My mother had absolutely nothing in her name – she doesn't exist on paper. All her credit cards are linked to my father's, all the store accounts and property are in his name. She's never, ever filed a tax return. She has no idea how much my father earns or how much things like electricity cost.'

Appalling! we think. But along with a new openness in our partnerships, we've created some new pitfalls. For a start, juggling two careers isn't easy, and a shortage of time is the biggest threat to modern relationships. Sex is ignored as we tumble into bed, exhausted from work. The workplace is still number one venue for affairs. As many women as men are being tempted at late-night meetings and on business trips by colleagues with whom we spend more time than we do our partners. People split up more easily and often. There's no stigma attached to divorce and we're surrounded by a score of newly single friends to play with. It's hard to keep perspective and work hard at our relationships when it's less effort to keep trading in on new models.

So how do you manage to resist the temptations, shoulder the burdens, sort out all the differences and still curl up satisfied together at night? I spoke to a selection of long-term happy couples to find out the secrets to their success. It came down to the following five points:

1. **Talking things through and being 'heard':** Talking openly and honestly with their partner, knowing they're interested and listening hard, was listed as of number one importance in every single case. Being able to reveal all, without fear of

being judged, is, in a nutshell, the secret of long-lasting love. If you get that right, the rest is easy.

> 'He's the person I turn to when I'm in strife. I can do anything when we're together because he gives me strength and total support.'
>
> Carla, 23, shop assistant

2. **Commitment and trust:** These were also up there, with commitment defined as 'I know he or she's in it for a long time, not just the good times' and trust defined more as 'he or she will do the right thing by me' rather than faithfulness.

3. **Freedom:** All couples gave each other space to see friends and pursue interests separately, but also made an effort to do lots together. They made time for their relationship and consciously planned pleasurable 'dates', away from work and chores.

4. **Support and friendship:** When asked what they most liked about their relationship, almost all the couples listed support as one of their top three reasons. 'She helps me and I help her – we guide and advise each other on our careers and our problems,' was a typical answer. Most had 'got over' that initial in-love stage, and while they still loved each other, companionship and the joys of having a 'live-in best friend' were as important as sex. 'Because I love her so much, I'd rate my sex life as ten out of ten – though I've probably had better sex in a technical or lusty sense with other people,' said one happily involved man.

5. **Working at it:** Not one of the couples expected their relationship to coast happily along – all were prepared to put the effort in to get through the rough patches.

If communication is the most important, it makes sense to tackle it first. After that, I'll move onto discussing all the other elements that are essential ingredients in the true-love recipe.

COMMUNICATION: THE KEY TO EVERYTHING

When I was a kid, we had a party game. One person in the group wrote down a simple story on a piece of paper. They then had to whisper the story to the person sitting next to them, who whispered it to the next, and so on until it reached the last person in the room. They retold the story and the original 'correct' version was produced. We used to roll about the room laughing at how different the end version was. (Why, I have no idea.) But it was an early lesson in how information gets garbled very quickly.

The same thing happens when you talk to your partner. Even simple messages can get horribly confused because words have different meanings and connotations for different people. You say to your partner, 'Phew! What a bloody awful day.' To you, it's obvious that means you had a bad day at work, need a bit of TLC and a large glass of wine. Your partner might think it means a) you're prewarning them – no sex tonight; b) you had a dreadful day because they didn't call and were supposed to; or c) they should steer clear to give you time to cool off (when you'd rather talk to let off steam).

Couples who stay together learn how to 'read' each other. They don't just listen (really listen) to the words, they look for accompanying body language and are sensitive to each other's moods and soft spots. They speak clearly and specifically. They let their partner know where they're at, even if they're not really sure themselves. Instead of, 'I don't know why I'm moody. I just feel funny that's all,' they'll say, 'I feel a bit weird, honey, but it's nothing to do with you. I'm just a bit flat – maybe I'm coming down with a cold or something.' If they can't provide a reason for feeling 'off', they'll make sure each other knows it's nothing to worry about.

Communicating couples are also sensitive to 'problem issues' in the relationship: they sit up and pay attention if they're discussing a topic they've argued about before. But even if it's a volatile area, they're not afraid to reveal their feelings or fears and keep talking until they feel understood:

'I hated seeing you chatting up that girl at the party.'

'What do you mean chatting up? I wasn't chatting her up.'

'Oh yes you were! I know when you're chatting someone up. You didn't take your eyes off her face for a second and you didn't offer to get me a drink when you went to the kitchen.'

'No, because you had a full one. I checked. And as for looking at her for too long. To be totally truthful, I was trying to work out if she had caps on her teeth.'

Silence. Both laugh.

'Did she?'

Argument averted. She made it clear what 'chatting up' meant to her. He was then able to explain his behaviour.

Communicating is all about being specific. It's okay to trot out words like 'hurt', 'angry' or 'jealous', but you need to provide much more information to really be heard. Does 'hurt' mean you'll never trust them again and are going upstairs to pack your bags? Or that you feel you deserve an explanation and an apology? Is hurt really the right word? Perhaps what you mean is ignored, didn't feel special, slighted in front of their or your friends.

The real differences between men and women and why we communicate differently

I didn't want to write this section but felt obliged to. While I agree there are differences between men and women (I wouldn't have to write separate bits 'FOR HER' and 'FOR HIM' if there weren't!), in my experience, problems in relationships are caused by individuals rather than genders. So while you'll find lots in this book that says, 'Women are more likely to be victims of this one,' or, 'Sorry guys, this relates to you more than her,'

I'd rather focus on how to meet in the middle than promote the battle of the sexes.

Also, I'm loath to expand on what John Gray, author of *Men are from Mars, Women are from Venus*, has created: the concept that men and women come from different planets. Gray fans forgive me (and he does have a few valid points in his books), but I don't think it's healthy to think of your partner as an alien. It's negative and also incredibly sexist.

Sure, men and women think and act a little differently but the edges are blurring all the time. I have plenty of male friends who'll talk about nothing but relationships, when I might be more interested in discussing career or what shares to invest in (namely, can you buy shares in Coca-Cola for a pound?). While we're counting the wrinkles around our eyes, he's counting the hairs he finds on the pillow each morning. If women are the romantics, how come men fall in love quicker and out of love slower? And why do men always have the biggest collection of all those soppy female artists like Whitney Houston and Celine Dion?

Now I've got that off my chest, I'll happily admit there is one area where Ken and Barbie do have problems connecting: communication. Rolled up into the communication parcel is expression of emotion and how we relate to other people. Women and men *do* talk a different language sometimes, women *are* more adept at expressing emotion and tend to worry about others more. Which is why . . .

If you were a guy turned into a girl for the day, you'd:

*   **Listen more.** Women make more 'listening' noises, like, 'Really?' and 'Wow!' Possibly because they're not as comfortable with deep and meaningfuls, men try to turn the conversation back to themselves and onto lighter topics. Alternatively, they'll cut the conversation short by

trying to solve whatever's being discussed, not realizing women like verbalizing fears and anxieties, even if they already know what the solution is. Men are also prone to interrupt more, especially when a woman is talking. In one study, men interrupted 75 per cent of the time with women they'd just met and 96 per cent with women they knew.

- **Feel much more comfortable with expressing emotion.** Men are taught not to show feelings because it's unmanly or 'weak'. 'Manly' emotions like anger, indignation or pride are okay, but fear or vulnerability aren't. This is one reason why men think women have more emotional problems than they do. We don't – we're simply more open about talking about them.

- **Be able to tell how someone feels just by looking at them.** Women are twice as good at finding hidden meanings simply by reading people's expressions. So now might be the time to suggest that poker game . . .

- **Search for deeper messages.** Men take words at face value; women read between the lines. What men say is what they usually mean, but we'd rather delve into the *meanings* of human actions ('Why does Sue always end up with men who are bad for her?'). Besides, we love analysing. Men tend to be more curious about sport, politics, history or how things work. Women tend to like dissecting relationships.

If you were a girl who turned into a guy for the day, you'd:
- **Be angrier.** There's one emotion you won't have trouble expressing: anger. Women are taught anger is 'unladylike' so we tend to get 'hurt' rather than angry. We also value our relationships more, so we're far less likely to shout at someone in case we hurt their feelings.

- **Talk about different topics.** Men talk mostly about things while women talk mostly about people. Business, sports, politics, cars, gadgets, stereos, how they work, how to fix them – men include much more of this sort of talk in their average conversation than women do. Women talk much more about people: their problems, reactions, responses and feelings. Even if a male and female discuss the same topic – career, for instance – they'll probably take different angles on it. He'll be more interested in results and strategies, she'll talk more about the office politics and the problems of getting things to run smoothly.

> 'I used to go to restaurants and watch couples who didn't have a thing to say to each other and I just knew I'd never have a problem with Sylvia.
> I never tire of her company. I can sink my teeth into a conversation with her though we've been going out for four years. She gives me the zip to get out of bed in the morning and confidence on my down and vulnerable days. I can put myself in her hands to look after for life and she'll do the right thing by me.'
>
> Brad, 27, accountant

- **Deal out advice rather than sympathy.** Tell most guys a problem and he'll try to fix it before you've even explained what it is. Practical and solution-orientated, as a man it seems logical to focus on the facts rather than talk through every possible emotional consequence. Women, on the other hand, are often just looking for a sympathetic ear. The act of talking out loud to someone who understands is often all they're really after.

- **Put friends down – straight to their face.** Nasty, eh! Actually, it's the opposite. When men do it to other men, it usually means they like them. It's all part of the teasing and jostling that happened during his adolescence. Women aren't angels: we put down people too. But seldom to their faces because we show affection more directly. To insult a friend face-to-face for us means we really *don't* like them.

GETTING HIM TO OPEN UP

Relationships expert Dr Maryon Tysoe says one of the strongest binding elements between two people is their ability to reveal intimate thoughts and feelings to each other. She cites one study which tried to predict which couples would stay together over a four-year period by just one factor: how much they shared their feelings. The results were as expected: the more the couples shared, the more likely they were to be together four years on. Another survey of 400 therapists showed the largest single reason they thought marriages failed was the husband's inability to communicate his feelings.

Unless your guy's spent the last five years locked away in a dark room playing computer games (come on, he must have come out sometimes), he's probably got the message that he should be opening up. Then why doesn't he? Because deep and meaningfuls may not be that easy for him. Most women consider a good, long, deep conversation one of life's pleasures. It's up there with walking into your favourite designer's with a spare £500 to blow. For some men, a deep conversation isn't enjoyable at all because it's hard work. Men are 'doers'. When he meets up with the boys, they don't sit around in coffee shops chatting. They play pool, go to the football, go for a jog or a swim. He's not that practised at talking intimately so it requires effort. And say he stuffs it up? 'I worry I'll give the wrong answer.' 'It all comes out wrong and I upset her.' 'I don't know what she wants me to say.' They're the comments I got from from male friends who don't find it easy to talk to their partners. If talking doesn't come naturally to him, it's not surprising he's all for going to the movies rather than out to dinner (where you're bound to want a conversation). ➢

My idea of a good time is a good chat. My ex's idea of a good time was playing tennis. Personally, I would rather clean all the public toilets at the Olympic Stadium the day after the opening ceremony, than hit a ball around the court. Why? Because that doesn't come naturally to *me* – I'm embarrassingly pathetic at it. My boyfriend would say, 'I know – let's have a game of tennis!' expecting me to jump up with an enthusiastic 'Yes!', rush into the bedroom and pull on a short white skirt. Instead I'd do *anything* (even watch football on telly) to avoid it. The last time I was forced to play a game of social tennis I spent most of the day before sitting on the loo. If a 'deep' conversation for men is the equivalent to tennis for me, they have my sympathy.

Unfortunately, being able to have an intimate conversation is slightly more crucial to relationships than perfecting a backhand. Besides, once they do get the hang of it, most men admit having a good chat is an incredibly rewarding experience. Which is more than I can say for tennis.

How to help him open up? Encourage him by:

- **Letting him know talking is important to you.** Say, 'I know you don't feel comfortable talking about your feelings just yet, but it would mean a lot to me if you'd try.' Explain why. Get him to read this section of the chapter and other sections in the book which talk about communication issues.
- **Rewarding even the slightest hint of intimate talk.** If he usually says, 'My boss, Bob, is a bastard,' then one day comes out with, 'I don't know, Sally, sometimes I think Bob isn't happy with my performance,' let him know you're thrilled. I don't mean jump up, throw your arms around him and say, 'Honey! At last! You're talking to me' (he'll clam up for good). The trick is to acknowledge it but not make a big deal. Let him know a) you don't think 'less' of him for revealing a fear; b) it's normal; ➤

and c) it's great he let you in. Say something like, 'I think all of us worry about that sometimes – I sure as hell do. What makes you think that?' Let him tell you, then say at the finish, 'I'm glad you let me know. It's nice to know how you're feeling.'

- **The more open you are, the more open he'll be.** If you're comfortable with talking about 'embarrassing' things – topics which make you look a bit foolish – he'll take your example.

- **Ask him questions.** If you think he's worried about something, say, 'Are you worried about this? Tell me,' then truly listen to his reply. Guide him along by saying, 'What did you feel then? Angry? Confused? Frustrated?' Yes, you are putting words in his mouth, but you're also teaching him *how* to talk intimately.

- **Don't assume silence means disinterest.** This is the main difference between how men and women talk: women tend to think out loud, men tend to work things through in their heads. He might mention a problem he's got ('My boss is really getting up my nose'). The next time he mentions it, you'll probably hear the conclusion ('I've decided to apply for a job with another company'). The middle bit – weighing up the pros and cons – he does privately. That's why, when you ask his advice about something, he might say, 'Let me think about it.' He's not fobbing you off, that's just the way he handles problems. Women, on the other hand, verbalize thoughts. In fact, we're rather fond of expressing *every* thought that enters our head, not just important ones. So we might say, 'Okay, I've got to go to the bank, then the drycleaners. No, I'll go to the drycleaners first because it's on the way. Jesus! I nearly forgot! I have to drop in that presentation to a client, even though it is Saturday. Honestly, sometimes I feel all I do is work, work, work. Where *is* that bloody black ➤

How to talk and listen to each other

All the happy couples I spoke to said they talked intimately ('We fill each other in on what's been happening') for around one hour per day. If you're answering, 'Hi honey. I'm home,' with 'Shut up, *Ally McBeal* is on,' you aren't going to be watching reruns of it 30 years from now. If you don't talk constantly to each other, you lose sight of how the other person is thinking, feeling and looking at the world. You stop connecting because you don't know where you're both at. If he doesn't tell you he's irritable because his mum's just been tested for cancer, you'll give him a hard time about it. He withdraws even further, and before you know it there's a gulf between you that's bigger than the Grand Canyon.

Words are the glue that stick couples together. The more you talk and share what's happening inside your hearts and heads, the more you'll get out of the relationship. Let's face it: one reason why all of us want a special relationship is the joy of being able to share all our worries and fears and get reassurance.

Listening is even more important. After all, there's not much point in either of you rattling on about this, that and the other if it's all falling on deaf ears. It's insulting if someone's reading the paper while you're talking to them. Ditto people who switch channels on the telly or are obviously lost in their own thoughts, even though they

Six minutes – that's the amount of time most couples spend each day in meaningful communication, say Japanese scientists.

are looking straight at you.

A good listener isn't someone who sits there quietly, letting you talk. It's someone who *actively* listens. Their body language shows they're interested. They lean forward, eager to hear your next words. If you're telling them something funny, they laugh along with you. If you're worried, concern is etched on their face as well. They acknowledge the conversation every few sentences with an 'uh-huh' or comment on the subject. They ask questions and offer opinions. When you've finished the conversation, you know they've not only heard every word you said but tried hard to experience it with you.

> **What's the perfect position to talk intimately with your partner? About five feet away from each other, sitting face to face. Women are uncomfortable discussing personal matters from further away; men don't like it when women move closer. Five feet is the happy medium.**

Like most relationship skills, talking and listening properly requires a bit of effort at the start. Keep the following in mind until it all starts to come naturally.

Ⓜ Ⓕ FOR BOTH OF YOU

- **Be aware of each other's body language.** Watch your partner's body language and facial expressions and you'll learn to 'read' each other more accurately. Close couples can list each other's 'giveaway' signs. 'I know he's worried about something even when he doesn't admit it because he gets this red, angry line between his eyes from frowning.' 'I know when Sarah's uncomfortable when we're in company because of the way she stands. She's stiff and doesn't move her hands around as much as she normally would.' 'I know when he's lying because it's like shutters come down over his eyes and they go blank.'

- **Give each other time.** Sure, we're all busy, but if you truly can't spare an hour a day to sit and listen to someone you supposedly love, you shouldn't be in a relationship.
- **Ask lots of questions.** 'How did that meeting go? Did your idea get through?' is better than, 'How was your day?'
- **Offer solutions, not problems.** There's nothing more satisfying than having a good, long whinge about something, but constantly bitching about life to your partner drags both of you down. If you want to complain about something, at least finish it with, 'So I've decided in future I'm going to . . .'
- **Try not to let emotions stop you listening.** Your girl-friend says, 'There's a problem with our sex life,' and even if she continues talking for an hour, you're stuck back at the first sentence thinking, *Bloody hell! I'm a dud in bed*. If you are stuck, ask them to stop explaining and give some reassurance before continuing.
- **Be discreet.** What you reveal to each other isn't anyone else's business. Intimate secrets aren't fodder for your next meeting with best friends, no matter how discreet they are.

F FOR HER

- **Don't interpret silence as disinterest.** He's simply thinking about what you just said.
- **Touch, along with talk.** It helps keep him focused and it's easier for him to get in touch with his emotions.
- **Let him know you're not going to get angry** if things do come out 'the wrong way'. Don't get defensive, just ask him to repeat what he said using different words.
- **Tell him if you want to talk just for the sake of it.** Say, 'I'm just going to ramble on here because it helps me to work it out by talking out loud. I don't expect you to solve it for me.'

- **Don't rush him.** It's not as easy for him to express emotion, so he takes longer to 'search' for the right word or phrase or even think about what he does feel. Women analyse their relationships every few minutes, he might not have thought about the issue at all. Give him time to think – don't expect instant solutions.

Ⓜ **FOR HIM**
- **Be patient.** Women tell long stories, men summarize. Accept she'll take the long way round. Don't say, 'Can you get to the point?'
- **Don't jump in with solutions.** She's probably just off-loading. If you're not sure what's expected of you, say, 'Do you want my advice or are you just talking this through?'
- **Start small, aim high.** If you're uncomfortable expressing emotion, start by revealing not-so-intimate stuff ('I was so angry with my boss today', 'I really enjoyed last night with you') before working up to biggies ('I'd be devasted if we split up', 'I'm worried I'm not successful enough for you').

Talking through important issues
The next time you want to talk about something important, try systematically following these steps until they become second nature.

Before you talk to your partner
- **Work out how you communicate best.** Do you find it easier to explain yourself verbally or to write things down? If you're about to tackle something that usually ends in a screaming row, you might get further by handing them a letter, then discussing what's written. The beauty of the written word is that you can get it exactly right. Read it first thing in the morning and last thing at night before handing

it over, to make absolutely sure it clearly and specifically states all the points you want to get across.

- **Work out what you want to say before you say it.** Start with what you think the problem is: 'I swear I'll go stark raving mad if I have to sit through another boring work function of his.' Then think up at least three reasons to answer, 'Why?' You might discover it's not the work dinners that concern you but the fact that you're not spending enough time together, just the two of you. Maybe you don't like taking second place to his career. Maybe you don't like the person he becomes when he's around his work colleagues. They are the real issues. The work dinners are a symptom.

- **Put yourself in your partner's shoes.** Every time you talk about something important, imagine how it sounds on their end. Not how *you* would react if *they* said it to *you*, but how you think you'd react if you *were* them. Take into account their personality, their past, their vulnerable points: do they have a tendency to take a negative slant on any criticism? Is what you're going to say or write worded in such a way that they won't feel criticized and put up defences? Insult someone and they'll immediately stop listening.

- **Think up solutions.** What is it you want to achieve from this? What would stop this troubling you in the future? Is your solution practical or a wee bit selfish? Will it make both of you happy?

During the discussion

- **Wait until you're both calm.** It's crucial. The old saying, 'Don't go to bed angry,' doesn't always apply. Sometimes you're better off huffily sticking to opposite sides of the bed and talking it through in the morning than saying things you really don't mean in the heat of the moment.

- **Don't accuse.** Instead of saying, 'You're a ——' or 'You made me ——', say, 'I felt —— when you behaved in that way.' Start sentences with 'I' and criticize the *behaviour*, not the *person*. If you ignore all the rest and only take on board these two points, you'll still notice a huge difference.

- **Be specific.** Deliver your speech or letter and ask them to repeat back to you what it is they think you just said. When you're satisfied they've received the message you wanted to send, then move onto discussing the issue.

- **Take turns.** Give them full attention for five minutes and don't interrupt. Then repeat back what you think they've just said. Then it's your turn and they do the same to you. It's called 'parroting' and it's an easy, effective technique. Parroting each other has another advantage. If what you're asking or arguing over is silly, it'll sound even sillier coming out of *their* mouth.

- **Talk through the solutions.** Give a bottom line: 'I'm prepared to do X, but won't put up with Y.' Keep going until you reach a compromise you're both happy with. If it's incredibly important to you, your partner might decide to give up something. If they do, make sure it evens up. The next time something is important to them, you do the compromising.

SHOULDN'T COUPLES IN LOVE BE 100 PER CENT HONEST WITH EACH OTHER ALL OF THE TIME?

It's a sweet thought but horribly naive. Think about it. I don't care how angelic you are, would *you* want your partner to know your every thought? Because that's what being totally honest would entail: hooking them up to a 24-hour mind-reading device. ➢

Total honesty means every time they ask, 'What are you thinking?' you'd have to tell the truth. 'Actually, I was thinking you look a bit pudgy and wondering if you'll end up with a beergut.' Or, 'I was thinking I wish you'd bloody well stop going on and on about Christine. I couldn't care less what she said.' You ask what he thinks of your best friend, Michelle, and he'd be forced to say, 'Brilliant! If you weren't around, I'd shag her in a second.' He cooks you dinner and asks how it is. Your answer would be, 'It tastes like dog food but I suppose I have to eat it or you'll get offended. If I throw up, I throw up.' I could go on and on (and on), but I think you get the point by now.

No matter how much you love someone or how compatible you are, there are times when your partner drives you completely nuts. There are times when they don't look so hot. There are times when other people do. If you make a pact to be truly honest with each other, you'd have to admit to these thoughts. I don't know about you but I don't particularly *want* to know if my partner's spent all day imagining what the girl at the next desk would look like with her hair spread out over his pillow. So long as he has no intention of acting on it, that's his business, not mine.

Total honesty would reduce most of us to paranoid, blithering heaps within a day. Those fleeting desires and momentary doubts should be left unsaid. Spoken out loud, they're painful and hurtful and destructive. I'm not advocating lying to each other about big issues or issues you've been concerned about for a while, but I see no advantage whatsoever to making a pact to tell each other every thought. (Don't laugh: lots of couples *do* pledge to do this. It usually lasts about five seconds until one says something the other definitely didn't want to hear.)

There's one area in particular where it doesn't pay to be honest: your past sex life. 'What's the best sex you've ever had?' you ask them, smugly confident it's bound to be ➤

with you. 'Gosh!' they answer, truthfully. 'That's hard. I had sex in a lift once – that was *fantastic* – but if I had to pick just one I guess it'd be the time Trudy and I had sex on the steps of her parents' house. Just thinking about it makes me want to ——' Like, this is *not* the answer you want to hear. The answer you want is, 'The time you and I ——' If someone asks you that question, I don't care if your nose grows like Pinocchio while you're saying it, that's the answer to give.

If you and your lover get into that 'how many people were there before me?' discussion, stop it before it goes any further. It's pointless, anyway, because you'll be none the wiser at the end of it. Men subconsciously up the figure because they think it makes them more of a stud; women reduce it because they're worried they'll seem 'easy' or 'slutty'. (In fact, if you *really* want to know how many men a woman's slept with, researchers say you should triple the number she admits to. One study found women tend to 'forget' significant sex encounters, particularly one-night stands. Whether that's because we've deliberately blotted them out or they meant so little we just forget them, is beside the point.)

There's a huge difference between talking about your past and reducing it to a statistic. Telling each other about significant past relationships is healthy and necessary to get close to each other. Most people start asking the ex-lover questions when it's starting to get serious, and the reason we do it is to check how special we are. Like, am I as important to her as she is to me or does she act like this with every guy? We need and want to know what's happened to our partner's heart. If some girl led him along then dumped him, it explains why he's a bit nervous about commitment. If she's never had a relationship that's lasted more than two weeks, it says something about her. That's not prying, and you need to share stuff like that. If you focus on the feelings for the person, not your sex life, you probably won't get into too much trouble. ➤

You move into the extreme danger zone when you start talking about how *many* ex-lovers each of you has had, because then you're reducing things to a number and removing the emotion and circumstances. If a partner asks you how many people you've slept with, refuse to answer and don't ask them the question. If they hassle you, say, 'What I did *before* I met you really isn't your business and vice versa. It's what we do after we met each other that I'm interested in.' If you do confess, I guarantee no matter what number you say, it'll be too many, especially if you're female. If he's slept with 50 and you've had five, it'll still be four too many.

COMMITMENT AND TRUST

There are two levels of commitment: making a public statement you intend to stick around (moving in, marriage, the stuff we talked about in Chapter 3), and what I call *true* commitment. True commitment is making an emotional commitment to do the right thing by each other and the relationship. Just because you've got the first, don't assume you've got the second. Plenty of people commit to marriage and walk up the aisle eyeing up the bridesmaids. Others go through the motions of a relationship on such a superficial level, they don't even know what their partner's favourite colour is.

True commitment is about deciding you're going to make the relationship work, no matter what. It's called looking out for someone, being their number one biggest fan and best friend. Listening to their dreams, protecting them from 'the big, bad world', travelling through life together as a team. If you're truly committed to someone, their happiness is as important to you as your own. You say no to the 'this would be so easy to get away with' sex on the side because you couldn't face *yourself* in the mirror afterward, let alone them. In essence, it's about treating your partner with love, respect and kindness. The very best relationships are those where both partners are not only truly committed to each other, they both know it.

It's the same deal with trust. Trust isn't just about knowing someone won't bonk around on you. It's knowing they can be trusted to take responsibility, live up to expectations. You know they're not going to blow next month's mortgage repayment on a horse. Or forget to feed the cat while you're away. Or organize a stripper when asked to provide entertainment for Aunt Betty's eightieth. In short, you respect their judgement and can count on them to do the right thing in any situation. This sort of trust tends to be taken for granted in good relationships – you just assume your partner will behave responsibly and they do. It's when it's missing that you notice. Which reminds me, funnily enough, of an ex of mine called Rob.

Rob could certainly be counted on. Unfortunately, it was to do the wrong thing in any given situation. I took a day off work once to nurse a thumping hangover ('I've got terrible food poisoning'). My boss rang later to see how I was and Rob took the call.

'Oh, she'll be fine by the morning,' I heard him say reassuringly. 'She just had one too many down at the pub last night.'

I took him to a dinner party at my best friend's house. 'You're a fantastic cook,' he enthused. Casting an eye over her rather full figure, he winked and said, 'Now I know why you eat so much.'

Not only couldn't Rob be trusted to say the right thing, he couldn't be trusted to do it either. He'd push past little old ladies clinging desperately to their walking sticks, to jump the queue. He'd forget to pass on important phone messages ('Oh, your brother called last week to say he's getting married'). He'd promise to lock up before bed and then he'd leave the back door wide open. 'I'll be there on time.' 'I'll do the dishes in the morning.' 'I'll pay you back on Thursday.' None of it ever eventuated. He was a walking, talking verson of 'The cheque's in the mail'. Trusting Rob to do anything was about as sensible as giving your brand new leather sandals to a puppy to play with and assuming you'll be able to wear them to work the next day.

That's trusting (or not) on a basic level. Then there's a deeper, more intimate level of trust that's equally as crucial. It's about being able to trust your partner with your innermost thoughts, about feeling comfortable enough to expose your vulnerabilities, reveal those nasty and/or incredibly painful secrets from your past, and know none of it will be used against you later. This type of trust is earned and it takes time to develop. One of you starts the ball rolling in the beginning by disclosing something personal, the other responds by sharing something equally as intimate. Both of you hold your breath and wait a little while to see if it's safe to go further (you don't read it in the gossip pages, their friends don't look at you oddly, it's not thrown back at you in an argument). Once you've got the all clear, you go a little deeper the next time, and so do they. For a relationship to be healthy, trust needs to be reciprocated. Lopsided relationships don't work. If they know everything about you and you know nothing about them, you feel exposed and powerless. Not a great feeling.

It's impossible for me to give practical pointers on how to truly commit to and trust someone or get them to commit to and trust you. Only you know whether your partner's worthy of both. Only you can make these private pacts with yourself and each other. What I can tell you, though, is this: if you want a *really* good relationship, commitment and trust is all part of it. So if you or your partner have problems with either or both, I'd think about getting some professional help to get to the bottom of it.

According to Dr Maryon Tysoe, most people fit into one

of three categories. *Secure* people find it easy to get close to others and to trust them. *Anxious* types commit and trust a little *too* easily, become obsessively preoccupied with their partner and worry excessively that they don't love them back. *Avoidant* people are uncomfortable with intimacy and closeness and fight against both.

If you're a secure person, you're in an enviable position. (In fact, if you are having problems trusting or committing to someone, sit up and pay attention. If the act of committing and trusting doesn't frighten you, the problem obviously lies with the person you're nervous about committing to.) You're the anxious type? Back off and calm down. You tend to perpetuate your worst nightmare and drive your partner away by being overly jealous, possessive and clingy (see 'Freedom', below). If you're an avoidant person, you constantly run away from good relationships or deliberately sabotage them to justify leaving. Read Chapter 8 for some clues on why you've ended up this way, or book in to see a good therapist.

FREEDOM

Not one of the happy couples I interviewed lived in each other's pockets. They all saw friends separately and enjoyed activities solo as well as making an effort to do lots together. It's natural to want to velcro yourselves together in the first few months; not so healthy if you're still doing *everything* together a year in. Freedom in a relationship is allowing each other to keep your sense of self. Thinking for two as opposed to thinking *as* two: there's a huge difference.

'Come out to dinner with me tonight,' says your friend Sarah.

'I'll pass this time because Mike's a bit down,' you reply. 'He missed out on the promotion.' That's thinking for two: you're considering your partner as well as yourself.

Thinking *as* two is automatically assuming Sarah's asking *both* of you to dinner. 'We can't come because Mike's working late,' you say. It doesn't occur to you to go solo because, well, you're a couple, right?

Don't laugh – I've met several Tweedledum, Tweedledee couples: they come as a matching set or not at all. Quite frankly, they're the ones you only ask to a dinner party if you need a nice, pleasant pair to fill seats while you're entertaining that 'Oh God, when are they going home?' visitor. They're boring! I mean, if you haven't got the balls to say, 'Honey, order in some pizza and beer. I'm out with a friend tonight,' you're hardly likely to be one of those witty, vivacious, mesmerizingly passionate types who's *top* of everyone's must-invite list.

> 'She had a bowl near the door where she'd dump change and business cards and stuff. Every time I came over, I'd sneakily look through it. One day I found a note that said, "All those lunches meant the world. I love you. David." I thought the worst and dumped her without giving a reason. A few months later, we ran into each other and she asked me why. Turned out the note was from a gay workmate whose partner was dying of AIDS. She'd take him out every day to cheer him up but promised not to tell anyone. I apologized but she hasn't forgiven me.'
>
> Alan, 31, personal trainer

The healthiest, happiest relationships are those where both partners give each other the freedom to enjoy life apart from each other. She spends a week in Bali with a girlfriend with his blessing. He says, 'Count me in!' to the boys when they suggest a weekend fishing trip, knowing he doesn't have to ask permission. Just because you're now part of a couple doesn't mean you don't spend the odd Saturday night watching videos and scoffing chocolate with your best friend. Or he cancels his Tuesday night squash game with his. Quite apart from maintaining precious friendships, seeing people separately gives you the chance to vent. Let off steam when your lover's driving you nuts. Get a fresh perspective on how to handle a relationship problem. Talk about how delicious the man in the video shop is and you couldn't help but notice him noticing you when you happened to have to return a video on the way to the cocktail party when you looked pretty fab in that tight black number. And how (Jesus!) if you were single, Harry's secretary would be doing a lot more than taking bloody dictation if she worked for you. Let's face it: talking about doing something can be just as good as doing it (with far fewer complications). Saying it out loud makes you think, *I could do that if I wanted to*. And you realize you don't really. You just wanted it acknowledged somehow.

Freedom's also about not expecting your partner to be a clone of yourself. You respect each other's rights to have different opinions, likes and dislikes, and don't get all huffy because you were both on opposing sides during a raging debate with friends. You appreciate that just because you want something, it doesn't mean they will, too, at the exact same moment. That goes for everything from wanting to eat Thai that night to wanting to have kids before your partner's ready. You can't wait to play Dad but she's concentrating on her career right now? Fine! She's got her own life, you respect that and give her time. Freedom's about not expecting to be number one priority in your partner's life every single day of it. If studying four nights a week while working full-time will help them get their dream job, you'll encourage rather than complain. Remember those posters that were all the rage during the flower-power years? The ones that had naked bodies silhouetted against sunsets, with the slogan, 'If you love something let it free. If it returns it was yours, if it doesn't it never was,' blah blah blah? Sure, the person who wrote it was possibly stoned at the time, but it actually does make a lot of sense.

Of course, letting go of someone you love desperately isn't that easy for some people. If you're insecure or the jealous type, there's a temptation to keep them on as tight a leash as possible.

I went out with a guy once who couldn't bear to be separated from me. When I went to the loo, he'd stand outside the door talking to me. Initially, I was flattered. He was so besotted and devoted, my ego skyrocketed with all the attention. Flowers every week, phone calls to say how wonderful I was, how he'd never met anyone like me before, notes shoved in my wallet, under my pillow, inside the fridge. He'd come over to cook for me when I worked late, clean my flat if I was too busy to do it, ask my opinion on *everything*. Yup. It all got *too, too* much. After two months, it felt like he couldn't breathe without consulting me first. I pulled back and the phone calls went from two to ten a day. If I dared to go for a night out with the girls, I'd come home to find 12 messages on my machine, all saying how much he loved and missed me, when I'd only seen him a few hours before. I felt like I was being stalked.

American relationships guru Barbara de Angelis calls people like him emotional vampires. She says they're people whose hearts are like empty containers they desperately want *you* to fill up, except there's a hole in the bottom and it's never, ever enough. Emotional vampires feed off their partners, sucking up their energy, affection and attention like hungry puppies. Why do they do it? Usually it's because they've been hurt badly somewhere along the line and think being loved by you will make the pain go away. It won't. Counselling will. Do yourself a favour if you've hooked up with someone like this: send them off to a therapist and then bugger off to the Bahamas for a few months. (Maybe for good.)

Why clinging on makes people run away

We're all individuals with our own personal needs for space, time alone and privacy. What's affectionate for one person is suffocating for another. Ideally, we'd choose a partner with needs similiar to our own – but even then, it's not guaranteed you'll both feel soppy at the same moment. The trick is getting to know each other and learning to read each other so you know when's the time to cuddle on the couch and when's the time to leave them alone.

Most of us get the hang of it after a few months together. But there are people who seem to be in a permanent state of 'clingy'.

'I was paranoid about him seeing me without make-up on so I used to shut the bathroom door when removing it and slap on a new "face" before opening it again. One day it was so bloody hot I couldn't stand it. I left the door open and he came to talk to me while I was standing there, face bare. He smiled and said, "You look pretty and fresh without make-up on. Why don't you leave it off now and then?" I was like, *Oh God! All that effort for nothing!'*
Robyn, 25, music rep

They're permanently draped over their partners: get upset if they go down the shop without them, get all possessive and funny if they dare to talk to the opposite sex. Constantly asking for reassurance, they're like needy children tugging on your skirt, always wanting attention. If you're the clingy type, take note. Cling on too tight and no matter how much your partner loves you, they'll push you away. This sets off a rather unpleasant chain reaction. You feel insecure when they push you away, so react by being even more clingy. They feel even more suffocated and push you even further away, and so it continues.

The thing is, clingy behaviour isn't very attractive. If you're at a party and your partner spends the entire time glued to your side, whining, whingeing and asking, 'Do you love me?' you're hardly going to think, *Wow! I'm so lucky to have them.* You think, *They think they're so lucky to have me.* Watching your partner holding court, chatting and laughing and obviously being admired by others has the opposite reaction. That's when you think, *I'm so glad they chose me out of all the competition.*

It's all about insecurity. If you're the clingy type, you need to work on your self-esteem (see Chapter 1). Work out why you constantly need your partner's approval. Why does it mean so much to you? Chapter 8 deals with how past encounters, experiences and your childhood might have made you so dependent on others. If you haven't read it, do so now. If you have and it hasn't made a difference, see a counsellor.

If you're the smothered partner, try boosting your partner's ego to give them confidence to let go. Try reassuring them *before* they ask for it: how attractive they are, how much you love them, how you're still thinking of them even when they're not around. The more secure they feel of your love, the more space they'll give you. If this doesn't work, you've got little choice but to disengage yourself permanently or suggest they seek professional help.

Explain that time alone is good for the both of you. Solitude isn't just necessary for ourselves, it allows us to connect with others in a far richer way. Being alone gives you time to think things through, readjust your life if necessary. It restores energy, lets you rest and most importantly, gives you time to dream and make plans for the future.

SUPPORT AND FRIENDSHIP

Clock up a decade as a couple and you realize romantic relationships are based as much on friendship as they are on love. 'It's not about gazing into each other's eyes and whispering sweet nothings, it's about two people who are best friends.' 'It's about liking your partner as well as loving them. I'd choose Michael as my best friend even if we weren't going out.' We're best friends: pretty well all the couples I interviewed said this about their relationship. And the same rules that apply to platonic friendships apply to romantic ones as well.

Closely linked to friendship was support. Support means helping each other out: taking half the responsibility for everything to do with the relationship. Sometimes support means carrying the *entire* load on your shoulders to give your partner a break, knowing they'll do the same for you when you need it. In short, it's about thinking for two. If you can't put yourself in

FOUR RELATIONSHIP NO-NOS

1. **Reminiscing about an ex during your special moment.** You're lying in bed watching the raindrops trickle down the window pane when she says, 'This reminds me of the time John and I were lying in bed in this great little hotel in England.' They know you've been around the block – spare them the addresses.

2. **Betraying each other's secrets.** You introduce her to your work colleagues. She says, 'Trevor was right: you *do* look like the woman out of *Two Fat Ladies*.' Anything derogatory said about friends, pillow-talk, those intimate, highly embarrassing childhood confessions: none are to be repeated.

3. **Criticizing when they're doing their best.** It might not occur to you to marinate the steak in gin or wash the chicken with detergent but he's doing his best. Let your partner have their big moment.

4. **Constantly apologizing.** 'Sorry honey, I shouldn't have said that / done that / breathed so loud.' Women seem to have far too many polite genes. He knocks a cup of coffee out of your hands and you're the one who apologizes. Like, sorry for existing.

your partner's shoes, see how life and the relationship feels on their side, you haven't got a hope of making them happy. A psychologist friend of mine takes this even further. She says the true secret of great relationships is when each partner lives their *life* as if they *were* in the other's shoes. Every single thing they do and say they look at from their partner's perspective rather than their own. 'If everyone concentrated on keeping each other happy, we'd all be happy,' she says.

I say, 'Bollocks!' It sounds dreadfully romantic and some couples could pull it off (the sort that say no to an all-expenses paid trip to their dream destination because it wouldn't be fair to go alone – nutters). Most of us would have major problems being that selfless. My version of thinking for two would be to first think what would make you happy, *then* see it from their side. What objections are they likely to have to what you're suggesting? Are you taking their feelings into account?

Thinking for two also has a calming effect in arguments. The bastard completely forgot about your anniversary so it – and you – obviously mean nothing to him? From your side, this would be true. You place great store by significant dates. But looking at it from *his* side, you realize he's just not a 'date' person and never has been one to make a fuss on birthdays and Christmas. It might still piss you off something dreadful, but you know it *doesn't* mean he doesn't love you. Instead of confronting, you'll say, 'John, I know anniversaries don't mean much to you but they do to me. It upsets me that you forgot. Can you put it in your diary for next year so it doesn't happen again?'

If your partner doesn't think for two, ask them to. Say, 'Look at it from my side, just for a minute,' or, 'Think about it: how would *you* feel if I did that to you?' The more you remind each other there are two sides to everything, two ways of looking at things, the more natural thinking for two will become.

WORKING AT IT

This whole book's about working at it because working at it simply means putting effort into the relationship to keep each other happy. Working at it includes satisfying each other sexually, splitting the household chores evenly and dividing finance commitments fairly. It's about being interested, attentive and thoughtful. Expressing affection by telling and showing your partner you love them through words and actions. Loving each other warts and all. Turning a blind eye to things that annoy you about your partner, focusing on things you do like. Solving problems before they turn into crises. Partners who actively work on their relationship, constantly check with each other: 'Are you happy? Is there anything you're not getting that you need?' It's about putting all the things I talk about in this book into practice. Again, the energy both of you put into the relationship should be fairly even, or resentment creeps in.

Working at it is a lot about making each other feel special. It seems trite to say be nice to each other, but you'd be astonished how many couples aren't. Some spend their lives playing

You consider yourself a tennis pro, they beat you. Do you a) slap them on the back and say a genuine 'Congratulations!' or b) secretly seethe? According to US researchers, your reaction to a partner's win could predict the long-term future for the two of you. If you take joy in their achievements (especially if they beat you in an area you excel in), start booking the reception. You're happy with reflected glory and think of the two of you as 'one'. Feeling resentful and wanting to outdo each other means you're still sorting out the power balance – a long way to go yet, guys!

a game of one-upmanship, in a constant struggle for who's got the power. Others *think*, I love you often but rarely say it. There are two ways to let someone know you think they're special: through words and actions. I'd suggest you use both.

At the start of relationships, couples spend an extraordinary amount of time talking about how they feel about each other. 'The relationship' is often the favourite topic of conversation. Unfortunately, this tends to wear off rather rapidly once a major commitment is made. One study cited by Dr Maryon Tysoe dramatically demonstrated how affectionate behaviour decreases after marriage. Within the first year of 'wedding bliss', saying 'I love you' dropped by 40 per cent, approval and compliments by 30 per cent, doing something nice for each other by 28 per cent and touching and cuddling (non-sexual) by 39 per cent. Don't fall into the same trap.

Say, 'I love it when you laugh, it makes me laugh.' Say, 'That's so sweet of you, darling. It's just one of the things I adore about you.' Give loads of compliments about your lover's physical appearance as well. 'I was watching you walk back to the car and thought, *Yum!*' and 'Do you know how fab your arms look in that shirt?' Every time you *think* something nice, say it.

Say thank you as often as possible: 'Thanks for being so patient, darling', 'Thanks for listening', 'Thanks for being so nice to me'. It's the equivalent of giving the dog a pat when he's been good. The more positive feedback you give, the more

> 'We kept it quiet for ages, terrified it would be frowned on to date a co-worker. One day, my boss called me in and said, "I thought maybe you'd like to work with Mike on this one since you get on so well." I went red, she laughed and said, "You've amused the entire office for months by pretending nothing's going on. But it's fine, really." The relief was enormous.'
>
> Janet, 19, journalist

they'll keep on being nice to you. There's a reward at the end which makes *them* feel good!

The other way to make each other feel special is to *do* nice things. I'm not just talking flowers and impromptu pressies, even though they *are* heaven, but also caring enough to find out what your partner's idea of heaven is. Do you know what their all-time favourite thing to do is? Do you know their favourite food, which of your (and their) friends they like best, what they'd like to do more of together or less of? If you don't know, ask – or watch. Does their face light up when you suggest dinner out? Or do they look longingly at the video store and takeaway when you drive past and wish they were curled up on the couch?

Another gift you can bestow that costs nothing but means everything: give them permission to have fun *without* you. What would they like to do solo that perhaps they're nervous about asking? A girlfriend and I dearly wanted to run away for a weekend of pampering at a resort but she felt guilty about deserting her partner. She wouldn't even suggest it. One night, we were out and I was talking about how much I needed to get away for two days but now my best girlfriend was attached, well . . . Her boyfriend turned to her and said, 'Would you like to go? I wouldn't mind because Joe really wants to go fishing and I know you'd hate that.' I knew I liked that guy!

Also keep an eye out for the little things your partner does that maybe you don't notice. Like him getting up half an hour early so he can drop you at work. Her coming home early from a night out with the girls because you were feeling down. These small, seemingly insignificant gestures are the things that hold couples together. Men, especially, are more prone to showing love than verbalize it. In one study researchers asked a group of men to show more affection to their wives. One man decided to wash his wife's car. Hardly romantic, but the intention behind it was.

Working at it also means keeping the fun happening. We all need routine in our lives and there's definitely something appealing about knowing you'll be tucked up in bed asleep by 10 pm this Friday, arms wrapped around your partner, when the week's been a nightmare and you're knackered. But if you can predict pretty accurately what the two of you will do every night this week, every week of the year, you're heading for a fall.

Psychologists call it 'emotional deadening'. The average person calls it being bored out of their brain. Both mean the same thing: let your relationship get *too* routine and life takes on a hum which is comforting and pleasant sometimes but dull for the rest of it.

It's not so much *what* you do together, but how often you vary your routine. If you've eaten out every single night for the last three weeks, a night *in* can be unbearably exciting. In fact, couples who are always running out the door to yet another social event aren't any better off than those who stay home. The idea is to aim for a balance. Just the two of you, stress-free evenings combined with novelty and what I call kick-up-the-bum outings.

They're places you go together where there are people you don't know of the opposite sex. They're necessary to remind each other of how attractive your partner is out there in the big wide world. I'm not talking singles bars, it could be a dinner party: anywhere you're forced to dress up, get out there and socialize. It's good for you to see your partner across a crowded room and realize you'd still go home with them every single time.

Money's tight? No excuse. If finances or time mean you only go out a fortnight, just vary when you do it. Make it a boozy lunch on Sunday instead of Saturday night dinner. Don't mix with the same old friends, over and over. Throw in a few people neither of you know very well or mix friends in different combinations. Do things apart as well. Do they really have to come to that family Sunday lunch? If they don't get on with a group of your friends, see them on your own. If you do everything together, what are you going to talk about that's fresh and new?

Set aside one weekend a month and take it in turns to plan it. Deliberately turn it into a game of who can come up with the most interesting itinerary. The more situations you put each other in, the more interesting you'll both seem. Watching her screaming with hysterical laughter while riding the rollercoaster reminds you how much fun she is. Watching him build a campfire reminds you of how resourceful he is. If the only time you see each other, you're both in slob-around clothes saying things like, 'Honey, hurry up, *ER* is about to start,' you'll end up in the emergency room yourselves. Comatose.

SEVEN SIGNS YOU'RE GOING TO MAKE IT

1. **After arguments you feel closer.** You both feel raw, exhausted and a little fragile but closer than you did before it. You've managed to talk it through rationally, listened to each other's viewpoints and come up with a solution that suits both of you.

2. **Jealousy isn't a problem.** Instead of losing it and storming out or trying to get even by flirting with someone else, you confess jealous feelings and allow yourself to be reassured. You become less jealous of each other the longer you're together. While both of you dabble in a bit of harmless, occasional flirting you try not to do it in front of each other. If one does get caught out, you turn it into a joke because you *know* it's harmless.

3. **If in doubt, you'll take it as a compliment.** If your partner says something that could be misconstrued, you'll put the best possible light on it and ask if ➤

that's what they meant. She says, 'All I want to do is curl up and read a book. I'm sick of everyone.' Instead of getting huffy and assuming he's included in 'everyone', he says, 'I know what it's like. Take some time out, sweetheart, then let's go down the road for dinner and a glass of wine.' If your partner doesn't feel like sex, you think, *They must be tired*, not, *They don't fancy me any more*.

4. **You think first, react later.** Everyone sees the world differently, through a different filter. If you truly accept each other, you'll allow for differences. If your partner's being extraordinarily critical of someone or something, you'll listen first to what they have to say, take into account any stresses and how tired they are, *then* throw in your two cents' worth – if at all. Important issues are worth fighting over; trivial differences aren't.

5. **You don't change to suit each other, you work with each other.** You're both aware of each other's bottom line – what they will and won't put up with – but allow each to be individuals. There's a certain standard of behaviour that's expected, but you're not rigid. Neither of you compromise *those* standards, but you are prepared to put their needs before your own occasionally.

6. **You know how to say goodbye.** They're about to head off for a two-week work conference overseas. You don't cling on, sob and feel miserable and resentful they're having time away from you. You take them to the airport, kiss and hug, then wave them off cheerily. A graceful exit is the best preparation for the next grand entrance. Smart lovers keep each other hungry for more.

7. **You both feel you're getting a fair deal from the relationship.** Ask yourself this: Who's getting the best deal from this relationship: me or my partner? Are they getting much more out of it than you or vice versa? You're on the right track when you can honestly answer, 'It's fairly equal.'

Sex: Do It or Kiss Goodbye

Why hot sex makes for a hot relationship, and how to handle loony libidos, lousy lovers, and being too zonked to bonk

••

'To tell you the truth, Trace, I'd much prefer to read my book,' said my boyfriend of three years, lifting the duvet to peer down at me.

Call me sensitive, but when you've got your mouth wrapped around some guy's penis, it's rather insulting to be told to stop. It's sort of like a shivering street kid holding up the fur-lined leather jacket you're offering, when it's snowing and minus 30 degrees, and saying, 'What, *this*? I wouldn't be seen dead in it!' Mustering up all the dignity one can when forced to emerge, *un*triumphant, from the darkness, I tried desperately not to be offended at being passed over for Jeffrey Archer. I failed.

'Sorry, honey, what was I thinking? I forgot we'd had sex once this month already,' I snapped.

'When are you going to grow up?' my lover (actually, scratch that and make it 'roommate') retorted, waving the hated book madly about. 'Honestly, we're not 17 any more, in case you hadn't realized.'

No. Twenty-eight – practically in our graves.

'*No-one* has sex all the time when you've been together as long as we have,' he said with that superior 'I'm trying very hard to be patient' look.

'John and Alice do,' I ventured.

'Phhhhtttt! You're holding *them* up as an example!!!! The couple who *tongue*-kissed in front of our guests at the last dinner party? They're . . . well, they're . . . sex maniacs!'

I knew there was a reason why I liked them so much.

'Perhaps,' said the about-to-be-dumped-big-time boy-friend, 'you'd be happier living with *them*, if you think they're so great. You can all have a . . . a threesome or . . . something.'

Actually, that's not a bad idea, I went to bed thinking (the living with them bit, not the threesome). And I did shack up with John and Alice (though, I hasten to add again, not in the sense *he* meant) for a month until I found another flat. Solo this time. That way I could have sex as often as I wanted to, even if it was just with myself. Funnily enough, I'm still friends with John and Alice but appear to have lost contact with Mr Sex-is-for-Teenagers. After all, us sex maniacs have to stick together, and anyone who expects it more than once a month (I really wasn't joking), obviously qualifies as one. Not.

At this point you're (hopefully) having a bit of a chuckle but maybe feeling a tad guilty as well. Like, you can sort of identify with the wanting-to-read-rather-than-bonk bit? Relax! It really is normal. *Everyone*, even that hussy who works in the off licence and licks her lips and thrusts her chest out at *anyone* in trousers, occasionally thinks, *If I have one more fag maybe he'll give up and start snoring*. She, like you, isn't always as eager when she's shagged out from carting around one-too-many cartons of beer. Believe me, after a long day writing about sex and/or relation-ships, the *last* thing I want to do is actually do it or have one. The only stiff thing I feel like at the end of a long day is a drink.

But – and it's a BIG but – while it's okay to give an exaggerated yawn now and again when your partner turns to you with that unmistakable twinkle in their eye, constantly and consistently saying no to sex is not a good idea. For you, them or the relationship.

Making love isn't a luxury, it's essential for your relationship to survive. According to research, we get about a quarter of our total enjoyment of a relationship from sex. That's if you're having *good*, regular sex and the rest of your relationship's in pretty good shape. If you're having bad sex, or none at all, the other three-quarters of the relationship that *was* good, gets cancelled out. Why? If your sex life is in drastic dire straits, it spills over into the rest of the relationship and ends up poisoning everything.

What's the one thing that differentiates good friends from lovers? Sex. Think about it. These days, when we see friends separately and share lots of ourselves with same- and opposite-sex friends, it's the *only* thing we do with our partner that we *don't* do with anyone else. Good sex builds a close, intimate relationship – and it does a lot to smooth over the rough parts. Sex is good for us, both physically and mentally. It decreases stress, boosts the immune system and gives us a sense of well-being. We feel loved and nurtured when we're having satisfying, regular sex. More relaxed with each other and prepared to put up with more.

Stop having good sex and you stop feeling connected to your partner. If someone doesn't want to make love to you, you don't feel sexy or attractive. Your self-esteem plummets. Sexual frustration makes you irritable. Resentment means you start getting angry over things that previously didn't worry you. Without sex, intimacy disappears. Both of you feel increasingly isolated. You start fantasizing about other people. You may take it further and actually have an affair. Or you might just up and leave.

Bad sex really is bad news. Put the relationship first and sex last and you lose the most effective way of nourishing yourself and each other. Give it the same importance as the relationship itself and everything falls into place much more easily.

SEX – that's what 50 per cent of men said when asked their favourite thing to do in bed.
READ – that's what 75 per cent of women answered when asked the same question.

I'm not saying you should expect great sex *all the time*. Sometimes career and children have to take priority, and all couples go through phases when sex isn't as good. Just don't ever give up on *trying* to make it as good as humanly possible.

I found this chapter incredibly difficult to write because my first book, *Hot Sex: How to Do It*, afforded me 400 pages to dispense advice. This is but a mere snippet of what I'd like to tell you, so if you're interested in more, you might like to check that out as well. I'm not shamelessly self-promoting (well, maybe a bit) – I honestly think sex is such an important part of your relationship it deserves the full treatment. So, if you don't already have a few good sex books tucked in behind the *Intellectualization of a Modern Species* stuff you bought for show, do yourself a favour and buy a couple. If you've already read *Hot Sex* (God love you), forgive me if I'm being repetitive.

FIVE STEPS TO A GREAT SEX LIFE

Sex is a bit like typing. Anyone can sit down and bash something out using two fingers, but you'll never be as good as the person who uses ten and took the touch-typing course. This quick step-by-step guide is the equivalent of the touch-typing course (except a hell of a lot more fun). Once you're firmly established as a couple, it's a good idea to work through the following program to set up a strong foundation for your sex life and open the lines of communication. You don't have to do this in order, just pick whichever suits the mood at the time.

1. Put it on paper

Each of you grab a notepad and pen and write down, being as specific as possible, what you do and don't like about your sex life. You can do this together or separately, but no talking as you're writing!

Divide the page into sections with different headings: 'What I need to get in the mood for sex'; 'What I'd like more or less of during foreplay/oral sex/intercourse/during orgasm/after sex'. At the bottom write general comments: are you happy with when, where and how often you have sex? Are there any new things you'd like to try (acting out fantasies, sex games like tying each other up or renting an erotic film)? Also include relationship issues: what you do and don't like about the relationship, areas you think need work. Be as honest as you can but be a little tactful. Try to think up as many positive things as criticisms, and word it carefully. 'I'd like more foreplay,' rather than, 'You don't give me enough foreplay.'

When you've finished, it's not a case of swapping lists and skimming to see how you rated as a lover. Instead, read them to each other, talking through each point as you go along. Obviously, the best time to do this is when you've got time to talk and both of you are in good moods. Attempting it after a weekend with your mother (lovingly nicknamed 'that old bitch' by your partner) is asking for trouble. You'll be crucified. So pick your time. One goes first, then swap. Try to be as clear and non-judgemental as possible when you're talking. Saying, 'I hate it when you're too rough,' is guaranteed to make your partner prickly. Saying, 'I like it when you're really gentle,' (even if they never are) is a nicer way to give them the hint.

When both of you are finished, each summarize what the

other has said so there's no room for miscommunication. The more specific you are during the discussion, the more you'll get out of it. Saying, 'I'd like intercourse to last longer,' isn't enough information for him. You need to spell out exactly *how much* longer, or he'll still be thrusting away six years from now after buying a lifetime supply of Sta-Hard-Forever.

Give each other a few hours to digest what's been said, then come back with at least five ways you think you could make sex better for your partner, based on what they've told you. Don't try to put all ten suggestions into the one sex session – you'll end up confused (not to mention exhausted). Instead, consciously try to introduce one new thing each time you make love in the future.

It's a good idea to repeat this exercise a few times during the first year or so. After that, you should be in the habit of talking openly and honestly and able to tell each other what's working and what's not, as it springs to mind.

2. Give each other permission to let loose
When you sleep with someone purely for sex, you can be as wicked as you like because you don't really care what they think of you. Once you fall in love, it's like the censors moved into the bedroom. Will he think I've been around if I suggest that? Will she think I'm kinky if I do this? We switch from being lovers to auditioning as potential Mr and Mrs Rights. Hell, if she could bake a few scones during intercourse, she probably would. The only way to stop the censorship is to talk to each other. Confess your fears, have a laugh about them and reassure each other that there'll be no judging going on. Each of you has the green light to suggest whatever wild, weird or wonderful activity you'd like.

3. Don't stop masturbating
In fact, do it more. Lots of people think they shouldn't need to masturbate once they're getting regular sex, and if you've just

had it 25 times over the weekend you probably *won't* be locking the bathroom door Monday morning. But when your partner's away, they're not in the mood or you just feel extra sexy, masturbating's a great way to keep your libido running hot.

I'd also strongly suggest you take it one step further and do it *in front* of each other. Yup. That's right: a live performance of something you usually do in private. Why? Because partners can't read minds. Body language can speak volumes, talking to each other is essential, but a picture really is worth a thousand words. Watching each other masturbate, you get to see first-hand what technique you each use – the pressure and speed, how you speed it up or slow it down on approach to orgasm, how you stimulate yourself (or stop) when you're actually having one. All you need to do then is copy each other.

You'd like to try but are too scared to suggest it? If your partner's pretty open about sex, simply start touching yourself the next time you make love. Chances are, they'll sit back and watch, entirely fascinated. If they ignore you or don't notice, say, 'This is how I do it when you're not around,' or, 'I've had fantasies about masturbating in front of you. This feels great.' As you're doing it, get them to put their hand over yours so they can feel the pressure and rhythm you're using. Then remove your hand and let them copy you and give lots of (hopefully positive) feedback.

If you or your partner are a little shy, talk about it first. Tell them you read a magazine which suggested you can improve your sex life by watching each other masturbate. Follow it up with, 'I'm sure they're right, but as much as I'd like to, I think I'd be too embarrassed.' If they admit they'd also be a little uncomfortable, say, 'This is silly. Why don't we at least try next time?' The more confident partner goes first, prefacing it with something to break the ice ('If you laugh, I'll kill you'). If your lover's really embarrassed, ease them into it. Get them to put their hand on top of yours as you're stimulating them. Once things heat up a little, move your hand out of the way and say, 'Show me, it's easier.' Let them keep their eyes shut if they want: it's *you* that needs to be watching, not them. And, by the way, don't be surprised if you can't orgasm in front of each other when it takes a mere two seconds solo. It's just because you're self-conscious. Persevere though – there are plenty of reasons to give it a try. Watching her masturbate is a popular male fantasy and plenty of women also enjoy the experience. More importantly, it's a guaranteed way to find out how to give your partner an orgasm.

4. Take a guided tour of each other's body

To be the best lover they've ever had, you have to know *all* their hot spots, and this is how you'll find them. Each take turns, but I'll presume here that you're the one doing the exploring first. Get them to lie back, naked and comfortable on the bed. You then use your hands and tongue to explore each part of their body, while they give you a running commentary on how each sensation feels. They don't have to call it like the Grand National – just say, 'Ahh, that feels great,' or, 'That would feel nicer if you did it gentler.' You, of course, are listening and watching intently, discovering what sort of touch turns on what part of their body. One touch won't do for all. Lots of women like their breasts massaged quite firmly, but want a so-gentle-it's-like-a-tickle touch on their clitoris. Start from the top and work downward. And no cheating: skimming straight to the good bits isn't allowed. Slide palms up and down their arms, lick their armpit (both shower first), stroke and kiss their neck, run your fingers through their hair. Move down to the breast area, using fingers, mouth, tongue (maybe even teeth) to find out what they enjoy. Stroke their stomach, down the outside of the thighs, explore behind their knees. Massage feet, suck toes, then slide your palms up their calves and the inside of their thighs. Now – and only now – can you go to work on their genitals. Remember: the idea isn't to make them orgasm, it's a

Men are able to recite, in detail, what they do once they're in the bedroom, but it's women who remember each and every step in the flirtation game that got them there.

learning exercise. If you feel they're getting too close, switch to a less sensitive area. Once they've climaxed, they won't be half as interested in playing the game.

5. Show him how to stimulate your clitoris

What worked for Jane won't necessarily work for Mary, and it's crucial he gets this bit right for you to orgasm easily. If you did the masturbation exercise, he'll know how to manually stimulate you. But it's dark down there during oral sex and it's also easy for him to lose his bearings during intercourse. So let him have a good look in daylight.

If you're one of the majority of women who can only orgasm during intercourse with extra clitoral stimulation, speak up NOW. Explain it's just the way women are built – a matter of biology rather than penis size or his technique – then, the next time you have intercourse, take his hand and guide him to the spot. Choose positions which allow easy access. It takes more than a few seconds of stroking, so make sure his hand's not twisted or cramped. He should be comfortable while he's doing it so it doesn't detract from his enjoyment. Share the workload: stimulate your clitoris yourself sometimes so he doesn't have to. Or put your hand over his while he's stroking it. You can guide his strokes better and it seems more of a together, two-way thing.

YOU LOVE THEM TO DEATH, BUT . . . : SOLUTIONS TO SOME COMMON SEX SNARLS

The same couple who'll sit down and talk for hours to solve their relationship problems sometimes adopt an ostrich approach when it comes to sex snarls. 'I'm too embarrassed to say something.' 'Say I upset him/her?' 'Oh, it'll sort itself out somehow . . .' Hmm. *How* exactly if *you* don't do something about it?

The right time to fix sex problems is when they arise (or don't). The longer you leave it, the harder it is to speak up and the worse the problem gets, leaving you both even more sensitive than you were at the start. I agree, it's not pleasant telling a much-adored partner they're possibly the lousiest lay you've ever had. But what's the alternative? Put up and shut up and the frustration and resentment will simmer away nicely until one day, on your fiftieth wedding anniversary, the pot will runneth over and *you'll* run off with the milkman or babysitter.

Here's a few hints on tackling delicate subjects like clueless lovers and mismatched libidos plus how to rescue sex drives buried under the pressures of everyday life.

Your partner's awful in bed

You're crazy about them but think you really will go mad if you have to put up with ho-hum sex for the rest of your life? Take heart – and take action by trying the following.

Pick your time to talk

Make sure it's out of the bedroom. The absolute worst thing to do is erupt into a frustrated, fiery stream of criticisms while the bedsprings are still bouncing. Wait until you're both comfortable, happy and chatting freely. Then say, 'Darling, I really love our relationship and adore making love with you. Is there anything you'd like me to do in bed that I'm not already? There's so many things we can explore together.' It's less threatening to kick off the chat by talking about new things you'd both like to try, *then* you can gently work it around to how satisfied each of you are. If they're not terribly forthcoming on this point, you go first to give them an idea of how to word things. 'When I give you oral sex, I never know whether to keep going while you're climaxing or stop?' Most people are polite enough to then ask, 'What about you? Are you happy?' If they don't, turn it around yourself by saying, 'I love it when you ——. Can you do it more often?'

Concentrate on what they're doing right

Saying, 'Harold, if you keep on doing that weird thing with your tongue I'll go completely nuts,' won't get you very far.

Saying, 'Honey, it feels fabulous when you do X, but it would feel even better if you moved a little to the left/did it for longer,' will. Even if your partner truly is pathetic, there must be something nice you can say about them. Even if it's, 'It turns me on so much watching your muscles flex when you're on top of me.'

Let your body talk

The next time you have sex, use body language to show what you do and don't like and you'll get the point across far more effectively. When they do something you like or they're on the right track, exaggerate your response: moan loudly, move closer, kiss them harder so they can't help but get the message you like what they're doing. If you don't like something, make that obvious as well. Twist away, lift your body away from their touch or (better still) redirect their hand or mouth or whatever. Most people do to their partners what they'd like done to them. If you like having your neck kissed or bitten, kiss and bite theirs. If they don't get the hint, say, 'Do you like that? I love it, too.' Remember to ask, not order. Boss them around with, 'Do this, do that,' and they'll feel resentful. Besides, it's about as satisfying as asking someone to tell you they love you.

You thought everything was fixed but they seem to have forgotten all you've said three sessions on? It's very easy to get carried away in the heat of the moment and forget your partner

> 'For years, I put up with truly awful sex. It was like being served up broccoli and peas for dinner every night when you hate the stuff. Eventually, I plucked up the courage to tell him I wasn't happy.
> Predictably, he stormed out. But he came back in an hour and said, "Okay, let me have it." We talked for hours and haven't stopped. I'm happy and he's enjoying sex so much more as well.'
>
> Fiona, 39, journalist

needs their left toe sucked at the crucial moment. If this happens, just remind them. Whisper in their ear, 'Honey, remember you said you'd ——'

You're too zonked to bonk

Who's got time for sex? Juggling jobs, friends, bills, housework, families: is it any wonder a lot of couples end up having it about once a month unless they consciously make an effort? You're both working hard to establish your careers. You're *desperate* for that to-die-for-but-horribly-expensive couch so take on overtime. Stripping the paint off the walls of your brand new apartment seems more important than stripping each other. Just as sex is given a low priority after having children, it can get pushed to the bottom of the heap *way* before then by young couples who've just moved in or married.

Putting sex on (what you're convinced will be) a temporary hold seems justifiable when you're both totally exhausted by life. But if you want to stay together, it's possibly the stupidest thing you could do. Because if sex is given a low priority, even for a little while, it rarely creeps back up again unless both of you make a concerted effort. And who knows when you'll have time to put *that* much effort in? We all talk about how we'll have more time when this is done or that happens, but it never quite seems to eventuate, does it?

Ironically, couples starved for time tend to think the little they do have left for each other is better spent talking and communicating. Wrong. If you've only got five hours a week to devote to the relationship, put a good portion of that into your sex life. Sex is by far the quickest way to feel connected to each other, and if you're after maximum closeness with minimum time, that's the way to go. Talk all you want, but one good sex session can achieve the closeness you get from four hours of intimate conversation in five minutes flat. And yes I did say five minutes.

You don't have to have marathon sex sessions every single time. You're better off having three quickies a week and one long session a month than four long sessions a month and

Where do most Australians prefer to make love?
• *The shower – 36 per cent*
• *On the beach – 29 per cent*
• *Their parents' bed – 16 per cent*
• *The boss's desk – 6 per cent.*

nothing in between. The more your body has sex, the more you want it. The more sex you have, the more time you'll make for it. The more effort you put into making sex great, the quicker you can both have orgasms. If you roll into bed dog-tired but know there's one hell of a reward for five minutes of effort, you'll be far more inclined to keep your eyes open just that little bit longer. I'm not saying *all* your sex sessions should be that short, just that you're better off having a quickie than nothing at all.

Grab it whenever you can

A quickie is fast, hasty sex of any kind. Get the hang of it and you might find it can be equally as satisfying as those long, drawn-out sex sessions. Apply lots of lubricant (a quickie doesn't allow time for the vagina to produce its own lubrication) and you're away. She's tighter than usual without foreplay so it feels great his end, and the quick, instant shock of pleasure is great for both of you. Even better, you've only taken three minutes out of sleeping/decorating/feeding the kids time. If you're *only* having quickies, you're missing the point but they are a great way to supplement a time-restricted sex life. Don't restrict them to intercourse either. Oral sex, when you're still clothed, also feels fabulous.

Make sex a priority

Even during *serious* stress times, when you can't find the energy for a midweek snog or don't have the time for one, you should make time for sex on the weekends when you're not so tired. Set aside one hour – come on, even the busiest couple can manage that one! – and spend it having sex.

Try something new every third time you have sex
It really doesn't take much effort, once you're in the habit of varying one thing. It can be as simple as lights on or lights off. Music on or off. Clothed, half-clothed, naked. A different position. Different location. If you're so busy you can't even manage this, buy a copy of *Hot Sex*. It's got enough ideas in it to keep you going for years, with zero imagination on your part.

Again, the better sex you have, the more you'll make time to do it. If it's boring, it hardly seems worth finding the energy for. Constantly changing the scenario ensures each time's as hot as the last, so you'll be more eager to have it the next.

Educate yourselves
Good sex requires good technique. You both need to know how your body *and* your partner's body works and be reasonably educated and experienced about what to do with your fingers, tongue and genitals to turn someone on. If you aren't sure or confident of your technique, buy a few good sex books and read up on it.

Talk about sex together
Do the exercise suggested in point one of 'Five steps to a great sex life' (see page 208). Good technique alone isn't enough – you need to be able to communicate your needs to your partner and make them feel comfortable enough to do the same. Tell each other what you do and don't like. If you're not sure how, see 'Your partner's awful in bed', page 215. Even if they're not, the same principles apply.

WHEN I WAS SINGLE, I WAS DESPERATE FOR REGULAR SEX. NOW IT'S ON TAP, I'VE GONE OFF IT. WHY?

It's a bit like Christmas. You can smell that turkey cooking and you're practically *drooling*. Come the day after Boxing Day, you'd rather eat mashed-up grasshoppers than face another slice. You really *can* have too much of a good thing. Most couples gorge themselves on each other's bodies when they first get together. They've overfull, then keep topping up.

When you're single, sex isn't always available so that's all you think about. We want what we can't have. When you live with someone, you can have sex whenever you damn well please. Add to that, *he's* (I'm not being sexist but it is usually the guy) almost always ready, willing and able for sex, and you start to see why desire can wane. At first, being woken up by hands on your breasts and an erect penis sticking in your back is sexy. You think, 'Brilliant! Regular sex again.' Six weeks in, it's like, 'Oh for God's sake. Does that thing ever go down? Get *off* me!'

If your partner *always* wants sex, you never get time to build an appetite for it.

'I never, ever get the chance to initiate sex because Mark's always suggested it before I have the chance to *think* a sexy thought, let alone carry it through,' says a girlfriend of mine. 'We never go without it, so I never have time to miss it.'

If you never get the chance to reach out first, if you're always asked before getting an opportunity to do the asking, your sexual feelings wither. You start to feel pressured and used and lose interest altogether.

'I was totally bored with our sex life until my boyfriend lost interest because he was working so hard,' says Annette. 'After a week of him falling straight to sleep instead of hassling me for a bit, I suddenly realized I missed sex and started kissing him hard.

He said, 'Sweetheart, I'm too tired,' which fired me up ➢

Your libidos don't match

Some people have naturally high sex drives: given the choice
between winning Lotto and hot sex every day of their life,
they'd kiss the cash goodbye without a moment's hesitation.
Sex is as essential to them as oxygen, food and water. Deprived
of it, they're like dogs on heat and just as likely to start humping
your leg. For others, sex is a pleasant enough experience but not
one they'd knock back a nice, hot cup of cocoa for. They enjoy
it when it's on offer, but tend to forget about it if it's not. At
the bottom of the desire scale are people who are so uninterested or put off by sex, they'd be quite happy if their last
legover was their last for life.

In an ideal world, we'd all
find our libido equivalents. After
all, if you only want to have sex
every two months and that suits
your partner, it's not a problem.
Hook up with a twice-a-day
person and it's a huge one. If you
find you're a perfect match
outside of the bedroom but not
in it, this section's for you. It's all
about evening up mismatched
libidos so you're both a little
happier.

'Whenever I came near
her, she'd push me away,
even if all I wanted was a
cuddle. She made me feel
like there was something
wrong with me, like I
was immature for
wanting regular sex. We
split and I'm now with a
woman who enjoys it as
much as I do. I'm
marrying this one.'

Aaron, 27, plumber

They're hot, you're not

You're the one saying, 'Not tonight, honey, I've got a headache'? The first thing I want to say to you is this: it's not your fault. There's a tendency to blame the low-libido person for any sex problems, and that's not fair. Our sex drives are influenced by genes, hormones

Would you sleep with the boss to keep your job? More than two-fifths of men would. Forty-two per cent said they'd bed a female superior if forced to choose between sex and redundancy. But she has to be attractive. Half would reconsider if she wasn't dishy.

and past experiences, and not all of it is in your control. Having said that, there *are* ways to kick-start a naturally lazy libido so you'll feel like sex more. The idea, as always, is to meet your partner in the middle. You boost your desire while they learn to manage theirs (and stop hassling you).

I've aimed this section at both men and women. 'What???!!!' I can hear you splutter. 'A man knocking back sex?' True, it never happens on *Melrose Place* – but it does in real life (as I humiliatingly confessed earlier). Men aren't sex robots: they're human, and affected by stress and feelings just as much as women are. Besides, we're demanding little beasts these days and some men find the pressure of having to perform puts them off entirely.

1. Pinpoint the reason why you don't often feel like sex.

It's the obvious place to start. Plenty of people who think they've got naturally low libidos actually haven't. With the right partner, under the right circumstances, they're as randy as the rest of us. So do a bit of soul-searching. Are you simply bored by sex and happy to let other things in life take precedence? Most of us move out of that can't-get-enough stage after a few months. Unfortunately, we replace it with lovemaking that's as predictable as Aunt

Martha's gall-bladder operation story. In other words, if steamy, sexy, raunchy sex with George Clooney or Pamela Anderson was on offer, would you be more interested?

Are you tired and physically rundown? Working long hours, staying out too late, too many drinks and ciggies, a diet based around McDonald's – none leave us feeling terribly energetic. Is it temporary disinterest or permanent? At some point, all of us have found the thought of sex about as appealing as filling in a tax return, so think about what else is happening in your life. Are you putting all your energies into something else? If you're trying desperately to score that promotion or working extra hours to pay off the mortgage, there's not much energy left for romping around the bedroom. Stress and tiredness affect our hormones, blocking those that give our libidos a kick, increasing those that make us anxious. (Taking time out, making priorities and planning for sex can solve the problems in a flash.) Are you happy with your body? If you don't feel sexy, it stands to reason you won't feel like it. If you don't like what you see in the mirror, either see a dietician and start exercising or get help if you've got body image problems.

Another biggie: are you in the right relationship? Hooked up with a nice person who does nothing for you below the waist but plenty above? Or trying to force desire for someone who treats you badly? Sex slumps aren't usually just about sex, they're a sign your relationship's gone awry as well. If you have problems outside the bedroom, they leak under the door. Equally as important is your partner's skill as a lover. A bad lover

> **Men with symmetrical features give their partners more orgasms but they're also more likely to be unfaithful. Why? They're more attractive to women, so have had more practice, but they're also spoilt for choice.**

is a common cause of sexual disinterest for women. If he's selfish, inexperienced or incompetent, in other words a bore or boorish in bed, why would you want to initiate a session?

If you've never enjoyed sex, only ever have it because 'you have to' and it rarely satisfies or arouses you, there could be deeper psychological factors at play. An earlier traumatic experience, a strict religious upbringing or growing up being told 'nice girls don't do it' could be responsible, and a visit to a good sex therapist might help. If the thought of sex frightens you or you often feel as if you're 'watching yourself' – you're there but not really there – again, go and see a counsellor.

2. Get back in touch with your sexy side. If it's a temporary lack of desire, consciously concentrate on feelings and sensations when you are having sex, and don't get too hung up on having an orgasm. Start masturbating if you've stopped: the more orgasms you have, the more your body will crave them. Deliberately focus on your erotic self. Read some sexy books, watch erotic movies. Buy a book on sexual fantasies (*The Joy of Sexual Fantasy* by Andrew Stanway is excellent). Start writing down your favourite fantasies and use them to turn yourself on before sex. Prepare for it mentally. Anticipate what's going to happen. Have a bubble bath instead of a shower and read an erotic book while you're soaking. When you're out with your partner, imagine what that tongue will do to you later. How much better his fingers would feel cupping your breast than wrapped around a beer glass. How she'll look when that sexy little black dress is stripped *off* . . .

3. Make sure you know what turns you on, then tell your partner. Read 'Five steps to great sex' on page 208 and work through each. Initially, it'll be an effort. You're not used to giving sex a high priority so you'll need to do it deliberately. Ask yourself regularly: what would I like more of in bed? What would I like less of? Keep a diary and jot down thoughts over a two-week period. Think back to sex you've had in the past that you enjoyed. What was it about it that turned you on? How can you recreate this with your partner? Then pass on what you've discovered. Don't be scared to speak up, to ask for more foreplay or a different oral sex technique. Think outside the square. If you don't feel like intercourse, offer to give your partner oral sex instead. More than one person has changed their mind once they see their partner having such a good time.

4. Learn to receive pleasure. If your problem's long term, you may have grown up feeling guilty about sex and never been 'woken' erotically. In other words, you simply don't know how to respond to sexual sensations in your body. A sensate focus program is what sex therapists use to help you learn to receive pleasure. This simply involves replacing sex with a series of sensual massages, spaced over a month or so. During the first, you rub oil over your *own* body, to find out what feels good and arouses you. In the next stage, you and your partner massage each other, avoiding the genitals and breasts, reporting back on what feels good and what doesn't. During stage three, you're allowed to touch each other's naughty bits, but still no intercourse. The grand prize at the end is a long overdue, deeply satisfying, good old-fashioned bonk.

5. Ask your partner to be supportive. Explain that you're trying new things to boost your desire but they can help by not pressuring you to have sex when you don't feel like it (see 'Why doesn't she initiate sex more', page 229. It applies to both sexes). Get them to help you relax and feel sexy by reducing the stress level in your life. Sexual desire appears to originate in the brain. If you're juggling so much your brain feels like an amusement park, there aren't too many cells free for fantasy. Ask for some 'pamper time': an hour or two a week when they massage and stroke all the stresses away. (You can return the favour. Just because their libido's not affected, it doesn't mean they won't appreciate a massage.) Ideally, you'd both take a holiday. A few weeks lounging around can revive a lagging libido quicker than *you* can say, 'Let's skip dinner and have sex instead.'

HONEY, WAKE UP! I JUST HAD AN ORGASM

Make no mistake about it. That *was* an orgasm, even if one hand is wrapped around your partner and the other's clutching a teddy bear. It might take ten arduous minutes to masturbate yourself to orgasm in real life, but in your sleep – 'Look, Mum! No hands!'

Around 40 per cent of women experience wet dreams, according to sexologist Alfred Kinsey. It's just more obvious when he's had one (do I really need to explain?). Men have erections once every 90 minutes during the Rapid Eye Movement (REM) stages of sleep, coinciding with the dream period. It now appears women's sexual rhythms mirror those of men: our genitals also become swollen and lubricated. For some women, night-time orgasms are the only ones they'll have. British sex expert Anne Hooper says she's encountered women who could orgasm in their sleep, but couldn't through masturbation or with a partner. Why? It's the old cliché – the brain is the ultimate sex organ, and when we're asleep any emotional blocks (like sexual hang-ups) are removed.

According to Hooper, we're more likely to have a wet dream when we're not having regular sex. If we're single, our partner's away or been too busy with work to indulge, wet dreams are a wake-up call: you're not getting enough in real life. They can also be the result of having unsatisfying sex with a partner before falling asleep. Your body, very politely, finishes the job for you.

If you can remember the content of a dream that resulted in a bonus orgasm, pay attention. Force yourself to wake up and write down everything you can remember: ➢

where was it, what were they doing, how were they doing it, what were you feeling? When we dream, our subconscious allows us to fantasize guilt-free: you'll come up with scenarios you'd blush at if you'd daydreamed them. Often, it's your subconscious desires tapping you on the shoulder, saying, 'Hey, boring, be a bit more adventurous will you?' You dreamed of making love outdoors? Introduce some alfresco sex into your real life. Being seduced forcefully? Play out a slave–master fantasy. The only thing you *shouldn't* pay too much attention to is *who* you were having sex with in the dream. Dreaming of sex with a member of your family or of someone the same sex as you, for instance, doesn't mean you've got secret incestuous desires or gay tendencies. It's more to do with what they represent. If you adore your brother, he could simply represent sex with someone you feel comfortable with as opposed to a partner you're uptight about. If you're in bed with someone of the same sex, it's sometimes a narcissistic dream: you're actually making love to yourself. So don't get too hung up on the weird, freaky elements – concentrate on the yummy nice bits.

You're hot, they're *not*

'Is that all you ever think about?' 'Stop mauling me!' 'I get it, you're pissed off because you didn't get it this morning, aren't you!' Just as your partner's feeling the pressure of not wanting sex enough, you're getting a battering for wanting it too much. And since we always want what we can't have, constantly being knocked back only seems to fuel your desire more. What to do?

1. Take matters into your own hands – literally. Masturbate often to take the edge off. And drop the 'why should I have to when I'm in a relationship?' attitude. Your partner's not there to service you, it's not their *job* to keep you sexually satisfied. You're together because you love each other and want to make each other happy. Constantly hassling them for sex does the opposite. Masturbate every second time you feel like sex. Ideally, you'd tell your partner what you're up to so you don't have to lock yourself away, but make sure you don't make them feel guilty. There's a difference between stomping off ('I suppose I'll have to do it by myself – again') and giving a wink as you head for the bathroom with a sexy mag ('Be back in a minute, sweetheart. Get ready for a cuddle'). Even better, get into the habit of doing it in front of them. Your partner might be more than happy to watch you pleasure yourself, even if they aren't in the mood for sex themselves.

2. Don't force your partner to have sex. Stop putting pressure on someone to have sex and you'll give them time to actually feel like it. That doesn't mean you can't be affectionate or sensual, just make it clear when you *are* innocently kissing or touching your partner that there's no hidden agenda. You should be able to snuggle up on the couch and watch a video together without immediately suctioning your hands to her breasts. Ditto his penis. Stick to stroking arms, shoulders and neck and you'll ignite desire rather than quash it.

3. When you do make love, focus on their pleasure, not yours. The better lover you are and the more enjoyment they get from sex, the more likely they are to crave it. Encourage them to open up and tell you what they need to get turned on. Do you need to brush up on your technique? Do they need more foreplay? Are you picking the wrong time for sex (like Saturday mornings, the only chance they get to sleep in)? Suggest you take a bath together or give them a massage first. Ask for feedback during sex and above all, give them *time* to get aroused. Lower-libido people often take a little longer. Just because your genitals can spring to attention while reading about cross-pollination in *Green Foliage: A Guide*, doesn't mean their arousal system is permanently on automatic.

WHY DOESN'T SHE INITIATE SEX MORE?

It could be because you jump in before she's had a chance to make the first move herself. Or maybe it's because she's worried she'll come across as 'unladylike'.

When I was at uni, every psychology student had to 'volunteer' to participate in a number of psychology experiments in order to pass the course. For one, we were all seated in a classroom, arranged in boy–girl format, then presented with large, blank notepads and a pen. The professor beamed down at us from his lectern and asked, terribly politely, for us to write down all the slang words we'd ever heard used to describe the male and female genitals.

Now, at 20, all of us knew plenty. The guys scribbled ferociously, constantly checking the competition in a bid to be the last in the room to stop writing. The more he knew, the more sexually experienced he'd seem. The girls did the opposite. Twirling our hair and gazing innocently out of the window for supposed inspiration, we made the odd pathetic scribble, then crossed out whatever it was we'd written. After eavesdropping on my big brother for years, I could have filled the entire notebook. Sue, queen of dirty jokes, could have filled six of them but even she feigned disinterest and a complete lack of knowledge. Why? Because it wasn't done for females to be seen as too in touch with the raw, primitive side of sex. None of us could bear being thought of as a 'slut' by filling the page.

That's what may be at the bottom of your girlfriend's reluctance to initiate sex. If she grew up in a religious, strict household, I'd bet that is at the root of the problem. Tell her you'd love it if she was the one to make the first move and see how she reacts. If she opens up and confesses she's worried about being judged, reassure her profusely. You could also try buying her some erotic fiction, written by a female (try Anaïs Nin as well as modern writers), so she'll get the message it's okay these days for women to feel and be ➢

sexy. Incidentally, you're not alone in wanting her to initiate sex more often. Relationships expert Dr Maryon Tysoe cites a US study where psychologists asked dating or newly married couples what they'd like more of in bed. Men, much more than women, wanted their partners to have more experimental sex, spontaneous sex, initiate sex more often and play the dominant role.

FIRESTARTERS: REIGNITING PASSION WHEN THE FLAME'S GONE OUT

There are two common reasons why sex dies: No 1, your relationship's gone sour (in which case, read the whole book); No 2, sex has become so routine and predictable, it's just not fun any more. I know plenty of couples who just give up at this point. 'Sex? Oh, we stopped doing that years ago. Done everything. What's left to explore? Right, honey?' 'Honey' usually grunts and decides now's the time to freshen their drink. Quite frankly, I'm with them. If sex is no longer on offer, you might as well drink yourself stupid.

Now while I accept it's *common* for long-term couples to lose the sexual fizz, it's not written in stone. You won't find, 'And in the seventh year, thou shalt no longer desire thy partner,' painstakingly etched into some ancient granite tablet somewhere. It *doesn't* 'happen to everyone eventually', only to those too lazy and uninterested to put the effort in. Sure, maintaining a great sex life isn't easy when you've been together years. As we've already discussed in this chapter, you need to give sex priority, spend time thinking of ways to make it better and be able to talk to each other about what you need to keep *your* fire burning brightly. But it can be done and there are plenty of couples out there (the ones who always leave the dinner party early *and*, incidentally, John and Alice) who are still shredding the sheets 20 years on.

How? For a start, they focus on what's great about couple sex rather than focus on what's not, namely, the 'I'd kill for some new flesh' thing. Believe me, even happy couples complain about that one. It may come as a shock to you, but falling in love doesn't provide bulletproof protection against finding others attractive. *Very* attractive. Saying 'I love you' or even getting married doesn't mean you've signed a contract which says, 'I will never fancy anyone else,' and window shopping is fine. It's when you start handling the merchandise, buying it or taking it home with you that there are problems. So accept that occasionally lusting after someone else is normal. No matter how much you enjoy sex with your partner, they're still your partner. You've (hopefully) been there and done them hundreds of times. Exploring a new body for the very first time *is* heaven on earth – I'm not arguing with you.

But think about this for a moment. What if you succumbed and got caught? Would you really swap all the other pluses of being with someone you love just to satisfy that momentary craving? For a split second now and then (after being chatted up by an Elle MacPherson or Billy Zane lookalike), you'll probably answer, 'God yes!' Force yourself to think about it for a full five minutes, however, looking into your partner's face and imagining them finding out, and you may find *that* fire burns out pretty quickly.

Just in case you need reminding, couple sex has it all over singles sex in some areas. First up, if you've put effort in, orgasm is pretty well guaranteed for both of you. You know each other's bodies so well, it's a matter of pushing a few buttons to make each other climax. You know each other's preferences and are comfortable enough to speak up and say what you feel like. You've got a vested interest in pleasing each other. You want them to enjoy sex as much as you do because you care about them. You trust each other. You can share those kinky sex fantasies because they know in real life, you're not weird or perverted, it's just a fantasy. Couples enjoy more varied sex than singles. As well as lust-driven sex, there's lazy, sleepy Sunday-morning sex, romantic sex and sex when you both laugh each other stupid.

The trick to not letting the urge to stray turn into reality is to keep an erotic edge going long term. The trick to doing *that* is to constantly recreate, reinvent and rediscover sex.

Recreate

Sex with someone new is naughty – that's half the appeal. Recreate and satisfy the 'naughty' craving by being naughty together. Act out fantasies, have sex where there's a hint of being caught. Behave like you're having an affair with each other. Plan what you're going to do to them that night then tell them about it as you wave them off for work. Anticipation can be just as heady as newness.

Rediscover

Remember in the beginning how you used to try *anything* just so you'd both climax together? Continue the quest to slow his orgasm down and speed hers up. Ideally, give her a head start by making her climax through oral sex or masturbation before intercourse. If he orgasms too fast during intercourse, give him one orally, then let him give you oral sex to allow him time to get another erection. He'll last longer if he's onto orgasm number two.

Have more foreplay, not less. It's not a luxury, it's necessary for the women's vagina to physically prepare for inter-course. Relax, take your time and enjoy it for what it is. It's not something you do in the beginning; it's even more essential later when the 'newness' has gone.

Spoil each other with massages. It's a sadly underused

way to reignite the laziest libido. Women, particularly, like the slow build-up. Again, take your time. A five-minute massage isn't fun, that's just a token gesture. Instead of rushing, put something slow and

As much as we don't like to admit it, women are turned on by porn almost as much as he is. Our testosterone level shoots up by 80 per cent when watching a flesh flick. His goes up by 100 per cent.

sexy on the stereo, grab some oil (a water-based oil, sold at sex shops, is best because you don't need to wash your hands before touching the genitals – oils can cause things like thrush), a few towels and settle in for at least 30 minutes. Start with non-erotic touching, sliding your hands over their back, shoulders and neck, massaging all the tension away. After 20 minutes or so, you can start teasing. Slide your palms up and down the inside of their thighs, across their stomach, skim the breasts. Don't even think about touching the genitals until they're straining toward you.

Also, up her orgasm quota. Men usually climax each time they have sex, women often don't. If you're the one always hitting the jackpot, it's understandable you'll be keener for sex than the less lucky one. Devote a lot of time to foreplay and keep searching until you find that secret spot or technique which guarantees it for her.

Reinvent

Saying you're bored with sex is like saying you're bored with reading because you've read all the books in your library. There are as many varieties to sex as there are new authors to discover. Swap roles, for instance. If they normally seduce you, you seduce them. Even if you've already done the tie-each-other-up thing, try a twist. Add a blindfold – or take it off. Masturbate for them *while* they're tied up. Or both of you wear blindfolds and make love 'blind'. Your sense of touch is tripled, you're much less inhibited about what you're doing because your partner can't see you and you can let your fantasies run riot. Speaking of which . . .

Fantasize like mad. Sexual fantasies are the cheapest, most effective sex aids around. Pretending you're bonking the guy on the building site or the girl in the café isn't being unfaithful (though best keep your mouth shut), it's a way of introducing variety into your sex life without the disastrous consequences of actually doing it.

Enlist some help. Buy a few good sex books and how-to videos and try out some of their suggestions. If nothing else you'll have a good laugh together.

> 'I got dragged along to one of those dreadful parties where they sell sex aids, but once I got there, thought, *Why not?* I came home with crotchless knickers, a vibrator and a pair of rather pathetic looking handcuffs. Mike was still up when I got home and he stayed up all night, if you get my drift. It was brilliant!'
>
> Sophie, 28, producer

LIGHTEN UP A LITTLE: EROTICA CAN BE EROTIC

Oh come on! I don't care how posh you are or how intellectually brilliant or politically correct, I bet *you* sneak furtive glances in the window of those sleazy but oh-so-fascinating 'adults only' stores, just as the rest of us do. There's something macabrely fascinating about sex shops. Even when you are inwardly cringing, the urge to pick up that huge, black, throbbing, 'talking' vibrator and switch it on is pretty appealing. (Not to mention hanging around the entrance hoping your stuck-up neighbour will emerge clutching a brown paper bag.)

If I'm offending anyone, I'm terribly sorry. Sort of. But ➢

seriously, I'm not talking about hard-core pornography that involves children, animals or violence, more the saucy stuff even your family video store stocks. And I'm not talking make-your-eyes-water torture gear either (though, if you're into it and use it sensibly, I'm not bagging that either). While there are a lot of sex aids out there that are a complete waste of money, I personally think the kick you'll get out of blowing £100 at a sex shop is well worth the money. It's naughty. It's forbidden. Sneaking into a sex shop, a few sheets to the wind, is *not* what your average well-to-do couple does. And that's exactly why you *should* do it. It's fun, and sex is supposed to be fun. So don't be prudish. Have a laugh. Have *fun.*

At the risk of making fellow feminists' hearts pound with fury, I really think us 'girls' should lighten up a little in regards to erotica and pornography. Again, I'm *not* talking about the full-on stuff. But I don't think the sisterhood spiel needs to be dragged out just because your guy happens to like freeze-framing Kim Basinger during the strip scene in *Nine-and-a-Half Weeks*. Sorry to be sexist here but I'm yet to meet a man who's outraged to discover his girlfriend watches the odd sexy flick. It's women who usually have problems with it. Some think their partner is comparing their body to the woman on the screen, and they're worried they're not measuring up. Others believe if their partner watches or reads porn, it means he doesn't love them or they're not satisfying him sexually. Not true.

Let's set a few things straight here. The majority of men don't watch porn for the sinister reasons women think they do. They watch it because it's fun. Porn to men is no big deal. They honestly can't see how watching a sexy film can be any sort of reflection on their love for their girlfriend. Most don't understand why she takes offence because, as far as they're concerned, *every* guy does it.

They're right. Research shows the infrequent porn user is your average guy – 90 per cent of them. He's not a deviant, he just likes looking at sexy pictures. It's got a lot to do with what turns each sex on. Usually, men are turned on more by ➢

pictures and visual images, women are turned on more by words. Now, that's a massive generalization, but true in a lot of cases. That's why we'd prefer to curl up with a steamy blockbuster and he prefers to look at pictures. In most cases, it's pretty harmless.

Your partner not only watches it but – OHMIGOD! – wants you to watch it with him? If you truly have vehement moral objections to pornography, you're well within your rights to tell them you're not interested and not to pressure you further. If you just feel a bit embarrassed about it, try it once. You wouldn't be the first couple to use mainstream erotica to spice things up a little. Of the estimated 30 million dollars Australians spend annually on X-rated videos from Canberra, 60 per cent are consumed by couples. So give yourself time to get used to the idea and then at least give it one try.

Start by watching an R-rated movie rather than diving straight into X-rated. And it's one thing watching a sex scene together, quite another having sex while watching it. Get over the awkwardness before moving into the more explicit films (and if you don't want to go further, fine). If you get one out and find it laughable or dead boring, just have it playing in the background and look up at the good bits. It's more the thought of doing something naughty than what you're actually doing that's the turn-on. You could also try renting some women's erotica (films made by women, for women – it's made pretty clear on the back). They're pretty mild and – surprising, I know – actually have a plot.

If you give it a go and don't like it, be honest. Tell him what he does in private is his business but it's not something you want to share: you tried it but it's not for you. If your partner hassles you constantly or puts the pressure on after that, *then* feel free to put him and his videos out on the street.

NO SEX PLEASE – WE'RE MARRIED

Picture a happy husband and wife. It's a rare person who'd imagine the couple in bed – unless, of course, they're reading books and sipping tea. Why does marriage have such a bad reputation when it comes to sex? Well for starters, you're living with

Turn on the stereo to turn on each other. When researchers asked men and women worldwide, 'What gives you the most pleasure in life?' the majority said listening to music. Sex came a close second. For the ultimate pleasure experience? Bop while you bonk.

the label. If you lived together before getting married, you were 'living in sin' as 'lovers'. Slip that band of gold on your finger and you become 'husband and wife'. You're respectable, and for some couples that's the equivalent of pouring a bucket of cold water all over the bed. What is marriage if it's not official permission to bonk away to your heart's content? God won't mind, your mother won't mind, the neighbours won't mind because you're married – you're *supposed* to have sex.

'People say it's just a piece of paper, but marriage is a mental attitude,' says Anna, a 32-year-old receptionist who's been married for six years. 'Before, John and I would think nothing of spending all Sunday in bed. Now we're married and have bought a house, it's like we feel obliged to get up and do something like work in the garden. Sex seems frivolous, it's almost like we should be over that by now.'

Anna's not the only one who thinks of sex in marriage as of the Saturday-night-only-and-don't-disturb-the-children variety. Check out the bumper stickers that scream, 'No sex please. We're married.' The plots of TV sitcoms that constantly reinforce the get-in-bed-with-PJs-on rather than slinky lingerie. How many times was he slapped on the back by his mates on the stag's night and told, 'This is the last time you'll have fun, mate. Make the most of it.' Why do girlfriends organize a stripper for your 'last night of freedom'? There's a definite perception that fun – and that includes sex – ends once you're married. And this is where the secret to a good marital sex life lies.

All the couples I've interviewed who are still romping about the bedroom have a healthy disregard for the traditional views about marriage and sex. In the bedroom, they cease to be husband and wife and, instead, revert back to being individuals with very real needs and desires. In other words, they refuse to act 'married'.

Here are some other things you might also like to keep in mind.

Make the most of the 'recharge'

Make-or-break point for a lot of marrieds is when the newness of sex wears off – again. Getting married can add a nice, new edge to it for the first few months of being Mr and Mrs. The trick is to keep it going rather than let it lapse and fall back into the same old sex ritual. Think, *That's what happens*, and put up with ho-hum sex from now until your fiftieth wedding anniversary (if you make it that far) or start working at sex as hard as you should be working on the rest of your relationship.

Speak up if you're not happy

Keeping quiet if you're not sexually satisfied for fear of hurting their feelings won't help either of you in the long run. When Mandy, 27, found she was dreading going to bed with Andrew, she confronted the problem head on. 'When we first got married it was wonderful – then it quickly slid into familiarity. I knew we had to explore our sexuality or it was all over.' She told Andrew how she felt – that she was bored and wanted more – and they ended up talking for three hours about their fantasies and expectations. 'The result is we now let ourselves go and try stuff that would have made me hot with embarrassment at the start.' It is possible to pull your love life out of the deep freeze, all you need to do is reach in there and get it.

Don't get complacent

Most couples who rate their sex lives highly say they are proactive in sex. They think about when, where and how they'll have it and think up new things to try.

> 'I went to the loo at a party and when I came back some guy was all over Sue. I admit, I stood back and watched for a minute to see how she'd react. The guy was good-looking and seemed really nice but her body language said "taken", and her look of relief when I came back was obvious. I loved her even more after that.'
> Mark, 31, chiropractor

They spend time thinking about sex and what they'll do that evening. It's like a gourmet who'll spend half an hour deciding which dish on the menu to choose. They imagine what the food will look and taste like. Their senses are heightened. Savouring what's coming is almost as good as eating it (both puns intended).

Don't think of sex as just intercourse

Move away from the all-roads-lead-to-intercourse theory and make a conscious effort not to follow the same pattern in love-making. It's not all about orgasms, it's about giving and receiving pleasure – orgasm and intercourse are but a mere part of that. Substitute oral sex for intercourse more than occasion-ally. Manually masturbate each other to orgasm. Enjoy a deep kissing session without feeling pressure to 'finish it off' with anything.

In short, marriage isn't a sexual death sentence and monogamy doesn't have to be boring. It's all in *your* control.

Devote time and effort to making your sex life as varied as possible and it will reward you back.

always tried to think up something new for us to try. The more imaginative she got, the harder I'd try to beat her at it. It turned into a competition but a friendly one with a great spin-off!

When Claire arrived, I remember feeling jealous because all her energy went into being a mother. But I was always confident our sex life would go back to normal and it did. There was only one other time it's suffered and that was when my father died. I slid into depression, but Catherine was brilliant. She didn't complain, just talked and listened and gave me lots of TLC and massages. She knows when to be sexy and when to be understanding.

My advice to other long-term couples would be accept that sex can't be wonderful all the time but always try to make it so.

Love Landmines

Surviving the inevitable blow-ups over housework,
families, money and just about
everything else

●●●

You meet her parents and they're as cool to you as the chilled potato soup they're serving. It's 5 am and the bastard's still out partying with his friends. She's turned out to be a workaholic. You open the cupboard and discover his idea of washing the dishes is rinsing off the really big bits and now there's an entire ant colony whooping it up on the pots and pans. Yup – the blinkers have fallen off and you're seeing your partner for who they really are: human.

One minute you were cruising happily along, the next you're lurching from one argument to another. Remember all those lonely nights in bed when you dreamt of finding someone to share it with? Now's the time when you start dreaming of being single again. We've all got faults (yes – even you!) and, not surprisingly, most centre around the same old trouble spots, like housework, money, not getting on with friends or family and when or whether to get married and have kids. The rough spots are what sort the flings from the in-it-for-a-long-time-not-just-a-good-time couples because you need a lot more than deep breathing and counting to 100 (ten? You've got to be kidding!) to survive. Chapter 4 taught you about communication skills – this is the bit where you'll get to use them. I'll start with how you handle arguments generally, then talk about the specifics of what you're arguing over.

I WIN, YOU WIN: FIGHTING FAIR

The first step to surviving the fights is to remember that every couple argues. If you don't, there's something very wrong with your relationship. You're either the first human clones out of the lab (and gosh, you grew up fast!) or one of you is agreeing for the sake of it. Arguments are healthy: they show you're secure enough to question each other's beliefs and behaviour. So long as they're balanced with good times (relationships guru John Gottman's theory on a healthy relationship is five good times to every bad one), you're doing just fine.

On the other hand, arguments aren't up there on anyone's 'how I'd like to spend next Saturday night' list. So the aim of this section is to try to change the *way* you argue, so there are less of them. Plenty of couples argue about the same old problems, over and over again. Hopefully, this will help you solve things the first time round.

There's a right way and a wrong way to argue. You won't get anywhere by:

- **Being aggressive and attacking your partner verbally**
  'Sorry I'm late home again, honey.'
  'Do you realize what time it is? You're such a selfish bitch/bastard. You care more about your job than you do me! Arsehole!'
- **Avoiding the argument by walking out and refusing to discuss it**
  'Sorry I'm late home again, honey.'

'That's fine,' as you storm into the kitchen, lips pursed.

- **Trying to smooth things over simply for the sake of peace**

  'Sorry I'm late home again, honey.'

  'It's nothing really. You're only an hour late. I didn't mean to upset you by complaining.'

- **Being sarcastic**

  'Sorry I'm late home again, honey.'

  'That's okay darling. Of course work should take first priority over a night home with me. After all, we did have those two hours together two months ago.'

- **Looking for solutions too early: instead of discussing the emotions behind it you skip straight to the end**

  'Sorry I'm late home again, honey.'

  'Right. Look, in future, I'll eat dinner before you. How does that sound?'

You *will* get somewhere by problem solving. Discuss feelings directly and openly, look at the reasons behind the argument and search for a solution both of you are happy with.

'Sorry I'm late home again, honey.'

'That's fine. Have a shower then let's have a drink.'

Later: 'Do you think we could talk about this a little? I know your job is important to you, but sometimes I feel like I'm always second priority. I need some reassurance and we need to come up with ways to stop the arguments we've been having when you arrive home later than expected.'

Think you can get the hang of it? Here's a step-by-step guide to how to have an argument *successfully* – and survive.

The five-step plan for the ideal argument

I don't expect you to sit there, book open at this page, and solemnly work through this step by step. But if both of you give it a quick read at some stage and try to memorize the key points, then check back *after* arguments to see how you've done, it'll soon become second nature. Don't worry if, to begin with, you feel a bit stiff and as if you're reading from a script.

The way I'm asking you to word your criticisms does sound formal and excessively polite. It's not – it just looks that way written down. While it may feel a little unnatural in the beginning because you're deliberately choosing words, it's amazing how quickly you'll find yourself adopting 'win–win' speak.

> 'We argued about everything from whose car to drive and whose turn it was to do the shopping through to how much his mother hated me and I hated his profession. It was like dating your worst enemy: neither of us was allowed to get away with a thing.'
>
> Jan, 29, secretary

1. Define the issue

Make sure you know what you're arguing about. Ask, 'Why is that important to you?' and, 'Why do you want that?' and the argument could be over before it's started. A psychologist friend of mine explains win–win perfectly. 'If you have an orange and both of you are arguing over who'll get it, the obvious thing to do is to cut it in half – with both of you losing half,' Eric says. 'If you ask each other what you want it *for*, you may find he or she wants the pulp for juice and you want the rind for a recipe. That's win–win. It's not always that simple, but quite often it is.'

Rate how important the argument is. Each of you give the issue a mark out of ten for importance. Whoever gives it the highest score should get the lion's share of talking time.

If it's something you're sensitive about, admit it. Say, 'Look, this is a sore point for me because of something that's happened in my past. Maybe I am overreacting so forgive me if I am but it's still really important that we talk this through.'

Be specific. Make sure your complaint includes three elements: a) what it was your partner did or didn't do; b) what situation(s) it happened in; and c) how it made you feel. 'When you didn't pay attention to me in front of your friends, it made me feel ignored and not very special,' rather than, 'You don't make me feel special any more.' Instead of, 'You never give me compliments,' say, 'Last night I wore a new outfit and I felt upset that you didn't notice or comment.'

Word it so you're giving the reaction you would have liked, rather than what you didn't like. 'I'd really appreciate it if we could spend more time together,' rather than, 'We don't spend enough time together.'

Don't automatically lash out if your partner says something unkind or tactless. Force yourself to wait five minutes before responding. Research by American psychologists Nancy Yovetich and Caryl Rusbult found when men and women are asked to say what they'd do if a partner behaved badly, they're more likely to respond destructively if asked to give a fast response. A pause of as little as six seconds was enough to make them think more constructively, calm down and weigh up the consequences of what they were about to say. Fighting fire with fire often doesn't work: you need to pour water on the situation instead. It's not a sign of weakness to react to an insult rationally, it's a sign of strength.

2. Move into discussion

Take turns. One of you gets centre stage for a full five minutes (time it). They talk, you listen (and no interrupting). It's cheating to spend that time mentally planning how you're going to word your bit. Instead, try really hard to give them full attention and listen to what they're saying – you'll have your chance, uninterrupted, at the end. When their five minutes is up, repeat back to them what they've just explained to you. If they're happy you understand, it's your turn. If you've got it wrong, keep on asking questions until you get it right. *Then* it's your turn.

Keep reminding yourself: stop pushing my point, listen to theirs. Resist the urge to take over the conversation, even if you're better at articulating. The key to solving problems isn't about making your partner understand your feelings, it's understanding theirs. If each of you shifts the emphasis from talking about how you feel to listening when the other speaks and asking questions, you'll get a lot further.

Stick to the issue. If you find yourself saying, 'And another thing . . .' or, 'This is just like how you behaved with Linda,' stop right there. One problem per argument.

Criticize the behaviour not the person. Keep your criticisms focused on what your partner did (or didn't) do, not on what sort of person they are. 'I felt upset when you . . .' not, 'You're so self-centred, you didn't even notice when . . .'

Stop blaming by removing 'you'. Say 'I feel,' not, 'You made me feel.'

Don't say, 'If you hadn't slept in, I wouldn't be late for work. Now I'm in trouble and it's your fault.' Instead try, 'I was late for work this morning and it caused no end of problems. We need to look at ways to ensure it won't happen again.'

Don't use threatening statements. 'That's it then, we might as well call it quits,' or, 'Well, I don't know why we're even bothering going out if we can't agree on this.' It instantly makes the argument seem much more serious and hackles rise. It's very easy in the heat of the moment to come back with, 'Fine! Bloody well leave then!' if someone threatens to.

Listen for trigger phrases that make the other's blood boil. Just last week, a pleasantly stimulating debate with my boyfriend about relationships turned into a raging row. He told me I was being condescending and patronizing. I thought I was simply letting him know the latest research on the topic we were discussing (after all, I was in the middle of writing a book about the topic!). One simple phrase turned out to be the problem.

This is how I thought I was coming across:

'Do you know, I read a study recently which actually said quite the opposite.'

This is what I was saying:

'Listen, honey – the research actually proves quite the opposite.'

The phrase 'Listen, honey' does sound condescending. I don't know where I got it from but whenever I used it he'd stop listening to what I was talking about and think, *Rotten cow's trying to lord it over me!*

Check you mean what you say and say what you mean. Most of us pull words out of the air, particularly when we're angry, that sort of express what we mean but not accurately. We'll call someone 'stubborn' when we really mean 'You're not acknowledging that I have a point even if you don't agree with it.'

Don't mind-read. If you're not sure what your partner's trying to say, ask them to put it in another way. Don't assume you know what it is.

Recognize that men aren't as good at arguing as women are. Strange isn't it? Men are supposedly more aggressive, yet they're the one's who'll do just about anything to avoid having a row. Why? It's probably because arguments involve discussing feelings and we're usually better at that than they are. One study also suggests it's because men find feelings of anger more unpleasant to deal with than women do.

3. Check your progress 20 minutes in

Who's doing the talking? Are you both getting enough time or is one dominating the conversation? Do you feel the other person's still really listening to you?

If you're feeling really angry, take a 20-minute break. Relationships expert John Gottman's research proves discussions fall apart when heart rates soar. If your blood's pumping furiously and your heart's racing, talking is pointless – you're too angry to listen. Gottman suggests taking your pulse every five minutes during an argument. If it starts racing, take some time out. It's probably not enough to just put the kettle on or go to the loo – it takes at least 20 minutes for our body to return to normal. Spend it doing something that soothes you. Go for a short drive, a walk or call a friend and make small talk (don't sound off about the argument). *Don't* spend the time out planning what to say when you resume the conversation. Instead think calming thoughts like, *This is just a bad moment. We'll work it out.*

Check your body language. British relationships expert Susan Quilliam believes happy couples use very different body language when fighting compared with unhappy matches. Even though they're angry, their attention is still focused on each other: they face each other, make eye contact and talk. The body language says, 'We still love each other so let's face this now.'

Unhappy couples do the opposite. They jab fingers at a partner's chest while trying to make a point: annoying as hell and also quite threatening. They cross their arms and roll their eyes which sends a clear signal: 'Talk all you want but I'm not listening to a word of it.' Gazing around the room means they're not just uninterested, they're looking for an escape route.

Quilliam suggests the following to ease tension during an argument. Lean forward toward your partner, leave your arms loose by your side and nod your head: that way they'll feel you're listening. If you're talking and your partner seems to be drifting off, take their hand and *ask* them to look at you. Use soothing gestures if they're getting overheated. Lay a hand on their arm and say, 'I know you're angry and I wish we weren't arguing.' Let them know you also want the argument over with even though you're prepared to discuss it and resolve it for good.

4. Continue the argument, this time looking for solutions

By now, the anger should have evaporated a little. Try including conciliatory phrases. Saying, 'I see your point even if I don't agree with it,' will get you a lot further than, 'I don't agree with you.' Let your partner know you've at least heard and understood what they're trying to say. Include phrases like, 'I see where you're coming from,' and, 'I know you probably won't agree with me but I just want you to understand why I feel this way.'

If you now think you're in the wrong, admit it. It's natural to want to defend yourself but if you really have stuffed up, your partner will be much more inclined to listen to your reasons if you apologize *first*, justify later. Say, 'I apologize for not calling to say I was going to be late. I should have made the effort. But the meeting ran late and I raced out of the door so I could get home more quickly. My intentions were right but I can see now I'd have been better off taking those extra few minutes to let you know.' Put it this way and your partner's likely to come back with, 'That's okay, sweetheart. I know you did your best.'

Ask each other: 'How do you think we can avoid this happening in the future?' Listen to their side. If you're confident you can do what they're suggesting and are happy to, simply agree. If not, put your solution forward. Then talk about how they feel about it. You might well combine both ideas or ditch both and come up with another. Alternatively, the solution might well be to think about it over the next few days so you can rationally think it through.

Don't play shrink. 'You're defensive about this because your father left you,' or, 'This is all about your ex-wife isn't it? She's made you this way.' There's a difference between exploring underlying reasons together and feeling like you're on a couch and your partner's taking notes.

What's your fighting style?
- *The scream and sulk: 37 per cent of us rant then completely ignore our partner.*
- *The name callers: 28 per cent ignore whatever it is they're arguing about and trade insults instead.*
- *The talk and walk: 25 per cent have shouting matches – which end when one of you walks out.*
- *The long bicker: Only one-tenth of couples surveyed bickered for hours and hours after the event – but at least they ended up solving whatever was bothering them in the first place!*

5. End the argument
Once you both feel understood and have found a solution you're both happy with, stop talking about it. Sometimes you'll agree *not* to agree on something: you understand each other's viewpoint, have worked out how to deal with it but it's clear you have differing opinions. It's tempting in that case to keep thinking up evidence to support your side. Don't – no matter how fab it is. Drop it.

You don't have to solve the argument to end it. Even if you haven't come up with a solution, don't beat it to death. If you've been at it, hammer and tongs, for two hours, that's enough. Call a truce and resume the conversation later.

Don't expect to kiss and make up immediately afterward.
You've both taken a few steps backward from each other and feel emotionally exhausted, maybe even a little frightened ('For one moment there, I really thought we *were* going to split'). Personally, I think it's best you stay together: even if you turn on the telly and the other reads a book. But if one needs to be alone for a little while, that's their way of getting back to normal. Don't object – but do set a time limit. One hour is enough (any more and paranoia sets in: you'll think the relationship's damaged for good. Either that, or feel abandoned and get angry all over again).

If you're fighting about the same thing, over and over, try taping your arguments. This is incredibly effective for two reasons. First, if you know every word that comes out of your mouth is being taped, you'll think before you open it. Secondly, playing back the argument gives both of you a chance to hear what you *really* said rather than what you *thought* you did.

Do something nice for each other the day after an argument. Give a small gift or a nice card, or even make a phone call to say how much you hated arguing and how much you love each other. Failing that, just give each other an extra big hug when you wake up the next day. Smile and say, 'We survived. We're stronger than ever before. Isn't it great!'

DO ULTIMATUMS EVER WORK?
Exactly two years after Lisa met Paul she received an eviction notice from her landlord. Secretly, she was delighted. For months, she'd been hinting to Paul that she wanted to live together and this was the perfect way to cement the issue. That night, she insisted they go to their favourite restaurant, held his hand across the table and told him her rental flat was sold and she had two weeks to move out.

'That's a drag,' Paul said. 'But hang on, I might just have an idea.'

Here it comes, thought Lisa, *he's going to ask me to move in.*

Except he didn't. Instead, Paul suggested she call a friend of his who was looking for a flatmate. 'I was so utterly humiliated that it didn't even occur to him, I just mumbled something and ran for the loo,' Lisa said. 'Once I'd got myself together, I decided it was now or never. The minute I sat back down I gave him an ultimatum: either I move in with him or it's over.'

In Lisa's situation, many of us would be tempted to do the same. Most people don't enjoy issuing ultimatums, absolutely no-one likes receiving them but just about everyone has opened their mouths at some point to say, 'Do this or that or it's over.' Sometimes, ultimatums are logical, well-mulled-over requests delivered in a calm I-mean-it tone. More often than not they're outright (often outrageous) demands, heavily laced with expletives, that spill out during a hot, vicious argument. When all else fails and frustration reaches boiling point, ultimatums seem the most effective weapon we have, bar a loaded gun. Unfortunately, they're just as dangerous. Not only can ultimatums be turned and used against you, they have a nasty habit of backfiring. So if you're about to read your partner their last rites, do so at your own peril – and take a few tips first.

Why we give them

On one level, ultimatums work. They bring a situation to a head and show your partner how important something is to you. Trouble is, they're the poor man's means of communicating – and one of the least effective methods around. People who constantly dole out ultimatums are behaving like children. They're usually emotionally immature and aren't very good at communicating or working through problems. Top that off with poor listening skills.

If you're always saying, 'Do this or else,' you lose power and respect. Most times you don't follow through with your threats and your partner starts to see you as pathetic. There are far better ways to solve a problem. My friend Melanie agrees. 'I stopped delivering ultimatums because they proved mortifyingly embarrassing. Once I was at a party and told my boyfriend it was all over if he didn't leave with me there and then – in front of a huge audience. He refused and I stormed out and went home only to discover he had the keys to my flat. I had to slink back in, in front of all those people, and ask him for them. They all laughed and I felt like a complete idiot. Now, if I feel strongly about someone's behaviour, I tell them calmly that I won't put up with it but leave off the "or else" bit.' Threatening someone is dictatorial. You're not consulting with your partner, you're telling them. Most people understandably respond with resistance and, 'How dare you tell me what to do!'

> 'She'd clam up the minute an argument started, making me feel like a complete ogre. But she was passively aggressive. While she wouldn't come right out and criticize me, she'd make smart, snide comments then tell me I was being oversensitive when I picked her up on them. Give me a partner who screams and yells over someone like her any day.'
>
> Tom, 36, designer

Why they backfire

Word them as nicely as you like but they're still thinly disguised threats. Which is why our natural reaction is to do the opposite to what's being asked, if only to retrieve some sort of pride. If someone delivers a 'you do this or else' ultimatum, people often refuse even if it is reasonable. It's so demoralizing to say, 'Okay, dear.'

Brett, 27, broke up his marriage over an ultimatum delivered by his wife. 'She told me to stop drinking or leave. I didn't have a problem with drinking though, she did. Her father was an alcoholic and she considered a few beers on the weekend unacceptable. I tried talking to her but there was no compromise. I had to do all the changing. In the end, the only thing I did change was my address and marital status.'

The fact that you're forced to issue an ultimatum usually means your relationship is in dire straits anyway. Sometimes it's a symptom of basic incompatibility. It's certainly a sign neither of you are clear about what you want from the relationship. If you're doling out ultimatums over trivial things – like taking out the rubbish – you really should ask yourself, 'Am I overreacting here?' Better still, 'Should we be together if I have to issue an ultimatum over something so stupid?'

Ultimatums aren't necessary in healthy partnerships with strong communication because problems are discussed and solved before they get to make or break point. If you can't solve a problem by talking about it, you're unlikely to solve it by threatening. As Karen found out – the hard way. 'I'd been going out with Karen for about three years and we spent the last one arguing bitterly,' says David. 'It was obvious we were headed for a break-up, which is why I was so astonished when she told me, "Marry me on my birthday or it's over." How she could even consider settling down when we were getting on so badly astounded me. In a sense it gave me an out: on D-day I told her it was over.' Karen's ultimatum was a last-ditch attempt to save a dying relationship. She put her cards on the table and lost the game.

Never say never unless you mean it

Never, ever give an ultimatum unless you're prepared to follow through. You won't be taken seriously again and you strip yourself of any power in the relationship. 'My girlfriend issues loads of ultimatums and never means them so I don't take any notice any more,' says Robert. 'Like she's hardly going to dump me for turning up five minutes late! It's the old boy-who-cried-wolf scenario: one day, she might be serious but how am I supposed to know?' Packing your bags today, then turning up on the doorstep tomorrow doesn't just make you look silly. By coming back you've effectively said, 'I'll not only put up with this situation against my will, I'll hang around no matter what you dish out because I don't have the strength to leave.'

Commitment ultimatums – move in/marry me/say you love me or else – are perhaps the diciest of them all. There's a reason your partner's not moving the relationship forward: they're not ready, they're still thinking about it or you're not 'the one'. Giving them a jolt, trying to shock them into realizing how much you mean to them by imagining life without you, will certainly give you an answer. Problem is, it might not be the one you want. Pressure someone too early and you could lose a partner who would have been ready a year on, when they felt comfortable and ready for commitment. Behaviour ultimatums – stop putting me down/stop looking at other women – are usually more successful, but even then, use them as a last resort. You don't start by dishing out ultimatums, you finish with them. There's a whole heap of things you should try first. Let's say your boyfriend flirts outrageously at parties. Instead of ending the evening with, 'Flirt with that blonde once more and your clothes will be on the pavement,' keep calm, go home together and talk about it over lunch the next day. (How? See 'The five-step plan for ideal argument' on page 244.)

When an ultimatum is the only way

Tried talking, exhausted all angles and your partner's behaviour is still intolerable? *That's* the time to give an ultimatum. If it's serious – your partner is hitting you or has a severe drinking or gambling problem – issuing an ultimatum isn't just a good idea, it's advisable. What's imperative is that you follow through.

And if there's one situation that *only* an ultimatum will solve, it's when your partner is having an affair or you're having one with someone who's married. Most people with a spouse and a lover won't change anything unless one of them says, 'It's them or me,' and stands by their word. This time, you really don't have anything to lose except someone who's making you miserable anyway. Even if it's not the answer you want, at least you know where you stand.

Which was precisely how Lisa felt when her boyfriend said no to her ultimatum of moving in. 'If he wasn't ready by then, I knew he never would be,' she said. 'At least I wasn't hanging on for ever, wasting my time.'

If you must give an ultimatum, do it the right way

- **Don't deliver one without forewarning.** They're a last resort and should only be used after many discussions have failed. If you've spent several weeks (or months) talking about the problem with your partner, they'll at least have given it some thought before being forced to make a decision.
- **Write it down.** Think hard about what you want to say, then write it down as clearly as possible. Use non-threatening language and talk about changing the behaviour not the person. Instead of, 'I'm leaving if you don't see me more often,' try, 'I feel the relationship can't progress if we don't see each other more often. If you can't give me more time, I can't really see the point of continuing.' Tell them what you'd like them to do more of, rather than what you want them to stop doing. 'I want you to be sober,' rather than, 'I want you to stop drinking.' Word your demand as best you

can, then leave it for a few days. Does it still seem reasonable? Is there a better way of saying it?

- **Don't deliver it when you're angry.** If need be, leave the situation until you've calmed down. Ultimatums issued in the heat of the moment, when you're both tipsy or tired after a long argument, won't be taken seriously. Leave it until you've both calmed down, can talk reasonably and think logically.

> **Myth: Women nag more than men do.**
> *Reality: It's true. And we do it twice as often. Researchers say it's because women have got more to complain about, especially if we're married. Even if you both work, it's still usually the wife who's saddled with most of the domestics (and the kids). He doesn't nag because he's got little to gripe about!*

- **Don't drag other people into it.** Tacking on 'and all your friends agree with me' won't get you anywhere: your partner will feel even more ganged up on and defensive. Checking that your ultimatum is reasonable with someone you trust and who also knows your partner, however, is a good idea. Do they think you're overreacting or is your stand understandable and necessary?

- **Leave yourself room for compromise.** Tell them honestly that you're not prepared to put up with the current situation but if they have any other solutions, you'd like to hear them.

- **Be prepared to follow through.** Think about the worst possible outcome (they refuse to do what you're asking) and decide if it's worth it. If it is, be prepared to stick with your decision and have some good, supportive friends on standby.

- **Put a time limit on it.** If you want to get married or move in, tell them how long you're prepared to wait. There's a big difference between 'immediately' and 'six months'.

- **Pick the right time.** If they've just lost their job, have the flu or found out their best friend's moving town, they may say no to whatever you're suggesting simply because they're emotionally exhausted.
- **Reward your partner for changing.** If they do make an effort to get their act together, give some positive feedback. Pay attention and let them know how much you appreciate it. Otherwise, they'll slip straight back into old patterns.

CAREER CLASHES

I freely admit it: I'm a workaholic. It's not that I wouldn't prefer to be snuggled up watching trash telly with a partner than bashing away at my computer, it's just necessary at this point in my career. (Actually, sometimes I *would* prefer to be writing. Sick, isn't it?) Some of the guys I've gone out with understand this commitment and encourage it, probably because they're equally as busy and ambitious themselves. Others think I'm unhealthily obsessive about my job (which is probably true) or a selfish cow (which hopefully isn't). I talked about the importance of matching career aspirations and attitudes to work in previous chapters. But even if you did do as you were told (add bossy to selfish), circumstances change. The laid-back and disenchanted can turn into mad career-heads if they hit on the job of their dreams; some put their feet on the top rung of the corporate ladder and realize they suffer from vertigo. Whatever, if your relationship's suffering from unbalanced work schedules and commitments, the following will hopefully help even it up.

If one of you is a workaholic

If it's you that's being accused of working too hard, don't dismiss any career complaints without giving it a lot of thought. Few people complain for no reason in these sorts of situations and they might be right: you may well have become a workaholic and a martyr. Ask others you trust if your partner's got a point, then make up your own mind about what career sacrifices you're willing to make. The fact is, you have to spend time doing enjoyable, relaxing things to bind you and your partner together; if you've lost sight of that, rework your priorities. If the relationship is important to you, be flexible – but don't be coerced. If it's not justified, talk together about why they're feeling ignored. Are they insecure about your feelings for them? How much time do they want with you? Be understanding, but don't relinquish your career for demands that aren't reasonable. You'll only end up resentful later.

If you're the one putting up with a partner talking into a dictaphone at 8 am on Sundays, ask how long they expect to be working weekends and evenings. Say you realize their job is important but it's also important to have time together. Work together to try to achieve more balance in their life and be flexible. If their job requires them to work weekends, spend quality time during the week: meet for lunch at a café near their office or get up a bit earlier to have breakfast together. But don't put your life on hold just because they're entrenched in work. If you're never, ever given priority and there's no light at the end of the tunnel, you might want to reconsider whether the relationship's worth it. After all, it's not really a relationship if you don't see each other, is it?

If you're doing better than he is

If it's you saying, 'Honey, I'm home,' and dropping your brief-case on the floor while he's in the kitchen preparing dinner, you encounter your own set of problems. While it's hardly unusual for the female to be the one with the company car, expense account, glamorous job and high salary, it takes a liberated guy to cope with it. A traditional man might feel he's lost power –

particularly if you were both even-steven at the start of the relationship.

Women tend to feel proud of their partners when they achieve success; men often feel threatened. 'Whenever we went out, it was always Katie who got the pats on the back,' says Pete, a friend of mine whose partner scored a highly desirable promotion. 'Her career was flourishing, mine was stagnant. I found it really difficult to smile when people asked me if I was proud of her. Of course I was, but I wondered if they were really thinking, *What's she still doing with him? She could score someone much better now.* Her success became my failure.' Often, men won't even approach women who are more successful than they are because they think, *How can I attract a woman like that? She's too good for me.* (Which goes a long way to explain why lots of successful women are single.)

And it's not just him that feels weird. Women often feel put out if they're paying the lion's share of the bills, because there's a little part of them that still says, 'Hey! Isn't *he* supposed to be looking after *me*?' Resentment increases if they're not just the breadwinner but prime caretakers of the relationship and chief cook and bottle washer. 'I'd work my bum off, I was paying the bills, he'd have been home for hours and yet it was me who was expected to look after him and the house as well,' says Patricia. 'It wasn't fair.'

It's a lot harder for couples who started out on an even job status than those who met when she was more successful or financially well-off. After all, if he's the sort of guy who can't handle it, he probably wouldn't have asked you out again once it became apparent. If it is a case of your career taking off suddenly, approach him tactfully. Saying, 'Honey, I know you're a bit put out that I earn ten times as much as you do,' will have him immediately on the defensive. Don't play down your own achievements, but boost up his. Remind him constantly of all the reasons why you love him so much, how much you appreciate his support. Encourage him to chase his own career dreams but don't push. Forcing him to go for higher-paid positions will make him even more paranoid that he's not measuring up to your standards. Broach the subject, tentatively, when he's relaxed and in a good mood. Kick off the conversation by saying, 'I know you realize how important my career is to me and you're incredibly supportive, but are you happy with the amount of time we spend together?' Keep it light and non-threatening and he might well open up and talk about any fears created by your success.

You've come a long way, baby – if you're a woman that is. A recent survey comparing gender stereotypes common in the 1970s to those held in the 1990s show our image of women has improved while his has soured. Twenty years ago, women were viewed as indecisive, passive, unworldly and feelings-focused. Now, we're seen as intelligent, logical, independent, adventurous and dependable. Men got positive adjectives first time round – objective, savvy, assertive – but not-so-nice ones have been added to the list: jealous, moody, narrow-minded and deceptive.

HASSLES OVER HOUSEWORK

I can't say I've ever met anyone who said, 'I broke up with my boyfriend because he wouldn't wash the dishes,' but men not sharing domestic chores is a major cause of resentment in relationships. So while it seems like a trivial topic, it's not. You both make the mess, it's logical that both of you should clean it up, and being treated like a servant is not fun.

Before I go any further, though, I have to say all the responsibility doesn't rest squarely on the shoulders of that lazy bastard who never makes the bed. Women are half the problem. We mother men. We're always saying things like, 'Don't forget to pick up your drycleaning,' and, 'Did you remember to pay the electricity bill?' and, 'How many times have I told you not to leave wet towels on the floor.' If you treat someone like a child, you're giving them the message that they aren't capable of looking after themselves. If someone always cleaned up after me, I'd be inclined to sit back and let them do it, too! Men get lazy because they're used to us doing the running around. Conditioning's also part of it. Young girls are encouraged to 'play house'. If you come from a home where your Mum mothered your Dad, you're 80 per cent more likely to think housework and fussing over someone is what females do.

It sounds crazy, but not splitting the chores fairly is incredibly bad for your sex life. (There, that got your attention!) For a start, the quickest way to kill passion is to mother your partner. He starts behaving like a son, you start thinking of him as one; you start behaving like a mother, he starts seeing you as his. And who wants to sleep with their mother or their son?

Sex and housework are the two things just about all couples argue about at some stage. Generally, men want more sex and women want a fairer division of the housework. Relationships guru John Gottman believes one feeds the other. He's right if you think about it. Both sex and housework require energy, and most of us have only got so much left at the end of a hard day. In plenty of relationships, *he'll* come home from work, flop in front of the telly and relax with a beer while *she* organizes dinner. She'll cook, clean up, do the dishes, work out what's needed for the next night's meal then – Gee! – it's time for bed. Guess who'll feel more like sex?

The quickest way a man can boost the amount of sex he's having with his partner is to do his share of the housework. It's a fact: men who do more housework and involve themselves with the kids have better sex lives and happier relationships than those who don't. If he does his bit, she not only has more energy, she feels more valued and respected. The spin-off? She's in the right head space to feel sexy. Treat her like a servant and she'll feel as resentful as hell and carry *that* feeling into bed with her. Ever noticed how the rubbish feels heavier and the pile of dishes seems higher when you're thinking, *Bastard! He should be helping me with this!*? Ever jumped into bed after feeling like that and said, 'Give it to me, big boy!'? I didn't think so.

I bet if you're a new-age sensitive guy reading this you're feeling rather smug. Don't. Gottman did a survey on 50 guys who considered themselves 'liberated' and compared them to 50 guys who admitted they thought it was a woman's job to do the housework. Do you know how much more housework the liberated guys did compared to the chauvinists? Four minutes a day! Like, wow, what a tremendous help that'd be.

Housework isn't a woman's job, it's a couple's job. You aren't 'helping' her by making the bed, you're sharing the necessary chores that make both your lives more comfortable. So it's a very good idea to sort out the housework thing the minute you move in together. Don't just assume you'll each pick up your fair share – it rarely happens. Instead, grab a pen and paper and write down all the things that need doing every week – not just the cleaning but stuff like grocery lists, washing, ironing, shopping and who plans the weekend's social activities. Everything you do as a couple should be shared. Women tend to be the social organizers. We're the ones who remember someone's birthday, buy the present, wrap and write on the card, arrange a dinner and bake the cake. We're also the ones to organize who we're seeing on the weekend, when, where and what time. We juggle friends so they're all happy. That takes time and effort as well, so it's imperative this is also taken into account.

Write it all down then each go through and pick what you like doing best (or rather, what you dislike doing least). If you don't mind washing up and he doesn't mind ironing, split it that way. If you detest cleaning the car and the other doesn't like it much either but hates it *less* passionately, that chore goes to them. So mark what you both don't mind doing or hate doing so you can split things fairly.

Finished that? Now go through the list and make it as even as possible. Take into account the time it takes to complete the chore and likes and dislikes until you're both happy it's split evenly and fairly. It doesn't have to be 50–50. If one person works full-time and the other part-time, you might decide a 70–30 split is fair. Some couples swap chores from week to week to even it up that way. Others take one look at the list and decide they'd rather fork out for a cleaner and get their ironing done than waste precious weekend time.

Also remember you can use trade-offs. You might put up with doing all the washing and ironing if he gives you a weekly massage. He might take on more cleaning if you do all the social stuff like keeping up with friends. The bottom line is as always: compromise and communication.

FED UP WITH EACH OTHER'S FRIENDS AND FAMILY

I asked a psychiatrist friend of mine what advice she'd give to a couple who love each other but can't tolerate each other's family. 'Move to the other side of the world,' she said wryly. 'If you can't do that, at least keep a sense of humour.'

Squabbles over parents and siblings are both common and damaging. It's very easy to get into situations where you and your own family side against your partner and vice versa. So it's important to work out any differences – or at least ways of handling them – early, so there is no ganging up. I touched briefly on the initial meeting in Chapter 3. This is a more detailed version (for the truly petrified) plus some tips on handling the relationship once it progresses.

Meeting their family
First up

- When you're introduced, smile, shake their hand and say warmly, 'I'm so glad to meet you. I've heard so many nice things about you.' If the relationship with your partner and their family is so strained they'll know you're lying through your teeth, drop the 'heard so much about you' bit. But still smile a lot. It's not uncommon for a tactful, liked in-law to turn a bad partner–parent relationship into a great one.
- Try to treat them like you would anyone else you'd just met. If they start firing questions at you, calmly answer them. Assume they're nervous rather than attacking you. Try not to get defensive.
- Lay on the compliments. What a great job they did raising someone as wonderful as your partner. How delicious the meal tastes. What a nice house they have. There's no need to be gushy but a few white lies designed to ease *their* discomfort (remember, they may be nervous too) goes a long way.
- Ask questions. Who are the photographs of? How long have they lived in the house? If you're getting on well, ask them to tell you what sort of child your partner was. He or she will be as embarrassed as hell but you'll win their parents over immediately.

Later on

- If they start nagging your partner (they don't see enough of them), resist the urge to join in. It's not your business to interfere and you're in a no-win situation. Side with their parents and your partner will feel resentful; side with your partner and they'll feel put out.

- If any member of the family is openly hostile, take a deep breath and try to steer the conversation to safer topics. Ignore the chill and see if they warm up over time.

- If they compare you to an ex, making it clear that's where *their* loyalties are, swallow all pride and say, 'I know how much you loved Linda/Lyle and it is a shame they broke up. But it's over and who knows? You might grow to like me as well.' Only the truly cruel won't be disarmed by that sort of statement.

- Don't forget it's your partner you're in love with, not them. You don't have to adore them, though it's certainly easier if you do. If you've truly tried but can only manage a superficial politeness, fine. That's enough to get through the family get-togethers.

- Don't criticize their family, even if they do. The unwritten rule is this: it's okay for them to pick fault but not okay for you to agree. Say, 'Oh well, honey, that's brother/sister/mother/daughter-love for you,' even if you are dying to say, 'I agree – your mother should be shot at close range. Can I be the one to pull the trigger?'

- No matter how much you dislike them, you owe it to your partner to be polite. They owe you the same courtesy. If their family was particularly vicious and destructively protective of their offspring, you're well within your rights to simply refuse to see them again. If you behaved like an obnoxious brat, it's totally acceptable for them not to see you again.

- You both get on with each other's families to the point where you feel torn between the two? Aim for a compromise that satisfies you both and keeps the peace. If both sets of parents expect you for Sunday lunch, visit one set together one week, go separately to your own parents the other and do the other set the following (not forgetting to save the odd Sunday just for the two of you).

Introducing your partner to your family

- Fill your partner in on any family eccentricities. Your dad probably won't even take his eyes off the telly? Warn them so they don't feel slighted. Your mum's a little over-the-top? They're both liable to assume the wedding's planned for next year? Forewarned is forearmed.

- Fill your family in on your partner. If they're a little shy and cover up their shyness by talking a billion miles an hour. What they do for a living. Any significant vulnerable points: a parent who's recently died, a promotion that's just fallen through. That way, they'll know to steer clear of certain subjects. It's also a good idea to let them know how serious the relationship is, especially if your partner's more serious than you are. They'll already think meeting your family is the green light for commitment. Your parents smiling and saying things like, 'Well, you're part of the family now,' will have wedding bells ringing in their ears.

- Grin and bear it. If your Mum accidentally calls them by an ex's name, give your partner's hand a squeeze and laugh. She's not trying to sabotage, just vague. If they drag out highly embarrassing photos, laugh along with them.

- If you're going to stay the night, make sure you've had the where-you're-both-going-to-sleep discussion beforehand.

- Don't quiz your partner afterward to find out what their impressions were. Give them all time to get used to each other.

Juggling friends and lovers

You book the restaurant and warn the waiter your table's likely to be the rowdiest and the last to leave. After all, you love your friends, you like your partner – they're all bound to get on, right? At 9 pm, you're in a cab, sitting in stony silence. 'I don't know what you see in them,' your partner says. *I think they're wondering the same about you,* you think. *What the hell do I do now?*

It may come as a complete surprise but researchers have discovered men like to dominate conversations, hate being interrupted and want to be seen as the 'expert'. Women, on the other hand, co-operate with each other to tell a story, finish each other's sentences and make more encouraging noises than men.

Why those first few meetings are tricky

Being able to get on with each other's friends doesn't just make life easier, it's a good indicator you've chosen well. We surround ourselves with people we like and admire. If your partner doesn't like them, there are probably things they don't like about you. Having said that, don't be too hasty to jump to conclusions. There are lots of other reasons why those first few meetings might not go as well as you'd hoped. Here are some of them.

Your partner feels like they're under the microscope. Some friends deliver a very obvious message to new partners: you're on trial until *we* decide whether you're good enough. If they're sitting on the edge of their seat waiting for your friends' seal of approval, it's no wonder they're a little nervous. If you think your friends will be ridiculously over-protective, take the pressure off by ensuring you all *do* something together first time round. Invite a friend over to watch a video with you and your partner, play a game, get both to help you prepare dinner. Get them focused on a task rather than on each other so they're working as a team rather than fighting for your attention. Don't make your partner the centrepiece – especially if they're shy and reserved. A big group of friends is sometimes better than the two of you and one best friend. Warn them if they're likely to be over-protective. Tell your friends to back off if they give your partner a hard time. Say you realize they're trying to protect you, but you are quite capable of doing it yourself.

Your partner feels they don't measure up. Are you dating 'down'? Is your partner less intelligent/trendy/financially secure than your usual dates? If you and your friends all have masters degrees and your partner left school at 16, they'll obviously feel out of their depth. *You* might not rib them about their lack of education, dreadful dress sense or bad grammar but friends often aren't as tactful. If they treat him or her like the village idiot and are patronizing, your partner's understandably going to feel rather insecure.

Your friends will contrast and compare. Your partner knows your friends have seen all your other dates and they're being measured against them. Help ease the situation by making it very clear they don't have to impress your friends, just you: it's what you think about them that matters.

If it is a case of 'pick the person who doesn't belong', pay attention. If your friends are very different from the sort of person your partner is, it's not a great sign, because it means you probably are too. An introvert matched with a party animal; dating someone who's so shy you need a can opener just to talk to them – it's worth reassessing whether it's worth it. Statistically, people who are alike have a better chance of making it than people from completely different worlds.

Your partner sees something you don't. Friends that only see you when they want something. Friends that put you down. Partners are more objective and they'll sometimes see what should be glaringly obvious: this person isn't a friend, they're an enemy in disguise. Partners give us another angle and perspective. If they love you and feel you're being taken advantage of, they've got good reason not to be in raptures over the friend you treasure so much. The trick is to weigh up the comments and make sure they're not motivated by jealousy but your well-being. Then make up your own mind whether you want to keep the friend in your life. Some friends are worth making allowances for. One of my friends is notoriously unreliable and breaks two dates out of three. But she's there in a flash when I need her, and to me, that's more important. Boyfriends have never understood why I put up with her, but who cares? The bottom line is she's my friend, not theirs.

It's none of the above and they still don't get on with anyone? If your partner despises every single person you've introduced them to, sirens should be wailing and red lights flashing WARNING! WARNING! They're on an ownership trip: the 'I love you so you shouldn't need anyone else' one. If their comments about your friends are getting nastier and nastier, get out. It's one thing to say they don't like Sarah but quite another to call her a fat slut. Slagging them off mercilessly is your exit cue.

How to make it easier on everyone
Be loyal. If a partner forces you to *choose* between them and your friends, choose your friends every time. If they simply grumble each time you want them to go out with them, ask why. Is it the whole group they don't like, one particular person – or the fact that you ignore them? Usually, there's at least one or two people they'll take to (or at least tolerate), so

see those friends together and the rest solo.

Set limits. Can't tear him away from the boys? It's healthy to have time apart for girls' or boys' nights, but if they want to do it *every* Friday and Saturday night, it's immature and unacceptable. You think you've got a relationship, but you haven't. How much leeway you give each other depends on the relationship and where it's going. But do let him out once in a while. 'Relationships are hell,' says Pete, a friend of mine. 'You have to be polite, politically correct and charming. On boys' nights out you can relax, swill beer and bourbon, joke around and punch each other in the shoulders. All the stuff she thinks is childish.'

> 'I remember going out with the boys one night and all I could think about was how much I wished I'd stayed home with her. I bought some flowers at a convenience store, let myself in, and spelt out "I love you" with the petals on the lounge room carpet. In the morning, they were all withered and rather pathetic but she thought it was just wonderful.'
> Phil, 25, law student

Spell out expectations. Talk through how much time spent seeing friends solo is acceptable, what's not. Also, what activities are off limits. She might think a night playing pool down the pub is fine, a night cruising the strip joints isn't. He might give the thumbs up to dinner out but be not quite as understanding about you and the girls hitting the nightclubs till 5 am.

If there are fights over time, think about whether they've got a point before getting defensive. Are you spending too much time with friends and not enough with your partner? Are their demands reasonable or childish? A mature partner will say, 'Can you change your night out with your friends tonight? I'm working all weekend and won't get to see you otherwise.' That's a different story to, 'What are you seeing them for? You should be spending time with me!' Some partners expect their partners to sit at home and be constantly available.

Sometimes, it's a good idea to give each other designated nights. Say, 'I'm happy to see you Wednesday nights and over the weekend, but I need to see my friends during the week.' For a relationship to work, you need to make time to be together, alone, with your partner and their friends, and with you and yours.

Accept there will be personality clashes. People clash for all sorts of reasons but there's often nothing sinister about it. They subconsciously remind us of that abusive teacher, nasty cousin or dreaded ex. We also slot people into existing stereotypes, sometimes on sight, for silly reasons like what they're wearing. If it's instant dislike, your friend/partner/both may well get over it once the real person starts to take over their preconceived perception. If they've met five or so times and still can't get on, accept it's not going to work. Mix the two together as little as possible and see the hated friend on your own.

Don't stress too much. Is it really that important they get on? Not every relationship is meant to run for a lifetime. We're drawn to people throughout life, go down a little road with someone for a few months, realize we're at cross purposes, then split. If they're only going to be around for a little while, does it really matter if he hates Mandy or she hates Joe?

Demand respect from both sides. You can't force people to like each other but you can demand respect. Both should be polite to each other.

Allow for first-time nerves. A little bit of nervousness around friends is a compliment: it means it's important to your partner you all get on. Avoiding even meeting them isn't. It could be a sign of commitment phobia: meeting your friends means the relationship's moving forward.

Look for reasons. If your partner says they don't like your friends, they could be trying to diminish their importance. If they're dead keen on you but sense your friends don't like them, they know damn well the verdict will be thumbs down. By saying they don't like them, they're trying to reduce your friends in your eyes so you won't listen to their opinion.

Make your own judgements. Don't be swayed by a friend's judgement of your partner but do think about what they've said. It's normal for friends to offer an opinion and for you to ask for one. Listen to what they have to say – they might well see things you don't – but don't buy into the 'so when are you going to leave them?' game.

Remember you have the benefit of time. Partners often don't see friends the way you do. You think they're supersuccessful, he thinks they're career obsessed and stuck up. You think they're a laugh a minute, she thinks they're vulgar. Give both time to see the person behind the façade.

Use reverse psychology. Tell your partner the hated friend said how nice or cute they were. Tell the friend your partner said what a great smile they had and that they enjoyed their company. Of course it's all lies but they don't know that. If your partner thinks a friend likes them, they're more inclined to like them – and vice versa. They both start being nicer to each other and before you know it, they're best buddies!

Don't drop your friends every time you meet someone new. Juggling best friends and a new lover takes the tact, military precision, psychological analysis and manoeuvring skills of a foreign diplomat. If they're squabbling over your time and affection like two hungry seagulls fighting over a crust of bread, it's tempting to tell both to fly away. Instead, make the effort to keep both happy. Your friends will understand you both want to hide away from the world in the beginning, but will be peeved if it lasts more than a month. Catch up, even if it's just for a coffee, and don't spend the entire time raving about your new love affair. Show you're as interested in them as you were before you became a couple.

See best friends and partners together sometimes. If Tuesday night was telly night with a girlfriend, invite him along. If Fridays was drinks with the boys, get her to bring along a few girlfriends.

Remember to give friends time separately. There's nothing worse than always having to see your friends with their other half, so be a little sensitive. If a friend rings and wants to talk, go solo. Most of the couples I know see friends alone at least two nights a week: your friends are happy, you get breathing space from each other.

MONEY MATTERS

Money can't buy happiness. I absolutely agree. There's no way I'd marry some old bloke with a red, bumpy nose and shiny head just because he happened to be loaded. On the other hand, I know I'd be much happier typing this in a waterfront penthouse apartment than the flat I'm living in. It's a dilemma but I look at it this way: I decided years ago that the only way I'd ever have money is to make it myself. Even if I did marry someone rich, it would still be *their* money, not mine. Having said that, I have to say it would be rather nice to hook up with a partner who's got at least as much as I have (which isn't difficult). I've worked hard for the little I've got and I don't really fancy handing over half of it to someone who hasn't. That doesn't seem fair to me. Also, I reason, if we're around the same age and have accumulated similiar assets, it shows we share the same attitudes to money and are responsible about it.

I know plenty of women (and a few men) who think differently. I met one girl at a function who openly admitted she'd never date anyone who earned under six figures. (I couldn't quite see what she had to offer in return, but perhaps under that hard veneer there was a heart of gold. Actually, scratch that because she'd have cashed it in already.) But, let's face it, money's always been attractive. Rich men and women always top the 'I wish he/she'd ask me out' list because it's a lot easier to be happy, loving and affectionate to someone while sipping champagne on board a yacht than watching a black and white telly on a lumpy couch, eating baked beans out of a can.

Money affects relationships at all stages. If you're rolling in it, you've got the cash to dress well, look after your appearance and treat people to nice things so you're instantly more desirable to date. Two or three dates into a relationship, even couples who haven't a clue what the other earns find out fast because your incomes determine what you do together. If you're both reasonably affluent, eating out at posh restaurants is *de rigueur*. If they go deathly pale as you order the lobster, it's a fair bet they're mentally counting the bills in their wallet to check they've got enough. Date for long enough and situations like these can breed resentment. 'You're such a snob,' the poorer partner says. 'I had enough of cheap eats while studying,' the other snaps back. 'I deserve better now.' The relationship's particularly vulnerable if she's the richer of the two. The old 'he should earn more' attitude might be buried, but it's still there at the back of people's minds. He may feel 'less of a man' because he can't afford to take her to places she'd prefer to go or spoil her with expensive gifts. She'll be told constantly, 'You could have done better for yourself.' Income determines lifestyle. If you decide to move in together and one's looking at £500 per week apartments while the other's checking out £125 bedsits, it suddenly becomes horribly apparent you're used to different standards of living.

Even if your incomes don't differ, your spending styles might. Match a penny-pincher with Ms Splash-it-around and there's bound to be trouble. She's insulted by his 'cheap' gifts; he gives her a hard time for 'wasting' money on designer clothes. Then there's the saving-up-for-a-house-deposit part of the relationship – guaranteed to cause arguments. One of you is 100 per cent committed, taking lunch in a bag to work. The other's still buying three new CDs a week.

Let me give it to you straight: just as matching libidos mean less problems in the bedroom, matching incomes and attitudes to money mean less problems out of it. Unfortunately, Cupid has a nasty habit of shooting arrows into financially non-compatible hearts. Fortunately, there are ways (as always) to solve the problem. The first step is to identify your spending styles and the cause of the fights.

Spending styles of the rich and not-so-rich

The money miser

They'll drive two hours out of their way to get 20p off a packet of biscuits. They don't just watch their finances, they're obsessed with them, tallying up every penny which they hand over (begrudgingly). Usually from homes where money was tight or Mum and Dad were also penny-pinchers, often they'll have the last laugh: while you're still living in a rented, run-down flat, they've bought their second investment property. You, however, had a lot more fun along the way. It costs money to travel, look good, socialize with friends and have a good time.

The overgenerous spender

You bought them a card and piddly bunch of flowers for their birthday; they buy you a TV. You drop in for coffee at their house clutching stale cream buns from the local shop; they drop in for a drink clutching Veuve Clicquot and caviar. Amazingly, they often earn the same as you do. How do they do it? Let's put it this way: entire forests are felled just to print their credit card bills. Usually, their parents splashed money around. Sometimes, it's the opposite: their parents were scrooges and they're totally sick of not having nice things. Overgenerous spenders also tend to equate money with love. The bigger and more expensive the present, the more liked they'll be by the recipient.

The skin-of-their-teeth spender

They're always just a few pounds short of meeting their budget so borrow from friends/family/the bank to make ends meet. They use one credit card to pay off another, have six different personal loans going and, understandably, feel anxious whenever money is mentioned. Living anywhere from slightly to way above what their income allows, they're not prepared to make the lifestyle sacrifices to live within their means because somehow they always scrape through.

Mr or Ms Average

Most bills are paid on time, they've got a little saved up for emergencies and a vague, if optimistic, financial plan for the future. Occasionally they'll splash out on something expensive but pull back on spending for a little while afterward to compensate. They don't tend to have money worries but aren't rich either. Mr and Ms Average make ideal partners. They're sensible with money and likely to be proactive with their finances when they're in a settled relationship and want to buy property.

The money lover

Other kids were kicking a football around; they were on the sidelines selling soft drinks and sweets and creaming off the profits. Fascinated by money, their hobby is watching it grow. They make smart decisions because they research their investments but are prepared to take risks, so get higher returns. Entrepreneurial, they're to be admired if they're not obsessive about it. If they are, the terms 'heartless bastard' and 'shallow' are probably more accurate.

Why couples clash over cash

If you're arguing over money, it's usually because of one of the following:

There's a power inbalance

In plenty of relationships, the person with the money has the power in the relationship. They're seen as the better 'catch'. If they're constantly paying for you, you're constantly thanking them and you're expected to feel eternally grateful and dependent on them for the lifestyle you're leading. In short, you feel like the poor cousin dressed in their hand-me-downs.

You've got mismatched incomes

If one earns way more than the other, it's usual for your lifestyles to also be worlds apart. The simplest decision – like whether to go to the movies on (full-price) Saturday night or wait for (half-price) Tuesday night – causes conflict. Also, the more money you earn, the more likely it is you've developed more expensive taste. The lower earner is used to 'making do' and can't quite understand why it's imperative you serve Beluga caviar when who likes smelly old fish eggs anyway?

You spend at different rates

Even if she does earn a quarter of what you do, she'll spend more in one day than you would in a week. Some combinations of spending styles are disastrous: Overgenerous will bankrupt

Skin-of-the-teeth in a week as they struggle to keep up. Money also has different value depending on your wage. If you're earning £25,000 a year, 'expensive' to you might be a pricey takeaway. If you're on £150,000 a year, 'expensive' might be splashing out on the £150 bottle of wine, rather than the £50 vintage.

Gender-perception problems
He earns less and she still thinks the man should pay (as mentioned above). The obvious answer to solving this one is to have a long, hard think about how important it is to you. If he's got enough other positive qualities to overlook it, do it – and be gracious about it. Don't rub it in or make snide remarks. If you decide you can't accept the situation, do him a favour and stop the relationship so you can search for Mr Money-bags.

Your personalities affect your spending
Some save for a rainy day; others would rather lounge around expensive resorts in the sunshine while they can. Born worriers tend to worry about money: they'll make sure they've got more than enough to cover the impending disasters they're convinced are about to happen. Happy-go-lucky types don't expect bad things to happen to them, so tend not to plan for them.

One of you is more image conscious
A rip-off Rolex watch might be good enough for some; others want the real thing. It's a lot to do with image: wanting to be seen to have all the props of success like the right car, the right clothes. It can also be about reward: if you slog it hard, you want to enjoy at least one benefit which is, of course, the money.

One 'respects' money more than the other
It's the old you-get-what-you-pay-for thing. Some people believe that, others don't. A suit's a suit to some; others believe

the fabric, cut and design of Armani is worth knocking off their mother for. One parent might consider private schooling a waste of money; the other believes the child's education will obviously be better because money buys better teachers and better facilities.

One's a habit spender

This is the most infuriating problem of all for someone who can't relate to addictive personalities. If your partner's a big drinker, smoker, compulsive clothes shopper or thinks nothing of blowing £200 a night at the races, it can feel horribly unfair if a majority of your joint income is going (literally) up in smoke.

Managing money as a couple

If you can identify your spending styles and pinpoint the reason you're arguing over money, you're halfway to solving the problem. Combine that with some practical solutions and it's all but smoothed over.

In the old days, the minute you got married all accounts became joint accounts. These days, most couples keep their own personal accounts and open up joint accounts for shared expenses and/or future goals. It's a nice blend between retaining individuality and working together, and it also allows for different spending styles. (If you both agree on an amount to deposit in the joint account, it doesn't really bother you what they do with the rest of it.) It makes sense to me, so this is the model I've based the following exercise on. If you decide to do it, set aside a few hours for part one: you'll learn a lot about each other, so settle in and enjoy it. Part two is the boring mathematics part. Don't attempt it without a calculator and prepare to be depressed afterward (you earnt *that* much and now have *that* much left? What happened to it all?).

Setting some ground rules

Work out your spending style. Decide which category best describes each of you, referring to the section above. Talk about what influences have made you both this way. If you know your partner's overly careful with money because times were tough during their childhood and they seriously did survive on bread and dripping, you'll be far less inclined to get angry.

Define the problem. See 'Why couples clash over cash' on page 280 and work out which problem best describes your situation. Write down your own version of it. Her side might be: 'I get upset when John wastes money drinking down the pub with the boys because that could be used to put toward a house deposit.' His side might be: 'I resent it when Sarah nags me when I've been out drinking. I know we're saving, but aren't I allowed to relax once in a while?'

Look for underlying reasons. Is the argument *really* about money? In the above scenario, it could be that Sarah interprets John's 'wasting money' as a sign he's not as keen on buying a home together as she is. That makes her nervous about his commitment to the relationship itself ('Doesn't he want a home so we can start a family?'). Couple that with him wanting to drink with the boys instead of be with her and she starts to think, *He'd prefer to be single.* John and Sarah aren't arguing over him wasting money – they're arguing over a commitment issue.

Make a pact to solve fights over money once and for all.
Once you know each other's spending style, you know the
reasons behind it and you've isolated problems that really are
about money, the next step is to work *together* to come up with
a financial compromise that both of you can live with. Write
down how you think you can improve your spending style and
how you think your partner can improve theirs. Then swap lists
and talk it through. Keep talking until you're both happy with
the solutions and, wherever possible, try to meet in the middle.
For example: he wants to buy a £30,000 BMW; you think
a car's to get from A to B and want him to buy a rattly runaround
worth £3,000, putting the rest toward an expensive holiday. The
compromise might be to settle for an average-priced new car
worth £13,000 and a less-expensive holiday destination.

Remember to take into account people's passions. If
fresh flowers once a week make all the difference to her, let her
trade something else. She might cheerfully agree to cut back on
clothes spending to keep her 'indulgence'.

Decide who's best at managing money. They get the job
of being the person in control of the budget. This doesn't mean
the other person hands over their paypacket and closes their
eyes, simply that one's usually better at remembering when
things are due. If you want to share responsibility evenly, set
aside one hour at the same time each week or fortnight to sit
down together to pay bills and revise where you're at.

Decide when you need to check with each other. While
no-one wants to answer to their partner for every pound they
part with, you might like to 'check' on major personal
purchases. Decide what's none of each other's business
(presents for best friends) and what is (a £10,000 stereo system
for the car).

Practical stuff

Do a budget plan. Once you've done all this, you can get down to the nitty-gritty, that is, work out where your money is going and how much is left over. I'd strongly suggest you ask your bank for a budget planner to get the most accurate picture. It's basically a chart which you fill in. On one side, you list your monthly income, on the other what you spend it on. Most planners also include information on how to calculate expenses (wild guesses tend to be pathetically wrong). The budget planners are also great because they remind you to include things like holidays, presents, gym fees, medical expenses. (Not accounting for the 'little things' is why most people blow their budget.) If in doubt of what something costs you, overestimate. Some expenses can't be altered (like electricity), others can (mobile phone bills, daily facials). Decide what both of you are prepared to cut back on.

Set some goals. Do you simply want to free up some cash so you don't both have coronaries when the gas bill arrives or are you saving for a holiday or house deposit? If you're saving for something together, it makes sense to plonk that cash into one account specifically for that purpose. The balance will rise twice as fast and it's a nice bonding exercise.

Make a savings plan. Once you have a good idea of what each of you needs to contribute to cover shared monthly expenses, you'll know how much cash is left over for saving. (If there isn't any, you might like to make an appointment with a financial planner to help you consolidate any debts and manage things more efficiently.)

Decide what accounts you need. Most couples open several joint accounts. The first is to cover shared monthly expenses (electricity, phone, contents insurance), the second is usually a savings account for future goals. If you've got a shared mortgage, that counts as the third. Decide what accounts you need to open and what facilities you require (do you really want cash machine access on the savings account?) – but don't get too carried away. Keep an eye on bank charges.

Decide who contributes what. If you're both on roughly the same income, it makes sense to split things down the middle. If one's on £15,000 and the other £60,000 it doesn't. Make it proportional to be fair.

Check it's liveable. Go through your budgets and make sure they're realistic. Are the amounts you've agreed to contribute fair and attainable? Are you both comfortable with what you're committing to joint accounts?

Consider income protection. Could you afford to support each other if either became ill or lost their job? Would you want to? Income protection will cover your salary for a specified period against unemployment or illness. (Read the fine print very carefully – policies vary hugely.)

Put the plan into action. Open the joint accounts, arrange for the specified amounts to be deducted straight from your existing bank accounts so you don't forget – then sit back and congratulate each other on taking the first step to financial freedom!

MOVING IN AND MARRIAGE

Plenty of people consider marriage an outdated, religious institution that's quaint and cute but pretty irrelevant these days. I mean, all that standing up there before God bit – isn't it a tad old-fashioned for us? Others would crawl on hands and knees for a week to get the chance to play princess for a day and flounce around in a big white dress. Which is best for you? Only you know that – but read these statistics anyway.

About half of all couples play house before getting married. Living together is more popular than marriage – but de facto couples split up quicker, usually in the first year. If you're married you tend to split (if you are going to) within five years. The perception that it's far more sensible to live together before marriage and that you've got a better chance of it lasting if you do isn't backed up by statistics (even if most of us, including me, still believe it). The most recent studies show that if you live together before marriage, you're 50 per cent more likely to divorce than those who don't live together first. But don't rush up the aisle just yet, because it's actually not the living together part that's the problem. It's more that the *type* of people who choose to live together first tend to be less traditional and less likely to believe in marriage as a concept. If you don't have any religious or moral objection to 'living in sin', you're not usually as committed to the institution of marriage and much more likely to leave if you're not happy. Couples who head straight for the altar often stay together just for the sake of 'the marriage' and because they made a vow before God. But although they have less divorces, whether they're *happily* married is another story.

Over 161,000 divorces are granted each year in the UK. People are pretty cynical about marriage and it *is* a little offputting when you know one in three marriages ends in divorce (and that stat's fast moving toward one in two). Just about ready to slit your wrists with that engagement ring? Why not look at it this way: two out of three marriages *do* succeed and who's to say you and your partner won't be one of them?

Convinced you'd make it but your partner's not so sure? More on that and marriage later. First, let's talk about moving in together because the same advice applies even if you do head down the aisle beforehand.

'Let's live together'

You're sick of trying to find something, then realizing it's at *their* place. You're tired of carrying a change of underwear around in a plastic bag. Suddenly it seems like a complete waste of money to be paying two lots of rent when you're spending every night at each other's place anyway. You love each other, the idea forms and then it's said out loud: 'Perhaps,' one of you says tentatively, 'we should think about finding a place together.'

Break out the champagne – you've officially moved the relationship forward about six million paces. But don't be too hasty: there's much more to moving in than finding a place to move into. Like, are you really sure you're ready to give up the courting bit just yet? 'One minute, we were dating – I'd doll myself up, he'd arrive on the doorstep with flowers – the next, we were flopped on the couch eating takeaways with greasy hair,' says Anna. 'We fast-forwarded through those fizzy, sparky bits into domesticity. I felt ripped off. I know it would have happened eventually, but it happened too fast.'

Thinking of getting married after years of living together? If you're doing it because all your friends are, your friends and family want you to, you think it'll fix your relationship problems or simply because you want to have kids, you're on the way to joining the 50 per cent of couples who split within five years once they become Mr and Mrs.

He sees you plastered in night cream instead of make-up; you see him out of his suit and trimming his toenails. Hardly the stuff of lust but all part of being human beings who can't look or act perfect all of the time. (One word of warning: don't get *too* comfortable together. It's okay to pull on the tracksuit some of the time but break out the glad rags occasionally.)

Apart from noticing what slobs you both are, you'll also notice a loss of privacy. It's one thing going out and spending just about all your time at each other's place. It's quite another officially moving in. Before, if you felt irritable or tired and fancied a night by yourself, you simply stayed home. Give up your own place and there *is* no time out from the relationship.

The first week or two of living together is heaven. You

throw a house-warming party, feel all grown up, cook lavish meals for each other, snuggle in at night. Then you move into the 'who left the cap off the toothpaste' period and it's *hell*. There's a massive adjustment period for both of you. You might think you're 'one' but in reality, you're two individuals with different ideas on how to run a house and your lives. You'll fight about the housework, sex, general cleanliness, moan about money and who takes the rubbish out. Each of you will be struggling for power, trying to be the one who's boss. Which is one reason why I wouldn't suggest either of you move into the other's house unless it's so wonderful you'd need your heads read to give it up. Finding a new place together, with both names on the lease, puts it on an even power keel. 'It seemed obvious to move in with Maryanne because her place was bigger,' says Matt, 24. 'But I never ever felt like it was my home because it had always been hers. I think she also found it difficult because she was so used to living in the flat alone.'

Prepare, also, for a change in your sex life as first-time flatmates. Your sex life could improve dramatically once you move in – or fall in a big heap! 'After years of sneaking around corners – hiding from his flatmate or my parents – to finally be able to have sex somewhere other than bed was a fantasy come true,' says Leonie. 'Our sex life definitely improved when we moved in simply because we were free to make love when and where we wanted to.' Others couples feel somewhat differently. 'Jess and I definitely had more sex before we moved in because we'd grab the chance whenever we could. Now we know we can have it every night – and that's sometimes a huge turn-off,' says Jake.

This whole chapter talks about practical ways to sort out moving-in matters like housework and money, but I suspect you'll need to read the entire book to get through all the tough parts. *Expect* to argue, *expect* to feel resentful, sulky and irritable for the first little while and you won't be disillusioned. Give it a good four months before throwing in the towel (in the laundry basket, please!): it really does take that long to settle in. (Desperate to give it a go but unsure of how to suggest it? Read how to bring up 'The "m" word' on page 292 – the advice applies to living together as well. If you've been ready for *ages* and your partner's not sure, read the commitment section in Chapter 3, page 147.)

Here are some things you might like to think about *before* rushing straight to the real estate agent, pens poised to sign a shared lease. If you can't agree on issues like this before you move in, you haven't got a hope afterward.

- **Spell out very clearly what moving in means to each of you.** Is it for convenience and a temporary thing? Is it because you want to spend the rest of your lives together? Is it a trial run to marriage? If it is, how long do you want to live together before tying the knot? Personally, I wouldn't advise moving in with someone unless the intention is to move the relationship a stage further on. If it's money problems that are forcing you to move in, get a flatmate – that's what you're truly after. It takes great tolerance to live with someone else and cope with all their personal habits. It's difficult enough when you're madly in love, let alone when you barely even like each other.

- **What furniture do each of you have?** Can you stand living with each other's stuff? If one person's got designer taste and the other mismatched hand-me-downs, will you feel resentful? If the bad-taste partner doesn't mind, whack the not-so-nice stuff in storage for a year or so (and good luck deciding which of you has the bad taste). Don't sell it until then: you never know, it may not work out and that bright purple coffee table might come in handy.

- **Decide on what you need to buy and who's going to foot the bill.** It's romantic to go halves on things like fridges and sofas, but a complete pain to split it all up if it doesn't work out. Instead, write down the items you need to buy and split the list. You buy the fridge, he buys the telly. You buy the dinner service, he buys the saucepans. If it doesn't work out, you take whatever you bought and there's no messy arguments over who owns what. If you're really sensible, you'll make a list of all your possessions, including books and CDs, before you move in. It's easy to forget who originally owned what.

- **How will you split expenses?** See 'Money matters' on page 276. Differing money styles can cause a few arguments when you're just going out, but neither of you have the right to criticize. Once you've moved in or start buying shared possessions, however, who's stashing cash and who's blowing it is important.
- **Can you afford to live together?** Sit down together and talk about your existing financial commitments. Can you both *afford* to split expenses evenly? Work out a budget plan (again, see above, page 285). It doesn't matter whether you plan to keep separate accounts or not – household and entertainment expenses still have to be shared.
- **How will you split the household chores?** See 'Hassles over housework' on page 263.
- **How will you handle friends and visitors?** Are you the sort of person who craves time alone while they're the social type? Do you have friends who are prone to drop in for a coffee, stay for hours and maybe even crash the night? How does the other partner feel about it? Set some rules for friends and visitors and stick to them.

The 'm' word

If I could give you one piece of advice about marriage it would be this: make sure you both go into it knowing what the other wants out of it. Have a good, long talk about your expectations of marriage. How being married will be different from the relationship you have now. In other words: what does marriage mean to each of you? *Don't* just assume you know because you've been living together for ten years.

Something happens to people when they get married. Everyone has preconceived ideas of how a 'husband' and 'wife' should behave. What was acceptable for you to do as a girlfriend – wear miniskirts, be independent, have a great career – might not be acceptable once you're his wife. And vice versa. She'll put up with boozy nights with the boys from a boyfriend, but a husband? That's different.

> ❶ *The term 'settle down and get married' is truer than you think. Men's levels of testosterone (the hormone which contributes to aggressive, dominating behaviour) test high when they're single, drop when married and rise again on divorce. Other research shows alcohol and drug use decline in both sexes after marriage, probably because it encourages a sense of responsibility. Live-in lovers don't alter their lifestyle habits and neither marriage nor moving in stops smokers lighting up.*

It's also extremely sensible to talk through your attitudes to parenthood and if you both want to be parents. If one's anti the idea, it could be the result of a less than idyllic childhood: a few counselling sessions could banish any baby blues. If they don't want children because they're committed to a career, it might just be the timing that's off. But if after long and rational discussions, you're still vehemently arguing for opposite outcomes, reconsider your long-term compatibility. To have or not to have children is an emotive issue that can unglue the closest couple.

Another hot tip from someone who's been there, done that:

don't kid yourself it's the same as living together and if it doesn't work out it'll be just as easy to walk out. It isn't. It's hard splitting up when you've been living together – it's devastating when a marriage fails. You don't just have to separate your lives and your hearts, you have to separate legally: handle the pain of filling in those divorce papers (which include delightful questions like 'Who ended the marriage?' – not a great feeling when your spouse has already ticked 'She did'); you might need to change your name back, make property settlements, sort out the mortgage. You can't just divide up your possessions and get on with your lives – it's a long, drawn-out, intensely emotional process to untangle once you've said 'I do'.

Sorry to sound negative but I'm trying to save both of you from being hurt. For this reason, don't get married because your parents want you to. Don't get married because all your friends are. Don't get married because you've been together for ages and it seems like the logical next step. Don't get married because your partner's pressuring you or even if you want kids together. Get married for these reasons instead: you are both convinced you love each other, for all the right reasons; you're both convinced you want the same things from marriage and can live up to each other's expectations; and the relationship's lasted long enough for you to be sure of all this. In short, you can't imagine being happy without them by your side. Phew! Now I can say congratulations!

WILL THEY EVER ASK?

There's one other thing you need to get married: a proposal. These range from the partner on one knee, serenading violins and diamond ring popped in a glass of champagne variety to the '"I suppose we should get married," muttered while you're climbing into your jammies about to go to sleep' sort. If ➤

neither are happening to you and you'd like it to, how do you bring up the subject of marriage without feeling like a desperate twit? I'm going to address this section to women, since it's still usually men who do the asking-to-marry bit, despite so-called equality. But I want to make something clear first: there's a perception out there that women get more out of marriage than men do. I'd have to agree women probably get more excited about the wedding *day*, but once all the hoo-ha dies down, men actually get a lot more from marriage than women do. Most surveys show the two happiest groups of people are single women and married men. Men are also much more likely to want to stay married. In one survey, husbands and wives were asked if they'd marry each other again, knowing what they do now. Fifty-six per cent of women said yes, compared to 71 per cent of men. Married men drink less, take fewer risks and live longer than single men. Men take much longer to get over a divorce than women do. Ironic isn't it? Here you are reading this, hoping it'll result in him on bended knee, when he's the one who's most likely to benefit from it.

Anyway, here's my advice on working out where your partner's head is regarding marriage, without losing dignity.

• **First, look at your own motives for the conversation.** Are you bringing this up because you want some idea for the future or because you want a commitment NOW? If you'd simply like some feedback because you're curious and deciding whether to hang around long term, just say, 'I was reading a story/watching a TV show and it started me thinking about relationships. What do you think about marriage? Can you see yourself doing it someday?' Get some feedback, then switch topics ASAP. If you want to continue the discussion make it very clear you're talking about marriage in theory, not the two of you skipping off into the sunset.

You're hoping the discussion will end with a proposal? Check you're up for it before going any further. Are you ➤

really ready for this? Have you been together at least two years? Are you wanting it for the right reasons? Do you honestly think your life will be enriched 20 years on from now by being with this person? Do you honestly believe they feel the same way about you? Once you're satisfied *you're* sure, work out your own theories on why they haven't asked you already, before putting your partner on the spot. That way you're prepared and able to talk logically rather than emotionally about the issue. Be honest with yourself. Could it be they haven't asked you to marry them because they're not ready or not sure?

• **Introduce the topic.** Personally, I'd be up-front about this one. You're better off being honest than sending out subtle signals. For a start, most men don't pick up on subtleties, so all that gazing in shop windows while holding his hand is useless. He's checking out the sports watches, not the solitaire diamonds. If you know each other well and talk openly and honestly (and if you don't, you're not ready to make plans for next Christmas, let alone the rest of your life) wait until you're having a particularly good time together and introduce the topic generally. Start with the same point I mentioned previously – something like, 'I was reading a story/watching a TV show and it started me thinking about relationships. What do you think about marriage? Can you see yourself doing it someday?' But this time, follow it up with, 'Have you ever thought about *us* getting married?'

His response will be one of three. The first: absolute horror. If he shoots you a 'you've got to be kidding' look, forget it – and him if you want commitment. This guy's either deleted the 'm' word from his vocabulary or you're definitely not his idea of Ms Right. The second reaction is one of confusion. He hasn't really thought about it but that doesn't mean he won't in the future. All you need to say then is, 'I'd like you to think about it because I'd like to know where we're heading.' Unless you're planning on doing the ➢

proposing yourself, drop the subject right there. Let him think about it for a few months and see if he wants to take it further.

If you've been together for ages, the third reaction is probably the one you'll get: he has considered it but he's not ready right now because of – whatever reason he has. Resist the urge to jump straight in with, 'Oh, for God's sake, that's ridiculous! I don't care if you haven't finished your law degree/built up a bank balance/still live with your mother. Let's do it anyway,' because it really doesn't matter how trivial *you* think the reason is, it's important to *him*. You'll get a lot further with, 'I understand where you're coming from but just for the record, it's not important to me.' If you're prepared to wait for whatever it is he's waiting for, again, stop it there. If you're not, you'll need to add another sentence onto the previous statement: 'And John, I'm really not happy to put our plans on hold for another five years, so could we talk about this further?' Have the discussion, then:

• **Ask for a time frame** of when he'll be ready to commit, then set your own – the maximum amount of time you'll wait for him. Tell your boyfriend you're giving him six months, a year, whatever, to make up his mind. Don't issue it as an ultimatum; simply say, 'John, we've been going out three years now and I'm asking you for a serious commitment. I love you but marriage is important to me. I'm prepared to wait another [whatever] but then I'd like an answer.' Drop the subject but stick to the deadline.

• **Mark the date in your diary** and let him know a week or two before D-day. If he comes up with a good reason not to commit then, you might want to reconsider. Then it's up to you to decide whether he's worth another wait or not. If you decide he is, mark another date in your diary and make it your personal deadline. Tell him. If he won't commit then and you still need that commitment, it's time to move on. You've given it your best shot but it just isn't going to happen. Hang around after that, and you could be waiting for ever.

AND ONE MAKES THREE: KIDS

In our grandparents' day, no-one asked questions and just about everyone popped out at least one child by their second anniversary. One minute, the radiant virgin bride, the next, a housewife elbow-deep in dirty nappies and formula. The concept of 'waiting' to have children was alien. After all, what were you waiting *for*? Most women didn't work; those that did couldn't wait to escape the mundane tedium of a boring job. Travel was a luxury, and simply postponing motherhood to enjoy your partner and marriage was unheard of. 'If you could have babies, you did,' says my Mum, who was pregnant with twins by 21. 'No-one thought about putting it off for the sheer enjoyment of life. No-one ever, ever talked about how difficult and disruptive children are – which is why we all got the shock of our lives when the babies actually arrived.'

Modern women approach motherhood warily. Not only do we have lots of life options, the mere mention of children is often greeted with a tirade aimed at convincing us *not* to succumb to the maternal urge. As a new mum, you'll not only have no sleep, no time, no money and no sex, your career will be in ruins and your marriage a mess! The truth is, parenthood *is* a time of emotional turbulence when everything from sleeping and who does the groceries becomes renegotiable and ripe for argument. Which is one reason why many couples postpone it until they feel they – and the relationship – are mature enough to withstand the pressure.

It's also true that having a child enriches your existence in ways you can't begin to imagine. I've never had a child but I do have a niece and nephew who make my heart pound whenever they say 'Aunty Trace'. Looking into their faces, I believe those stories about mothers suddenly possessing superhuman strength and lifting cars off trapped children. Even the most harrassed Mum has told me one smile can make weeks of torment seem worth it. The joy of being a woman nowadays is you get to weigh up the good and the bad and choose what's right for you and when. Not only can you decide not to have children until much later in life – you can also decide not to have them at all. About the only thing that isn't flexible is this: once they arrive, there's no turning back. Children will alter your life utterly and irrevocably. So, if you're thinking of taking the plunge, read on. It ain't *just* about standing side by side with sloppy grins on your faces, watching the little one sleep.

The first shock: a brand new partner

You'll notice changes in your relationship the moment you break the happy news. Anxious fathers-to-be are prone to lecture on how you should be treating your body: frowning if you so much as *look* at a glass of wine, overloading your plate with 'food for two', tut-tutting if you dare to eat a curry ('Don't you realize it upsets the baby?'). Your sex life alters. Many couples report no change for the first few months of pregnancy (here's some good news: plenty say orgasms are deeper and more intense). But when the baby grows larger, intercourse becomes uncomfortable and he starts to worry he'll 'hurt the baby'. He looks at you differently as you change from lover to mother. Then, of course, there's the labour – an experience guaranteed to turn him off sex for at least a few months. For many men, watching their wives writhe about in agony is harrowing and upsetting – even if the moment of birth *does* rate as the best in their life. 'I must admit I felt really strange about Anna after the birth,' confides Steve, proud dad of a six-month-old baby. 'Before, well . . . I'd only go down there for pleasure. Then, I'm down there and there's a baby coming out of it. Her vagina changed from a place that gave me great pleasure to a place where babies came from.'

Once the baby's born, you're loath to leave him or her with just anyone, so may not get the time or opportunity to talk through all these things together and share common fears. Arranging to be alone a few months in – even if it's just for a drink and a quick dinner – can work wonders to revive your relationship and your sex life.

The next shock: where did my life go?

'Mick and I haven't had a decent conversation in months. Before Billy was born, we'd sit out on the balcony and have a glass of wine while we talked about our day. Now when he comes through the door, I push Billy at him and race around doing the million things I'd planned to do that day and couldn't,' says Jenny, a 34-year-old management consultant who's been married seven years. 'Everyone warned us our relationship wasn't going to be as flexible. But we had no idea just how much it would change.'

Jenny put off having children until she was in her mid-thirties because she was worried about the inevitable loss of independence, automony and freedom that having kids would cause. 'I liked the world I was in: ordered, organized, child-free. We had such a nice lifestyle.' Remember those fabulous, impromptu weekends away? Late-night movies, stimulating dinner parties, popping down to the local café for a cappuccino mid-morning on Sunday? Hell, remember being able to go to the loo on your own and relax for two minutes? Hold on to those memories because, if you have kids, that's all they'll be for a while. The longer you've become accustomed to a luxurious dual-income, no-kids lifestyle, the longer you're likely to put off having children. Which really isn't such a bad thing. A good marriage needs a strong foundation and a few years child-free, when the two of you can enjoy each other and live life to the full, certainly helps keep things on solid ground when you do decide to turn two into three. Besides, unless you've married in your forties, there's plenty of time to hear that pitter-patter later on.

Becoming parents

Having a child dredges up a lot of unconscious feelings about our own parents and hidden expectations about what being a parent means. 'Suddenly John wasn't my husband but a *father* and little things that didn't bother me before took on immense importance. Everything from his erratic driving to watching sport took on new meaning,' says 26-year-old Mandy. The fact is, all of us have deeply ingrained ideas about how mothers and fathers should act – one very good reason to find out each other's opinions *before* you have children, rather than after, when emotions are raw.

You'll both feel very confused in your first few months of parenthood. You may be unsure of your ability to be a good parent (you're having enough trouble bathing the child without drowning it, let alone guiding it through life, while he's just getting the hang of picking her up properly and already panicking like mad about how to explain the facts of life). Often, you won't feel love or that magic 'maternal bond' for months, until your child develops a personality. Many parents find that quite alarming. While you're coping with these emotions privately, too scared to admit them to your partner, he's feeling left out. Men are often cast aside (quite necessarily) and may resent the attention and affection you're lavishing on your child. You resent him because his life really doesn't seem to have altered at all while yours has been put in the washing machine on a never-ending spin cycle. Your roles have changed dramatically and the transition – however temporary – from equals to carer and provider isn't easy. 'Whatever you argued about before, you'll argue about even more,' warns one new mum. 'Except all the old arguments now become centred around the baby.'

You may also find your friendships changing. Suddenly, you understand the automatic bond parents have with other parents and start to see less of childless friends who don't understand the expense of baby-sitters and the fact that although you once raged all night long, now you need to be in bed by 10 pm because the baby wakes up around the same time you used to go to bed. You may also feel lonely during the day – especially if you were the consummate career girl and all your friends work. They're out there getting ahead while you're at home pushing a stroller and feeling awfully left behind.

> 'Since our baby was born, I tend to think about my wife a lot more. My love has grown – it's almost like I'm getting in touch with my emotional side. It's a different type of love, one that includes more respect for everything she has gone through.'
> Adam, 36, stockbroker

Kids and careers

'I used to run an office of 40 without any problems at all – now I can't organize to get myself and the baby down to the local shops without bursting into tears,' says my friend Jenny, struggling to open a pack of disposable nappies with a child on her hip. 'No-one tells you how useless you feel. My self-confidence is shot.' Careers are a source of satisfaction, identity and self-confidence and giving this up can be terrifying for some women. It may also be the first time you've had to be dependent on your partner and the first time you've not felt in control of your life.

Your career – and where you are in it – is often the major factor determining when you'll have children. As a rule of thumb, if you're planning to have one at all, it's generally best to postpone having kids until you've at least earned yourself some sort of reputation. The longer you've been in your job, the better your chances of returning to the workforce. But it's hard to say which is the hardest: giving up your job completely for a few years after a child or going back to it within a few weeks or months. For many career women, returning to work seems the most attractive option, but it's difficult. Quite apart from childcare problems, just when the child starts to become interesting, it's time to leave them. You may feel confused and not sure you're doing the 'right thing' by your child. If, on the other hand, all you're dreaming of are baby-free days back in the office, you'll feel guilty for different reasons. Either way, that first week back in the office is likely to be awful. You'll either feel jealous of the person who's looking after your child and wish you were at home or question what sort of mum you are if it gets to 5 pm and you haven't given the baby a thought.

There's also the stress of money worries. Having a baby is horrendously expensive. Not only have you been reduced to one income (even if temporarily), you've had to fork out for a cot and changing table, then dug deeper for a stroller, pram and baby seats for the car. Not to mention nappies, baby clothes, potties, formula, baby food, toys, books, babysitters and childcare.

Not working also has an effect on your relationship with your partner. If you're ambitious and adored your job but agreed to take time out to stay home and look after the baby, it can be frustrating to see your partner getting ahead while you're feeling left behind. Your end of day conversations are different. They've been out there in the 'real world', mixing with all sorts of people; you've been home alone mixing up formula. You hear yourself saying, 'Marjorie and I took the babies to the park,' and feel like a Fifties housewife. Which makes you wonder if he sees you as one. After all, you're no longer the sexy, go-getting career girl, dashing out the door with briefcase in one hand, make-up bag in the other. You're a mummy: incapable of dashing anywhere with a baby on one hip and the six tons of baby paraphernalia you now have to lug around.

If the whole parenting thing's starting to sound expensive, restricting and overwhelming, you're right – it is! Which is why you shouldn't even think about it unless you're prepared to make all these sacrifices. So think long and hard about the ifs before you even start on the whens.

> **More and more men are opting to swap the suit for an apron and stay at home to look after the kids. In 1997, more than 33,700 Australian men were the primary carers for their kids. Why the shift? Unemployment, wives who earn more money and choice.**

Tick, tock: that's your clock

A woman's fertile life peaks at 25, then declines *slowly* for the next ten years, gathering speed after that. At 24, it takes an average of six menstrual cycles to fall pregnant, at 34 it can take ten. Both these figures are averages which means you could fall pregnant after one month's unprotected intercourse at 39 while your 22-year-old sister tries for four years. The only problem with being older is that if you do strike fertility problems, there's less time to sort them out.

As we get older, our eggs get older and our hormones are less efficient. You might have a problem with cervical mucus (which stops the sperm passing successfully through the cervix to meet with the waiting egg) and may not ovulate every cycle. You might also have been a victim of diseases like endometriosis and pelvic inflammatory disease – both can cause infertility at any age – or your partner might have a low sperm count. The risk of chromosomal abnormality (like Downs Syndrome) rises with each year after 35, and prenatal screening by amniocentesis is routinely offered to women over this age, sometimes women over 30. Amniocentesis is a procedure which takes a sample of the amniotic fluid around the foetus. You usually have to wait until the third or fourth month of pregnancy before having the test which makes the decision of whether or not to go full-term very traumatic. Older mothers are also more likely to be affected by high blood pressure and diabetes, have longer than average labours, inductions or Caesareans. In vitro fertilization – IVF – is an option but it's costly, time-consuming and physically and emotionally exhausting. Having said all that, putting off children till your mid to late thirties really isn't a problem if you've had no major gynaecological problems. Plenty of gynaecologists will be more than happy to reassure you that you're not putting yourself or your baby at risk. And if you are thinking of delaying having children there are ways to protect your fertility as much as possible. Keep fit and generally healthy. Don't smoke, keep alcohol to a minimum, avoid taking prescription drugs unnecessarily, exercise regularly and eat a varied diet. If you're single, use condoms every single time. The more people you have unprotected sex with, the more chance you've got of picking up sexually transmittable, fertility-damaging diseases like pelvic inflammatory disease. Find a good gynaecologist early in life and stick with them for regular Pap smears and general check-ups.

Once you've done all you can to protect your fertility for as long as possible, try really hard to stop panicking. Take a look around you and you'll see plenty of mums who've managed to produce a small army after age 35 or later. Even if you *are* the wrong side of 35, it's still not a terribly good idea to let your biological clock dictate your relationships. Sure, it's tempting. You celebrate your thirty-eighth birthday, shed a few tears with a girlfriend, sobbing, 'Oh God! I still haven't found anyone and time's running out,' then you start dating some semi-decent guy you'd have ditched in the past and your mind plays tricks on you. You think, *He is nice. Maybe what I'm looking for doesn't exist, so he'll do. He's responsible, dependable, he'd make a great Dad*, and before you know it, you're up the aisle and up the duff. The problem with all this is that, while you might adore the children you create together, it sort of helps if you adore the father as well. Children link you for ever, and divorces and break-ups are even more messy and painful when there are children involved. So you've got two choices if you've hooked up with the wrong person: live a miserable life together or bring up the children on your own. Which is probably what you should have done in the first place. If you're *that* keen on having children, time is running out and you're not in a relationship, my advice would be to consider a sperm donor rather than 'make do' with a man you don't love.

Another point I want to make is this: when and if to have children is a huge decision and not one anyone else should or can make for you. If you're still happily playing the field in your late thirties with no great desire to 'settle down' yet, don't let family or friends change your mind for you. Settle down when *you* want to. If you don't end up finding your perfect partner until it's way too late, well, that's a shame but it's not the end of the world. Plenty of people have happy lives and great relationships without reproducing.

Don't be pressured by existing partners or well-meaning friends and family when you're *in* a happy relationship either. The right time to have children with your partner is when *both* of you agree it's the right time. Fall 'accidentally' pregnant to a partner who's not ready or doesn't want children, and you risk your relationship. At the very least, you – and the child – are going to be the focus of resentment. It's him that's keen but you're not? Explain the reason why you're not ready, say when or if you will be, then keep talking until you can reach a compromise which both of you are happy with. If you can't, you might need to get some couples counselling or admit you've both got separate dreams and separate.

THE PLUSES OF HAVING KIDS EARLY

- Your body is in peak condition and carrying and coping with the baby will be easier on you physically.
- You're at peak fertility and able to fall pregnant easily and with little fuss.
- You get to 'grow up' with your children so you may find it easier to relate to them because you're closer in age.
- By the time the kids are grown up and off your hands, you'll be young enough to enjoy your freedom and do something with it rather than simply retire.

THE PLUSES OF HAVING THEM LATE

- You're more established in your career so your chances of re-entering the workforce on a high level are better.
- You're financially better off and able to give your child a good education without skimping on your own lifestyle.
- You've had a chance to enjoy each other child-free and your relationship is more likely to withstand the pressures of parenting.
- You're mature enough to handle being a parent.
- You're unlikely to feel like you've 'missed out' on all the fun things in life because you've accomplished a lot of your goals (like travel or a nice house) already.

THE STATISTICS

Relationships expert Maryon Tysoe cites one study which looked at marriage a year after the birth of a first baby. The couples were asked to rate how satisfactory their marriages were. For about 60 per cent of the couples, the child did little or no marital harm. But about 40 per cent reported a damaging effect on their sex life. There's other evidence to suggest that, on average, marital happiness is lower when there are children in the home. This doesn't mean it's going to happen to *you*, but you're sticking your head in the sand if you don't expect some rough spots.

'Sex? Did someone say sleep?'

What really happens to your love life when you've had a child?

My girlfriend Tina was determined to be the sexiest mum around. 'So many people said to me, "After kids, it's just not the same," eyes averted in a way that suggests the subject is closed. I was determined to prove them wrong. I worried about sleep deprivation, whether I'd ever be able to fit into my Morrissey miniskirt, how having a baby would affect my career. But I never, ever worried about sex because we were such sexual creatures, my husband and I, I didn't imagine anything could take that away.'

And then the baby arrived. Turns out Tina did fit into her mini after a few months but 'who the hell wants to wear a mini after having a kid? All I wanted to do was slob around in trackpants and a T-shirt stained with baby vomit. I hadn't shaved my legs in three months. I didn't know when I'd last had sex and who bloody cared, anyway?'

Having a child creates a violent upheaval in your sex life. A bouncing baby (emphasis on the word bouncing) is incredibly demanding. Ask any mother how her sex life is three months after the first child and she'll look at you, dazed and bewildered and mutter something like, 'Sleep? Can I go to sleep now?' Things do return to normal but it takes effort and a very long time.

It's not surprising neither of you is sprinting to the bedroom when the magic six-week abstinence period is over. You're both tired, she's sore from breastfeeding, both of you are confused about your new roles, she's teary and anxious from all the hormones racing around her body: sizzling between the sheets is about as appealing as wanting to go to an all-night rave party.

No sane women is dying for sex when she's had two hours sleep in six weeks. The gyno says it's okay to do it, but her body is still recovering from expelling (let's face it) something the size of a small watermelon. Post-pregnancy haemorrhoids, hot flushes, lubrication problems, scarring from an episiotomy or a vaginal tear – like, *hullo!* These are hardly lust-inspiring conditions. A tummy that never quite goes flat, varicose veins, breasts that swelled magnificently during pregnancy and now shrink to the size of grapes – changes like that don't make you *feel* very sexy either. Add a child that needs your attention 24 hours a day, seven days a week and you can see why lots of couples don't resume a regular sex life until a year after the birth. Even then, it's hardly like the old days. Bang goes spontaneity and the freedom to bonk in the lounge room. Weird things happen: like, your child seems to have been born with a well-tuned sex radar. 'It's uncanny,' says a friend of mine ruefully. 'Babies can sense an erection six rooms away. If sex even *vaguely* seeps into your subconscious, they pick up on it and wake up, cry, throw up – do *anything* to demand your attention.'

I don't know about you but even researching this makes me wonder if it's all worth it! But there is good news. Plenty of couples get through all the angst to rediscover a new, improved sex life. To up your chances, try doing the following:

- **Do Kegel exercises to tone your vagina.** During childbirth, both the cervix and the vagina stretch. The cervix narrows and firms up again after about seven days but the vagina needs pelvic floor exercises to tighten the muscle. Your gynaecologist can advise you on how to do Kegels or refer to any good sex book.
- **Don't stress about it.** Pretty well all mums lose the desire for sex after having a baby.
- **If you don't want sex, talk.** Your partner's feeling strange too. He's sharing you with someone else and is probably feeling left out because no matter how involved he is, there's a bond between mother and baby that he can't

SERIAL MONOGAMY: THE WAY OF THE FUTURE?

There's a relationship pattern emerging which might well become the norm: serial monogamy. Serial monogamists spend years with one person in a committed, monogamous relationship, split, then start another, split, then start another. Instead of matching with one person for life, they might have five or six serious, long-term relationships, which might well include a marriage to provide security when having children.

In a sense, most of us already are serial monogamists. Few people commit to marriage without a few long-term relationships under their belt. Plenty of others try hard to stay with one person but end up serial monogamists by default: they start relationships thinking they'll last a lifetime, then when that doesn't work out, they try again.

The difference between true serial monogamy and a series of relationship blunders is the intention behind the partnerships. A serial monogamist believes *all* relationships have a use-by date. 'If I'm lucky,' they figure, 'I'll get a good ten years of true happiness out of it.' They don't go into the relationship thinking it will last a lifetime, they *expect* it will end after a period of years. In a sense, it's taking the in-love-with-love phenomenon even further. Lots of people leave relationships when real life kicks in and the fun falling-in-love bit is over. Serial monogamists take it a few stages forward: they move ahead into true commitment and leave when contentment gives way to habit. It probably *is* impossible to maintain a very high level of marital satisfaction over a lifetime together. And if that's what we're after (and it seems most of us are), this is certainly the solution.

One part of me believes serial monogamy is sensible. The other part rebels against it. For a start, it's unlikely both of you will decide you've reached the use-by date for the relationship at the same point, so it won't stop people getting hurt. Secondly, while being in raptures over your partner does feel fabulous, there's something to be said ➢

for pleasant companionship based on shared history. At 50, not everyone wants to go through the drama of moving house, splitting possessions, jumping on the love rollercoaster and starting all over again with someone new. It takes energy. Most of us are knackered by 30 – God knows how we'll feel 20 years on. Last but not least, every time a relationship fails – even if you do split amicably – a little part of your heart and soul go with that person.

There's a difference between being dumped after a few months and being dumped after ten years. I've got several long-term relationships under my belt, including a marriage, and although I'm quite sure none were meant to last for ever, I certainly hope it's not a pattern I'm destined to repeat for the rest of my life. I'd rather give all my heart to one person for good than hand over a slice of it once a decade. Perhaps you agree with me.

share. Assure him that your libido and sex life will return, that it's not gone for ever. Be loving and affectionate and let him know he's as important as the baby is.

- **Avoid intercourse initially and concentrate on gentle oral and manual stimulation.** Keep up the massages, long baths together – even if you don't feel like sex, you can do sensual things.
- **Experiment with new positions.** What you enjoyed previously might have altered. Try side by side and use bucketloads of water-based lubricant: breastfeeding drains the body of oestrogen which can cause vaginal dryness.
- **Book a weekend away, minus the baby**, six months in and one year on. The first weekend, you'll probably drop the bags on the floor and sleep for two days solid. One year in, gently re-explore what you enjoyed previously.

- **Plan time for sex.** If you can dump the child with family or friends for an hour or two on weekends, do it. Be selfish about your sex life. Give it priority. Have sex even if you're not champing at the bit for it: once you start being stimulated, you'll probably be glad you did.
- **Turn your attitude around.** So you've only got three minutes to make love? Great! Turn it into a raunchy quickie.
- **Give it time.** It takes a while to make the transition from two-of-you to three-of-you.

THE SMALL STUFF: TRIVIAL BUT STILL AS IRRITATING AS HELL

If your partner's just drained the joint bank account and disappeared to the nearest casino, you feel (and are) totally justified in ranting, raving and generally behaving like a rabid dog while simultaneously packing your bags. But, somehow, turning up to your parents' house with an overnight bag saying, 'I found one too many crisp packets shoved down the couch,' doesn't evoke the same sympathy. Still, beware those petty, annoying little grievances: they have a nasty habit of piling up, one on top of the other, until the whole lot topples and the relationship falls in a heap. It might seem unimportant and nit-picking on your part, but if you also know if they don't stop doing it, you'll go completely nuts, it's worth fixing. Now.

Slob versus neat freak

While you don't expect the slob to plump up cushions, wet towels dumped on top of your drycleaning turn you into The Shrew. The secret to domesticating a slob? A simple storage system that a child could manage. Make it as easy as humanly possible for them to be neat and they might just fall for it. Shoe organizers, no-fuss tie-racks, huge lidless laundry hampers and toss-it-all-in shower caddies should keep the bathroom and bedroom in order. As for the rest of the house, compromise: the neat freak fights the urge to wipe under their coffee cup, the slob should at least lend a hand to clean up the mess they've created before turning in for the night.

'I can't believe you're wearing *that*!'

Their dress sense is either outrageously inappropriate or does nothing for them. She turns up to an important work function in a gold lurex miniskirt and bright red bra. He turns up to meet your girlfriends looking like he rolled around in the gutter on the way. A bit of devious planning can fix this one fast. Ridiculing your partner will just make them defensive: instead, buy an item of clothing as a gift. Don't make it too far from their natural style, just a more tasteful version of it. Start by replacing whatever item you hate the most. If his jeans have creases down the front, buy a pair of bog-standard Levis. If she wears skin-tight tops slit to the navel, choose a top in a slinky fabric that shows off her curves without revealing them.

The next step is to take them shopping. Get them to try on things they wouldn't normally and they might well see themselves in a different light. Lots of people with bad dress sense don't know what suits them so they give up before they even start. With a bit of help and a few compliments, they might well get the hang of it.

But what about a partner who insists on policing your wardrobe and telling you what to wear? If it's your boyfriend, he'll try to influence you in one of two ways: get you to cover up or reveal more. If he's asking you to dress less sexy, he's worried you're too attractive to other men. The guy who wants your hemlines higher and neckline lower is suffering from the 'look what I can pull' phenomenon. You've become the outward representation of his sexual prowess.

Girlfriends influence their partners for different reasons: they're more interested in turning you into the man they secretly wish you were. If she wants you to dress up – swap the Mambo gear for suits – she wants you to be more ambitious and financially successful (or at least appear to be). If she wants you to dress down, she'd like you to be a little more laid back and not so uptight.

While it's healthy to pull on outfits you know your partner loves, feeling nervous about their approval every time you get dressed means it's gone too far. Ask a trusted friend if your dress sense really is *that* bad. If it is, see an image consultant. Decide if your partner really is trying to help or trying to turn you into someone you're not. There's a huge difference between giving a partner some guidelines for things like family functions or work dinners and constantly ridiculing. If they do, refuse to even buy into the discussion. Shrug and say, 'Oh well, *I* like it.' If they continue to harass you, challenge them head on. Say, 'Excuse me? I can't believe you said that. Are you really telling me what I can wear and what I can't?' If they won't shut up after that, ship out.

Turn it up – turn it down

You need quiet time, they like noise. If you'd rather wake up slowly to the sounds of nature and he opens his eyes and automatically turns the radio up full blast, you start each day irritable with each other. Equally as annoying are people who always have the TV blaring even when they're not watching it, when you're a curl-up-and-read person. Again, it's all about compromise. Put a TV in the bedroom so they can watch it without disturbing you. Agree on a volume level for the stereo (your neighbours will also thank you). Take it in turns with the radio. One morning silence, the next the Morning Crew.

Faction fights

You get along famously – so long as you don't talk about politics, religion or the death penalty. You're Labour, she's Conservative. You're all for capital punishment, she's a humanitarian – but both of you will argue to the point of death. Why waste energy on topics you're both passionate about and refuse to budge on? Save the debates for like-minded friends and agree to disagree. After all, if it's an issue you feel so strongly about you can't go out with someone who feels that way, you wouldn't have got this far.

Taste tantrums

They're a meat-and-three-veg type, you're into exotic fare. Women are usually more adventurous with food, probably because they're usually the cook. We tend to pick food on a menu that we can't make at home while blokes invariably choose the big rump steak with mushroom sauce. Educate a bland palate by demystifying food. Call Osso Bucco a casserole and they'll happily tuck in. Scallops in cheese sauce sounds a lot less threatening than 'Coquille St Jacques'. Take it in turns to pick restaurants and ease them gently into new tastes. Immediately dragging him off to a vegan restaurant to eat chickpeas and lentils is going to have him sprinting to McDonald's. Instead, pick a classy restaurant where he can have oysters, a well-cooked steak and a glass of red. If he enjoys that, he might even choose the veal next time round!

Pet hates

You don't go anywhere without your dog; they've never owned one and don't ever want to. Do they truly dislike animals or are they secretly a bit nervous of them? If they've never had a pet before, initiate them into the joys of animal companionship gently and they could well grow to love you and your dog. Dog hairs all over the couch, chewed-up shoes and suspicious stains on the table leg aren't going to endear anyone to Fido, so restrict your threesomes to walks outside to begin with. A few loving slobbers later and they'll be buying a water bowl for the nights you both stay over. If neither of you have had pets before and are considering owning one, spend time at your local animal shelter to find out what you're letting yourselves in for. If you can handle volunteer work for a day – walking, grooming, feeding, bathing and cleaning out kennels – you can handle an animal for a lifetime.

> ❶ *Check out their dog to find out what they're really like, say social psychologists.*
>
> • *A typically aggressive breed: you're on dodgy ground – they could be repressing anger.*
> • *A cute little designer dog: they need their ego stroked – constantly.*
> • *A much-loved mongrel: Ahh! This person values and dotes on something that cost them little and does nothing for their image. Odds are they're the genuine article!*

Where there's smoke, there's fire

They smoke, you don't. There are polite smokers and smokers who'll puff away while you're eating and stub out butts on their bread and butter plate. Regardless, it is a habit that affects others so you have every right to insist on a little courtesy – not smoking in the car or the non-smoker's flat, for instance. Choose outdoor restaurants so it's not as annoying and ban smoking in the bedroom. Nagging someone to give up is likely to have them puffing away twice as furiously because the mere thought of quitting makes addicts nervous and want to smoke more. Stop-smoking clinics say that the decision to quit the habit has to be made by the person who has it. You can leave piles of anti-smoking literature on the coffee table so they're armed with the facts but, basically, they have to acknowledge they've got the problem and give up themselves. If your partner does decide to quit, schedule that Bali holiday you've been planning with your friends to magically coincide with D-day. Nicotine withdrawal isn't pleasant for anyone.

Hooked up with a smoker? It's not just their health you should be worried about. A recent UK study revealed adults who smoke are 53 per cent more likely to divorce than those who don't. Experts say smokers are riskier life partners because of the psychological problems that got them addicted to the drug in the first place.

FIVE COMPLAINTS YOU'LL NEVER HEAR FROM HIM

1. 'Honey, I wish you'd stop bringing home sexy videos.'
2. 'Why can't I hang around while you have the girls over?'
3. 'I wish you'd leave the dishes for me to do.'
4. 'I can't believe you went Christmas shopping and didn't take me with you.'
5. 'Must we? Don't you think sex is overrated?'

AND HER

1. 'I can't believe you didn't look at that girl – she was gorgeous!'
2. 'I'm so depressed your mother's stopped giving me so much constructive criticism.'
3. 'Do we *have* to talk about the relationship? I'd rather watch telly.'
4. 'I wish you'd stop buying me flowers. They're a waste of money.'
5. 'Not more oral sex! I'd much prefer to give it to you.'

IF ALL ELSE FAILS: COUPLES COUNSELLING

The room might be cheery but the two people nervously fidgeting on the couch aren't. He's still trying to figure out what he's doing in a shrink's office at the ripe old age of 26; she's wondering why she insisted they come. Now she's here, she can't think of a single thing to say and it all seems a little ridiculous. 'It's often uncomfortable to start with,' says the psychologist. 'Perhaps you'd like to begin by telling me how the two of you met . . .'

Yet another struggling couple fronting up to a therapist to save their marriage? Not quite. Peter and Collette aren't even living together, let alone married. But they are thinking about it *and* have been arguing, and unlike other couples who privately ponder, *Will we make it?*, they decided to seek an expert opinion. It's an increasingly popular trend. After seeing their parents and friends split, today's couples are fighting back. In a bid to understand relationships and learn the skills that will make theirs work, they're detouring to their nearest psychologist *before* they move in or walk down the aisle. It's an option every couple should think about (yes, even you two).

Danger points in a relationship

You might think your problems are individual but the likelihood is the counsellor's seen it all before. Most couples hit the same set of problems, around the same time. The first hiccup: when the relationship moves from fun to functional. 'Once people decide they're serious about each other, they start getting serious about life: get a house, have kids, get a mortgage,' says psychologist Phillip Gorrell. 'They stop concentrating on the relationship and concentrate on work and money.' Romance takes a back seat and people stop feeling special. It's sobering to realize that real love is more about having things in common and being able to talk than your partner walking in with flowers or champagne. But plenty of couples skid into boring behaviour patterns around the two-year mark: often the kiss of death. If you don't take enough holidays and keep the novelty factor happening, you'll soon get bored. This is what's usually happened when a person says: 'I don't know what happened but I've fallen out of love for no good reason.'

The next problem point is based around quality of communication. You feel your partner doesn't understand you, he or she doesn't listen, you can't talk to them. This often slides into the third danger zone: our tendency to focus on the negative. 'You say to people, "What percentage of your relationship is good?" and they'll answer 75 per cent. I feel like saying to them, "If that much is good, why are you focusing on the bad?"' says Gorrell.

Not only do we focus on the bad, we have a tendency toward the grass-is-always-greener syndrome. People compare their relationship with those of their friends and, on the surface, their friends' looks wonderful. But how do you really know? You're comparing your internal feelings with their external experience. Don't believe all you see.

They're the most common complaints that couples counsellors hear.

Can counselling save your relationship?

The sooner you get help, the more chance you've got and the less damage the problem will cause long-term. A big factor in how successful counselling's going to be is how much you both really want it to work – and how hard you're prepared to work at your relationship. It's incredibly difficult to break old habits and stop sliding back into them and counselling takes up an awful lot of time. It's not just a matter of rolling up there once a week, because there's no point learning skills unless you practise them at home. The average couple is in for anywhere between six and twelve hour-long sessions – with homework. It's not a quick-fix solution – which is, of course, why it works long term.

When doesn't it work?
It's not very successful when you're already in the middle of a *huge* crisis. Which is, of course, when most people trot along. What usually happens is, by the time you've sorted out the mess (usually an affair), you're too exhausted to work on changing, so you settle back into your old ways and the problem starts all over again.

If one of you has already fallen out of love or already decided to leave, again, the prognosis isn't good, though it can soften the blow and your next relationship(s) will benefit from it. The thing to remember is this: the therapist isn't going to magically solve all your problems for you. They're doctors not magicians: you've got to want to change and work hard at it for counselling to work.

What happens in a typical counselling session?
Usually, you'll spend the first session telling the therapist what your problems are and just by watching you, they can get an idea of your personalities and how you relate to each other. After that, they start problem solving and teaching you communication skills, like what we've been talking about throughout this book: how to talk to each other, how to listen and how to make sure the words that come out of your mouth are actually what you're trying to say. Often, simply being able to speak up is half the battle. People will say things in front of a therapist that they wouldn't dream of saying at home because it would end up in an almighty row. They'll also delve into your backgrounds and significant life experiences to find out what other influences there are on the relationship (the stuff I talk about in Chapter 8).

Will they tell you if it's best to split up?

No reputable therapist will tell you to go home and pack your bags, but they will say something like this: 'We've spent a lot of time on your relationship, I've given you homework exercises and nothing appears to be changing. Is it time now to look at going your own ways? Maybe that's what we should be working on.' According to psychologist Grant Brecht, couples have one of two reactions when given this speech. 'They'll either say, "What a terrible thing to say to us! We'll make this work just to show you" – and they do! Or one person will say, "I'm so glad you brought that up." ' There certainly may come a point where you're working on splitting up harmoniously rather than working to put it all back together. Relationships counselling isn't just about helping couples to stay together – it also helps them break up successfully.

How do you talk your partner into going?

Very tactfully! It's all in the way you approach it. Saying, 'You need to get your head read because we're in an absolute mess,' won't get you very far. Saying, 'Darling, I love you but I think we need to learn a few relationship skills,' could well do the trick.

If he's a bit nervous – and it's usually the guy who's not so keen – tell him you'll go along on your own to check it out first, so you can reassure him what it's like. If your partner refuses point blank to even consider counselling, it's a pretty good sign the relationship wouldn't have worked anyway. If they're that stubborn, they're not going to change. So like it and lump it or leave. They're the only two choices you've got, I'm afraid.

How do you find a good counsellor?

Call the British Psychological Society – their number's in the yellow pages – and ask for a list of qualified counsellors in your

area. Don't just go along to anyone – call and talk to the counsellor first and see whether you like the sound of them.
Counselling's not cheap and it's more effective if you like and
respect the person who's helping you. Private counselling is the
most expensive, but lots of community groups offer it free or for
a minimum charge.

Jealousy and Infidelity

Taming the green-eyed monster and what to do if your partner cheats (or you're tempted to)

••

I play it pretty safe with relationships. My Dad had an affair so I've had first-hand experience of the pain of betrayal and would rather stick red-hot pokers in every orifice than be on the receiving end of *that*. Any guy who even looks dodgy doesn't get to first base. But I did make one exception.

When I met Jason, all my instincts said, *Run away – NOW!* Smooth, rich and oozing sex appeal, he had 'I will bonk around' written all over his Armani suit. God knows why (okay, it was lust), but I dated him even *after* he told me he actually did have a problem with infidelity and had cheated on his ex-wife and every single girlfriend he'd ever had. I, as always, was to be the exception: I was the only one he'd ever truly been in love with, after all. With me, it just wouldn't happen. He *knew* it. I don't know where my brain was at the time (possibly skiing in Aspen) but I guess I was trying to prove something. That the scars from my parents' divorce really had healed. That I didn't have a problem with jealousy.

That I wasn't so paranoid about someone cheating on me, I couldn't take a chance.

I wasn't entirely stupid, though. I kept my eyes open and I knew exactly where he hid his stash of condoms (we'd both been AIDS tested and since stopped using them). There was one unopened packet and two loose. For ten months, they stayed that way. Then three were missing. 'I gave them to a friend,' he said.

'Which friend?' I asked, and dialled their number. That's all it took for him to confess to a one-night (three bonk?) stand which, of course, meant nothing. Jason could not understand why I left him. Three years (one for each condom) and a lot of therapy later, he regrets what he did.

I simply regret going out with him. It was pointless because I never did trust him and (as I discussed in Chapter 4) trust is an essential ingredient in a good relationship. You can have matching

It's official: no-one likes an overtly jealous partner but most have a touch of the green-eyed monster themselves. When researchers surveyed 6,800 people in 20 different countries, they found:

- *Eighty-three per cent of people believe jealousy can ruin even the best relationships – though 49 per cent found 'mild' jealousy flattering.*
- *Forty-nine per cent would never stay with a jealous partner – but only 39 per cent trust their partners implicitly and wouldn't check up on them.*
- *The most jealous people live in Turkey and Spain, though 90 per cent of Portuguese spy on their lovers.*
- *What if you never get jealous? Fifty-four per cent of those surveyed say you're not in love!*

libidos, the same interests, dreams and goals, share a fetish for garden gnomes and both enjoy wearing green patterned jumpers during sixty-niners, but if you spend the whole of your life together looking suspiciously at each other through narrowed eyes, it means nothing.

For some people, jealousy and worries over infidelity aren't a problem. They work on the assumption that someone will be faithful until proven wrong. If this is you, count yourself lucky. Sure, you might get an almighty kick in the teeth now and again, but at least you're giving relationships the best chance they've got to succeed. Trusting someone means putting your heart in their hands for safe keeping. It's a precious present and it takes guts to do it.

Then there are the rest of us: the battle-scarred. If you'd rather sign over your firstborn than trust your partner, one of two things has happened. That person has done something to justify your mistrust – cheated on you or has a history of cheating – or something's happened in *your* past to make you jealous of *everyone*.

You may find this chapter painful to read because there's a lot in it that isn't terribly pleasant: like the shocking statistics on how many of us *are* sneaking around behind each other's backs. And while I'd love to, I can't give any guarantees *your* partner will be faithful (for a start, I don't know them). They might well betray you and yes, it will hurt if they do. An awful lot. But what's the alternative? If you never let down your guard, you'll never be able to truly fall in love. So arm yourself with knowledge and by all means look for warning signs, but after you've done that, take a deep breath and take a chance on *someone who's worth it*. Once you've read this chapter, don't look at it again unless you need to. Be sensible, but there's no point in being paranoid.

JEALOUSY: TAMING THE BEAST WITHIN – OR THE BEAST YOU'RE INVOLVED WITH

If you're an extremely jealous person, prepare to hyperventilate. Fact one: jealousy won't stop people being unfaithful – it makes it more likely they will be. If you accuse someone often enough of having an affair or fancying so-and-so, they eventually think, *Hey, they believe it, I might as well do it.* Fact number two: the biggest fear of a jealous person is that their partner will leave them, but if you continue to make their life hell, they probably will. Feeling completely paranoid? Good. Let these two facts sink in and you might well decide it's time to tame that green-eyed monster.

There's another reason why it's a brilliant idea to get jealousy under control. If you're a jealous person and in love, life is pretty bloody miserable most of the time. I've been there. I, like you, spent every minute of every day looking for evidence. A car parked down the street can't belong to a neighbour – it must be a secret lover visiting my boyfriend. His phone's engaged at work? He's not talking business, he's whispering sweet somethings to someone else. A girlfriend of mine used to put hairs across the phone to see if her boyfriend was making any dodgy calls while she popped out to get the milk. Some people ask their friends to come on to their partners to see if they'd take them up on it. An extremely silly thing to do, since it can spark an unacknowledged attraction that would never have surfaced if you hadn't forced them into it.

Extreme jealousy is an ugly emotion. A doctor friend of mine tells the story of a woman in her thirties with terminal cancer who had to spend a lot of time in bed. She bought some pretty nighties so she could look good for her husband but instead of being complimented, he flew into a jealous rage and accused her of trying to attract the hospital staff. A psychiatrist told me about a patient who wired up his entire house with microphones so he could tape the supposed sex sessions his wife had while he was at work. They weren't rich and he spent their life savings doing it. All he recorded was her doing the dishes and gossiping on the phone to girlfriends. (Bang went that holiday they'd been saving years for.) There's another quite bizarre case of a man who was so jealous he was convinced his wife was being unfaithful during the few minutes he left the bed during the night to go to the toilet.

You can pick the couple where one or both partners are jealous: they don't go out. The only stress-free environment is to stay home with a video and a bottle of wine because any public place – pubs, restaurants, even shopping – has potential rivals (that is, people of the opposite sex). Some people can't even bear their partners watching attractive people on television. Even the news becomes a problem if the newsreader happens to be attractive.

Hah! I hear you say, I'm nowhere near *that* bad. True (or maybe not). But solve the problem now, while you can. Jealousy is insidious. It grows like a weed and only needs the odd drop of water to spread. It's dangerous to think you're in control. It's like smoking. One day you're smoking one fag, the next week two, then three and before you're know it you're a two-pack-a-day person.

What makes someone jealous?

We all get a bit put out if our partner's drooling over some blonde at a party. But really jealous people have usually had something happen to them in the past. If either of your parents had an affair or you found your partner in bed with the next-door neighbour, it stands to reason you're going to be a tad suspicious.

Experiences like these leave us with cynical attitudes about relationships and we make massive generalizations based on them. If you're female and an ex-lover was unfaithful, you think *all* men will sleep around if given half the chance. That might be true of *some* men, but it's certainly not true of *all* men. Jealous people look at the world through distorted lenses. They see danger where there really isn't any. It's also got a lot to do with self-esteem. If you're happy with yourself, you're much more likely to think, *Why would my partner want anyone else when they've got me?* A healthy ego is great protection against jealousy.

The inability to trust other people affects both sexes, all socio-economic groups and all cultures. It doesn't discriminate in intelligence or looks. In fact, a lot of jealous people are actually above average in attractiveness and are often successful. The average person might look at them in astonishment when they throw a jealous tantrum (thinking, *Why would they have any need to worry? Who'd want to play up on them?*), but it's all about feeling like you measure up. We all measure ourselves against a personal ideal which is slightly above what and who we are. The more beautiful/clever you are, the higher your ideal. So the reason that gorgeous girlfriend never feels good enough – when she's a million times better looking than Ms Average – is because she doesn't measure herself against Ms Average, she measures herself against the truly extraordinary: the super-models. God knows who *they* measure *themselves* against, but the mind boggles, since few of them seem secure.

Everyone gets jealous occasionally. Match a 'normal' person with someone who presses all the wrong buttons and they might become outrageously jealous – but only with that person. Sometimes jealousy and distrustfulness *are* warranted. If your partner's got a history of playing around, you're wise to keep your eyes open. But truly distrustful people experience jealousy with *each* and *every* person they go out with.

Because of this rather obvious fact, most jealous people

know they're the ones with the problem. Once they've calmed down, they realize they've been irrational. But

when you're in the *middle* of a jealous rage, you lose all sense of logic and perspective. Jealousy is an incredibly powerful emotion. You can't control it because it's being fed by one continuous thought: is my partner being unfaithful to me? That's why you start opening their mail, listening in on phone calls and interrogating your partner when they're five minutes late.

There are lots of reasons why you've ended up this way. Here are some of them.

Insecurity

Jealousy and distrust are often rooted in insecurity. It's logical. If you truly thought you were fabulous, you wouldn't think for one moment your partner would fancy someone else. Insecure, jealous people react one of two ways to their insecurity. They turn into scared-little-mice partners, convinced their partner's about to run off with the 80-year-old cleaner at their work. Or they overcompensate by being bullies. If you're a quivering mess inside, the best way to make yourself feel better is to try to control everything and everyone around you. Playing tough guy and putting down your partner at every opportunity momen-tarily makes you feel tough. Besides, if you drag them down far enough, they'll become as insecure as you are and won't have the courage to leave you.

Childhood

Middle-child people are frequently jealous, according to the experts. It sounds like something Freud would say (and probably did), but often the middle child feels left out and overlooked.

Similarly, if your Mum or Dad had an affair, it stands to reason you're going to be suspicious of your partners. We tend to judge our relationships by what our parents had.

The past

If you've been dumped before or cheated on constantly, you've got good reason not to trust a partner. You've learnt by experience that (some) people aren't trustworthy and/or your judgement's not fab. If the last time your partner stayed out all night, they slept with someone else, it's obvious you'll assume that's what your new partner is doing, even if it's actually quite innocent.

'I always kick myself after the rage has worn off. It's like, "Why am I so jealous? How can he stand to put up with me?" Once I've calmed down it becomes painfully obvious that I've ruined a perfectly good evening for nothing. I feel embarrassed and remorseful – and then even more insecure than I was before. It's a catch-22 situation because I'm even more likely to be jealous the next time.'

Sharon, 28,
make-up artist

Your own history of faithfulness

If you find it incredibly difficult to stay faithful to one person, you may assume others are the same. Psychologists call it 'transference': seeing our own qualities in someone else. You don't trust yourself (now or in the past), so you don't trust your partner. If you've cheated on other people numerous times and got away with it, it seems logical that others could be doing the same to you.

Get a grip! The do-it-yourself jealousy cure

You've got two choices if you've got a problem with jealousy: get professional help or try to help yourself. Which should you do? Hopefully, it'll become clear as you read through this section.

1: Identify the reason

Pinpoint the reason(s) why you're jealous by checking the section above. Is it insecurity, your childhood, your past, your own cheating history or a combination of all four? If the answer's not obvious, force yourself to think outside the square. It might well stem from sitting through all the gory details when your best friend's heart got smashed to smithereens by a lover who cheated. ('Jesus! I hope this never happens to me!')

If you truly don't know why you're jealous and/or you've grappled with jealousy for years, you need more than this book. Get professional help by calling the British Psychological Society (their number's in the yellow pages) and ask for a list of qualified counsellors in your area.

2: Work on your self-esteem

The more highly you think of yourself, the less likely you'll believe your partner would dream of risking you and your relationship by playing around with someone else. Chapter 1 talks about self-esteem. If you've already read it and it hasn't helped, again, get yourself along to a good counsellor.

3: Change your behaviour

This program was put together by one of the world's leading experts on jealousy, UK psychologist Dr Nicholas Tarrier. It's hard work and takes up an awful lot of time but it solved my jealousy problem. Hopefully, it will yours.

The plan only works if you do it *every single time you have a jealous thought*. You need to follow it faithfully, religiously and without exception. Doing it every second time or even four out of five times renders it totally ineffective. It will take over your life for a few weeks or months, depending on how jealous you are. It means you have to carry a notepad and pen wherever you go. It might mean you'll be disappearing to the loo a dozen times during a dinner party. But even if it meant taking off your clothes and dancing naked at the local bus stop, it's worth giving it a go.

If you have a good relationship with your partner, it's sensible to tell them what you're doing. If they love you and want the problem fixed as much as you do (believe me, *more* than you do), they'll support and cover for you when you have to disappear. You might also consider telling close friends to explain any long absences while you're out together. But don't make the mistake of turning it into a party trick. It's acceptable to do this exercise with your partner after you've done it alone at least a dozen times. It's okay to work through it with a best friend. But no more than one person at a time: you'll feel silly, they'll make hurtful jokes and it'll backfire Big Time. Being jealous isn't fun. It's degrading and humiliating. You can do without being bagged and trivialized. Ready, willing and (yes you are) able? Here's how to do it.

Every time you have a jealous thought, write it down and rate how strongly you believe it on a scale of one to ten. For example: *My boyfriend is chatting up the girl behind the bar*: 9/10 [I'm certain this is true].

Underneath this sentence, list all the reasons why you believe this. Think of as many as you can:
- *He's been talking to her for ages – much longer than necessary.*
- *He smiled at her.*
- *He gave her 'that look'.*
- *She's his type/she's really attractive.*
- *Everyone else at the table looked really embarrassed – like they knew what was happening and felt sorry for me.*

Even if you know how silly it sounds as you're writing it, write it all down. Wait two minutes and dwell a bit longer on how upset and angry you feel. Deliberately stay in the 'rage' point a little while so every single one of those paranoid thoughts comes to the surface for you to write down.

Beside these reasons, now write logical, alternative explanations. Wait another two minutes but this time try to calm down. Breathe deeply, remind yourself of how you felt *after* the last jealous rage (unjustified). Then force yourself to challenge each and every point you've listed with a logical explanation. If you find this difficult, imagine your best friend is there with you. How might she or he challenge those thoughts? Write down the explanations even if you don't believe what you're writing.

- *He's been talking to her for ages.*

  It seems like a long time but that could be my judgement is way off.

- *He smiled at her.*

  He's friendly and polite. I also smile at people in that sort of situation.

- *He gave her 'that look'.*

  Let's face it: I'd interpret any sort of friendly expression as 'that look'.

  Don't stop until you've listed a plausible, remotely believable explanation for every single reason you've listed.

Read through what you've written – focusing on the logical explanations – and rerate how strongly you now believe the initial thought. Accept that there's as much possibility *they* are true as your jealousy-inspired accusations.

Keep going. The more logical explanations you can think of the better. Try to list at least two, preferably three explanations next to every jealous thought.

Again, rerate how strongly you now believe the initial thought. Don't rejoin your partner until you've reduced your initial rating (example: 9/10) at least one point. Don't be alarmed if the minute you walk out of wherever you've been hiding, it all comes flooding back and you shoot back up to 9/10. Just congratulate yourself that you regained a small amount of control when normally you would have stormed out immediately.

Now you're back in the situation, see how you feel. If you have to ignore your partner or look in the other direction to stay calm, do it. If your partner's aware you're following this program, tell them why you've been gone so long. Let them give your hand a squeeze even if you can't squeeze it back, try to smile when they reassure you you've got nothing to worry about, then change the subject.

If you still feel out of control, repeat the exercise or leave. Go back and go through everything one more time. If it's not working, go home – with or without your partner – and try it again there.

Keep repeating this exercise. If you're an extremely jealous person it will have little effect during the first few weeks. One month on, you'll notice a small improvement. Two months on, a significant change. Three months on, you're well on the road to living life as non-jealous people do. Please don't give up.

Keep writing things down until you can do the exercise mentally. Follow exactly the same steps but do it in your head rather than on paper.

Congratulations! It worked. One miraculous day, you'll find your brain does the exercise for you – without you even being conscious of it happening! Your brain has been trained to challenge silly thoughts with logic and it starts working through the process subconsciously and automatically. This is how non-jealous people's brains work. Their subconscious sees a potentially threatening situation but before they're even aware of it, the logical side of their brain clicks in and dismisses the idea if it's not based on reality. If there is good reason to be jealous, the thought will filter through anyway. So don't panic: you won't suddenly stop seeing *real* threats, you'll just stop seeing those that aren't.

You're fine, it's your partner who's out of control

A very good friend of mine went out with an intensely jealous guy for one, long, miserable year. Before Melissa met him, she was a happy, well-adjusted, fairly typical 24-year-old with no particular problems. Within a month of dating this loser, she suddenly wasn't 'allowed' to go out to dinner with me alone. Since the main reason I wanted to see her during this period was to conduct my own one-woman leave-the-bastard campaign, I was more than a little worried when she agreed to do as he said. Once, Melissa did sneak out – and paid for it heavily. He found out, accused her of all sorts of things and smashed their coffee table against a wall. They argued all night, she was late for work (again) and missed out on the promotion that should have been hers. It was my fault of course – not his. He made sure he convinced her of that.

After six months of virtually no contact, I called around unexpectedly. Melissa had lost close to ten kilos in weight – not a good look when she was a size 10 to start with. I had five minutes before the ogre was due home.

'Look at you. *Please* leave this guy,' I begged her.

'Logically,' she said, 'I know you're right. But I don't have the energy or the confidence any more.' Who else would want her when she was obviously such a bad person, someone who couldn't even be trusted to have coffee with a girlfriend at a local café? Her boyfriend was okay. Really. He just loved her too much, that's all.

I'm ecstatically happy to report there is a sort-of-happy ending to the story. When the man who loved Melissa too much decided to show it by breaking her nose in two different places, she finally upped and left. But she's still got scars – and I'm not talking about the ones left by plastic surgery.

What was wrong with the girl? I'd never stay with someone like that! you're probably thinking. Don't be too sure. The moral of this morbid little tale is this: be careful, because it *could* happen to you. Don't believe for a minute you're immune to the appeal of jealous, possessive lovers. That's right, *appeal* . . .

Jealous partners come in all sorts of disguises

That intense, wonderfully attentive man who spoils you rotten with impromptu gifts, rings just to say 'Hi' several times a day and wants you 'all to himself' seems terribly romantic in the beginning. He hates 'sharing' you with other people? Wow! How romantic! So you cancel that planned girls' night out and secretly feel a little smug about having a boyfriend who doesn't want to go out with the boys. Even his first jealous tantrum seems somehow, well, evidence that this guy really must like you. Heaps. Before you know it, you're spending every second together, alone with him.

Early warning signs you've hooked up with a jealous lunatic aren't as obvious as you think. In the 'honeymoon' period of healthy relationships, it's normal to live in each other's pockets a little. It's only when you try to return to normality – re-establish your life *apart* from your partner – that you realize they won't let you. You'd like to think this is when you take the nearest exit. But sometimes you feel a bit wobbly and unsure of what to do. *This person loves me so much – and it's obviously upsetting them when I do things alone, so best put up with it for a little while. Once they become more secure of my love, they'll settle down.* And your perspective starts to get warped. It's around then that Mr or Ms Fabulous starts deflating your self-esteem.

Jealous partners erode your self-confidence

They might not even be conscious of doing it, but they start manipulating, trying to make you needy and dependent on them. 'I don't know about that haircut,' they say. 'It doesn't do much for your chin. If Laura was half the friend you say she is, she wouldn't have insisted you cut it so short.' The message: *My chin's ugly and I can't trust Laura.* They set the seeds of doubt, then water them regularly. Your family tell you how to run your life, your girlfriends are secretly jealous of you, that workmate is trying to sabotage your success and pinch your job. After a while – and if they're clever there's always a grain of truth in there – you start to believe them. You see less and less of family, friends and workmates until your social support system is gone. You start to feel unsure of yourself, vulnerable. The only person left in your life is your partner so there's no-one to balance those irrational, poisonous accusations.

They've now got you where they want you. Your life revolves almost entirely around them and their opinion counts. It has to – it's the only one you're getting! That's why you don't up and leave when it turns really ugly – your confidence has dived lower than theirs. (Believe me, just about *all* severely jealous, possessive people have self-esteem below rock-bottom.) It suits them for you to doubt yourself because you're less likely to leave. And if someone tells you often enough that being unfaithful to your childhood sweetheart in primary school was unforgivable, that you're a *bad* person, you eventually start to believe it. You start to question your own motives for wearing that LBD, and forget it's not normal for your boyfriend to accompany you to the dentist.

Exhausted from fighting and constantly defending yourself, you haven't got the energy to do much else but hang around and put up with whatever is dished out. You're pushed to breaking point, your friends are fed up and appear to have forgotten you, your family are annoyed because you don't see them any more. You feel stressed, emotional and trapped. They've effectively cut off all your escape routes: there's nowhere to turn so you stay.

> 'I used to be jealous until it cost me a great relationship. Now I understand you get what you reap. If you expect someone to play up, they probably will. Why wouldn't they – you think they are any way. If you trust them and they know it, they'll try much harder to live up to that.'
>
> Diana, 24, writer

If you're reading this and thinking, *Oh my God, she's talking about me!* please, read the next section that deals with severe jealousy very carefully. If your partner's nowhere near that bad but you recognize it's a problem, skip to the section that follows it.

Your partner's severely jealous and you're miserable but you don't have the strength to leave
Understand the problem
Understand why you feel so bad about yourself and powerless to leave by reading the previous section, then put it on paper. Write down how you felt *before* you met your partner, how you felt in the first few weeks, two months in, six months in and so on. Record when they first started interfering with your friendships; when you stopped seeing friends and family on your own; when you started to feel isolated; when they

started to put you and people close to you down; when you began to doubt yourself. If you've managed to maintain any friendships, get that person(s) to sit down with you and jog your memory.

Let the facts sink in
Read your list over and over until you accept what's happened to you. Knowing how you got into the situation will give you the power to get out of it.

Get angry
Keep reading and rereading the list until you start to feel angry. How dare this person have done this to you! It will gradually start to dawn on you that your partner's behaviour isn't normal or acceptable. This is not how someone who loves you would treat you. They'd want you to be surrounded by lots of people who love you, who give you compliments and encouragement, not insults and fears.

Get organized
Make concrete plans to leave if you live with the person. Call your friends and family, even if you haven't called them for ages. Simply apologize for not being in contact and tell them you need help to get out of the situation you're in. Ask them to stop you getting sucked back into 'saving' your partner again. It's a good idea to stay with a friend for a few weeks, or your family, rather than try to organize permanent accommodation immediately. Leaving a jealous partner is emotionally draining: just get yourself out of there and worry about things like bonds and flats later.

Once you have somewhere to stay, decide *when* you want to leave. If you're female, arrange for a friend to wait outside in the car at a certain time (a male, the bigger the better). If you don't come out within ten minutes, they knock on the door. (If you don't have anyone to call or a place to stay, call the police or a community support group like Careline and ask for their help. They will direct you to the appropriate support service. If you think you're in physical danger, ask your local police to organize a restraining order.)

Are you a jealous female? Try spending the first 14 days after the start of your period with your girlfriends and the rest of the month with him. You might think it's his nights out with the boys that cause those jealousy attacks; researchers say it's your hormones, which are particularly vicious at that part of your menstrual cycle.

Break the news and leave quickly
It depends on your partner and how you think they'll react to the news as to when you should tell them you're leaving and it's over. If you're expecting trouble – and it's extremely unlikely they'll let you go without a battle – it's safest to tell them you're leaving two minutes before you walk straight out the door (all possessions packed and removed while they were out). Don't get drawn into a long, involved discussion about the relationship. They've had enough chances and there's nothing they can do at this point to fix it. If they swear they'll solve the problem, tell them to book in to see a good counsellor and call you through a mutual friend in a few months.

Don't see them
Once you've left, don't see them under any circumstances. Surround yourself with good friends, don't answer the door until you know who's there and hang up if they're on the end of the phone. Forget friendship – if it is possible, it'll still be years down the track.

Your partner's got a problem but it's not out of control and you're not feeling threatened

Even if the problem's not severe, constantly defending every move you make and not being trusted to go down to the local shops takes its toll on the most devoted partner. Jealousy ruins most relationships eventually, so the time to have a serious chat to your partner about it is *now*.

Explain it's their problem

Tell your partner you want to help but essentially, it's up to them to solve the problem. Jealousy is like any other habit – you can't make someone kick it if they don't want to. Your partner's got to want to change and be prepared to do some DIY therapy (see the program on page 330) or get professional help.

Set a time limit

Set yourself a time limit relevant to how long you've been going out. If you've been dating seriously, six months is about right. If they haven't improved by then or are still refusing to get help, bail out. Tell them you're setting this deadline.

Stop reassuring them

Stop reassuring – you're reinforcing bad behaviour. If every time they have a tantrum, you run after them saying, 'Of course, I don't fancy John in computers,' you're rewarding bad behaviour. If a tantrum results in you telling them how wonderful they are, how much you love them and how you'll never stray, of course they'll keep on having them – the end result is fabulous. Instead, treat them like a two-year-old. Refuse to be drawn into inquisitions, go to bed early or disappear until they've calmed down. In other words, leave them alone until logic returns. Do your reassuring *after* the rage has subsided.

Help them make a list

Sit down with your partner and make a list of situations they'd find difficult to cope with. Rate them from nightmare (you out on the town with friends), to hard (you out with an opposite-sex friend who's an ex) to relatively easy (you've gone for coffee with a same-sex friend). Put them in order, then try them out – working from the easy end. If you come back from coffee the same loving person who left, they'll probably be fine next time round. Wait until they're comfortable with that situation before moving onto the next, more difficult one. Eventually, they'll realize you're trustworthy no matter what situation you're in. The other bonus: you're working together as a team and can see the light at the end of the tunnel. You'll one day be able to go out without having to face a red-faced lunatic when you get home.

> 'All men look. If one guy says, "Look at that," we all jump in with a comment. It doesn't occur to any of us to say, "But George! You're happily involved with Mary! What are you checking out other women for?" That's not to say we'd act on it though.'
>
> Stuart, 24, sales rep

Build their self-esteem

The better they feel about themselves, the less likely they'll believe someone would want to betray them.

Be reliable but realistic

If you're going to be an hour late, call. But having to ring someone three times during a movie while you're at the cinema is ridiculous.

Be sensitive

Be sensitive to their problem. Don't flirt, even harmlessly, while they're around.

HELP! MY BOYFRIEND'S A PERVE!

There's the casual once-over and then there's the look that starts at the top and moves downward very slowly, very obviously undressing someone with your eyes. If your partner's checking out the talent using technique No 2, they're out of line.

It's a natural human reaction to look at really beautiful people, and admiring them doesn't mean you don't love your partner or are about to run off with them. But spending all night at a party chatting someone up and leaving with their phone number isn't okay. Even more exasperating is the guy who tries to justify outrageously flirtatious behaviour with the old 'but I was only being friendly and you're being insecure or jealous' comeback. It's like dog owners who say, 'He's just being friendly,' while Rover's madly humping your leg: it's bloody obvious Rover wants more than just walkies. If your lover's doing the human equivalent of humping but trying to make it seem like *you're* the one with the problem, he's being manipulative. Don't put up with it! Read the following to check you're not overreacting, then follow the fix-it plan underneath.

What's acceptable

- **Checking out other women when you're not around.** He knows a comment like, 'Look at the chest on that one,' is guaranteed to get him a slap on the back from the boys at the pub. It's pretty harmless if you're not with him.

- **Doing a double take when a girl walks in wearing a micro-mini and bikini top and has breasts the size of watermelons.** You can't help but look at people like that. If Manpower walked in wearing G-strings, you'd do the same.

- **Giving others compliments.** 'Sharon looks great tonight,' is fine. 'Sharon looks fantastic. It's a shame your legs ➤

aren't good enough to wear dresses like that,' isn't.

- **Lusting after celebrities.** Even if he dribbles while watching Cameron Diaz on video, it's not something you should feel threatened by. He's just expressing a healthy appreciation of the opposite sex. If he goes on and on about it, tell him it upsets you, and hopefully he'll just gaze adoringly at the screen rather than give a running commentary on how great she looks.

- **Catching your partner exchanging meaningful glances with a stranger across the room.** There's nothing essentially wrong with smiling at someone gorgeous as if to say, 'Yes, I find you attractive, too, but we're both with other people,' even if few of us enjoy seeing it. If it's not followed through by flirting, it's probably best ignored. After all, you probably do it too. It's an ego boost, a way of affirming to ourselves that we're still attractive and could pull a date if we weren't with our partner. If it seems like your partner's doing it deliberately, they might be trying to give you a good kick up the bum. It's the equivalent of saying, 'Hey! Don't take me for granted. I'm not cemented to your side, and other people find me attractive.'

What's not acceptable

- **Checking out other women in front of you.** If every female gets the once-over and he spends more time looking over your shoulder than looking at you, take a trip to the ladies and don't bother coming back.

- **He's just started drooling over women when he didn't look twice before**. This is a danger sign. It can mean there are real problems in your relationship and he's subconsciously – or even consciously – thinking of leaving and moving into singles mode. Singles scan the room; happily attached people cast a lazy look ➢

around but it's not obvious. It could also mean your boyfriend's not getting enough sexually out of your relationship. If he's got a high sex drive and you don't, he might do a lot of mental lusting even though he wouldn't dream of acting on it. Therapists call this 'leaking': he's got sexual energy that's not being used up, it overflows and he starts fantasizing about other people. If you've been fighting a lot, also beware. When people are constantly criticized, they're very vulnerable to temptation. The message you're giving him is, 'You're not good enough.' He's looking around for someone who thinks he is.

How to fix it

- **Check with a trusted friend to make sure you're not being paranoid.** You can't expect someone to totally ignore all other members of the opposite sex, and if you put unrealistic restrictions on people, they will rebel. If you're unable to look at their behaviour objectively, ask a trusted friend and get their opinion. Are you overreacting or are they being an insensitive jerk?
- **If you're certain your partner's out of line, call them on it.** The standard answer is, 'You're jealous and overreacting.' Reply calmly. Say, 'No. I've thought about it and I'm not. I won't be treated this way. Look at other women when I'm not around if you have to, but don't do it in front of me. Serious flirting is out of bounds all of the time.' End of conversation.
- **Give him one more chance.** See if he's taken your feelings into account. If he hasn't and it happens again, repeat your speech and say you're giving him one more chance. Ask him, 'How would you feel if I'd been staring at that good-looking guy over there as long as you have the girl in the black?' It's underhand and stooping to his level but it will get his attention. ➤

- **If he does it again, give an ultimatum.** This is one of few situations when an ultimatum is necessary – so give him one. Next time he does it, no matter where you are or who you're with, you'll walk out and the relationship will be over. Nothing he can say at that point will change your mind.
- **Follow through and leave if it continues.** He's had three chances to get his act together. If you've rationally and logically explained why you find it unacceptable and he chooses to continue, you're better off without the guy. Put up with him openly drooling over other people at the risk of losing respect for yourself.

AFFAIRS: HOW COULD THEY (OR WHY DID YOU)? AND ADVICE ON THE 'OH GOD! WHERE DO WE GO FROM HERE?' PART

Okay, be brutally honest here and imagine yourself in this scenario. You've been married for 15 years. You dearly love your partner, have two wonderful kids and appreciate how lucky you are. But you're struggling, as most couples are, just a little. Sex is pleasant but all too rare because who's got the energy or the time? The mortgage reminds you of Jack and the Beanstalk: no matter how much money you pour in, the end's still out of reach. The kids are from Land of the Giants – they're growing up so fast, you're forking out for new shoes every week. Work pressures are mounting, you're arguing and honestly can't remember the last time you had *fun*. Then your company sends you away on a four-day conference overseas.

It's hot, you're lying by the pool thinking, *Oh my God. I'd forgotten what this feels like*. Later that night, you and a single work friend have dinner and he or she convinces you to go for a nightcap in the hotel bar. They start chatting up some gorgeous young thing who also happens to have an equally

> 'He'd check out other women and it was like he had a ten-second orgy with them in his imagination. He'd disappear for a little while and I knew exactly where he'd gone – into fantasy land. He told me it didn't count as unfaithful because he didn't act on it, but it was so destructive to watch, I left him.'
>
> Trudy, 19, promotions

gorgeous friend. The sort you would have gone ga-ga over if you were single. You're polite. You tell them you're married, they continue flirting. *Jesus!* you think. *It would be so easy.* But you do the right thing, excuse yourself and go up to your room. Ten minutes later, as you're harmlessly fantasizing about what you'd like to have done if you weren't married, there's a knock at your door. It's them.

'Did my friend tell you my room number?' you ask.

'No. I saw your room key,' they say. 'No-one knows I'm here. I know you're married. I'm not interested in a relationship, all I want is sex. Now. No strings. I don't even know your last name and I don't want to know.'

You've had six too many drinks. You think, *My spouse and the kids are thousands of miles away, literally. There is no possible way they can find out. I've been faithful for 15 years, I have every intention of being faithful for the next 15. Would it really hurt so much to give in just this once?*

Do you:

a. Say, 'Thanks, I'm awfully flattered but I'm married,' and shut the door.

b. Start out with every intention to do the above, but instead of shutting the door you invite them in for a drink because you feel a bit rude and immature sending them away like that.

c. Do both of the above, while secretly hoping like hell they'll convince you it doesn't matter and what's the harm. You know you're going to wake up feeling as guilty as hell tomorrow, but at that very second it seems worth it.

Don't think about what you'd like your *partner* to do in that situation – what would *you* do? Go on, admit it – I can't read minds and your partner can't either (even if they are looking at you with an 'I know all' look right at this moment). If you're honest, the answer is c. I don't think too many of us would honestly say no in that situation. We might like to think we would – we hope like mad our partners will – but we probably wouldn't.

If you're like most people, this little self-exploration exercise has left you feeling simultaneously guilty and turned on – and also terribly suspicious of your partner. I apologize, but I'm doing it for a reason. Because, before we start exploring the darker, sinister side of affairs – those that *aren't* so innocent in origin – I wanted you to realize something. We're *all* susceptible to an affair, given the right (wrong?) circumstances. Yes, even you.

I'm quite harsh on people who cheat in this chapter and extremely sceptical about staying with someone who's cheated. If asked the question, 'Should I leave if I find out my partner's been unfaithful?' my knee-jerk – and often correct – answer is yes. That's because *most* partners only find out their partner's been unfaithful after they've been bonking around repeatedly. *Very often*, even saying 'yes' in the situation above leads to a repeat performance. You get a taste, get away with it once and continue. The skies don't fall in after all. But I'm the first to admit this doesn't apply to every couple.

I really have come across the odd person who's strayed – or their partner has – under circumstances like the above. A one-off, never-done-before, never-repeated-afterward experience. Maybe even two slip-ups over a very, very long period. Do I think couples like this should split if that's the case? Throw away 15 good years, two kids and what they've built together for a genuinely-not-proud-but-it-happened slip-up? No, I don't. So if this is why you're reading this chapter – you've done similar or your partner has – there's your answer straight up. When I use the word 'affairs' from here on, I mean sleeping with someone you shouldn't on more than the odd occasion. There! Now I've made myself clear, I'll move on.

Most of the advice in this chapter is aimed at the entirely innocent who want to know how to avoid affairs, people who've been seriously upset by their partner's infidelity – and those of you who don't want to be unfaithful but can't seem to keep your zip done up. (If you're the latter, please read Chapter 8 and forgive me for unashamedly trying to 'cure you' by showing how it feels to be on the other side.)

Depending on which category you fall into, the word 'affair' will conjure up one of two very different sets of emotions. Some of you immediately think of hot, steamy sex and erotic encounters: others think pain, betrayal, deceit and heartache. Quite frankly, I think pretty well all of us would prefer our partners to think the latter.

If you're in a long-term, committed relationship, affairs are serious stuff, about as serious as it gets for most couples. Plenty of counsellors will tell you it's possible to repair the damage caused by serious infidelity; personally, I'm not entirely convinced. So if you're contemplating having an affair, I'd strongly advise you read the next section *very* carefully. In it, you'll find the latest research on affairs and the effect they have on relationships. A fair portion of the ideas are a result of studies by Shirley Glass, a leading US expert on the subject.

What constitutes an affair?

If you're unsure, ask yourself, 'If my partner caught me doing this, would they be upset?' If the answer is, 'yes,' it's an affair. You don't need to bonk, kiss or even touch someone to be having an affair with them. You don't even have to meet in the flesh! You can have an affair via the phone, the post, the Internet, and carrier pigeon if you're creative enough. Basically, affairs are about sharing intimate, romantic and/or sexual feelings on a regular basis with someone other than your partner.

That's the true definition of an affair, but what's more important is that you and your partner agree on one. Lots of people I know use the old Bill Clinton logic: if you haven't had intercourse, you haven't been unfaithful. Penetration is the unforgivable sin; a bit of harmless 'mucking around' never hurt anyone (except their partner when they find out).

> 'I was in a café when I noticed a gorgeous guy sitting alone at the other table. I smiled, he smiled back. Two minutes later, his girlfriend appeared from the loo. When she turned the other way to talk on her mobile, he smiled again and shrugged, as if to say, "Hey, if I wasn't with her . . . " I held up my hand to show him my wedding ring. It meant nothing and it made both of us feel good. Attractive people don't go away when you're attached – you just don't do anything about it.'
>
> Mandy, 31, lecturer

Why do people have affairs?

Both sexes have affairs to get something they're not getting from the relationship they're in – it's that simple. What's not so simple is defining what it is that's missing, because often the cheating partner isn't aware of it.

Sometimes, it is obvious. If you're not particularly interested in sex and haven't been for years, the cute redhead at your husband's work who wears slit-to-the-navel tops and licks her lips is going to be pretty damn tempting. If your partner's a workaholic and your self-esteem's at rock bottom, you might have an affair to prove you're still attractive to the opposite sex and to boost your self-confidence. Other people cheat on 'perfect' partners for that reason alone: they're sick of perfection. Some people are searching for something they lacked as a child, others for lost youth. Whatever it is, few of us realize that's what we're really after while we've got our legs in the air in the motel room.

Q: Why do women outlive men?
A: Men bonk themselves to an early grave, according to a UK geneticist. He found the life expectancy of male worms increased enormously when separated from females – and claims human males are no different. Apparently, men use up so much energy pursuing sex, they 'wear out' quicker than women do!

Why do men cheat?

It must be because they're not happy at home: that's what most of us naively believe. Unfortunately, it's not necessarily true. According to Shirley Glass, many men who love their partners and have great sex at home, still *never* turn down an opportunity to have a bit on the side. Fifty-six per cent of the men she sampled who'd had affairs said their marriages were happy (versus 34 per cent of women). Men in long-term marriages who have affairs report very high marital satisfaction. Women in long-term marriages having affairs report quite the opposite – they have the lowest satisfaction of all. Everyone's marital satisfaction went down the longer they were married, *except the men who had affairs*. Horrifying, isn't it.

Why do women cheat?

There used to be a theory that men were genetically programmed to sleep around because their function was to populate the earth. We've evolved since then – like, we don't walk on four legs any more – and the other thing that blows that theory out of the water is that, these days, women are cheating almost as much as men are.

We have affairs for the same reasons men do. To recapture that 'newness'. They're forbidden, you're not supposed to have them and it's an unfortunate trait in both sexes that when we're told we can't have something, it immediately becomes more desirable than a family-size block of Cadbury's. Most affairs don't survive once they're out in the open: the whole point of them is that they're secret and naughty.

When *She* magazine polled more than 600 female readers (aged 18 and over), nearly one in five Australian women admitted to being unfaithful. The real stats are likely to be much higher. Most of us baulk at ticking the 'yes' box in surveys for fear of somehow being found out, and our definitions of affairs are also dubious. The same women who said they'd never had an affair, ticked the 'yes' box when asked if there was a guy other than her husband who she flirted with, felt a strong connection to or fancied. Whether these were in fact affairs (or about to become one) is debatable.

Why *did* they feel the need for someone other than their partner? Lots said they had an affair as a 'reward' for being such a supportive mother and wife. Others believed it was the direct result of a critical life event (like pregnancy, a new job or their partner changing jobs). Plenty of women said a partner who isn't affectionate, who won't listen or talk to them and failed to notice the terrible state the relationship was in was enough reason to justify having an affair. Sometimes, we do it to 'get back' at a partner who's betrayed us. Self-esteem was also right up there. Not convinced your partner finds you attractive? An affair gives a much bigger boost to the ego than a new haircut and a visit to the Revlon counter. Usually, women tend to have affairs with men who are the opposite to their partner or like them, but much younger.

We're far more susceptible to having affairs today than our grandmothers were. In the old days, women usually had one sex partner: their husband. These days most of us have premarital sex so it's not such a big deal to share our bodies with another man: we've done it before. We're financially independent and often work, spending our day mixing with the opposite sex.

We're also less religious than we were. According to the *She* poll and others, women who live with their partners (50 per cent) are more likely to have affairs than married women (15 per cent). De facto couples are less bound by religion or morals, so feel less guilty.

Both sexes are susceptible to having affairs to fix unhappy childhoods. If we lacked security as a child, we'll often seek out a marriage partner who provides stability. Once we're married and feel secure, we may have an affair with someone like the difficult parent who made us 'insecure' in the first place. It's an attempt to rewrite history: if we can make that sort of person love us, somehow it will make the parent love us. Odd, but the subconscious has a habit of working in weird ways.

Your partner dotes on you. Surely they're immune to the temptation of an affair?

More so than most – but *you're* not. The person who gives the most in the relationship – really looks after it and nurtures it – is the person less likely to have an affair. Trouble is, they can become so fixated on the 'relationship' – building a nice home and financial future – they forget the person they're having it with. The partner feels neglected and seeks attention elsewhere. As Glass puts it in a recent article, 'A relationship is like a fire. You can let it die down but not out. Even if you're in another part of the house, you have to go back every once in a while to stoke the coals.'

Can you make a relationship affair-proof?

You can certainly lower the chances (see page 367) but you can't reduce them to zero. *Choosing* the right person is probably more important than keeping them happy once you've got them, because their value system, morals and family background are such strong influences. Besides, sometimes one person thinks the relationship's going along wonderfully well and is totally unaware their partner is unhappy and looking for something elsewhere.

Who's most likely to have an affair?

If you work in a job where lots of colleagues play around, you're more likely to do it yourself. Why? Because you're being given permission. If you come from a family with a history of affairs, you're a bad risk because you've 'learnt' that's what people do in relationships. Cultural acceptance (in some Mediterranean cultures it's done for men to sleep around) is another green light. Your personal value system also contributes. Some people remain faithful to spouses who've been dead for a decade. Others believe affairs are justified under certain circumstances (if they fall in love with someone else).

People in high-drama professions (like ER doctors and stockbrokers) live life on the edge and are drawn to the excitement of an affair. Any job that requires travel and being away from home a lot, ups the risk because of opportunity, boredom and sexual frustration. The more money you have and the higher your status, the more likely you are to cheat. You've got more opportunities (high income usually means travel), you've got the cash to rent hotel rooms and an inbuilt excuse for being away (it's a work trip).

How do you prevent yourself having one?

Start by ditching that romantic but unrealistic concept that if you love your partner you'll never, ever fancy anyone else. You will. It's normal, it's natural and it doesn't mean you've fallen out of love.

The trick is not to let those attractions develop by creating boundaries to stop yourself being vulnerable. In other words, don't create opportunites for intimacy.

> 'My girlfriends don't understand me at all. I've really got no interest in playing around because I know damn well Steve would know the minute I walked in the door. Why throw away all we've got for one hour of what will probably be bad sex anyway?'
>
> Pamela, 23, student

Going to a very fanciable work colleague's house for 'one for the road' after a very pissy work function is not a terribly good idea. Personally, I'd avoid hanging around any room that has good sorts and alcohol in it, when you're feeling flirty, horny and a tad bored with your partner. If you can't avoid it, for God's sake don't drink.

How are most people found out?

If you're having great sex, your partner can't possibly be having an affair, right? Glass calls it 'the hydraulic pump theory': you only have so much energy for sex, so if you're getting it elsewhere, you won't want it at home. Wrong again. Some people are more passionate at home when they're having sex on the side. The affair sexually arouses them.

It's technology rather than bedroom performance that trips people up. Hit the 'redial' button on your partner's car phone. Look through that nicely itemized mobile phone bill and ring the number that's called most frequently. Pick up their beeper and see 'Darling. Call Me' displayed on the screen. More methods of communication mean more to cover up. Despite this, the fact remains that if you truly *don't* want to be discovered and actively cover your tracks, you probably won't be. If you get found out, you either don't care if you do or aren't being as diligent.

In the *She* poll, 50 per cent of the women who'd had affairs didn't get found out. Out of the 50 per cent who did, 37 per cent confessed.

Does it mean they don't love you if they're having an affair?

Not necessarily. But it does mean they don't respect you and they have a different value system. Generally, men have sex-based affairs; women have emotion-based affairs. Glass's research shows 44 per cent of men who'd had extramarital sex had slight or no emotional involvement. Only 11 per cent of women reported the same. A continuing affair for women usually does mean she's not having her emotional needs met and is growing apart from her partner.

Because both sexes have affairs for different reasons, we assume our partners have them for the same reasons. Men assume that if there's emotional involvement, there's sexual involvement. Women assume if there's sexual involvement, there's emotional involvement. Both could be, and often are, wrong. Lots of women have 'affairs' that don't include sex: lots of men have affairs that include nothing *but* sex. An affair is more serious for both sexes if it happens early in the marriage.

Is it ever just about sex?

Some affairs are and most certainly include it. If it is purely a sex affair, it's usually very *hot* sex. Let's face it: if your partner thinks leaving the lights on is risqué, a hint of something more erotic is very appealing. A girlfriend of mine said she was in the park, eating an ice cream one lunch hour and chatting to a guy from her office that she ran into. He told her she had ice cream on her mouth, leant forward and licked it off with his tongue. That one, simple gesture was enough for her to have an affair with him because her boyfriend wouldn't dream of doing something so spontaneous and sexy. That affair was definitely about sex. Believe me.

Do one-night stands mean anything?

Spur-of-the-moment, no-strings-sex may represent nothing more than a need for it and taking advantage of an opportunity. But it still breaks the trust bond and, if discovered, has the power to destroy a 20-year relationship in one second flat. Women tend to be better at coping with their partners having a one-night stand than men are. While few are thrilled, they find it easier to deal with an impersonal one-off fling than a long-term liaison where their partner shared feelings. Men think the opposite. They'd rather you stared lovingly into someone's eyes over a hundred romantic dinners than shred the sheets with a stranger for ten minutes. Again, it all goes back to the sex/love, male/female thing.

Is there anything positive about having an affair?

Glass says one of the things people like best about affairs is that they get the chance to start over and be who they want to be. If you've been with the same partner for ever, you're usually well and truly stuck in a role. You might have changed dramatically from the person you were when you first met your partner, but they're still likely to see you as you were, rather than the person you've become. If you like the person you've become with your lover, you might not want to return to being 'yourself': the 'old' you, the 'you' your spouse married. (Ironically, plenty of partners would love the 'new' you but rarely get the chance to see it. I know plenty of betrayed partners who say, 'What! He wanted to be more adventurous in bed? God knows I would have loved it if he had been!')

Glass says she rarely asks about 'him' or 'her' – the person they had the affair with – when she counsels couples after an affair. 'I ask about "you". What did you like about yourself in that other relationship? How were you different? What can you do to be that person with your partner?' She says an affair holds up a vanity mirror, the kind with all the little bulbs around it: it gives you a rosy glow to the way you see yourself. The marriage offers a make-up mirror which magnifies every little flaw. Ironically, it's the make-up mirror type of love that's the real one. It means you're loved *despite* all your flaws.

What if your partner has a history of infidelity? Does it mean they'll cheat on you too?

In a word – yes. If your partner has cheated on every person they've been out with – and nothing's changed in their life to make them rethink their behaviour – it's pretty guaranteed they'll do the same to you.

Why do affairs destroy relationships?

'Thou shalt not sleep with other people,' is a pretty standard couple clause. So, for a start, the guilty party is breaking a vow. They've taken what was yours alone – the sexual and emotional intimacy – and shared it with someone else. It's not special any more because it's not something you share exclusively together.

If you love someone and they supposedly love you, you feel safe. It's the two of you against the world. When someone has an affair, everything you trusted is gone and you have to rethink what relationships are all about. If you've been hurt in the past by someone cheating, being hurt by 'the one person I finally thought I could trust' is even more devastating.

It's also destructive, because lying goes with the territory and honesty is the basis of most good relationships. Glass says there are two types of lying people use when having affairs. The 'lie by omission' is when you say, 'I stopped in at Jenny's on the way home.' It's the truth but you've omitted the fact that you were at Jenny's for five minutes and licking Brad's thigh (and other bits) at his house for the rest of the hour. The 'lies of commission' are those 'what a wicked web we weave' type of lies. 'My watch stopped on the way home and the jewellers' was shut and I've got a really important meeting tomorrow and needed to be on time so I drove three hours out of my way to find another jeweller and it turned out they were shut as well so I ——' The long, elaborate, made-up excuses which get more and more complicated to remember.

Even if you do pull through after an affair, there's a loss of innocence and a scar. It takes years of hard work to rebuild trust, if indeed it can be. Couples who do end up staying together often find the relationship's tinged with resentment, sadness and guilt. If most people stopped and mentally pictured their partner's face if they found out, they wouldn't have an affair in the first place. If you're tempted, it's a good tactic.

How can you tell if you're partner's having an affair?

You've got good reason to be suspicious if:

Your instincts tell you something's wrong

Most people who *seriously* suspect their partner is cheating turn out to be right. If you can't put your finger on it, but you *know* something's up, call them on it. If you feel anxious and 'not quite sure of them', it could be a sign they're distancing themselves. Particularly listen to your intuition if you're female and don't have a problem with jealousy. We've got great inner radars.

Your partner's behaviour has changed
If they're less interested in talking generally, it could be because they're scared of slipping up. If you're trying to cover your tracks, you'll volunteer the minimum of details in case you slip up. Is your partner more or less affectionate than usual? More could mean guilty, less that they're withdrawing from you.

They've changed their routine or habits
If your boyfriend used to run at 5 am and now he's running at 7 pm, with aftershave on, you don't need to be a rocket scientist to figure out something's going on. Do they check the answering machine privately, instead of in front of you?

They've changed their appearance
Forget the obvious (the wedding ring's accidentally replaced on the wrong finger or they dropped it down a drain) – look for subtle changes. Have they suddenly lost those few extra kilos? Are they hitting the gym and revamping their wardrobe without a word of criticism or encouragement from you?

They desire sex more or less frequently
If you're having it less, they might be getting it elsewhere. Sometimes, they'll want it more because the affair's boosted their desire for sex in general, not just with their lover. In the words of one (charming) womanizer: 'It's a real turn-on for me to have been with someone else then make love to my wife when I get home.' Remember, though, none of these clues mean anything if they're the *only* clue you've got. If you're having sex more often, it might simply mean your partner has decided to make a bit of effort or invested in a good sex book.

You've found a clue
A box of matches from an unfamiliar restaurant coupled with a guilty reaction. Unexplained florist bills. The friend who calls to

say they haven't seen your partner in ages yet they were supposed to be out to dinner with them the night before. Finding a condom in their wallet or purse – then noticing it missing. All are *Warning! Warning!* signs.

If they're in love with the person they're having an affair with, sometimes your partner will *deliberately* leave clues, hoping to be discovered. Or the person they're having it with will. It's rumoured Jackie O found a pair of women's knickers stuffed into her pillowcase at the White House while she was married to Kennedy.

Also beware the person who smells impossibly fresh and clean after a hard day at the office (they've had a shower after sex at their lover's place). She smells decidedly like after-shave/he smells of a perfume you don't wear? Again, it's a clue all might not be as wonderful as you think and they're rubbing up against someone else.

A new 'friend' is suddenly invited into your home

It sounds bizarre and it is: in an attempt to cover up an affair, some people introduce the person they're having the affair with to their partners. (The logic being you won't possibly suspect if it's not hidden.) Often, it's done to placate the bit-on-the-side. Other times, it's because they both get off on fooling you in front of your eyes. You'll be in the kitchen, removing the lovingly prepared Beef Wellington from the oven, they're in the lounge room having a furtive feel. Be warned if you have children – they notice more than you think ('Mummy, why is Daddy holding that woman's hand under the table?').

There are too many 'wrong numbers'

Wrong numbers happen a few times a year, not once a week. Also beware the 'I'll have to call you back' when the phone rings while you're together – and the old giveaway, 'I realize you've got a problem and you're upset. But I can't fix it right now, if you know what I mean. I promise I'll call first thing from work tomorrow.' The tone of their voice is often a dead giveaway.

It's also not a great sign if your partner's always 'popping out for a few minutes'. Years before mobiles were *de rigueur*, a friend of mine forgot to ask her husband to pick up some milk along with the papers, so drove to the local shops. He was in the public phone box at the bottom of the street, calling his lover.

'I'd suspected for a while but the first I *knew* Gary was cheating was when I got a call from his mistress's husband. "Your husband has ruined my marriage," he said, sobbing on the end of the phone. "Do something." I did. When Gary walked in the door, all smiles and, "How was your day, honey?" I handed him a packed suitcase and said, "Leave."'

Shirley, 42, mother

Your friends drop hints

Men tend to cover up for each other; women feel obliged to give some sort of warning, no matter how subtle. While few people will blurt the news out, many give themselves away by making indirect comments. Pay attention. That passing remark from a friend ('I was reading a story today about infidelity. God, you just never know, do you?') is sometimes a warning.

Your body warns you

Suddenly plagued by thrush and/or urinary tract infections? Having problems getting an erection? It could be because you're suddenly exposed to your partner's lover's infections or your body's accepted what your heart doesn't want to.

You find yourself deliberately not thinking about 'it'

Most people know when their partners are unfaithful – they just don't want to admit it to themselves. But what you don't know *can* hurt you – both physically and mentally. If your partner's not practising safe sex, you're at risk of contracting an STD or, worse, HIV. If you're crying 'for no reason', getting headaches, feeling rundown – again, it's your body's way of saying, 'Hey, you might not want to admit it. But *I* know you think they're cheating and I'm suffering for it.'

They're reckless, ruthless and unreliable.
Constantly late, they check their reflection in the mirror frequently, interrupt while others are speaking, leave the lights blazing when they walk out of a room, run up debts, play hurtful practical jokes and aren't kind to animals. Who are they? According to US sociologists, this is a portrait of people most likely to cheat on their partners. After interviewing 107 couples, they discovered infidelity wasn't the only thing straying partners had in common. They also shared these key personality traits.

Are you overreacting?

Some people will answer 'yes' to all of the above without any reason to do so. Totally innocent acts can take on ominous over-tones if you've got a history or family background of infidelity. Even if you don't have a tarnished background, some people mistakenly think love means never doing *anything* apart. If their partner wants to do something solo, it *must* mean they're having an affair (it doesn't).

If you've got low self-esteem, you're also far more likely to think your partner is being unfaithful. Who could blame them for sleeping around when you're boring/fat/stupid/unsexy/

unattractive? The easiest way to find out if you're being right-fully suspicious or ridiculously paranoid is to ask yourself this: is it normal for me to think my partner's playing around or is it unusual for me to mistrust someone? If it's the latter, keep your eyes open.

How do most people react once they find out their partner's betrayed them?

Most, understandably, go a little nuts. They cry easily. A tape of what their partner got up to plays, and replays, in their head, over and over (and over). They want to know all the affair details (over and over). They don't believe *anything* their partner says any more. Even 'You look nice' is open to conjec-ture ('What do you mean, nice? Obviously I don't look that nice or you wouldn't have had an affair'). They'll alternate between hating their partner, desperately loving them in a sad way and absolutely despising them.

How their partner reacts to this erratic behaviour dictates whether or not the relationship is saveable. If they start saying, 'Oh, for God's sake, can't you just move on?' or blame you ('Well, if you hadn't been so cold, I wouldn't have done it in the first place'), there's little hope. And they're lower than scum. An affair isn't the way to draw attention to a problem, talking is.

Should you confront a partner who you think is having an affair?

If you truly want to know – and can cope with – the answer, definitely. It's the only hope the relationship has got of surviving. If your partner feels bad about what happened or is still happening, they may well feel relieved to be discovered. No more lies, no more guilt, and the chance to get it all out into the open and try to work it out. But if the affair is serious and they were considering leaving, the confrontation could tip them over the edge.

Should you ask for details?

Anyone who's had a long-term affair has led a double life. They've lied. Said they were somewhere when they were actually with someone else. It's natural to want to find out when you were lied to so you can go back, put all the pieces together and make sense of it all. Another reason we ask for details is because we want to know how good our instincts were. Were we right to be suspicious that night he was late from work? Did her car really break down?

Then there's plain old curiosity. What did this person have that I don't? We don't just want to see the bed where the dreaded deed took place, we want to see the kitchen where the coffee was made afterward. Where they both sat, whether she knew he took three sugars and not much milk. If we don't get the details, we make them up. She looks like Julia Roberts, he looks like a young Sean Connery. If the partner refuses to give details, our imaginations conjure up the most painful scenario possible. She's thinner/wittier/better in bed/more successful than we are. They loved them far more than they've ever loved us. The more details we get – good and bad – the more the affairee becomes human and less of a threat. Also, as Glass believes, the more our partner will tell us, the more likely we are to trust them again. If they withhold details, they're protecting them. Not a fab feeling when it's loaded on top of all the rest.

Repeating the story over and over until it no longer feels like someone's stabbing at your heart with sharp knives can be part of the healing process. Certain questions definitely need to be answered. Like: Who was it? Are they or were they in love with them? Why did they do it? Where did they have sex (in the bed you share together)? Is it now over?

Should you confess to an affair?

If your partner has evidence and confronts you, confess. Denying it when there's solid evidence is ridiculous. As for confessing when your partner has no idea, I wouldn't. It might make *you* feel better, like the guilt's been lifted off your shoulders, but all it does is cause them intense pain. If you want to confess because you want to save the relationship, don't. Instead, stop the affair and work hard at doing just that.

You're on the other side and having an affair with a person who's married. They've promised to leave, but will they?

The short answer: probably not. They're getting to have sex with two different people, with two very different positive benefits. Their spouse offers security. You offer excitement. Pretty fabulous, eh? Why would they choose to have just one when they can have both (and live with themselves). The real question is: why are you settling for someone else's leftovers?

Does it usually work out if the two people having an affair leave their partners to be together?

Not usually. In most cases, the appeal was the affair itself, rather than the person. Doing something secretly. Also, there's often a high level of mistrust. After all, they both know each other is capable of lying and cheating because they've had first-hand experience. Couples that do survive are usually the rare few who had an affair for no other reason but love. They finally found their special person but were unfortunately married or involved at the time.

EIGHT WAYS TO REDUCE THE RISK OF AN AFFAIR (YOURS AND THEIRS)

1. **Make sure you both agree on what monogamous means.** Sit down together and spell it out. Is kissing someone being unfaithful?

2. **Make it very plain, very early on in the relationship, that you would leave if your partner cheated, *no matter what the circumstances.*** If they're 100 per cent certain you're not going to hang around to hear the excuses, they'll be much less likely to take the risk.

3. **Have an affair with each other.** Meet during your lunch hours in a hotel room and pretend you're being naughty. Play the part: say, 'Darling, how did you manage to get away?' The couple who play together, stay together.

4. **Don't give in to impulses.** If you're tempted, picture your partner's face if they could *see* you sharing parts of yourself you'd promised to reserve for them exclusively. Move beyond the immediate attraction of giving in to the undeniably erotic appeal of a new body and instead think about the threat of AIDS, lying to your partner, the drama and heartbreak of getting caught, deciding who gets the dog, throwing away all that history and so on.

5. **If your partner says they're unhappy, take it seriously.** If you've got reason for doubt, watch for non-verbal signs that give you clues your partner's distancing themselves but don't ignore the obvious either. If your partner says they don't feel loved, *do something about it*. It doesn't mean the problem's gone away if they stop complaining, they've simply given up. You have been warned.

6. **Do a once-a-month check on your partner.** Ask them 'Are you happy? Is there anything you'd like me to do more of or less of, both sexually and emotionally?' ➢

7. **Do things as a couple, even if you've got kids.** Because our lives are so busy, most parents feel guilty if they don't spend every second at home doing things as a 'family'. But the most precious gift you can give to your children is for them to see Mum and Dad happy. Make time for being a couple as well as parents and make sure it's quality couple time. Studies of monogamy prove conclusively that couples who spend time together are less likely to stray. That doesn't mean just sharing couple 'chores'. Invest in a cleaner, turn off the TV and video and really talk to each other for at least 30 minutes a day and an hour each weekend day.

8. **Concentrate on what's good about being together as well as solving what's bad.** It's great to isolate problem areas and work on solving them, but don't forget to acknowledge the areas you're doing well in too. Make an effort after an argument to point out a 'plus' of being together.

Are they worth another chance? How to decide whether to stay with someone who's betrayed you

Couples hurt each other all the time. Sometimes it's accidental, sometimes deliberate. If you stay with someone for a long period of time, they will do things to upset you. They might forget your birthday or embarrass the hell out of you in front of your boss, be rude to your mother or selfish and self-absorbed when you really need support. Or they might sleep with someone else. And that's the hardest of all hurts to forgive.

Some couples do survive infidelity but *only if both of you honestly think the relationship is worth it and the guilty person is prepared to do everything it takes to win back your trust and love.* If your partner has cheated on you, I want you to think long and hard about whether it's worth staying with them. A lot of the time, cheating partners don't deserve to be forgiven. Sit down for a few hours, somewhere quiet and private and ask yourself the following questions:

Have they cheated on other people in the past?
If your partner's got a history of being unfaithful and they've just done it to you, forget it. You gave them a new chance and they failed dismally. They've always cheated, they've cheated on you, chances are they'll do it again (and again) until someone – hopefully you – tells them to Sod Off and they realize they can't get away with it. Even then, they're a far worse bet than the average person.

Why did they do it?
This is crucial: it's your best indicator of whether someone deserves a second chance. A one-off incident with seemingly genuine reasons to explain it is a lot easier to forgive than repeated slip-ups or a long-term affair. Perhaps it was very early in the relationship and there was an unspoken rather than verbal commitment between you. An ex showed up at their house, they ended up drunk and in bed together. You might decide it's not worth throwing a perfectly good relationship away over this. I'd agree with you in this case. If they're sorry, they accept what they did was wrong and there's no evidence it's been repeated or ever will be, hang in there. But if it happened *after* the relationship became serious, and both of you knew it was, that's a different story.

Don't, whatever you do, fall for the old 'I was drunk and it just happened' story. What utter crap! One-night stands don't 'just happen'. Women don't suddenly decide to take their clothes off without a good reason. They don't 'force' him into having sex. And what was she doing in his bedroom/hotel room/car in the first place? (Don't feel too smug, girls, we use the 'I was drunk' line just as often, and the same applies to us.)

The fact is, no matter how drunk you are, if you've bonked someone you shouldn't have, there were several points along the way when you decided to take it further. Even if it was a drunken *'Oh, what the hell,'* you made a decision to do something you *knew* would hurt your partner.

Do their reasons justify their behaviour?

Put yourself in their shoes. If you were them, feeling the way they did, in the situation they were in, what would you do? Can you understand it? Could you see them being in the same predicament in the future? How would they react then? What's your gut reaction? Does it seem out of character or aren't you really surprised? Knowing all this, do you think, with time, you could trust this person again – or would you always feel insecure? What guarantees can they give you that it won't happen again? What would be different next time?

Also ask yourself this: Why do I want to stay with someone who behaved in this way? Why did I deserve to be treated this way? Was the relationship really over before the affair started – and is way beyond saving now? Or do you think there's a good, justifiable, I-can-live-with-this reason? Don't cling on just because you're scared of being alone. Don't let fear rob you of logic and dignity.

What state was your relationship in when it happened?

As we touched on earlier, you'll be much more likely to forgive (if not forget) if you were aware your partner was unhappy, the relationship wasn't great and you were suspicious. If, on the other hand, you didn't notice a single sign that anything was wrong – they seemed happy and affectionate and you thought you were living *The Brady Bunch*, it's incredibly hard to trust again. If there were no clues last time round, how will you know in the future if it happens again? What sort of person are they if they can sleep with someone behind your back and not show the slightest hint of guilt?

If the relationship was struggling, sometimes (very, very rarely, but it does happen) an affair can bring problems to a head and you finally solve them together.

> So much for male bonding. One in five men would make a pass at his best friend's girlfriend. But only one in 30 women said they'd do the same.

Do they obviously regret what they've done?

I mean *really* regret it. A cut-off-their-right-arm-if-they-could-take-it-back kind of regret. Are they as, if not more, miserable about the pain it's caused as you are?

If you decide to stay

Leave them – if just for a few weeks

If you understand why they've cheated and don't honestly think it will happen again, by all means give it another go. But don't make it easy.

Your first reaction will be to cling to each other like limpets. Don't. If you live together, get them to move out for a few weeks. It'll show you mean business and give you a chance to sort through your emotions. If you don't live together, say you don't want to see them for a while. If you don't trust them enough to behave themselves without you for a few weeks, forget it now. Keep in touch with phone calls during the time apart, but that's it.

Think about why they strayed

During this time, think about the reason why they sought sex and/or intimacy elsewhere. Are there things the two of you could do to improve your relationship to ensure it won't happen again?

Write down all the questions you still need answers on
Keep a notebook handy and write down every single thing you don't understand about the affair or want further explanation on.

Meet after two weeks (minimum) or when you're feeling calmer
If they don't show up with black circles around their eyes, looking like they've camped out at Weight Watchers, forget it. You've been torn apart by this – so should they be. They should spend the time apart worrying themselves stupid whether they've lost you for good. If they don't think there's a good chance of it, they haven't taken it seriously and probably will do it again.

This won't be a pleasant meeting. Warn your partner there are lots of questions you still need answered, then whip out that notebook and hit them with all of them. This will be incredibly painful. When you see each other again, you'll probably both burst into tears. The reality of what they've done will hit both of you all over again. But you need to spend a few hours thrashing it all out so you can clear the air as much as possible.

Don't be surprised if you end up storming out when you hear some of their answers. Take five minutes to calm down, then try again. If you can't, arrange to meet in a day or two and try again. Don't go home together whatever the outcome.

Wait for the anger to subside
That might take a day, a week, a month or longer. When you're feeling logical, rethink the situation. Now you have *all* the facts or at least all the answers you're going to get, how do you feel? Are you still sure you want to try again? Still reasonably confident you'll both pull through and there's enough to work with? Now's the time to move back in or start seeing each other regularly again. You're ready to start healing. Read this book cover to cover, especially the parts on building good communication

skills. Get your partner to do the same: you need to talk and listen to each other to get through this.

Healing: when will the pain go?

'How long will it take before the pain goes?' Louise asked me, one month after she found out her much-loved husband had a year-long affair. She had lines on her face that weren't there last time I saw her. Her eyes were weird: she had the look people get when they've just witnessed a horrific car accident and can't forget it. She'd lost at least ten kilos and had on one brown shoe and one black shoe. The pain she was feeling was so intense, if you reached out you could touch it.

It's pretty hard to answer a question like that. My honest

response would have been 'never'. As it turns out, the pain went after two years – when she left her husband. The wound was too deep to heal. How quickly *you'll* heal depends on the level of betrayal. The more intense and intimate the relationship, the harder an affair hits. If someone cheats three months in, it hurts, but if someone cheats three years in, it hurts horribly. For this reason, I've directed this section to couples who've been together for a couple of years before the incident – and want to stay together a long time.

> 'The absolute, total indignity of it all was that I suffered through two months of couples' counselling, trying to work it all out with him. Two months of pain and heartache and at the end of it, he dumped me anyway.'
>
> Kate, 25, nurse

Some people recover quickly from an affair, others will take longer. Your personality has a lot to do with how quickly you'll heal. If you're a happy, 'up' type of person who recovers from life's knocks easily, it will take you less time to get over a betrayal than someone who tends to dwell on the negative – or has been betrayed before.

Taking blame

One of the most common questions after an affair is, 'Will our relationship ever be the same again?' The answer is no. Your old relationship is dead and you need to build a new one. That's not necessarily a bad thing. The new relationship might be even better than the first in lots of ways, but make no mistake about it, it's never going to be as 'pure' as it was. The innocence and trust have gone and can never be resurrected. The aim is to replace it with other qualities, like, 'We are survivors – even this didn't break us up.'

You will feel angry and insecure for months, maybe longer

if you've been together a long time. Your natural inclination will be to take it out on your partner – and rightly so. If they're truly worth giving another chance, they'll put up with whatever you dish out and reassure you each and every time you get upset. If they don't do this, tell them, 'You caused this. You're the one who betrayed me. You're the one who broke the trust. It's up to you to get us through this.' Again, the onus is on the person who strayed to fix the relationship – not the innocent victim.

Working together

According to Shirley Glass, one of the goals of healing the damage from an affair is to let the unfaithful person express all the parts of themselves they were able to satisfy within the affair. This might be the freedom to be the 'new' them, or reworking the relationship to satisfy something they were craving. Lots of men married to super-competent women, she says, have affairs with weak women so they feel needed. This doesn't mean you have to ditch the business suit for an apron, but letting him see more of your vulnerable side might be a good idea. If she had an affair because you spent every waking hour at work, set limits. Take weekends off, bring work home rather than working late in the office.

Rebuilding trust

The only way to regain trust is to be honest – about everything, but most particularly about anything relating to the person involved in the affair. If you work with them, that means coming home and saying, 'I saw Rachel today and she was hassling me to have a drink. I told her, "I'm so *not* interested it's not funny. I'm going home to the person I love."' If you don't reveal things like this, you run the risk of your workmate, John, seeing the two of you talking intimately, going home and telling his wife, Joan, it's all on again. Joan tells Shirley, her best friend, who happens to work with your partner's best friend. Get my point?

Your partner shouldn't have to ask for information like this, you should offer it freely – and follow it up with bucketloads of reassurance. Eventually, you'll talk about the affair and events and people relating to it, less and less. But it will always crop up again in conversation, even if it's once every five years.

> 'I got propositioned by a real babe once. There was no way Karen would find out but I didn't care. I loved her so much I didn't give it a moment's serious consideration.'
>
> Ian, 33, architect

A well-on-the-way-to-recovering couple, says Glass, will have moved past the basic details ('Did you have oral sex?') to searching for meaning ('If you knew it was wrong, why didn't you stop?'). Work on taking the positive view that your relationship could be better because of what happened. It's forced you to talk more openly, to spell out needs and expectations clearly.

The signs of recovery

US psychotherapist Mira Kirshenbaum puts it perfectly when she says time heals all *healable* wounds. In other words, if you're not feeling better after a period of time, it's not going to work – ever – with the person who betrayed you. These are some signs time is healing your wounds. I've included some of Kirshenbaum's ideas in this realistic timetable for positive healing.

After the first month

- You have moments when you can calmly discuss couple issues (not relating to the betrayal) with your partner without dissolving into tears or feeling angry.
- You have a feeling things will work out in the end.

- There's some sign of 'cooling off'. You're still as angry as hell, but it's not consuming your life.
- The cheating partner shows obvious signs of guilt and accepts blame.

After two months to one year
- You can discuss the incident for a few minutes, quite rationally, before you start feeling upset.
- You forget about it for hours at a time.
- You've gone back to doing some of the things you used to enjoy together before 'it' happened.
- You find yourself being affectionate, like you used to, for a day or so, 'forgetting' to punish them by withholding affection.
- You can imagine trusting them 90 per cent.
- You don't feel like vomiting every time you think about what happened.

After the first year
- Your relationship reverts back to 'normal' for months at a time. There are still rough patches when the pain resurfaces but it goes away again.
- You can listen to your partner's explanation of how and why it happened without getting very upset. When you discuss it together, you feel hurt but not as hurt as before. The intensity has eased to a 'liveable' level.

After the first five years
- You both feel you've learned from your mistakes and are confident they won't be repeated in the future.
- Your partner still accepts responsibility for what they did but you've stopped pointing the finger of blame.
- You feel good about yourselves as a couple, despite what happened.

Bad Love Habits

Always falling for people who are wrong for you
or treat you badly? The reasons why and how
to fix it

● ●

By the time we've got our heads down the loo, throwing up our first triple Scotch and Coke, most of us have a pretty good idea of who we think we are and how we think the world's going to treat us. At 18 years old, we're already 95 per cent emotionally programmed: a trillion life experiences have moulded our personality. If all *your* life experiences have been wonderful, you're liable to be bursting with self-confidence, optimistic and enviously free of any emotional baggage. Relationships will be a breeze for you. You'll be able to trust, love and commit without a problem; go on to marry, raise children and die happy. Good for you – if you exist.

It's a rare person who has a dream run along life's highway. It's practically impossible to avoid the potholes, detours, traffic jams and roadblocks, and all of them leave their mark. Every time we have a bad or good experience or relationship, it affects our perception of the world. Mum and Dad were sweeter than a bowl of Jelly Beans, you won the lottery at 21 and date super-models? It's a bloody marvellous place! A different story if your Mum died young, you dropped out of school, ended up on the dole and still haven't lost your virginity at 26. Unfortunately, just as good life experiences tend to set you up for more (happiness makes others happy), bad life experiences do the same (misery loves company).

How you feel about yourself is strongly linked to how nurturing your parents and siblings were to you when you were growing up – Mum especially. Stable, healthy mothering is great protection against most emotional problems.

If you're depressed and insecure or angry and suspicious of people and their motives, you're hardly likely to be top of happy people's must-invite-them party list.

What's *really* unfair is that you can't control all of the things that happen to you in life. Death and love are two obvious examples. We can't stop people from dying and we can't make people fall in love with us or stop them falling out of it. We also can't stop people treating us badly when we're a child, sometimes even as an adult. What you *can* do, though, is analyse what's happened to you so you understand the influence it may be having on your life now. The next step is to challenge those destructive attitudes, either by simply being aware of them or by seeking professional help.

Whatever's happened to you in the past doesn't *have* to dictate your future. Whether you had doting, fabulous parents or a mum and dad fresh from hell, loving, long-lasting relationships or a series of horrendous disappointments, you still have the power to be the person you'd like to be and live the life you want to live.

This chapter is by far the most serious in the book because I cover truly devastating past influences like sexual and physical abuse. But it's also worth reading if you simply want answers to some of those niggling questions. Like why you always go for wild types, why the people who adore you are always the ones you *don't* want, and why it is that you seem to fall for the same type of partner over and over and over again, even though you know it'll end in boredom or tears.

KID STUFF: THE MESSAGES ABOUT LOVE AND LIFE YOU GOT FROM YOUR FAMILY

Parents are often given all the credit – and the blame – for how their children turn out. You get accepted into university, your parents are congratulated on producing such a smart child. You decide you'd rather be a Gothic and do weird things with goat's blood, people say, 'I wonder where George and Martha went wrong?' We all do it. If some snotty brat's wiping chocolatey fingers all over your skirt in the supermarket queue, it's the parent you glare at, not the child. As adults, plenty of us blame our parents for any (or all) of our shortcomings. But how much is their fault – and what can you do to change it?

What nature gave you: genes

The genes you inherit influence your personality and your relationships with other people. One of the longest, most thorough studies of child development showed genes have a much greater effect on your personality than previously thought. They're responsible for how well you do in school, how you get on with others, whether you choose a career as a corporate or a life of crime. There's zilch you can do about genes, except be aware of what you've inherited and consciously fight against those that don't work for you.

What your parents gave you: environment

We don't just hatch out of an egg and raise ourselves. We're dependent on people around us, and no matter how much our parents love us or how good their intentions, they're human and make mistakes. After all, they have *their* own set of genes inherited from *their* parents, and how *their* parents brought them up influences the way they brought you up. Unless you've done some serious soul-searching (which is what this chapter is all about), we're all products of the generation before.

Ideally, parents are loving, supportive and affectionate while simultaneously encouraging their children to be independent and make their own decisions. That's the theory. Unfortunately, not too many of us grow up with Mike and Carol Brady as parents. Some parents are cold and distant, others cruel and abusive. Most muddle their way through, alternating between Parents of the Year and 'Oh, for God's sake, what do you want *now!*' parents, depending on how far behind on the mortgage payments they are. All parents have some flaws, and as a little child, you are like a sponge, soaking up whatever their attitudes are and reacting to the way they treat you.

Mum and Dad in the bedroom

One of the most important influences on the romantic relationships you have now is the relationship your parents had. We learn how men treat women, how women treat men and how a relationship functions by the way our parents behaved toward each other. Scary thought, isn't it. Now here's the really scary part: *no matter what sort of relationship your parents had, you'll subconsciously search to find a replica of it, or (if you've consciously thought about it) the complete opposite.* Sometimes that's healthy. If you admired your parents' partnership, it's sensible to look for the same. It's also sensible to want something completely different if you didn't. The problem with all this is that we're naturally programmed to look for mum and dad clones. As I said, unless you're intensely aware of what your subconscious is up to, you aren't even aware of what's going on.

I went out with a guy once who said the most attractive thing about me was my independence. Yet what did we fight about the most? My independence and him feeling like he wasn't needed. When I met his parents it all fell into place. Look up 'doormat' in the dictionary and there was a picture of his mother: he spent the entire visit telling her to stick up for herself. So while he admired me because I was capable and strong, he was *used to* the opposite scenario. Intellectually, he thought it was great; emotionally, it felt uncomfortable. Being aware of influences like these can make sense of those confusing conflicts.

> 'I hated my father for years – it's only now I realize he did the best he could. He wasn't around as much as he should have been because he had to work seven days a week to pay the bills. No-one can be purely a parent 24 hours a day. I now accept it wasn't choice that stopped him from being there for me, it was necessity.'
>
> Sven, 24, physiotherapist

Your opposite-sex parent: who you're modelling your *future partner on*

🅕 FOR HER

The way you feel about your father affects the way you feel about all men. He's the first man you meet, the first you get close to, so we tend to judge all men by him. My father is a good-looking, successful businessman. He's always impeccably groomed, has travelled the world and mixed it with the best of them. He also happens to be refreshingly down-to-earth, has always looked out for the underdog and couldn't really give a damn about money so long as he's got enough to brew his own beer. Growing up, I thought all men would be like him. It's only now I realize you don't often find all those qualities in the one person, and measuring boyfriends against his ideal is unfair.

If your father was successful, you go out there thinking all grown-up men will be. If he was nice, all men will be nice to you. If he

wasn't so nice, you think quite the opposite. In fact, if you don't trust men, Dad's usually got something to do with it.

The old theory that women who love their fathers marry a man just like him does have some truth to it. If Dad looked like Sean Connery on a good day, you probably are attracted to good-looking men. If he looked like Mr Bean on a bad day, you'll probably be less impressed by looks and more attracted to personality. But your partner doesn't have to *look* like dear old Dad to be similar to him – they might be similar in personality.

Often, it's the *type* of relationship you had with your father that you're trying to replicate. If he was warm and wonderful and loved you no matter what, you'll probably try to find a guy who'll do just the same. If Dad was distant and didn't show any love or affection, unfortunately, the same thing can happen. You may find yourself drawn to guys just like him – cold, uncaring men – *because that's what you're used to*. That was your first male–female relationship, so it feels normal to you.

Ⓜ FOR HIM

It's worth reading the 'For her' section above because most of it also applies to mothers and sons. If your mum was a stunner, she could well be your blueprint for what you consider attractive in a partner. Again though, it's more likely you'll seek out the same *type* of relationship.

If you had a good relationship with your mum, it's likely you'll choose to settle down with someone who has the same personality type as her. If she was a homebody and Dad revelled in being looked after, you'll probably be attracted to a traditional girl who's happy to stay home, bring up the kids and warm your slippers by the fire. If you thought Mum sold herself short, you may consciously search for someone who's kicking arse in the boardroom.

The way your father treats your mother is your blueprint of how you'll treat women. You learnt from Dad when and how often to send flowers. Mum's response will dictate just how far you think wooing will get you. The more carefully you look at the dynamics between your parents, the more you'll discover about your own relationship strengths and weaknesses.

YOUR OPPOSITE-SEX SIBLING
For her

Women learn a lot from a close relationship with a good brother: it can set you up for a lifetime of easy, comfortable relationships with men. Having a brother means you've got a walking, talking, live specimen of manhood to study, experiment and practise on during those angst-ridden, sexually formative years. As an adult, you've got the male perspective covered by someone you know and trust.

If you grew up with a brother you admired, you're likely to relate better to men in general. It's because you've seen men as real people rather than knights in shining armour. Women with brothers tend to have a more realistic, rational view of men because they've spent time around males they're not sexually involved with. You've seen that men can be competitive and seem to think more of their mates than their girlfriend, but also that they cry and have bad-hair days. If he puts a brotherly arm around your shoulder now and then, you'll also learn that men can be supportive. There are lots of nice messages a brother can give you about how men treat women. ➤

If you didn't have a brother, it's hardly your fault. Just be aware that you'll be more likely to view men as future boyfriend or marriage material rather than potential friends. If you attended a girls-only school and didn't have friends with brothers, your contact with men was even more limited. Men were – and still may be – mysterious creatures who made you giggle, blush and hide your face. Very often, the only males you may have mixed with were those who asked you out. Because of this, you've got higher romantic ideals: men bring flowers and chocolates and smell of aftershave and hair gel. Girls with brothers know what teenage boys really smell like (and it ain't pleasant!).

Feeling sorry for yourself if you're brotherless? Sure, you missed out in some areas but you're still better off than the girl who grew up with a not-so-nice male sibling. Some brothers are outright cruel or unbalanced. They drill holes in bathroom walls to watch their sisters shower, get drunk and make sexual passes at them. Trusting your brother is important, and if he breaks this trust, especially with sexual boundaries, you can end up with long-term difficulties and bad messages. Often you'll shut down your sexual side altogether, to be safe.

Brothers who are cold or dismissive of sisters also leave their mark. If your brother treated you as a second-class citizen, ridiculed you, criticized or ignored you, he sent a strong message about how other men will treat you. If you're lucky enough to go on to date caring and sharing types of boyfriends, it will dilute the effect. Date a bastard and your initial impressions will be confirmed. A good brother–sister relationship celebrates the differences between men and women; a bad one reflects the age-old battle between the sexes.

For him

Read the 'For her' section – the principles are the same. While your sister was surreptitiously studying you, you were ➤

doing the same with her. Your sisterless friends were still trying to figure out how to get to first base, you were streets ahead in deciphering what makes girls tick. You saw that women tend to be more emotional, noticed that she talked a lot, took a long time to get ready and that her girlfriends were important. When you went out with a female, you understood her a little better. Later in life, your sister's often the one you'll turn to for clues on why your girlfriend's upset when you wouldn't have the foggiest why.

As with women, if you didn't have any sisters, the opposite sex may seem a bit confusing. If your mates were sisterless as well, you may have grown up to be one of those men who are fond of saying, 'I just can't work women out.' As a child you probably ran around the playground passing 'girl's germs' onto others; as an adolescent you were probably shy on dates, the shoe-shuffling, blushing adolescent with a constantly bobbing Adam's apple.

If your sister was an out-and-out bitch, you grew up being highly suspicious of women. The message you got from her: men are the enemy. That doesn't seem true (you're nice, your friends are nice), so you reinterpret it to read: women are the enemy. Again, a few experiences with understanding, open girlfriends can break the mould. Dating ice-queens reinforces your worst fears.

The parent–partner checklist: how much influence do your parents have on your love life?
Ⓜ Ⓕ FOR BOTH OF YOU

It's worth analysing the effect your parents have had, to make sure your instincts are guiding you in the right direction. Spend an hour or so doing this exercise – you might be surprised what it turns up!

How do you feel about their relationship? Do you want the sort of relationship your parents have or had for yourself? If you do, follow your instincts: you're already programmed in the right direction. If you'd rather stay single than endure a carbon copy of your parents' marriage, write down all the qualities you dislike about it and be on the alert. That's what you'll subconsciously try to turn *your* relationships into, because it's familiar to you. It's a good idea to show serious partners what you've written down and to ask them to do the same with their parents' relationship. Both of you can then watch the other doesn't lapse into unwanted behaviour patterns.

How did your parents treat each other? Was it an equal relationship or was one partner dominant and the other submissive? It doesn't matter which sex was which: your brain's already chosen which role *you'd* prefer to play and is seeking out the matching bookend. If Mum was downtrodden and you looked at her in disgust, wondering why she let herself be treated badly, you may well pick a man who *you* can boss around.

Did either parent have affairs? Pay particular attention if the answer is yes. Parental affairs have a dramatic impact on your future relationships. If you're female and Dad had affairs, you've learnt not to trust men like him. If Mum was the one getting more than just tennis lessons, you might find yourself severely tempted to play around when you're given the opportunity.

If you're a male, watching Dad cheat as a young boy sent you this message: this is how men treat women. You'll grow up thinking that's what all men do – or, if you were disgusted with him, turn out to be as faithful as old Rover (perhaps, hanging around when you actually *shouldn't*). Work out what attitude their affair left you with and decide if you like what you discover. If you don't – it's left you oversuspicious or scared of getting close – again, you'll need to actively fight against it.

Did your parents split? If your parents split up, you've learnt how to leave. When your own relationship hits a problem patch, you may well bail out rather than stick around and try to sort out the mess. If your parents stayed together even though they were miserable, you're likely to stay put, even if you're as unhappy as they were.

How do your partners measure up? Write down ten adjectives to describe your opposite-sex parent, then do the same for past or current boyfriends or girlfriends. Are they unerringly similar or completely the opposite? You should be able to work out from this whether you're trying to find a partner just like Mum or Dad – or steering clear of anyone like them.

Check you're heading in the right direction. If your opposite-sex parent had great qualities and you're trying to find a match, that's healthy. Just check you're not looking for the impossible and don't look at Mum or Dad with huge rose-coloured glasses on!

If your relationship with your opposite-sex parent wasn't so great and they weren't someone you looked up to, it's obviously not a good idea to seek out the same personality type. If your lists suggest you're subconsciously drawn to men or women like them and you feel like jumping off the nearest cliff at the thought, don't panic. You've just taken the first step to breaking their hold by recognizing the pattern. Keep your eyes open when you first meet someone new and check the lists after the first date, one month in, three months in and every six months after that. Ask a close friend to also check they aren't another Daddy or Mummy clone.

Let go of the blame. Once you've done the deep analysis and know what legacies they've left you, stop blaming your parents for making you this way. The quicker you accept it wasn't intentional and forgive them, the quicker you'll reduce the influence they have. Take responsibility for your life. It's pointless blaming your mother for being attracted to bad boys even if she did marry one. She had her own influences. Instead, count yourself lucky for recognizing the pattern *before* you name your first child. Look for the positive things your parents gave you. Even if Dad was an arrogant son of a bitch, maybe he taught you how to stand up for yourself.

> 'I stopped looking at my parents as Mum and Dad and started relating to them as friends. I let them into my life and stopped censoring conversations, gave them a chance to see who I really was. They surprised me by how interested they were – then *they* started opening up.'
> Judy, 26, writer

Your mother may be clingy and dependent but she *was* always there for you when you were a child. Recognize that, despite their flaws, your parents did their best.

GO OUT WITH WHO YOU WANT, NOT WHO YOUR PARENTS EXPECT YOU TO

Everyone who's close to their family would prefer to get the golden seal of approval on their partner and sometimes they *can* see things you can't. But part of growing up is a healthy emotional distance from your family – their opinion matters, but ultimately you should make up your own mind about who you go out with, and they should allow you to do that.

If they don't, it's up to you to make a stand.

If you're serious about someone, that relationship should come first, family second. If they don't like your choice, it's hard luck for them. You're well within your rights to say to your family, 'I've chosen this person and I like them. I expect you to treat them with respect and if you can't behave ➢

politely, I can't involve you in that part of my life. I want you in my life but not if you can't respect my decisions and my judgement.' If you feel silly saying this face to face, write your family a warm but firm letter along the same lines: 'Mum/dad/brother/sister, I felt you made X feel uncomfortable when we came over for dinner. I want you to understand how important he/she is to me' then add the speech above, putting it into your own words. Yes, it is formal but emotions run hot in situations like these and, in my experience, you're better off handing over a carefully worded letter than trying to talk it through.

If your family refuse to see sense, see them less frequently, minus your partner. Make it obvious you won't be seeing them as often as they'd like but if they insist you come solo, that's all you can offer. With time, they might well soften.

Now, this is all assuming you haven't hooked up with someone who's treating you badly or an obvious bad choice. If your partner turned up drunk or stoned, kicked the cat, insulted your mother and was sick on the lounge room floor, I'm with them. Ditto the girl or guy who doesn't make a real effort to get on with and be liked by your family. It's a two-way street – and it's also a good test of how serious your partner is about you. If they're a nice person and intend sticking around, it's in their interests to get on with everyone. The more effort they make, the keener they are on you.

DESTRUCTIVE RELATIONSHIP PATTERNS – AND HOW TO BREAK FREE

We all know someone who's been in a bad relationship. The girlfriend who married a nice guy, then left for *him*: the loser ex of hers, who everyone else hated. The bright, successful young lawyer who slays them in the courtroom but stays with a no-hoper girlfriend who's addicted to both drugs and other men. *Why did they choose them? Why don't they leave?* we think to ourselves. How someone so intelligent, attractive and *normal* could end up in that situation really is beyond us.

When people constantly go out with people who are bad for them, it's usually because they've developed a destructive relationship pattern. It's not rotten luck – they're subconsciously *choosing* people who treat them badly because of something which happened in the past.

How healthy are *your* love habits? Skim through the following to see if any apply to past or current lovers.

You've got bad love habits if:

- **You love your partner, even though your head tells you you're not compatible.**
- **You're putting up with bad treatment.** You tend to have an 'I want you whether you want me or not' attitude toward love. You keep on loving in the face of abuse, neglect and clear absence of any feeling on the other person's part.
- **You believe there is only one magic person out there who can make you truly happy.** All of us hope like hell it works out with someone new, but we give ourselves a safety net: we'd like it to work, but we realize it might not. Obsessive lovers have no safety net because they're convinced their partner is the only person who can make them happy. That's why they cling on so hard.
- **You've tried to leave in the past but can't.** Even though you're miserable in the relationship, you're unhappier without it.
- **They've left you but you won't accept they're gone.** Many people switch into denial. Even if their partner's married someone else, it means nothing ('They're living with them but their heart belongs to me').
- **Your relationships are always bad but the sex is fantastic.** If there's one thing destructive relationships do

have going for them, it's great sex. Because emotions are stretched to screaming point, sex can be nothing short of spectacular. 'I had sex every day for four years and loved every minute of it,' says Jan, 22. 'Even in the end, when I hated him, I still craved his body.'

- **Your friends and family often don't like the partners you choose.** If you get on with your parents and friends and respect their opinions on everything else except your love life, pay attention. If they're sensible about other things, they're likely to be right about this as well.
- **You sometimes feel like you're on an emotional roller-coaster.** Settled isn't a word that describes your relationships.
- **Other relationships suffer when you fall in love.** You stop seeing friends, family and other people who were important to you.
- **Your work and health also take a dive.** Does work come last when you're in a relationship? Do you become increasingly reliant on addictive substances like alcohol and cigarettes? Eat much more – or less – than you used to?
- **People who care about you often say your partners don't treat you as well as you deserve.** Sometimes, they'll come straight out and say, 'You're mad. They're treating you badly. You should leave.'
- **You constantly think about a past lover who you haven't seen or heard from in years.**
- **You find yourself returning to the same lover time and time again – even though it never seems to work out.**
- **You live for the day when you'll meet a perfect person and live happily ever after.** Your life won't officially start until then.

Feeling a little uncomfortable because most points are ringing true? Here's how to up your chances of making the next person you meet different from the last.

Ten steps to kicking the addiction

I'll go into specifics a little later, but whatever your particular destructive relationship pattern is, these general rules still apply to you.

1. Work out what your pattern is

Think like a shrink. All psychologists and psychiatrists do is get you to think past the surface and pinpoint what's really happening below. Try this DIY therapy.

Write down what usually goes wrong with your relationships at the top of one page. For example:

Problem: I always go out with men/women who dump me and treat me badly.

On a separate sheet, do the partner–parent checklist exercise (above). Take a long look at what's in front of you. Can you see a connection between your childhood and your relationship problem? Try to tap into the emotions you felt as a child. If your parents fought fiercely, you might have thought, *I have to be really good or they'll start shouting at me.* Twenty years on, you're still sugar-coating every sentence and timid about upsetting people. Is that the reason why you don't stick up for yourself and let people treat you badly?

Underneath your relationship problem, write down any influence your childhood has had. For example, for the problem list above, you might write:

Childhood influence: Because I grew up surrounded by anger, I avoid expressing anger now. I'm too scared to stick up for myself.

Underneath those two statements, write down your aim: what you want your relationships to be like in the future. For example:

> 'The rough times are there for a reason. Learn from them, toughen up if you need to, but don't carry around baggage for the rest of your life.'
> Sue, 42, flight steward

Aim: I want to be treated well. I deserve to be treated well.

Next, write down the sort of person you think would be able to achieve the aim you've written:

The sort of person who would be treated well in relationships:

- has respect for themselves: doesn't let others take advantage of them, has a high self-esteem and sticks up for themselves;
- walks proud and tall: has friends who admire and respect them.

Try to list as many personality traits you can think of and add to the list whenever you think of more. Watch friends who are in relationships you admire. What is it about them that makes their partner respect them and treat them well?

2. Play pretend

Every morning, look at these personality traits – this is the person you'd like to be. Now you're going to pretend you *are* that person by acting the part. That's right, pretend the person you'd like to be is a character in a TV soap and you've just won the role. Walk the way they would, dress the way they would, interact with people the way they would (and only the people they would). At the end of each day, record what happened. How did you feel? Probably like a complete twit to begin with! Did people react to you differently? Close friends probably thought you were a little weird. If they do question the 'new you', simply say, 'I've turned over a new leaf.' Keep friends who say, 'Good for you!'; ditch those who respond with, 'You'll never keep it up.'

Continue 'acting' for a few months and you'll notice two things start to happen. First, you're only acting part of the time because you're so used to the role you're playing, it's starting to feel more natural than the 'real' you. Secondly, people are reacting to you differently, as though you *are* this new person.

No prizes for guessing what happens next: you *become* this

person. You attract partners who treat you well because the new you doesn't put up with any less. Easy, wasn't it!

3. When you next meet someone, don't have sex too soon

Sleep together before you get to know someone and you risk being emotionally bonded to a person you really have nothing in common with. If you don't stop the affair when you realize your mistake, you'll end up addicted to the sex – and in the middle of another huge mess.

4. Don't slip back into old habits

Try hard to see people as they really are, not as you'd like them to be. Every single time a partner doesn't come through with a promise, think long and hard about if it's worth going further. They said they'd phone on a particular day but didn't? Challenge them. No-one's so flat out they can't make one phone call, even if it's just to say, 'The market's crashed. I can't talk now but I'll call the minute I can.'

5. Spell out your needs

Say, 'I understand why you couldn't call for a long chat, but next time, a two-second explanatory phone call would be appreciated.'

6. No second chances

One warning, then they're out. You need to be tougher on partners than the average person to break the doormat habit. Once you start giving second chances, you'll give third, and fourth and so on.

7. Listen to your instincts

If you feel uneasy and not quite right about your relationship, sit down and work out why. Is it something they've said?

Something they've done? A flirtatious look followed by a guilty one when you caught their eye? A comment by a friend of theirs, which they quickly glossed over? Do they seem like they're hiding something from you?

Keep analysing until you pin down the source of that funny feeling and have a good idea where it came from. Then look for evidence to back up whatever theory it is you've come up with. If you can't find any, it could be you're a little paranoid because other relationships went sour. If you do find evidence, challenge your partner with it. Listen to their explanation but if you're not satisfied, leave.

Do you dwell on bad past events and find it hard to talk about your feelings? You could have a toxic personality – one which literally makes you sick. Researchers found people who 'bottle things up' suffer far more health problems than those who let it all out. Yet another reason to work through any negative emotions.

8. Watch your self-esteem
Low self-esteem is nearly always the reason why people get stuck in obsessive, destructive relationships. Choose partners who make you feel a million dollars. If they don't make you feel good about yourself, they're not right for you.

9. Avoid drugs and alcohol
They skew your judgement.

10. Shift the focus from worrying about the relationship, to worrying about yourself
Become obsessed with *your* needs and desires instead of your partner's. Have your own life plan, which doesn't include a partner but is flexible enough to involve one if they're special.

This time, they're coming along with *you* for the ride, not the other way around.

Now, let's move into more specific problems and solutions.

Why do I fall for the same type over and over (instead of learning from my mistakes)?

Kate looked hard at the man sitting in front of her and wondered, as she had so many times before, why she didn't find him attractive. Tim was a close friend of hers who'd made it clear right from the start that he'd like more. Tall, blond and athletic, he certainly didn't lack for female attention. Tim was intelligent, gregarious and liked the same clubs and restaurants she did. He made her laugh, he listened to her problems, he had everything she was looking for, except . . . 'I guess he's just not my type,' Kate sighed. 'Pity.'

Her friends would certainly echo that sentiment. Kate's 'type' are dark, olive-skinned, handsome men who all have one thing in common: a tendency to stop calling once the relationship gets serious. At 28, Kate is keen to settle down, maybe even start a family, except the guys she likes don't share her enthusiasm. A case of looking for Daddy, who also happens to be a dark-haired bad boy? Low self-esteem from being dumped time after time? Or the end result of one hot night in Greece when Kate, a 17-year-old backpacker, happily lost her virginity to a dark, handsome local bartender who gave her more than free drinks? Knowing Kate's background, my guess is it's a combination of all of the above.

As more and more people are seeking help from psychologists to solve relationship problems, the more counsellors are discovering what shapes our sexual psyches. Why is it you think Robert De Niro is sex-on-legs and all your girlfriends see is an ageing movie star with moles on his face? This is what researchers have come up with so far:

We fancy people who look or act like other people we love or loved

Ever met someone and struck up an instant friendship because you feel like you've known them for years? That sudden familiarity is usually because they have similar features or gestures as people you've got on with in the past. They might laugh the same as your best friend does or have the same shaped eyes as your much-loved aunt.

It's the same with sexual attraction. From the moment we're born, we continuously feed physical data about people close to us into our subconscious. The brain divides these physical characteristics into 'people I like and were nice to me' and 'people I don't like who hurt me'; then it tries to generalize. If two-thirds of the people you've disliked have big noses, you'll be suspicious of those who do. When we meet a potential partner, our subconscious checks it against the 'liked people' list in our heads and tries to find the closest match. The more 'chemistry' we feel, the more matches we've found.

We do the same with gestures. Maybe a yearned-for ex had a habit of smoothing back her hair with the palm of her hand. If a girl standing next to you at the bar does the same thing, you'll look twice without knowing why. Your brain's telling you, 'Hey! Remember Maria? She did that, so maybe you could fall in love with this girl as well!' The more 'liked' gestures and physical characteristics a person clocks up, the more attractive we find them.

It's cute, but one that seriously can lead you to all the wrong people and stop you meeting the right ones. Why? Because you're on dangerous ground when you choose partners based on looks and gestures – and that's exactly what your brain is trying to do. Like Kate, my internal 'lists' constantly guide me to dark-haired, European-looking men. Blonds don't get a look in. When I meet a blond guy, I instantly throw him into the 'friend' basket rather than consider him as a potential partner, simply because when I was at school, every single blond guy I fancied didn't look twice at me. They didn't like me then so I don't lust after them now.

The problem with this unconscious imaging is that it's self-perpetuating. I don't flirt with blonds, so even if they *do* fancy me, they get zero encouragement to act on it. Understandably, most don't – and my theory about blonds not fancying me gets another tick. See how it can work against you? Who knows how many potential Mr Rights I've passed up simply because of their hair colour!

If you're convinced you've got the same problem, deliberately date against type to break the stereotype. One great love affair with a blond would probably break my subconscious fixation on hair colour (and if the dishy fair-haired guy in the Calvin Klein underwear ads is reading this and wants to volunteer, please feel free to write to my publisher). Ask your friends what they think your 'type' is – you might not be as eclectic in your tastes as you imagine.

The first person we had sex with strongly influences who we're attracted to

Who we lost our virginity to, what they looked like and how much we enjoyed the experience was a strong influence on who does it for us in the future. If your first experience was with someone blond and pretty and it was pleasurable, you'll subconsciously seek out people with the same build and looks over and over – even if they're not nice people. That's your 'type'. If it was a bad experience, you'll avoid anyone who looks like that – no matter how nice they are.

Again, it doesn't get you very far because we're being influenced by physical characteristics rather than choosing partners for healthy, logical reasons, like compatibility, shared goals and respect. Our personalized 'sexual blueprints' are also responsible for choosing 'bad' people who physically or mentally harm us. If the first time you had sex, it was a traumatic experience, sex may have become associated with violence. Even though the experience was horrifying and you have absolutely no desire to repeat it, you might find you can't get turned on when you're made love to in a gentle way. That first time set the blueprint.

If *your* first-time sex involved rape or extremely violent or unorthodox sex and you think there's a pattern emerging, get help from an expert. If you're having minor relationship problems because you can't seem to break free of a 'type' and think your first time might be responsible, try the following:

- **Recall when you lost your virginity in as much detail as possible.** What they looked like, whether it was good or bad. Are you avoiding people who look like your lover if the experience was bad? Avoiding people who *don't* look like them, if it was good? Can you see any patterns?
- **Be aware of your 'type' and actively challenge it.** Pick partners for reasons other than looks. If they treat you with respect, seem great company and are interested in you, give it a go.
- **Work on your self-esteem.** A bad sexual encounter can leave us seriously doubting our sexual appeal and attractiveness.

Why do I fall for people who need rescuing?
Some people continually and repeatedly choose partners with problems. Women are particularly good at playing rescuer (a lost puppy brings out all those maternal, look-after-him instincts), but both sexes are guilty of it.

Rescuers are attracted to people they can help. They

become saviours, putting their life completely on hold while they rescue their lover, cheerfully giving up work, friends and family to be at the beck and call of a person who often doesn't deserve such loyalty.

Why the need to play doctor and shrink? Because rescuers truly believe that if they love enough, give enough and do enough, they'll save their lover from their problem. In return, their partner will be eternally grateful and (the pièce de résistance) never leave because they're dependent on them.

Not surprisingly, saviours often come from homes where at least one parent had problems. They saw the other parent devote their life to fixing the problem, so that's what they go on to do. (It's quite common, for instance, for women who marry alcoholics to have a daughter who marries an alcoholic.)

Children who've been through divorce and had a mother or father rely heavily on them are also prime candidates, as are kids who took on Mum or Dad's role and looked after the family because Mum and Dad were too busy or didn't care. You've learnt to equate love with being needed. In order to feel loved you have to nurture and solve problems.

Giveaway signs
- If you keep telling yourself (and your friends and family) your partner just needs a little more time to get themselves together – and you're still making excuses months, even years in.
- If you put other people's needs before your own. Do you only feel happy when *everyone* around you is? Do you only feel good about yourself when you're helping someone else?
- Are most of your friends and current or former partners needy? Have you ever thought, *I can help them even if a psychologist or counsellor couldn't?*

Fix-its

- **Screen all potential partners.** If they start pouring out their troubles on date one, two or three, you've done it again – picked someone who needs rescuing.

- **Deliberately keep conversations with people you've just met on a lighthearted level.** Don't ask deep, personal questions. Don't invite confidences.

- **If someone tells you a problem, offer sympathy rather than a solution.** Say, 'How awful for you,' suggest they contact a support group or counsellor to get help, then change the topic.

- **Only help people who'll also be there for you.** Be aware you will attract people who'll take you for granted. Instead of being the first to jump up and say 'I'll do it', let others volunteer first.

Why do I fall for people who are married or involved with someone else?

Falling in love with one person who's married could just be bad luck, bad timing and bad judgement. But if you've had more than one affair with a married lover, you're deliberately picking them for a number of reasons. Top of the list is self-esteem. It's a boost to the ego to be able to lure a married person away from someone they supposedly love. You *must* be special if they're in your bed. If you rapidly lose interest the minute your married partner does decide to leave their spouse, it's definitely a self-esteem problem. You don't want them, you want a person who is attached to someone else. It's a power game that's over when you're the official winner: you could have them if you wanted to.

Another common influence: your childhood. If one or both parents abandoned you – they split, died or seemed to forget you were there – you're repeating the pattern by finding adults who can't be there for you either. A married lover who's always running away from you – home to a spouse – feels nicely familiar. Similarly, if your parents put you down or criticized you, the message you got was, 'I don't deserve to be loved.'

> *When your partner reacts strangely, they're often not reacting to you but to a parent's voice playing inside their head. Mum and Dad are the hidden audience who constantly watch our lives.*

Sharing a partner with someone else – and getting the bum end of the deal – is all you think you deserve.

A third possibility is you're scared of intimacy. People who've been physically or emotionally abused by their parents or betrayed by past lovers, often end up chasing married people. If you've decided – consciously or unconsciously – not to let someone get close to you in case you get hurt again, married people seem a great option. You've got an in-built excuse for not committing – they already have, to someone else – and the rejection factor is also lower. If they don't choose to continue the affair, it's not *you* they're rejecting. They're simply doing the 'right thing' by their spouse.

Fix-its

- **Look hard at your childhood and past** to work out why you're attracted to people who are already committed to others. If you can fathom a reason, constantly be aware of it. The next time you're attracted to a married person, think, *It's not them I want, I'm really looking for —* If you can't pinpoint a reason, ask close friends – they're often more astute than you realize. You've all drawn blanks? Consider getting therapy. A few sessions with a no-nonsense counsellor could uncover what you're really trying to get from these relationships.
- **Work on your self-esteem.** Let's be honest here, it's degrading to be 'the bit on the side' and no fun spending

Christmas and holidays alone while the person you love is playing happy families. Why anyone would voluntarily choose to be in this situation is beyond me. Why *should* you share someone you love? Don't you deserve to be number one, instead of in second place?

Why do I feel more confident dating people who don't quite measure up to my level?

You're scared of being hurt. If you're always better looking, more successful, financially superior and an all-round better package than your partners, you only feel comfortable in the power position. They'll never dump you, because you're such a good catch for them.

Again, first look at your past. Did your parents divorce? Did you watch Mum or Dad go through agony trying to get over it? Did you see a best friend fall to pieces after a much-loved ex left? Has someone in *your* past betrayed you? This is why you'll only go out with people who are guaranteed to hang around.

Next, rate your self-esteem. Why don't you think you're good enough to hold the interest of someone on your own level? Are you trying to boost your ego through 'sure-thing' relationships? Every time you leave someone heartbroken, your ego's getting fed. It's quite common for people who've been badly hurt in the past to climb back up the self-esteem ladder by dating from the bottom of the heap. The more superior they are to their partner, the less likely they are to be dumped. Each success (they dated but didn't get dumped) gives them a little more confidence to try someone 'better' until, eventually, they're back to dating people who are the equivalent of themselves.

Fix-its

* **Have faith in your own ability to survive.** Imagine the worst possible scenario: you took a risk on someone and they

left you utterly heartbroken. Sure, it would hurt for a while but you would survive – pretty well all of us do. Convince yourself you'd be okay even if your nightmare becomes reality, and you'll have the courage to take the risk.

- **Consider the alternative.** Dating an equal is far and above the most satisfying relationship of all. Do you want to share your life with someone who truly fulfils and stimulates you, or have a series of insipid, luke-warm love affairs that do little but make you feel guilty when you break it off, yet again?

> 'Mum always said she'd wasted her life by staying home to look after Dad. In a sense, I got the law degree for her, because she didn't have the opportunity to. She's proud of me, but I think I got the message too clearly. I cooked dinner for my boyfriend the other night and I was gritting my teeth. It's like I'm not allowed to look after people or else I'll end up like her.'
>
> Debbie, 34, lawyer

Why do I always choose the bad guy over someone who adores me?

For a start, they're forbidden. When you were young, your Mum said, 'Don't eat all the biscuits,' so that was the first thing you did the minute she wasn't looking. And they tasted damn good, even if you did feel sick afterward. When you're older, she says, 'Don't go out with bad boys or girls.' So you just *know*. If she says bad boys and bad girls are bad news, they *must* be fun.

Think about it. What do bad people provide that the nice types don't? Excitement. Drama. *Fun*. The freedom to let your hair down, kick your heels up and unleash *your* bad side. Because even nice girls and boys have one. Bad's always been appealing. Smoking, drinking, eating chocolate – we love doing things that are bad for us.

If your parents are really strict, you might deliberately choose someone who's a little on the wild side as an act of rebellion. If they've controlled everything in your life, bringing home someone with dreadlocks and a rude tattoo on their tongue is the equivalent of saying, 'Up yours! You can't control me any more. I'm about to turn all your nightmares into reality.'

Why bad is so appealing

There are other reasons behind it. Like, the sex.

We like 'bad' because it's sexy. Put a person with a bad attitude and a great bod into a leather jacket or a short, short miniskirt and our hormones go crazy. We look at people who live on the wild side and think, *I bet they'd be into everything in bed*. We'll do things with them that we wouldn't dream of doing with a potential Mr or Mrs Right because *it doesn't matter if they judge us*. If you're not interested in a long-term, serious relationship and simply want a hot, sexy fling, you don't really care if they think you're wicked (in fact, it's better if they do). It's incredibly liberating to be able to unleash the erotic side of yourself and let loose, without someone looking down their nose at you. The odd affair with someone from the other side of the tracks can actually be good for you – so long as you don't expect anything to come of it.

We've fallen for the rescue fairytale. It's also got a lot to do with ego. Not all bad boys and girls are bad underneath, and if you can be the one to change them, how fabulous must you be? We kiss the frog and turn them into a prince or we kiss Sleeping Beauty and she awakens to become the ultimate in girlfriends. It's the stuff of fantasies.

Opposites attract. If you're a 'good guy' matched up with a 'bad guy', you're both getting certain needs met – at least temporarily. Good guys usually have stable jobs, a bit of money in the bank and lead pretty sensible lives. They don't need someone for security, they want someone to spice things up a little. And that's exactly what bad guys do. The bad guy usually has enough excitement and drama going on – what *they* lack is stability, and that's what the good guy gives them.

The beauty of this relationship is that the good guy gets to live on the wild side – but from a nice, safe distance – and the bad guy gets the stability they need, without having to turn into one of those boring, nine-to-five morons they detest.

Short term, it works well. Long term, not so fabulous, because the bad guy's refusal to live by the rules usually wears thin for the good guy. The fact that they've got no money, you're always having to bail them out, you can't take them home to meet your parents – it's annoying. What you once saw as wonderfully spontaneous and unpredictable, you start to see as childish and irresponsible. In short, you want them to grow up – especially if you're thinking mortgages and kids. Even the hot sex loses its appeal over time unless it's balanced with a loving, snuggle-up sort.

Your self-esteem is low. You don't find nice guys appealing because, deep down, you honestly don't think you deserve to be treated nicely. Again, something's usually happened in your past to make you feel this way. Wild guys are exciting, but if your heart's being broken left, right and centre, it's hardly worth the joy ride. If this is you, skip straight to the section 'If you only ever go out with bad boys' on page 410. If you're hooked and hopeful it could turn into something worthwhile, keep reading . . .

Can you change a bad guy into a good one?

It depends. Have they always been wild or are they just going through a rebellious stage? Have they chosen to lead the lifestyle they do because it's their passion – or because they're secretly worried they won't measure up in the real world?

There are bad guys and bad guys. Some people appear bad just because they're leading alternative lifestyles. They have trouble meeting the rent and are a little too heavy on the booze and ciggies because they're geniunely frustrated. If they're trying to break into a profession that's difficult to crack (like acting or the music world), they might have to live rough to be true to their lifelong dream. This type of bad guy isn't bad at all – but still don't expect to change him. He won't – and neither should he – until he really has exhausted every avenue. The day he comes home and says, 'Darling, guess what? I've just got a job as a bank teller,' is the day he's given up. It's not a cause for celebration, it's the end of a dream. So if you're involved with someone like this and don't like the lifestyle, opt out now. It's not your right to change them, and if you do succeed, you'll be left with a shell and no substance anyway. Take away the dream and you take away the spirit.

The other type of bad guy has deliberately picked an alternative way of living through insecurity. If their goals are ridiculously high, they won't be judged too harshly if they don't make it. If they have no goals at all, again, they can't fail. If this is your partner, there is hope. You possibly can change them by giving them the courage to be themselves. But the bottom line is always this: do they want to change? You can't change someone unless they want to be changed.

The third type of bad guy is plain bad. Insecurity probably started it but the only way *he'll* change is with the help of a social worker, psychiatrist, rehabilitation or possibly all three. If your partner is heavily addicted to drugs, alcohol, gambling or sex, leave it to the experts to cure them, similarly if they're breaking the law, have a criminal record, are dealing drugs or involved in anything illegal.

I want to give him a chance but not get hurt. How do I handle it?

If you're going to survive a relationship with a bad guy, you've got to stick to five rules.

1. **Set limits.** Make it crystal clear what you will and won't put up with. Bad guys secretly want – and certainly need – discipline, so don't be scared to spell out the boundaries. The minute you let them walk all over you, they'll be off, anyway, because you're not a challenge any more.

2. **Make it safe for them to show their good side.** If a lot of the tough act is exterior only, the more you open up and talk about your feelings, the safer they'll feel to do the same.

3. **Don't be their partner in crime.** Don't rush to their rescue, don't pay their rent, bail them out of prison or cover for them or they'll never, ever learn to take responsibility.

4. **Keep your eyes wide open and know when to get out.** Some people are bad apples: rotten to the core. If they're disrupting your life and you're risking your job and your relationships with your friends and family, the rest of it simply isn't worth it.

5. **Ask yourself: what's he getting out of this?** Be aware that if you're a 'good guy', you may be a bit of a trophy for a bad guy. If you're successful, respectable and going out with them, well . . . there's obviously more to them than what people thought. They're not such a loser after all. Sometimes bad guys hook up with good guys when they *are* ready to change. They know you'll give them the kick up the bum

they need to get motivated. You'll encourage their ambition, help them get to where they want to be. Other times, they've hooked up with you for not-so-nice reasons. They get off on corrupting you and want to see how far they can drag you down. Why? It's a power thing. They secretly feel they're not good enough for you, so they'll try to bring you down to their level to get the ego boost they're craving. You're really no better than they are, after all.

Geneticists now believe there's a gene that makes women attracted to men who are bad for them. US researchers found women who carried the gene, aptly named 'PRIC 1', were five times more likely to date married men, 15 times more likely to back down in arguments with their boyfriends and twice as likely to fall in love with guys who never called. A simple blood test could identify susceptible women in the future.

If you only ever go out with bad boys

I'm going to mainly address this to women simply because we're more often the suckers in this situation. But keep reading if you're a guy with the same problem: the advice holds true for both. Whatever sex you are, grab a coffee and settle in: this one's worth taking a close look at because it's an extremely common complaint.

While just about *all* of us find bad appealing in an odd sort of way, some women seem to find an endless supply of partners who treat them badly. Each time it happens you probably think, *I've learnt my lesson. Never again*, but the next guy's just as bad as the last. If you're constantly being ripped off, cheated on, left or treated badly, it's time to face some facts.

Here's the first truth: in a way, it's your fault. If you *only ever* date men who treat you badly, it's not simply a case of lacking judgement skills. No-one's *that* unlucky. Believe it or not, you're unconsciously but *deliberately* seeking out a particular kind of man – and the most common reason for doing this – surprise! surprise! – stems back to your childhood. The first step to forging healthy relationships is to understand *why* you're choosing the men you are.

There are two basic childhood theories to explain your behaviour. The first is that you're attracted to men who break your heart because subconsciously it feels 'right' when a man makes you feel unloved. You might think, *Get out of here! Here's another one!* when you meet a bad boy, but your subconscious makes you stay. It whispers in your ear, 'Hold on. This seems nicely familiar,' and that's why you end up getting involved. This is what's happening when you feel like you can't help yourself.

As adults, we tend to seek out emotional situations similar to what we've experienced in childhood. In other words, the guys you're choosing now make you feel like you did as a child. Say Mum or Dad weren't around much: you're used to a lack of attention. Being ignored is a feeling you're most used to experiencing, so you unconsciously choose men who do just that. If your parents fought a lot, you might go for guys who *you* fight with. If your father put your mother down, it feels comfortable when men do the same to you. *It's what you're used to.*

The second theory is that you're searching for something that was missing while you were growing up: you're attempting to change history. Here's how it works. Say your parents were cruel or unloving. You'll tend to seek out men who are equally callous and try your hardest to make them love you. If they love you, somehow it makes up for Mum and Dad not loving you because, in the murky bits of your brain, they *are* Mum and Dad. You're also trying to convince yourself the problem was with your parents, not you. If a guy like them falls in love with you, you're effectively saying, 'See, Mum? See, Dad? He's just as cruel as you were, and he can love me. It's your fault you didn't, not mine.' You don't realize you're doing it, but you're actually not seeking love from the guy, but from one or both of your parents.

Some psychologists swear playing out this ritual can actually be good for you. If you can resolve unfinished childhood business by making a person like your father or mother love you, I guess it is a good idea. But it's not the sort of thing you set out doing. Like, 'Okay. I'm going to go out there and look for someone who's critical, moody and disapproving – all the characteristics I most hated in my parents – so I can finish my unresolved childhood business.'

A more sensible way to approach it is to work through your problems on paper. For this exercise, you'll need to make three lists.

- **List one**: List ten adjectives which best describe your childhood by writing down this sentence and finishing it for me: *As a child I felt* . . . You might write down *unloved, unwanted, lonely and sad*. Or you might write *happy, loved, supported and encouraged*. It could well be a mix of both good and bad things.

- **List two**: Now list ten adjectives to finish this sentence: *The atmosphere in my childhood home was* . . . Was it happy, boisterous and filled with lots of people? Or deathly quiet, tense and uncomfortable?

- **List three**: Now write, *My boyfriends usually make me feel* . . . and list ten adjectives to complete that sentence. Your past lovers may have made you feel unworthy of them, criticized or not good enough, but there might be some good stuff in there. Again, it could be a combination of good and bad things.

When you've completed all three lists, have a good look at

them. What's your initial reaction to seeing all this written down? Do the lists give you a nice, warm glow or do you feel quite sorry for yourself? If it's the former, your relationships are probably in pretty good shape: your parents made you feel good about yourself, your childhood environment was pleasant and your boyfriends are continuing the trend. You're reading this section because you've had one or two bad encounters with bad boys and are either curious or keen to avoid a repeat.

You're also on the right track if you can see negative feelings on the first two lists that have positive matches on the third. For example, if 'criticized' appeared on your parent and childhood home list and 'accepted' appears on your boyfriend list, you're doing fine. You know what you lacked as a child and need now and are choosing men who'll give it to you.

If reading all three lists makes you want to lie down in the middle of a six-lane highway, keep reading – and have faith, you can break the pattern simply by being aware. Concentrate on comparing lists one and two to list three. Can you see any words that match up? Are the feelings you've described similiar? Does it now seem obvious you're choosing men who are making you feel exactly how your parent(s) did? These are the reasons behind your behaviour; now let's look at how to break it.

1. **Go back to Chapter 1 and do your partner and relationship wish lists to work out what you want from both.** (Keep the three lists you've just done (above) as a reference point for things you *don't* want from a partner or relationship.)

2. **Stick the partner and relationship wish lists to your bedroom mirror** (or at least somewhere where you'll see them daily). Read them so often you don't need to: they're firmly etched into your brain.

3. **If you're currently involved with someone who doesn't have *at least two-thirds* of the qualities on those lists,**

ditch them. I don't care how much you like them, just do it.

4. **Tune your radar to spot men with fatal flaws.** Assume the worst, not the best of men. Avoid anyone who's addicted to something, men who get angry easily, have extreme mood swings or lose patience easily. Watch out for men who blame others for everything in their life, rather than take responsibility for their own mistakes, and men who want to control you, hate their family for no apparent reason and don't seem to have any friends. Be especially careful of anyone who won't open up emotionally. If the guy can't reveal the most trivial intimate detail, he's emotionally unavailable and off limits. It should go without saying that you should also discount anyone who shows the slightest sign they might be verbally or physically abusive. (See page 417 if you have a problem with either.)

5. **You think they're fine so have been on a date?** When you come home, think hard about what they revealed about themselves. Look at your partner list. How are they faring? Do they have most of the qualities you're looking for? Be absolutely ruthless and refuse to date anyone again who doesn't match on at least 70 per cent. Pay attention in the beginning of relationships when you're more objective. Ask lots of questions, look for warning signs and stay focused on what you're looking for in a partner.

6. **Don't have sex or make any commitment until you've known the guy at least six weeks** (and are averaging about three dates a week). I'm deadly serious – sex confuses things. As you get to know them, check your list constantly to make sure they're *still* measuring up.

7. **Enlist the help of trusted friends and family.** Take your partner to meet them at all stages of the relationship, not just in the beginning when they're on their best behaviour.

Listen to their opinions and answer any questions they have honestly. If you find you're making excuses about how he's treating you, you've slipped back into your old patterns. Ditto if you're knocking yourself out trying to please him.

> 'Her father opened the door and I thought, *Jesus!*: I was looking at myself 30 years on. Jenny was totally oblivious to the resemblance until I pointed it out.'
>
> Tony, 31, sales consultant

8. **If your date suspects he's being thoroughly checked out, admit it.** Say, 'My last two boyfriends turned out to be bastards and I'm making damn sure I don't make another mistake.' If he's a nice guy, he won't be worried: he's got nothing to hide and will be proud of you for looking after yourself. If he's not, he won't bother hanging around. Either way, you can't lose.

9. **Don't give second – let alone third – chances if someone treats you badly.** If they turn up on your doorstep with flowers, don't open the door. He's blown it – move on. Accept you've made a mistake, end it and don't have any further contact, no matter what he does or promises.

10. **Work ferociously on your self-esteem.** Stop focusing on finding Mr Right and focus on you and your life. Surround yourself with people who boost you up; get rid of those who put you down. Be nice to yourself and concentrate on what you're achieving every day, rather than your failures. Think you deserve the best and you'll get it.

REALLY SERIOUS ISSUES THAT AFFECT YOUR RELATIONSHIPS

If you've been sexually or physically abused in the past, or are suffering right now, you already know the dramatic and destructive influence it has on all aspects of your life – particularly romantic relationships. It would be ridiculous to write a book on relationships and ignore this serious (and tragically common) problem. Unfortunately, it's such a complex, complicated issue it's equally as ridiculous to claim to offer any real help in one section of an entire book.

Nearly one in ten Australian women say they've been emotionally abused in their current relationship. Almost one in four women who've been married or in a de facto relationship have been victims of violence by their partner.

Quite frankly, even if my entire book was devoted exclusively to this subject, I think you'd need more than written words to help you heal. You need a qualified therapist who specializes in sexual and physical abuse. Please, if you're a victim of either or have been in the past, call the British Psychological Society (listed in the yellow pages) for a list of counsellors in your area. I've seen many people's lives turned the right way up through good therapy, and *know* yours will be too if you just make that phone call.

All I've attempted to do here is try to encourage you to seek help by talking a little about the emotions you may be feeling. I've also included some signs to watch for, for anyone who's worried their partner might become abusive.

Sexual abuse

If you've been raped or abused, it's pretty obvious your romantic relationships will be affected, even if it did happen during your childhood. There's a school of thought that says if you experience or grow up witnessing abuse you'll seek out an abusive partner later in life. Opinion divides sharply on the truth of this statement. Some swear a girl who grows up in a violent family relationship will come to see the behaviour as normal and unconsciously be drawn to men who'll do the same to her. Others believe it does the opposite: the girl grows into a woman with a very low tolerance to abusive behaviour – and a highly tuned radar to spot it.

Whichever reaction you may have had to the experience, it's not uncommon to be struggling with emotions a decade or two after being abused – or to still feel it was your fault. *If I hadn't been walking down that dark street/If I'd been more convincing, people would have listened and stopped the abuse.* It's *never* your fault. We can't always control our lives, particularly in instances like rape and abuse.

If you've been abused as a child or adult and haven't had therapy, sex probably isn't a pleasant experience for you. It brings back memories of feeling powerless, betrayed, frightened and out of control. You might also feel angry, ashamed and embarrassed. Understandably, you'll have problems trusting outside the bedroom as well. Many abuse victims put up emotional walls to protect themselves: if they don't let anyone in, they can't be hurt. Unfortunately, it also means they can't love properly – and others can't love them back.

In my experience, it's a rare person who recovers from the deep, psychological damage caused by sexual abuse – either as an adult or child – without help from a therapist. If you haven't been through intense counselling and are having relationship problems, please do yourself a favour and get some – even if it has been years since the event.

Physical abuse

If you're in or have been in a relationship where your partner continually hit you, again, you probably need much more than the do-it-yourself style therapy this book offers. You might well be able to fix the problem solo, but you'll fix it faster and more effectively with a trained counsellor to help. The aim of this section is to encourage you to seek help because, God knows, you shouldn't be embarrassed about asking for it. Shocking but true: you certainly aren't alone on this one. In fact, you probably already know people in your situation – but they're just as good at covering it up as you are.

According to one Australian magazine survey, only 81 per cent of women would leave their partner if he hit them. It's suggested (though difficult to confirm) that around 1.5 million women in Australia have been hit by their partners. Although attitudes toward domestic violence are changing – thanks to campaigns like 'Zero Tolerance' – it's still rife. Domestic violence occurs in every suburb, among every social class.

In almost all cases of abuse, emotional abuse goes hand in hand with the violence. Being told you're ugly, useless, that you wouldn't get hit if you could only 'behave yourself', is eroding your self-esteem as fast as he's punching it out of you. Add feeling helpless if you truly haven't got the money or anyone and anywhere to run to – and a faint hope that the last time really was the last time – and it's not surprising you don't know how to leave. Plenty of you are plain terrified to walk out the door because you're convinced your partner will come after you and finish the job completely. It's a fear that is justified: authorities say half of all women who die in domestic homicides are killed when they threaten to leave or actually have left violent partners. That's not a reason to stay because it's still

> 'Six months into the relationship, I found out my boyfriend had been married before and had three kids. He said he forgot to tell me. He also forgot to tell me he'd served time for assault. I'm ashamed to admit, I still gave him another chance: he repaid me by sleeping with an ex.'
>
> Christine, 29, photographer

uncommon, but take it as a warning why you shouldn't leave without the help and protection of police, support groups and/or friends and family.

There are deep, psychological reasons why you're staying with someone who hurts you which are beyond the scope of this book to explore. These need exploring through therapy. But here is an action plan to help you break free.

1. Give up the dream
If he's hitting you now, he's going to keep on hitting you. Pretty well all studies show it almost never stops.

2. Prepare yourself emotionally
Look up Victim Support in the phone book or call your nearest hospital, Careline or a community support centre. Say you want to organize some counselling. It's more effective face to face but you can be counselled via the phone. The counsellors are well aware that you're in a dangerous situation, and won't ask for names if you don't want to give one. They will do their utmost not only to protect your confidentiality but to stop your partner finding out you're getting help by fitting in with your situation. They will also discuss fees with you – plenty provide the service free.

3. Gather evidence as well as courage
It's strongly advisable to report all attacks – even if you don't want to press charges – rather than just the one that breaks the camel's back (and possibly yours). Tell the police you want it on record but aren't emotionally ready yet to take it further and don't want your partner to know you've reported him. The more they have on record, the more chance you'll have of establishing a history of violence. If you don't want to involve the police, keep a diary and take Polaroids of all your injuries. Obviously,

keep them hidden somewhere safe. If you still have good friends that you see regularly, ask them to hold them for you.

4. Prepare to make the physical move
Your counsellor will advise you on how to make the move to somewhere safe – or how to remove your partner so your current home is safe. You may need to involve the police and obtain a restraining order which stops them re-entering the house until an injunction is issued by the courts. The number one objective is to get you out of the situation without putting yourself in danger.

5. Don't be dragged back in
Violent men can be exceedingly charming and persuasive – they have to be to keep you hanging onto a shred of hope. Don't stop counselling until a year or so after you've left your partner so he's got zero chance of talking you around. If you have friends or family who weren't aware of your situation, swallow your pride and tell them what happened. The more people around you who know and will protect you, the less likely you are to give in and go back.

THE DANGER SIGNS YOUR PARTNER MIGHT HIT YOU
Violent men come in all sorts of guises. You can't tell by looking at them – but you can watch for signs of potential abuse. A major US study on domestic violence found batterers came in two distinct types: men whose temper slowly simmered before erupting into violence, and those who strike out immediately. The study also found men who abuse physically nearly always start out abusing mentally. It's necessary to undermine a woman's confidence before she'll 'put up with' being abused. ➤

You're at risk if your partner:

- Is intimidating: he'll silence you with a look or angry gesture. You're not quite sure what he'd do if pushed.
- Puts you down: if he calls you names, insults you or plays mind games.
- Controls who you see and when: the more isolated and friendless you are, the more likely you are to put up with whatever he decides to dish out.
- Pretends you're 'imagining things': you're too sensitive, he didn't insult you, he was just playing around. Later, a punch was a 'slap', you weren't pushed, you fell.
- Blames you for any angry arguments: you were to blame for him losing his temper, it wasn't his fault.
- Directly threatens to hurt you, your family or children if you don't do what he says.
- Cuts off your finances: refuses to let you get a job or demands you hand over your paypacket because handling the finances is a 'man's job'. You're only allowed small amounts of cash at a time (if you had more, you might use it to get yourself somewhere safe).
- Seems dangerous to you, even though you've got no evidence to support it. Always trust your instincts.

Gay and Lesbian Relationships

Special issues homosexual couples face

•••

No relationship is easy but some are definitely under more pressure than most. Whether it's a huge age difference, matching up with someone from a different race or culture or dating the hired help when you're Lord or Lady of the Manor, being different from the norm isn't easy. Any couple combination who aren't the same colour or around the same age and with similar background, wealth and education are in for a tougher time than those who do find their matching bookend. Ditto for same-sex couples. While most of the advice that applies to male–female relationships applies to same-sex relationships as well (hopefully, you'll find the whole book useful), there are issues you face that straights don't. And this is what this chapter's all about.

To research it, I spoke to gay and lesbian support groups as well as gay couples and singles whose advice and judgement I trust implicitly. I also sought opinions from 'experts' in the field, most particularly Gerard Webster, a well-respected psychologist who's worked extensively with the gay community.

SOME COMMON QUESTIONS
I've been gay for years but still can't decide whether I particularly want to announce the fact to the world. I worry I'll lose friendships – on the other hand, I feel a bit hypocritical pretending to be something I'm not.

Coming out (which simply means openly and publicly announcing you're gay) could be the very best or the absolute worst thing you've ever done in your life. I can't tell you what will happen to you, but I can give you some things to think about.

First up, let's look at the bright side. By coming out, you're being true to yourself. It's important to take a stand on who you are in the world and there's certainly a great deal of satisfaction when you make a public declaration.

'To be able to stand up, with pride, and say, "This is who I am. I'm not what my parents and friends expect me to be. I'm unique," is a huge relief for a lot of people,' says Gerard. 'Along with declaring who you really are comes an acceptance that you're okay. It's okay to be gay, even if it might frighten others.'

It takes maturity to be able to do it, but for lots of gays, coming out of the closet has meant finally being happy.

'I know it's scary, but it's worth it,' says Mary. 'For me, family was a big issue. I was so scared I'd lose them. I told Mum first and she was great. She said she'd pretty much known and loved me no matter who I was. Then I plucked up the courage to tell Dad. Dad's quite conservative and he finds it hard to talk about his emotions, yet me confiding has made us closer than we've ever been. I remember he said, "Maybe it's better – there are so many bastard guys out there." So your family might well surprise you. Besides, if you don't tell them, you'll lose them anyway, because they can't share in your life if they don't know who you are.'

Living a lie isn't fun – as you well know. But then neither is living your life ostracized from people you love. Sometimes coming out is so disruptive and destructive, you'll wish you'd kept your mouth shut. Some people lose family, friends and jobs and are kicked out of their homes by homophobic landlords. Others are shunned by large sections of the community. They can't buy a loaf of bread at the local store without outright hostility or people nudging each other and whispering. This is one reason why many gay people tend to move to gay-friendly cities like Sydney, and settle in areas where gays are readily accepted.

What sort of reaction will you get to your news? That's a question maybe you can't even answer. If you are considering coming out though, keep the following in mind:

- Some people don't need to know, and you'll gain nothing by telling them: a narrow-minded boss for instance. If you're unsure of his or her reaction, why risk your job?
- Make sure your relationships are in good shape before confiding: are you already close to the person you're about to tell? If you're not, try moving the relationship to a more intimate level before announcing the news. The better you get on and the more honest you are with each other beforehand, the more chance you've got of being able to talk this through.
- Work out why you're telling them. If it's because you want this person to share in your life and they need to know who you are to do that, terrific. If you're doing it to punish, it won't get either of you anywhere. Blurt out, 'I'm gay!' in the middle of a heated argument with parents you've never seen eye to eye with, and they're liable to interpret it as, 'See? Look what you've done to me. I'm gay!' They'll think it's all part of an ongoing campaign to hurt and embarrass them rather than an admission designed to clear the air.

- Make sure it's your decision. Think through the worst possible consequences and be prepared to live with them. If you're not, you might decide to partially come out. Plenty of gay people move cities and

Lesbian sex is now legal in 63 countries and gay male sex legal in 71. Only five countries in the world recognize same-sex partnerships legally: Denmark, Greenland, the Netherlands, Sweden and Norway.

live happily in same-sex relationships without their 90-year-old parents ever finding out the truth. If you know they'd never, ever understand, it would ruin what's essentially a nice relationship and it's easy for you to maintain the façade, is it really necessary?

I'm 'out', my partner's not. I find it frustrating and insulting to have to pretend we're just good friends. Do I have the right to insist they come clean?

In a word, no. No-one has the right to force anyone to do something they don't want to: it's called the individual right to choose. Your partner will tell who they want, if and when they feel comfortable enough to. Force the issue or (God forbid) take it upon yourself to blab their business, and you deserve to get dumped. Big time. That would be like confidentially telling your best friend at school that you're gay, then realizing they've told all the other kids. The stakes are high, even as an adult. If your partner's a teacher, for instance, he or she could easily lose their job, not to mention risk treasured relationships with friends and family. Do you really want all that responsibility on your shoulders?

Having said all that, I *can* appreciate it's difficult. 'I lived with a couple once where one girl was out and had told her parents and the other hadn't. Every time they came to visit we had to "de-dyke" the apartment: rush around removing incriminating photos of the two of them together, get rid of any gay mags, make the spare bed up so it looked like they had separate rooms. It was hardly surprising when the parents finally arrived, no-one felt very comfortable,' says Erin. Feelings of, 'Are you embarrassed to be with me? Aren't I good enough for you to be seen with me in public?' are understandable but still, I think, unjustified. It's not the equivalent of some guy refusing to take his girlfriend home to meet Mum, even if it does feel like it.

Sit down together and talk through the reasons why your partner doesn't want to come out, ask if/when they think they'll be ready, then decide whether you want to continue the relationship. If you do decide to stick around, do both of you a favour and stop hassling them. Every time you open your mouth to complain, give them a big snog instead.

Should I tell people I'm gay? When I meet someone new, I'm never quite sure whether to mention it, and if so, when.

It depends on what sort of person you are and how comfortable you are with your sexuality. If you're proud of being gay and a naturally extroverted, confident person, it'll come out naturally and spontaneously in conversation. If you're not so comfortable in your own skin, or a little shy, you might want to hold back a bit and check out the 'safety factor' (that is, will this person make fun of you or put you down?). If you're easily wounded and hurt by criticism, it doesn't make sense to put yourself in the firing line unnecessarily. Because the reality is, while homosexuality is more accepted now than it ever has been, there are still a lot of people out there who are hostile to gays. And no-one likes to be attacked.

I'd wait until you've got a 'feel' for the person. Do they seem open, non-judgemental and understanding? Use your judgement. Telling your Mum's 80-year-old bridge partner what you and your boyfriend got up to on the weekend possibly isn't a terribly good idea. And don't feel obliged to confess. As a lesbian friend of mine said, 'Straight women don't run around telling people, "By the way, I sleep with men." You don't have to run around saying, "I sleep with women." It's not really anyone's business, so don't feel obliged to offer it up front.'

Do the same rules that apply to heterosexual relationships apply to gays?

In one sense, yes. In another, no. All relationships need a strong foundation built on trust, honesty, compatibility and mutual agreement on the 'rules'. So in that sense, it's no different. But you can't really follow the traditional straight couple path of dating, engagement, marriage and kids for legal reasons. Gays and lesbians are clearly disadvantaged legally. In the UK, it's not possible for you to marry, though it is possible for gays to adopt and foster children. You can try having a child through an IVF program, but it depends very much on the local philosophy of the hospital involved. Some are pro-equality; in others you wouldn't get past the initial screening interview.

Which is pretty sad. Because despite perceptions that children brought up by same-sex parents will turn out to be a) gay, or b) complete fruitcakes, research suggests they aren't disadvantaged psychologically. There's also zero evidence the child will grow up to be gay: the 'recruitment theory' (people who hang around gay people end up gay themselves) has no basis. On the other hand, there is some evidence that children of same-sex parents are actually advantaged in certain situations. It may be because gay parents make a conscious, very deliberate decision to have children: it's not a mistake, it's a carefully thought-through choice. 'In other words, they're in it for all the right reasons,' says Gerard.

Not being able to have children is one reason why many people fight the dawning realization they're gay. 'It was by far the hardest thing I had to come to terms with,' says Gary. 'I

> **What was that about gay relationships being short-lived? In Denmark, where it's been legal for same-sex couples to get hitched (and unhitched) since 1989, the divorce rate of Danish homosexuals is 17 per cent compared to 46 per cent for heterosexuals.**

can understand why some gay guys make a conscious decision to go straight – get married and have kids – then revert back. I'm not saying it's the right thing to do but I can understand the motivation behind it.'

Lesbians have their own set of problems. 'Quite apart from the frustration of not being able to produce a child together with someone you love, there are other issues on top of the usual ones all females face,' says Sarah. 'Like, which one of us will carry the child? And how does she get pregnant – by a sperm donor or by sleeping with a male friend? I also worry about the social pressure that might be put on the child if she's growing up with two mummies.'

Not being able to marry and have children can have a negative effect on your relationship. There's no institutional support and no mutual love of a child to bind the couples together. When the in-love feeling fades for straight couples, children unify them and give purpose to the relationship. The old 'we'd better stay together for the kid's sake' can get you through the rough patches and back on firm ground. Without that bond, it takes good relationship skills to stick it out. Another reason to read the whole book, not just this chapter.

Is it easier to go out with someone of your own sex? Do you get rid of all the gender differences that cause problems for straights?

Yes – and no. There's certainly a greater sense of camaraderie because you tend to relate to the world similarly. 'You reach a deeper level of understanding and a deeper level of intimacy,' says Pam. 'You understand each other's bodies, emotions and things like fat days, PMT, periods and sexism. Other bonuses: you can swap clothes and they already know how to give great oral sex!'

The downside is, it can cause an imbalance in the relationship. The heterosexual model of matching male with female works for the majority of people for a reason: each sex can teach the other a thing or two. It's the old Yin and Yang and all that stuff. 'If you've got two very blokey blokes together, there's obviously a bias toward masculinity,' says Gerard. 'They'll do blokey things together. If a blokey guy marries a woman, she may have got him in touch with his emotions more, given him a richer experience of life.' To balance this, make sure you've got a cross-section of friends – gay and straight males, gay and straight females – and allow each other to explore both feminine and masculine sides.

Straight couples hold hands in public and express affection, but when we do it, people stare. What's the solution: to only be affectionate in private?

Some say you have a political responsibility to openly show you're gay by being affectionate in public. After all, the more exposed the general community is to gay couples, the more accepted it becomes. Keep it behind closed doors and people continue to think, *It doesn't happen in my neighbourhood.* All well and good when it's not *you* and *your partner* who are being stared at by the table of 20 in the corner who are getting louder and more obnoxious with each bottle of wine.

As with everything, use your judgement. Why are they staring? If you sense it's sheer curiosity behind the looks, simply ignore them or try smiling in their direction. Check your gut reaction. 'People have internal warning systems but we tend to discount our gut feeling and go off and do what our head tells us – often at our peril,' says Gerard. If your gut instinct says you're in a potentially dangerous situation, trust it. Either leave or ask the manager of the venue to deal with the situation for you. Check you're not being paranoid though. A lifetime of putting up with people picking on you, particularly at school where you can't escape, can leave you more than a little self-conscious. Throw enough mud and it sticks: you start to feel everyone is talking about you.

Is there some way of telling if someone's gay or straight? What if I fancy someone, but I'm not sure of their sexual orientation?

It would be a lot easier on everyone if we all wore badges saying 'Straight', 'Bi', 'Gay' and 'Don't know, but you could be the one to solve it for me'. Unfortunately, most gay people are forced to rely on their 'gaydar'. 'You do get a sense after a while,' says Gerard. 'You'll notice they'll hold your gaze a bit longer. There's something in their voice. Body language can tell you a lot, and the more practised you are, the better you are at spotting other gays. Believe me, it's something gay people learn pretty quickly. Because if you get it wrong, you could be attacked, ridiculed or humiliated.'

If your gaydar's still being honed, it's probably best to stick to gay venues where you can at least make a safe guess. Otherwise, chat for a while to the person you've got your eye on and be generally friendly. Most people mention a boyfriend or girlfriend or make some sort of giveaway comment once you've spoken to them for an hour or so. If you think they're gay friendly but aren't sure if they're gay, drop into the conversation that you are. They've then got the green light to 'fess up themselves.

I'm a lesbian and find all my relationships get too intense, too quickly. What's going on?

What does a lesbian bring on the first date? A suitcase. There's a lot of truth in the joke. Lesbians *are* often rapidly and intensely intimate, simply because women generally are more intimate than men. There's also a common recognition that gay men are more into casual sex and casual relationships, simply because men generally are better at separating love and sex than women are.

Most of the lesbians I interviewed admitted their relationships tended to be full on, very quickly. 'Girls meet, then they disappear for months from the scene. The next time they reappear, you'll either spot them out to dinner, looking lovingly into each other's eyes, or one's back nursing a broken heart,' says Anne. And like straight couples who jump in feet first, you often jump out just as quickly.

Relationships need a solid base and it takes time to build one. If you gradually and gently take time to sort out the rules and understandings of the relationship, explore what shared history you both have and get to know each other, you've got something to hang on to when trouble comes. Get carried away too soon and you might find when the in-love bit fades, as it inevitably does, you don't actually know the person you're supposedly in love with.

Sure, I'm a lesbian, but I'm also a woman. If I wear make-up and a dress I sometimes get a hard time from lesbian friends.

'I went out the other night and my lesbian friends gave me heaps for dressing like a straight,' says a gay girlfriend of mine.

'My straight friends accused me of "not really being gay" because I don't "look it".'

Says another, 'I find it really annoying that the gay radio stations play dance music only. The dance scene is only a tiny representation of the gay community. It's frustrating to be pigeon-holed.'

There are as many stereotypes within the gay community as there are out of it. Not only that, many gays *do* fit the set images they've carved out for themselves. In Sydney, the most visible gay guy is usually gorgeous, muscle-bound and wearing trendy designer clothes which show off the bod (fabulous for other gay guys, frustrating for us straight females!). 'Then there's the drag queen, the S and M image, the avant garde artist type, the scene queen, and the list goes on,' says Gerard.

The lesbian community also tends to divide into masculine-looking girls with short hair and no make-up, through to the 'lipstick lesbians' who are more into dressing up than their peers.

But there is a hybrid emerging: the non-recognizable gay. 'There are a lot of people who don't want to fit any of the images because they don't particularly want to advertise their sexuality,' says Gerard. 'They're doing well in the community and in their professions and they want to move around freely without being branded.' Which is fair enough. The fact is, just because you're gay, doesn't mean you have to look it. Just as many gay men don't conform to the mincing, nancy-boy image, being lesbian and being feminine aren't mutually exclusive.

The next time gay (or straight) friends accuse you of dressing straight, tell them you're not a walking, live advertisement for the gay community, but an individual who has her own tastes and clothes sense. After all, isn't that what you're fighting for: the freedom to be yourself?

THE DOWNSIDE OF GAY RELATIONSHIPS

Plenty of gay couples enjoy warm, loving, intimate relationships that heterosexuals envy. Others don't. These are some issues that can affect gay relationships and may be harming yours.

The psychological cost

It's usually in relationships that psychological difficulties start to become apparent. 'Single, you don't really notice them. But once you start relating intimately to someone else, that's when all the baggage from the past starts tumbling out,' says Gerard. And for many gays, there's truckloads of it.

If you knew you were gay from an early age, you've probably had more abuse and insults hurled at you in ten years than the average straight gets in a lifetime. At school you overheard the other kids saying things like, 'He's a faggot,' or, 'She must be a dyke. She's weird and she never has a boyfriend.' Many work environments aren't much better. 'Having to listen to homophobic statements people make at work and not get too hung up about it takes its toll,' said one lesbian.

The gay male scene looks glamorous and ritzy – lots of partying and party drugs – but 'scratch the surface and you find a lot of pain,' says Gerard. 'It's a fast, hard life and too many drugs and too much extreme sex take a toll on the body.' It can also be superficial. If you're a pretty boy, the world's your oyster. If you're not, it's painful and depressing. Many gays have been through hell, hence the attraction of an excessive lifestyle that allows them to escape, albeit temporarily. Unfortunately, a drug habit or sexual addiction makes things worse, not better.

Living life as a minority can chip away at the healthiest self-esteem. There are few positive gay role models to emulate. Although gay characters in soaps are definitely finding their way into the plot line, Ellen Degeneres and her TV show *Ellen* were axed when she came out. Because of an 'us' against 'them' feeling, there's also a tendency for gays to segregate themselves. 'Most of us prefer spending time with other gays because they understand. But then we end up isolated from the straight community,' says Tim.

Many gay men are cautious in relationships, preferring to keep people at a distance. It hurts less when their partner moves on for younger, firmer flesh. They yearn for a close, loving relationship but lose hope they'll ever find it. Counselling sometimes helps; other gays put the energy they'd normally devote to a relationship into other areas of their life.

Domestic violence

It's as prevalent in gay relationships as it is in straight ones. Put two gay males together and you've got a lot of testosterone. Studies also show at least 50 per cent of lesbians have been physically abused by their partners. 'It follows the same pattern we see in heterosexual relationships,' says Gerard. 'The partner starts by stripping the other's self-confidence, dominates them, isolates them from friends and takes control of their resources. If you're HIV positive, for instance, they might take control of your medication.'

Then the physical abuse starts. Because the gay community has a reputation for not being terribly monogamous, there's a lot of suspicion and jealousy in gay relationships which can lead people into extreme behaviours.

Health issues

The arrival of HIV had an incredible impact on the gay community. 'The fire of the sexual liberation of the Seventies was smothered by the wet blanket of HIV,' says Gerard. 'If you were active with a number of partners, there was a very good reason to now be cautious.' While it's encouraged people to stay in monogamous relationships and reap the benefits of long-term love, HIV has made many gays even more afraid of the price they'll pay for being 'different'.

HIV-positive people face their own private nightmare. Not only do they struggle with health problems, they often feel they should only match with HIV-positive partners for fear of transmitting the virus or inflicting their suffering on someone else. If you're not infected but your partner is, you need to work out how to protect yourself during sex as well as decide whether getting close to someone who might not live as long as you is worth the pain. As Gerard puts it, 'It's difficult enough – this makes it even more so.'

AIDS and HIV affect the lesbian community as well. The virus is spread through unsafe drug usage (sharing needles) and bisexual women who may have had unprotected sex with men who are HIV positive.

TEN TIPS FROM THE TRULY GAY
In the old days, 'gay' meant deliriously happy. I spoke to a selection of gay people who also qualified in the old-fashioned sense. This is their advice for living it up as someone 'different', rather than letting life get you down.

1. Don't dive in at the deep end if you're not really sure of your sexuality
'Test the waters by checking out a few reputable gay clubs so you can get an idea of what gay relationships can be like. When the idea that I was a lesbian started to crystallize, I had an old friend who happened to be gay take me to a gay club. The minute I walked in, goosebumps appeared. I just knew. So if you haven't been to a club yet, this might help cement the issue for you.'
Jennifer, 28 ➤

2. Look for the good and you'll find it

'Because you all tend to hang around the same places, everyone tends to know each other's business. It's a bit like living in a small country town where your reputation and past history constantly precedes you. That's difficult in new relationships because everyone knows why you and your last girlfriend broke up and it can colour people's perception of you. That's the bad part. The good part is this: when you're down, it's like having a big family. Everyone rallies around to look after you.'

Lynn, 23

3. Your relationships with opposite-sex friends are great

'Women love gay guys: they feel incredibly comfortable around us because we're not "after something". I have so many close girlfriends who I have the best time with. My gay girlfriends say the same: once guys realize they're not man-haters, they open up more and talk about their relationships with their girlfriends.'

Andrew, 32

4. If you keep cool and rational, you'll get further

'There's a difference between coming out but still living your relationship behind closed doors and coming out and taking your rightful place in society by making your relationship known. Take "and partner" work functions. It's up to you to make sure your partner is not just invited but acknowledged. But you won't get anywhere by ranting and raving about gay rights. Just appeal to their logic. Once, a secretary at my work came to me and said, "Do you mind if I sit you and your boyfriend separately? I'm setting the tables up as boy-girl-boy-girl." She meant well and she'd been to dinner at our home but I had to point out the world isn't that simple. ➤

I asked her how she'd feel if her husband was at a different table and she understood how ridiculous she was being.'
John, 36

5. If in doubt, laugh
'Straight people ask lots of silly questions and it used to upset me. Now I realize, they're not meaning to be offensive and can usually see the funny side if you point it out. It doesn't necessarily mean they're not accepting you, they just don't understand. At least they're trying!'
Catherine, 21

6. Stereotypes often help people make sense of the world
'Lots of people will assume one of you plays "the girl", the other "the guy". Personally, I think it's a fallacy, but most people think that's the way it works. Once, I referred to my partner as "my husband" with a friend. It was a joke, but she burst in with, "Oh! I wondered who played the male and female role!" I don't think even young heterosexuals buy into the traditional male–female thing any more, but for older people it makes sense because that's what they're used to.'
Michael, 27

7. Give people time to get used to you
'I doubt we'll ever be the majority and I'm not sure I particularly want to be. I quite like being exotic and different from the norm. But like any other minority group, it takes a little time for people to relax and realize we're all God's creatures, no matter who you choose to love and have sex with. Be kind, be nice, be yourself and with time that nervous, homophobic work colleague could turn into a friend.'
Rachel, 25 ➢

8. Get help if you're not happy

'There are numerous free gay and lesbian counselling services at your disposal. Just knowing you're not alone, that others have been through what you're going through now *and* come out the other side, really does help.'
John, 19

9. Don't beat yourself up

'If I can't think of any other reason why someone's angry with me or doesn't want to get to know me, I catch myself thinking, "Maybe it's because I'm gay." I know it's silly but it's easy to slip into thinking like that. Don't beat yourself up about it or use it as an excuse to blame everything on.'
Helen, 18

10. Remember: no matter how hard it gets, it's better than living a lie

'It's not as if you can decide whether you're gay or not: you are or you're not – at this stage in your life anyway. If straight friends don't understand why you've "chosen" this lifestyle, say to them, "I didn't choose. Imagine someone telling *you* you have to live life as a gay person when you're straight. Can you imagine what that would be like?" Homosexuality isn't something you draft people into. It's not always easy being gay – but it's still preferable to living a lie.'
Paul, 40

Dumped!

How to get over a break-up and what to do if you're still hung up on an ex

• •

I remember it vividly, even though it happened about 13 years ago. I was working through my lunch hour in the office at *Cosmopolitan* magazine, when an Italian male model wandered in. It was the fashion editor's job to look through model portfolios, but I gave it a flick through just to be polite (okay, he was the sort you instantly imagined wrapping your legs around in a jacuzzi). Enrico didn't speak English very well, but we had what passed as a conversation (that is, we both smiled a lot). I watched his bottom walk out the door, sighed and went back to work.

About an hour later, the rest of the troops filed back in and when I looked up, he was there again. Walking right up to my desk. Standing in front of me.

'I sorry, but I have to come back,' he said. 'I say to myself, "Enrico. You like that girl." Will you go out with me?'

Ahh, what a glorious moment! Not only had a model asked *me* out but he did it in front of *everyone*. Of course I said yes. Of course everyone rushed over the minute he disappeared. Angels burst into song.

Enrico and I had three dates – every detail faithfully reported back to everyone who worked within a 10 kilometre radius. Our last date was spent at the zoo. He watched the animals quietly for a while then said, 'I think I take you home to see *my* country and *my* animals. You would come?'

Hell, I practically had my bags packed. Bugger the job, bugger my friends, I was on the next plane out of there if that's what he wanted. The next day, the office was a buzz of activity: the fashion editor worked on my travel wardrobe, I remember someone even called the Italian consulate to find out about a work visa. We all waited excitedly for what would happen next. And waited. And I never heard from the guy ever again. Not one sodding phone call.

Enrico disappeared into thin air and to this day, I have no idea why. Did he fall off his big, red motorbike? Have to hotfoot it back to Italy to sit at the bedside of his dying mother? Catch some killer disease from the elephant he patted that day? Was Enrico now horribly scarred and disfigured and flatting with the Elephant Man? I suspect – actually, scratch that – am damn positive it was none of the above. He was smooth, he rode a Harley, he was Italian, he was a *male model* for God's sake. Some other girl caught his eye, that was all (or maybe even a guy – like I said, he was a model).

I felt like a complete idiot. I'd told *everyone* this man had asked me to go to Italy, and now I had to tell them all I'd been dumped. Without even a phone call. The *embarrassment* of it all. The *public humiliation*. I'd never get over it. (I did, of course. Within two weeks, we were all making Enrico jokes: 'Where's that story disappeared to? Maybe it's done an Enrico.') But back then, I thought my heart would never mend. I'd never love again (blah blah blah). How could he do this to me? (blah blah blah). How pathetic – and how lucky would I be if that was the only dumping experience I'd ever have in my life!

Because while Enrico was my first taste of being rejected, being dumped good and proper feels twenty billion times worse than I felt back then. It's the difference between accidentally dropping your last pound coin down the drain

> **'I can't live without you'** isn't far from the truth. You really can die of a broken heart. Scientists have found a direct link between negative emotions like prolonged sadness and anxiety, and heart abnormalities.

beside the parking meter and losing your life savings on the way home from your retirement party. If a long-term, dearly loved partner leaves, everything you've counted on is gone. You look around the home you once shared and it's as though you've misplaced half your life in it – which perhaps you have.

All your life plans have to be rethought. You don't just lose the person, you lose hope – and also part of yourself. When they go, they take a part of your life with them, the bit they were a witness to. Sometimes, they nick off with real evidence of it – like that photo of you looking tanned and terrific on a beach in the Greek Islands, the only picture of yourself you voluntarily showed people. Broken hearts, broken dreams, a whopping great hole in your photo album. Is it any wonder most people find getting over a serious relationship split one of the hardest things they've ever had to do in their life?

The astonishing fact is, though, most of us not only muddle through the agony and survive, we go back for more. When we're hurting we think, *Not me! No sireee! I've bloody well learnt my lesson this time. I'm never falling in love, ever again.* But we do – and most of us know we will, even in that deep, dark lonely moment. Broken hearts heal, new dreams replace the old and a lot of people – including me – look back and realize most relationships end for a reason. If you'd stayed with Stan, you wouldn't have met Greg. (What were you thinking? You'd never have been happy with a man obsessed with model train sets.) If Susan hadn't dumped you, you wouldn't be with Sarah – and just looking at her turns the world the right way up.

Yeah, yeah, I can hear you thinking, *that's all wonderful.* But how do I get from the painful part to the Greg and Sarah scenario? I'd like to say it's easy but I'd be lying. It's a difficult, sometimes long road back to recovery, but there's plenty you can do to make the journey quicker. Reading this chapter's a good start.

BREAKING UP
Ten reasons you're about to split

Sometimes, the writing's so obviously on the wall, it might as well be in bright pink neon. Neither of you could possibly miss it. In other relationships, one person's eagerly planning next Christmas together while the other's planning to leave. There are vulnerable points in any relationship, and all of those listed below scream danger. Take them seriously. How you handle them (and each other) could mean the difference between a relationship hiccup and a death rattle.

1. Circumstances have changed dramatically

Change gives us a new perspective – and forces us to question just how happy we are. A new job, a move to a new city, the death of someone close: any major life change for either of you can put the strongest relationship in jeopardy. Sickness or death causes people to look deep inside themselves and at their partner, searching for true feeling. If you decide they're there for a good time, not a long time, you'll search for someone new. A new job exposes us to new people and, considering most people meet their future spouse at work, changing jobs can turn up more dates than a disco.

2. You're at a turning point as a couple

Everyone's asking when you're going to get married/move in/have that baby/buy a house. One of you is stalling because you're not entirely convinced you want to move the relationship onto a deeper level of intimacy and commitment. Sometimes, a nudge from others can make us push through silly fears and take the leap. But outright pressure and nosy interference can send us in the opposite direction – flying over the edge to freedom. Leaving seems the most sensible solution if you're not allowed the time you need to make a decision.

3. You don't want sex any more

Counsellors call it 'the cringe factor'. The thought of your partner touching you makes your skin crawl. You'll pick a fight, get drunk, invent exotic illnesses, *anything* to avoid the bedroom. If affection disappears along with the libido – you or they dive for the armchair rather than snuggle up on the couch – the relationship's a hair's breadth away from expired.

4. One of you cheated

Infidelity – discovered or not – means you're not just in troubled waters, the boat's sinking fast. If you're the guilty one and got away with it, you've satisfied your naughty side without the sky falling in. But you'll still feel differently about your partner because the 'specialness' has gone. You can't quite meet their eye, feel guilty, then end up resentful for feeling guilty and, before you know it, you're caught in a downward spiral. Lots of people bonk around to 'test' their feelings or have one last, final fling before settling down for good (neither are recommended); others do it because they haven't got the guts to say, 'It's over,' and think it'll be easier on their partner if they catch them out (it isn't).

5. The blinkers have come off

It's the 'new car syndrome'. When you want to buy a car, that's all you see: you're checking out makes and models all over the place. Once you've bought one, you stop looking. When you're in love, you don't focus on other attractive people because you're committed and happy. Once you fall out of it, you start 'shopping' again. The blinkers come off and good-looking people appear everywhere. Don't get me wrong, it's normal to look while happily attached, and occasionally testing your sexual attractiveness by flirting is also normal. But wanting to take it further and feeling trapped isn't.

6. People keep assuming you're single

If you're involved and adore your partner, you can run your fingers up and down the stem of a glass and lick your lips all you want: you'll rarely get asked out by other guys. Whether it's a chemical thing, pheromones or a wicked glint in your eye, we subliminally give out signals which tell others whether we're playing or dead serious. In other words, we advertise our availability. You may well have a ring on your finger or *appear* to be settled but, take my word for it, the minute you decide you want an affair, someone tempting will appear in front of you. As the saying goes, 'When the student is ready, the teacher arrives.'

7. You talk less

Your boss gives you a glowing review and you find yourself picking up the phone to call – anyone but your partner. Lately, you've forgotten to tell them significant things altogether. We naturally move closer to people who share their secrets with us, and the person who knows most about us is the person *we* feel closest to. If your conversation with your partner is now restricted to 'How was work?', they're not number one in your life (or you don't feel you're number one in theirs).

8. You stop arguing

In a recent university study, researchers asked a group of single men and women to name the opposite to love. Their answer, predictably, was hate. When the same question was posed to married couples, they answered 'indifference' – a far more realistic and accurate response. If you're still arguing – even bitterly and frequently – there's still hope. You're still trying to get your point across and your needs met. Once you stop, you've given up.

> 'Being dumped taught me to think hard about what I really wanted. I've stopped going for looks and put "nice" at the top of the list.'
>
> Alison, 23,
> financial adviser

9. Everything they do annoys you

That cute little habit she has of twisting her hair while distracted seems neurotic. You can't stop looking at his teeth and thinking, *Yuk!* Our tolerance level drops, and sometimes, we deliberately look for faults to try to justify why we're going to be mean and nasty and dump them. When we like someone, we think their imperfections are cute. When we fall out of love, it's like someone got up during the night and turned the 'nice' switch off. Instead of ignoring their imperfections, our brains zoom in like a camera with supersonic magnifying lenses, homing in on all the bad spots and leaving the good bits blurry and out of focus. Suddenly, you don't see the fabulous broad shoulders and washboard stomach. You see hands that somehow seem too small and feminine for a man, lips that seem thin and mean – get my drift?

10. You're seeing less and less of each other

Going out alone and leaving your partner behind because you feel more comfortable solo? Inventing excuses why they shouldn't 'bother' coming? You're either testing the waters to find out what it would be like single, or things are so tense, it's a relief to escape. Doing less together is one of the tail-end signs that you've drifted apart.

The four fatal fall-out signs for long-term couples

Psychologist John Gottman is a world-respected relationships expert who's spent 20 years studying what makes a marriage last. In his book *Why Marriages Succeed or Fail*, Gottman pinpoints four warning signs which he says signal a serious relationship is headed for disaster. They usually run in this order, with each feeding the next.

Criticism

All couples squabble, and complaining about your partner's behaviour is usual and pretty unavoidable. It's when, 'Honestly John, you spend too much money,' turns into, 'You're such a selfish person. All you think about is yourself,' that you're in trouble. Attacking someone's *behaviour* is different than attacking their *personality or character*.

Contempt

One step on from criticizing someone's character is intentionally insulting or verbally abusing them, says Gottman. Calling your partner selfish isn't great. Calling them a stupid, irresponsible pig is worse. If one of you starts flinging insults, the other throws back – if not with words, with body language. We've all been to dinner parties where one partner's telling you all about their latest achievement, while their other half is rolling their eyes and looking bored and uninterested.

Defensiveness

By now, you're both starting to feel understandably defensive. You feel victimized by each other and quite upset about it since you're (obviously) totally innocent. If you feel you're being picked on, the natural reaction is to defend yourself with, 'What are you picking on me for? It's not my fault.' It's the old, 'Yes, but.' He says you never invite his friends over for dinner. You say, 'Yes, but I would if you'd help clean up afterward'. Neither of you hear each other, no-one's happy.

Stone-walling

Exhausted by constant arguments, you both wearily stop having them – and give up altogether. If he shouts at you, you say, 'Yeah. You're right. You always are,' and pick up a book. You pick a fight with him and he says something similar and walks out.

All four of these warning signs create a cycle of negativity, says Gottman. There's still hope even if your relationship has well and truly progressed to stage number four (see Chapter 6) but only if *both* of you want to work on it. If your partner's not willing, expect a 'Dear John/Jane' letter sometime soon.

How to dump someone nicely

There are ways to kick someone out kindly. 'Sorry, but my gyno agrees with me – your penis is just too big,' would work wonderfully on most men (if only they'd believe it). 'Sorry, but you're just so beautiful I can't bear everyone gazing at you,' would do the trick for most women (ditto). Another alternative: if Hallmark came up with a series of terribly nice and well-worded dump cards. All we'd have to do then is sign their name at the top, ours at the bottom and shove it under their door. Alas, they're not yet available (actually, I have seen some but they were more of the 'sod off' variety) and, even if they did exist, I still wouldn't seriously recommend dumping someone via the mail (or e-mail or phone – so forget those options immediately).

WHY MEN DUMP WOMEN
Short term

- **You tried to change him.** In the beginning, you admired everything about him. Then you realized his table manners need fixing, he could do with a haircut, half his wardrobe is just *wrong* . . . The message he gets: I'm not good enough for her (so I'll find someone who thinks I am).

- **You're not interested in sex.** If you've been together four months and already feigning headaches, he sees the rest of his life stretching out before him. One of intense frustration.

- **You know him too well.** Some men guard those walls with machine guns. A girl that knows him better than he knows himself makes him feel emotionally exposed. Add immaturity and a battle-scarred past and he's out the door.

Long term

- **It's time to tie the knot.** Hell, even his mates are asking when he's going to make an honest woman out of you. He knows it's expected but the old ball and chain image keeps popping up. He's convinced he'll never get to play golf on Sundays again.

- **He meets someone else or realizes you're not 'the one'.** Women aren't the only ones with expectations about what marriage will be like. He loves you but you're *so* comfortable together, he hardly notices you're there. Then a new girl starts at his work. She's bright, sexy, attractive, *interesting.* She talks to him and asks him questions. He thinks, *There's more to a relationship than watching videos on the couch. This girl makes me feel alive.*

WHY WOMEN DUMP MEN
Short term

- **You don't turn out to be the person she thought you were.** Women are optimistic creatures and she'll think you're Mr Perfect for as long as she can kid herself. If it becomes painfully obvious you're not ever going to turn into the man she was hoping you would, she'll move onto a new project.

- **The timing's wrong.** She was just offered a great job – in another city. Her girlfriends are about to head off for a six-month trek around South-East Asia and she doesn't love you enough to wave them goodbye.

- **You don't treat her well.** She'll probably give you a few chances – maybe more than you deserve. But persist with bad behaviour and she'll realize that you're bad news.

Long term

- **You're – still – not ready to commit.** Sure, she knows, you need a bit more time before you're ready to (take a long, deep breath because I'm going to say the 's' word) *settle down*. But honestly, ten years is long enough.

- **She loves you like a brother.** Sex is important to her too but she sometimes gets so caught up in the emotional side of things, she forgets to look closely at that as well. If, after two years, she finally realizes as much as she loves you emotionally, physically it just ain't happening, she knows as well as you do: it's not going to work.

- **She catches you out.** Once or once too often, any girl worth her Clarins leaves when it's painfully obvious you're sleeping around.

Telling someone you don't love them any more *must* be done face to face. It's necessary for the person to see you saying the words 'It's over', so they can have some sense of closure. Your feelings are secondary in this situation – the idea is to make it as painless as possible for *them*. For this reason, do the deed as soon as you're sure it's finished. *Don't wait for their permission to leave.* It's normal to feel upset at the prospect of hurting them, but staying until you think they're 'ready' isn't helping either of you. (Undecided whether to leave or stay? See page 553).

Q: Why don't I ever get chatted up after a break-up? Is it because I'm feeling vulnerable and unconfident? A: Yup. It's all to do with pheromones and body language. When you're feeling up and attractive (and especially if you're in the mood for sex), your body lets off a musky scent that others respond to. Your eyes sparkle, you smile more, stand taller and project an air of confidence. Yet another reason to curl up with a video until you're over it.

🄵 FOR HER

Women *hate* hurting anyone. Dumping some guy who's madly in love with us is like shutting the door on that cute stray dog that followed you home to your no-pets-allowed flat and licked your nose when you bent over to see if it had a contact number on its collar. Actually, it's worse, because at least with the dog you can bring it inside and call your mother to convince her one more pet won't matter. Unfortunately, it's not done to ring all your single friends and ask if they'd like to adopt a house-trained boyfriend. Though it is a thought.

Look, you will feel guilty and like a bitch with a capital 'B' while you're telling him. But leading someone on is even more cruel. What's the alternative anyway? You don't want to share your denture glass with this guy, or even another Saturday night fobbing him off. So get to it.

Decide what you're going to say

Work out *exactly* how you're going to word it and put the plan into action *pronto*. Otherwise, you'll end up mothering the guy because you know what's coming. You say, 'You really are sweet, you know? Any girl that ends up with you will be very lucky,' thinking you're sending him a clear warning signal because it's obvious that girl's not going to be you. He thinks the opposite (she must want a commitment). So play it cool. Act off-hand. Don't be too nice. Do whatever it takes to get the message across to him that *you are not happy*. In other words, make sure he's had at least a few days (if you can manage it, a few weeks) warning he's about to be dumped.

Sit him down and deliver the speech

Most men react one of two ways to a dumping: they gaze at you with a hurt, glazed expression on their face, listen to what you have to say then leave without saying much at all. Or they get angry and accuse you of all sorts. (If he's the angry type and you're worried he'll become violent, do it in a public place with a male friend sitting outside in the car. Move in with friends or family for as long as you think it'll take for him to calm down and you to be safe.)

If he didn't say much, call him the next day

Women think on their feet and tend to ask the 'but why?' questions there and then. We're more in touch with our emotions and used to expressing them instantly. He may not be as articulate and/or he may be in shock. He probably only heard half of what you said because 'I can't believe she's doing this' took over his brain. It could take a few hours to sink in and often, he'll call you then or the next day to find out the whys. If he doesn't, and he didn't say much when you delivered your speech, you call him. Ask if he's okay and if there's anything he doesn't understand. If he doesn't want to talk and tells you to take a flying leap, fine. But he might need to know some answers, and could be too proud to pick up the phone.

Call one of his friends

The one you got on the best with. No need to go into details, just say, 'Look. I just thought you should know I've just broken it off with X. He might need a bit of cheering up.'

Ⓜ FOR HIM

Men hate dumping women because women cry. Most of you would rather go to a poetry reading than dole out the tissues – and that's why you always try the silent dump before anything else. This involves beam-me-up-Scotty type behaviour, that is, pretending you just don't exist any more. Trying to contact you is like trying to serve a summons, and when she finally *does* track you down (with sniffer dogs), you pretend she's imagined the whole thing. 'Honey, I told you. I'm busy at work,' you say, all wide eyes and innocence. Coward! The silent dump will work eventually. It has to. If she hasn't seen you in two months, even the thickest of us know it's over. But it's not playing cricket, and if you truly do want her out of your life for good, there are quicker, kinder and more effective ways.

Women need reasons for things. If you give us a pretty plausible reason why you don't want to go out any more, we'll still be upset, but at least we'll *know why*. We need to make sense of things before we can move on. That doesn't mean we won't cry and scream and call you names. But we're much less inclined to follow you around with mascara streaked down our cheeks, desperate to figure out why you gave us roses two months ago and can't even give us the time of day now.

First up, decide on a reason
If you don't want to tell the truth (you're bonking someone else) or your reason is so petty and trivial even *you* think it makes you sound bad (her new haircut is just awful), come up with a plausible lie. Even clichés like, 'I'm too busy at work for a relationship,' or, 'I must be commitment phobic because I just can't make a commitment to you,' are better than nothing. If it's possible, make it something that makes us believe you did once love us, even if you don't now.

Choose your time
Make it sooner rather than later, but be sensitive. If her father's just been rushed to hospital with a suspected heart attack, the emergency ward is not the time or place. Avoid significant dates like Christmas, her birthday, the anniversary of when you first met. Don't do it in a public place, and if you're really nice, check her best friend's not sunning herself in Bali on the weekend you choose.

Get it over and done with
Look at her and say, 'X, I'm really sorry but I think we should split up. I think you're a terrific person but I don't see this heading anywhere.' Follow it up with the reason you thought of, then wait for her to react.

Hang around long enough to answer her questions
She'll throw them at you like dinner plates (those too, possibly). 'Did you ever love me?' 'Is there someone else?' Then, 'How could you do this to me?' 'How could you hurt me like this?' There's not much you can say to a lot of this,

though you can ease the blow by at least looking suitably upset. Tell her the truth as much as possible. If you didn't ever love her, say, 'X, I loved you in lots of ways but not in the way you wanted me to.'

> 'Guys are better at covering up feelings. We form an emotional scab a lot quicker. But the hurt's still there and the scab gets knocked off pretty easily.'
>
> Andrew, 30, sales rep

When it becomes clear there's nothing more to say, leave. If she's in a real mess, ask her if you can call someone to come around. Even if she says no, get on your mobile the minute you're out of the door and call her best friend. Yes, they will give you a hard time, but that's all part of it, I'm afraid. What to do once you've done the hard bit? Keep reading . . .

After the break

Some people are out of your life before you've even finished reading the riot act: others have real problems accepting that it's over. Help reduce the risk by keeping the following in mind.

Refuse to feel guilty

It's not a criminal offence to fall out of love with someone.

Stop being their girlfriend or boyfriend

If you really like the person, it's natural to want to help them when you see they're hurting. You can't: after all, it's *you* they're trying to forget. Don't solve their problems after you've left. It's not your job and it's perpetuating their dependence on you.

Stop seeing them if there's absolutely no chance of a reconciliation

That harmless coffee 'just to check they're okay' will set them back months. If it was serious, wait a year or so after the break to suggest friendship. Semi-serious? Wait at least three months.

Beware of manufactured excuses to see you
If they're desperate, they'll come up with all sorts of imaginative ways to get together – and play on your guilt to force you to turn up.

Don't give them hope
Be cruel to be kind: tell them you don't love them and you're not going to change your mind.

Exes that won't go away
You've tried all the above and they're still hanging around? Time to pull out the big guns!

Write them a letter
Say that the relationship is well and truly over, there is no hope, and following you around is making you dislike them, not regret what you've done. Repeat certain sentences throughout: 'I don't love you any more,' 'There is no hope,' 'There is nothing you can do that will change my mind,' and, 'It is over for good.' It's better to write it down rather than say it over the phone. If they're in denial, it's much harder to dismiss something that's before them in black and white.

Ask mutual friends to back up what's in the letter
If your ex is constantly calling them for news, ask them to say that they have indeed spoken to you and they're afraid it really is over. Have a good chat to any super-nice friends you share. They might be giving them hope because they can't stand to see someone so upset.

Keep a diary
If it continues and they start getting heavy, keep a diary of what's happening. Record when, where and how they're harrassing you, especially any threats that are made.

Send them a letter from your lawyer
Explain to the lawyer that you're being hassled and would like them to send a letter on your behalf. It should be formally worded on official letterhead and state that you will seek a restraining order unless they stop calling/following/harrassing you. It won't cost very much, it shows you mean business and it'll scare all but the most stubborn exes into giving up.

Get a restraining order
If a letter from a lawyer doesn't help, you've got little choice but to visit your local police station and ask them to help arrange a restraining order. You'll need to go to court to get one. Take your diary with you so you can provide concrete evidence of how you're being stalked.

THE GET-OVER-IT GUIDE: DAY BY DAY, STEP BY STEP TO MENDING A BROKEN HEART AND WHY IT'S NEVER EASY

You knew it was coming. But hearing them say, 'It's over,' and imagining it are two totally different things. In your fantasy, they take both your hands in theirs and deliver the tragic news in a voice cracked with emotion. Invariably, they're leaving for a reason that has nothing to do with you (the army needs them, they've decided to devote their life to God). You nod quietly, delivering one, hauntingly touching parting line ('Go – but you take my heart with you'). They head for the door then stop dead as they hear you catch a sob. Their back still turned to you, one hand on the doorknob, they say (struggling for composure): 'I have to do this. I can't ask you to wait for me but . . .'

Reality is somewhat different. You both sit awkwardly on the couch because you know what's coming. 'It's just not working,' they blurt out. 'FINE!' you say. 'That's just BLOODY WONDERFUL!' Then you start screaming, 'You CAN'T *LEEEEEAVE* ME!' fall in a pathetic heap at their feet, wrap both arms around their legs and burst into a hysterical sobbing fit punctuated with unattractive hiccups and snorts. They start to head for the door, you're forced to endure the indignity of being dragged across the carpet because you won't let go of their legs. Desperate to get away, they kick you free and sprint for the door, slamming it behind them. You're after them quick smart, throwing yourself and anything else you can get your hands on in their general direction. Their parting words aren't 'Wait for me', but 'Get away from me, you psychopath!' You follow with a supremely clever 'Get stuffed, you bastard/ bitch! I hate you!'

Then the anger goes and you go back inside, slide down the wall, hit the floor and give in to total panic. You're crying so much you can't breathe. You feel dizzy, think you're going to be sick and are, right there on the carpet. Stumbling toward the bathroom, you visualize the packet of razor blades in the cabinet and sensibly do a detour to the kitchen in search of vodka. One swig and you're sick again. You think, *This is what dying must feel like.* Because that's exactly how you do feel: dead. What's the point of life if they're not going to be there to share it with you?

Getting through the next 30 seconds seems impossible when someone's put your heart through a mincer. But you *will* get through the next minute and the next hour and the next day and the next year. However painful it is now, *you will survive.* How do I know? Because I've been there, everyone I know has been there, and I'd bet money on it that you could fit all the people who *haven't* been there into one small, sad little room. You loved, you lost – but at least you loved. We all came out the other side – so will you. Clear the tears long enough to stop the page blurring and I'll tell you how it's done.

How to use the get-over-it guide

I admit it. The time frame of this guide is ridiculously optimistic, deliberately so. It's not just designed to give you practical advice on how to get through, it's designed to give you hope. The time frames I've organized it under are probably irrelevant, anyway, because every split-up is different and every person heals at a different rate. But most of you will go through all the different stages, usually in this order:

- **Stage 1:** the intensely painful bit. This can last anywhere from two weeks to two months, depending on your relationship. Getting through each day is difficult and you think you'll never be happy again.
- **Stage 2:** is spent adjusting to being single again. It might take a month to six months to stop yourself saying and thinking 'X and I', and come to terms with being 'one'.
- **Stage 3:** is when you start truly healing. If you went out for a year or so and thought it was for ever, this will probably happen about six months after the split. If it was longer, it could take up to a year. You feel normal most of the time but are still battling memories or analysing what went wrong every week or few weeks.
- **Stage 4:** you made it! Official recovery can take anywhere from one to two years.

Don't panic if you appear to move onto the next stage, then slip back one for a few weeks – it's normal. But that's what you're in for. Hopefully, the following guide will help get you from one to four in record time!

Week one

🕑 FOR HER: THE DAY IT HAPPENS

Get on the phone as quickly as possible, the minute he walks out of the door. Call your closest friend, your Mum, big brother, the *butcher*, if you have a special bond: anyone who will understand. Ask them to come over immediately, stopping only for supplies (tissues, alcohol, chocolate, poison to drop into his drink next time he's out). While they're hot-footing it to your house (allow time for speeding tickets), call another friend and let, 'Oh, poor darling,' and, 'I always knew he'd hurt you,' drone on in the background while you hiccup and create a mini tidal wave of tears on the floor. Don't put the receiver down until the doorbell rings, then (and only then) you're allowed to lose it completely. Cry, beat the wall, cling onto your friend for dear life but let out as much grief as possible. When you feel remotely calm, sit down, have a drink and pour out the whole sad, sorry tale over and over until they not only know what happened, they're living it with you. He said, then I said . . . Did I tell you he said then I said? Keep going until you can't analyse it any further or your friend falls asleep. If they can't stay with you, let them bundle you up and take you to their house. Tonight is not the night to be alone.

🕑 FOR HIM: THE DAY IT HAPPENS

Initially, you're in shock. You keep thinking, *She'll get over it. Any minute now, she'll call me to say sorry and everything will be fine.* You consider sending flowers – that's worked before. Except you know this is different. She doesn't call, and when you call her four hours later, she says, ever-so-gently, 'I meant it. I'm sorry. It really is over.'

If you can do it (yes, you can), let yourself have a good cry. When you're done, pick up the phone and call someone. If you've got a close female friend, she's first on the list. Tell her your girlfriend's left you and you're feeling down. Could she come over and cheer you up? She'll be over at your place in a nanosecond, dispensing hugs and all sorts of soothing there-theres (and no, she won't tell everyone how pathetic you were, so drop the macho act). No close female friends? Call a mate. He'll drag you down to the local pub for a game of pool, give you a slap on the back and say, 'You'll get over it – I did.' It's not much, but it is true. Whatever you end up doing, tonight is not the night to start the Liver Cleansing Diet. If a few beers make you feel better, have them but keep it under control. The idea is to send you to sleep – not stumbling over to her house drunk.

> 'Listen to friends but be careful. If they'd secretly prefer you single, they'll think up a million different ways to convince you he's a bastard, even if he's not.'
> Christine, 27, journalist

Ⓜ Ⓕ BOTH CLING TO THIS

Think back to when you helped someone get over a painful break-up. Remember how they said they'd never smile again, but you knew they'd get over it? They did – and so will you.

Day two
Ⓕ FOR HER

The first thing you realize when you open your eyes the next day is that you can't: they're swollen shut from so much crying. Reality starts to seep through when you get out of bed and stand on a mound of crumpled tissues. Instant tears. It hits with full force: he's gone, you're alone. Day two (sorry) is even worse than day one, so aim to simply get through it.

It's a weekend

Spend the day repeating the story (for the 45th time) to a friend, any friend. You'll feel raw, miserable and so sorry for yourself it's not funny, so surround yourself with people who care. True friends will let you tag along wherever they go: take them up on it. If they're cleaning the loo, hand them the Flash; if they're shaving their legs, the razor (actually, maybe you'd better skip that one). It's wallow-in-it day, so don't feel guilty about dominating the conversation totally and not having cleaned your teeth for 24 hours. The only no-no today: DON'T call him and don't persuade your friends to call him either. Resist the urge to park outside his house, do a drive-by *or* turn up at his best friend's hoping for some inside info. Make a pact with yourself that you can call him in one week if you still need to and get a friend to help you stick to it. (The deal: you have to call them before you call him.)

It's a work day

Get up, put your make-up on and get out that door. You'll be tempted to call in sick and pull the bedclothes over your head, but you're not doing yourself any favours. If you feel so traumatized you honestly can't make it, call in sick, but get yourself to a friend's house – don't stay at home alone. You've dragged yourself into the office? Great – but it's unlikely you'll be Ms Efficient, so tell your immediate boss what's happened. You know you won't perform well, but would prefer to be there and you'll make up for lost time later and so on. If you're on friendly terms with your workmates, let them know you're hurting (and accept all offers of lunch, cream cakes and cups of hot, sweet tea).

If it's a brisk, professional team and you don't feel comfortable blabbing all, put on a brave front and make calls to friends and family in your lunch hour. If you can't hold it together, disappear into the toilet and take your make-up bag to do a quick repair job. Call a friend to see for dinner tonight: their place or yours. If you can't face sleeping alone, crash in front of the telly with the sound turned *up*.

Ⓜ FOR HIM

Read the 'For her' section because you'll feel exactly the same. If you picked up the phone and someone said, 'Congratulations, you've just won the lottery!' your first thought would be, *I wonder if a million dollars would change her mind?* Fill up your day with activity. Play sport, watch reruns of old sitcoms, strip the car engine then put it back together again: anything to keep yourself busy and keep your mind off it.

It's the weekend

Get on the phone and don't get off it until you've organized non-stop entertainment for the entire weekend. Tell people you've split up, even if you do play it cool and insist you don't care (they'll make their own conclusions). If you don't want to talk about it, tell people. Say, 'It's over. I don't want to talk about it. I'll tell you the details later.' People will want to spoil you: let them. It's not being 'weak' to accept offers of roast dinners, it's what friends do. Your main aim today: convincing yourself that turning up at her front door with enough red roses to fill her entire flat really won't work. If she's serious about splitting, she'll just feel sorry for you.

It's a work day

You're one up on your female equivalent: chances are you'll get through the day without dissolving into tears. If you think you can get through on autopilot, do it. If you can't, tell your boss what's happened. If possible, arrange to meet a friend for lunch, but steer clear of the nearest pub. I don't care how fabulous she was or how bad you feel, she's not worth losing your job over by going back to work drunk.

Ⓜ Ⓕ BOTH CLING TO THIS

Before you finally go to sleep, tell yourself, 'I'm okay. I'm just upset. I will get through this. I survived today didn't I?'

Day three
Ⓜ Ⓕ FOR HIM AND HER

Okay, enough of this namby-pamby wimpy stuff: today is toughen-up day. I'm being cruel? Humour me, anyway, and give it a go. You've got nothing to lose except a day feeling powerless. Today it's time for some action: I want you to gather up all those relationship reminders and put them out of sight. That's right: books, cards, letters, photographs, CDs with your song on them, cute little notes, anything at all which connects them to you. If Special K brings back memories, plonk it in the bin. (If *everything* does, perhaps you'd better wait a week.) Put all that memorabilia into a big bag and either throw it all out (best), give it to a friend to look after (okay) or shove it in the back of a cupboard where you can't get to it without a huge effort (a cop-out, but better than leaving it in sight).

Wash the sheets and towels (yes, you must), then go through your diary and cancel any events where you're bound to run into each other. Stay away from all your old haunts: the secluded beach you both discovered, the great little Thai restaurant that was your favourite. Avoid anything that reminds you of your ex. Why? Because you really are

It used to be women who worried about relationships – now it's men. Fifty-eight per cent of Australian men say they'd like to improve a personal relationship. Only 47 per cent of women agree.

kidding yourself if you think lying around listening to 'your song' and rereading old love letters is going to help you heal or magically get them back. It won't. In fact, if there honestly *is* any hope of a reconciliation, seeing you get on with your life is far more likely to do it. It's been proven over and over: act like you don't need them (even if you do want them) and they may well realize they want you too.

So if they come over to beg forgiveness and notice their picture's been removed, you'll win respect not disapproval. *The quicker you accept they're gone for good – even if they aren't – the quicker you'll get over them, and the more likely it is they'll want to return*. It's a win–win situation. You're not only upping the chances of getting back together, you're upping your chances of happily getting on with your life if they don't. The reverse is also true: send letters begging another chance, pester them with phone calls, follow them around and they'll thank God they got out when they did. Besides, your ego's been bruised enough, it can't take any more knocks right now, so don't set yourself up for them.

Ⓜ Ⓕ BOTH CLING TO THIS
There are whole minutes – perhaps even two or three together – that you don't think about your ex. You are recovering.

Day four
Ⓕ FOR HER
From now on, you're only allowed five minutes crying time a day. Yup. It sounds bizarre but I want you to try really hard to hold it all in until you're allowed to let it all out. Schedule a time and once the floodgates open, set the timer because in five minutes you have to stop and reward yourself. Follow every crying session with something that makes you feel good. Slap on a face mask,

some empowering music (Alanis Morrisette, 'Jagged Little Pill', The Corrs, 'I Never Loved You Anyway') on the CD player and soak in a bubble bath with your favourite mag. If you're reading this and thinking, *I can't stop crying for five minutes, let alone restrict it to that*, you're officially allowed to move this step back a little. (And if you're feeling seriously out of control, get yourself an emergency appointment with a good counsellor.)

Ⓜ FOR HIM

If you're a typical bloke, you probably haven't spoken too much about how you're feeling. Now's a good time to call that female friend and pour it all out to her. If you don't have one, or feel uncomfortable talking about your feelings, write it all down. Get yourself a beer (or coffee) and take an hour or so to write down everything you're feeling and going through. No-one's going to see it (burn it afterward, if you're paranoid), so be totally honest. Record how you seriously thought she was the one, the plans you had, how you started reading the fine print at the bottom of the diamond ads. What you miss about her, how she made you feel ten feet tall and now you feel about one inch high. Why you think you broke up, how you'll never, ever trust anyone ever again or fall in love. Ever.

Yes, it sounds pathetic and you'll feel pathetic as you're writing it all down. But it truly will help. So just keep writing and let it all come out. You'll cry a lot and feel exhausted when you've finished but at least you've released some of the pain and it's not festering inside. Face your emotions *now*, feel the pain *now* and you'll give yourself a chance to recover. If you push them to some dark place deep inside you, you risk them resurfacing when you next meet someone you really like. It's hard enough making new relationships work without having to grapple with all the old stuff Jayne left behind at the same time.

Ⓜ Ⓕ FOR BOTH OF YOU

Keep as busy as possible and *don't sit by the phone*. Let's be logical here: if the former love of your life suddenly decides they want to live for ever in your pocket, they're not going to give up if you're not home when they ring. If they do, it was a spur-of-the-moment (they didn't score last night) thing. Or they're simply calling to see how you are. Don't return the call or pick up the phone if you're pretty sure that's all they want. Talking with them will send you straight back to longing-for-them land. Call a friend and ask them to relay a message: you're hurting but you're okay and don't want to hear from them for a little while.

By day four you're still utterly miserable – though more in a depressed than out-of-control way. Nevertheless, keep surrounding yourself with understanding friends and protect your heart. If a soppy song comes on the radio, switch stations. Ditch any novel that has love scenes for gutsy thrillers, choose your movies very carefully and buy some party music to replace those banned CDs.

Ⓜ Ⓕ BOTH CLING TO THIS

All this heartache has made you remember how bloody awful you felt when you split with another ex. You got over them – maybe, just maybe, you'll survive this one too.

Day five

Ⓜ Ⓕ FOR BOTH OF YOU

Today you officially take back control of your life by doing some spring-cleaning. If it's a work day, start with your office. Spend your lunch hour going through every single 'to do' pile and organizing it properly. Clear out your drawers, ruthlessly throw out everything you don't need or file it where it belongs.

When you get home that evening, turn the CD player up

full blast (boppy music, not sad stuff) and do the same at home. Empty all the cupboards and throw out or donate anything useless or stuff you haven't worn or used in the last two years. Rearrange the furniture. Make a list of things to buy that'll brighten up the place. You've just started on the kitchen and it's midnight already? Who cares? You're not sleeping that well anyway – you might as well completely exhaust yourself and have something to show for it in the morning other than knotted sheets. Tomorrow you'll wake up to a clean, organized flat and office and feel a sense of satisfaction.

Ⓜ Ⓕ BOTH CLING TO THIS

Believe in fate. Everything happens for a reason. Perhaps you broke up with your ex because someone even better is out there waiting for you or you're about to get that promotion and need all your energy for work. Trust in your future.

Day six
Ⓜ Ⓕ FOR BOTH OF YOU

Okay, you're still down and feeling terrible but after five or six days should have a little perspective on the situation. You did some physical spring-cleaning yesterday; today we're going to do some emotional spring-cleaning. If you're a guy (and did as you were told), you will have already written down all the emotions you're experiencing. If you're female, you've no doubt verbalized them to your friends. This list is different.

The best strategy to accept someone is gone is to collect as much evidence as possible to prove a) you're a wonderful person who deserves better, and b) they weren't as fabulous as you thought. I'm not being nasty or vengeful, just realistic. After all, if they were *that* perfect for you, they wouldn't have dumped you in the first place. There were obviously areas where you didn't see eye to eye and things you didn't like about them. They were human, weren't they?

Start with list number one: get a good friend to help you write down everything great about yourself, all your successes and achievements. You're a great friend. Popular. A terrific listener. Your family adore you. You were crucial in helping your team win the final. You can sink 12 beers and still stand. Write down big achievements, serious things, silly things – as many as you can come up with.

List two: set to work on your ex. It doesn't matter how much you did or do love them, no-one is perfect (not even them). Write down every single flaw and weakness you can think of. How they didn't share your passion for the sea, how your Mum never really liked them, the time you caught them admiring themselves in the mirror, how they flirted at parties, the embarrassing green trackpants that made their bum look six times bigger, how they'd give you a hard time for wanting to watch 'crap', how he vomited all over the bathroom floor after a night with the boys, how she used to leave little hairs from shaving all over the bath.

Every time a friend calls, ask them to help you add to the list – but make sure you explain your motives. Friends will be suspicious if you ask them to bag the person, because they're worried you'll use it against them if the two of you get back together. Explain that it's a silly little exercise you want to do to support you right now, and you'll be amazed what nasties they'll come up with!

Ⓜ Ⓕ BOTH CLING TO THIS

Look at yourself in the mirror every morning and evening and say to yourself, 'It's over. They're not coming back. I will survive.' Keep on doing this until you can look yourself straight in the eyes, speak confidently and believe it.

Day seven

Ⓜ Ⓕ FOR BOTH OF YOU

Get out your diary and phone book and spend the day calling all the people you've neglected during your relationship. Prepare what you're going to say when they ask about your ex (a simple, 'It didn't work out,' is fine). Make dates with everyone until your diary looks satisfyingly full. Give opposite-sex friends preference: they'll give you the ego boost you need, but be careful with exes. It's extremely tempting to convince yourself they really were 'the one' when you're feeling vulnerable and lonely. (They weren't.)

I wouldn't accept invitations to go out and party just yet – you're still too raw. Instead, plan evenings with good friends and happy couples. No, you won't look at them and feel envious – you'll see living evidence of people who've been through what you're going through and had the courage to fall in love again. Ask them (separately) to recount the details of their past break-ups. How they never thought they'd love again but here they are, doing just that.

Ⓜ Ⓕ BOTH CLING TO THIS

Do I honestly believe I'm not going to meet anyone else in the next ten years?

Week two

Congratulations! Here you were thinking you couldn't make it through a minute and you survived an entire week without a) joining the French Foreign Legion; b) joining a cult; or c) moving back to the country to live with Mum. A shred of self-respect should be resurfacing. By now, you're probably making about three 'God, I feel awful' calls to friends a day and are able to spend half an hour on your own without feeling suicidal. Now's the time to cut the umbilical cord completely. Ask mutual friends not to report back every piece of gossip about your ex – and vice versa. Don't spend your life trying to find out about theirs. If they're depressed, it'll give you false hope. They're out dancing until dawn – your ego will take another dive.

Beware of friends who encourage you to believe your ex will 'wake up to themselves' and come back: they're not doing you any favours, just trying to make you feel better. If your ex seriously does think they've made a mistake, they'll call you themselves. Don't believe it unless the words come out of *their* mouth.

On the subject of friends, remember they have lives too. Make sure they know how much you've appreciated their support and put up with you knocking on their door at 3 am and phoning 65 million times an hour. It's okay if your conversations are still largely dominated by your break-up, but make an effort to spend even a quarter of it asking about them. As for striking up a friendship with your ex, it's too soon. Leave it a few months or longer to put some distance between you.

With seven days under your belt, it's time to organize and make sense of the thoughts and theories about the split that are whizzing around in your brain. If you have a good friend whose judgement you trust implicitly, ask them to help you diagnose the break-up so you can learn from the experience. Was it just bad timing and incompatibility or are you constantly falling for people who are bad for you? Do you grab onto anyone because you're scared of being on your own? Encourage them to be brutally honest and take whatever they say on the chin: if they know you well, there's at least a grain of truth in their theories. If you have a history of bad relationships, consider seeing a counsellor for a few sessions. At the very least, flick through Chapter 8 for clues on why you keep getting kicked in the teeth.

Feel especially tempted to call your ex after all this analysis? Don't! If you really must pour out all your intimate revelations (and are they really any of their business?), write a letter and wait two weeks before posting it. Chances are, you'll decide they don't need to know after all.

Week three

Okay, you cried when you found his old T-shirt at the bottom of the laundry basket or an old lipstick of hers under the bin in the bathroom. But you may find sadness being replaced by anger – white-hot, good-job-you-don't-own-a-gun type of anger. By all means, fantasize about taking revenge, but don't do it. Instead, get rid of the anger in a constructive way. A girl-friend of mine started running. 'I was so angry, I didn't know what to do with it so I started pounding the pavement.' She now has the best legs in Sydney. Join a gym, take on extra work, get stuck into the garden: just do *something*!

By now, a certain amount of logic should be creeping in. Even if they came back, could you trust them not to leave you again? Even if you did call and beg for another chance, wouldn't you always wonder if they did it just because they felt sorry for you? Your brain's exhausted from diagnosing and dissecting the break-up and quite frankly, you're a bit sick of thinking about it. You stop taking all the blame for the split and realize it's rarely, if ever, one person's fault. Your friends stop worrying you're about to jump off a bridge and call less. Their eyes start to glaze over when you mention your ex's name. By week three, you're forced to spend nights alone and you feel okay about it. Not great, just okay. You still feel an overwhelming sense of loneli-ness and still wonder (for the 600th time) what they're doing at that moment, but it shouldn't be the focus of your existence. If it is, again, get yourself along to see a counsellor.

Week four

Life goes on. You're surviving without them, your heart is mending but this makes you feel despondent rather than satisfied. True love? Yeah, right. Forced to watch a soppy film, you scoff at the romantic bits and your friends accuse you of being cynical. You are – but that's normal. We all lose faith for a little while. If you're feeling depressed and unmotivated, take a good look at your health. You've probably been eating little and grabbing takeaways when you do. Resolve to eat healthily, cut back on the alcohol and ciggies and get a solid eight hours' sleep a night. The better you feel physically, the better you'll be able to cope emotionally.

If you find you can't stop thinking about your ex, try some aversion therapy. Put an elastic band around your wrist and flick it each time you think about them. You'll literally snap yourself out of it because it *hurts*. Your brain will start to associate thoughts of your ex with physical pain and subconsciously stop you thinking about them. When you flick the elastic band, say to yourself, 'I don't need you. I have my own life. I'm over you.'

The next month

Take a long look at yourself in the mirror. Are you happy with your appearance, your image and your wardrobe? The sort of person you are? If not, do something about it. Indulge in a personal trainer, get a friend with great dress sense to help you shop for new clothes, treat yourself to a course of massages and let a professional get rid of the tension of the last few weeks. Work on areas you'd like to change. Start being a better friend, work harder, take some evening courses. Get back in touch with your sexual side as well. Start masturbating again, if you've stopped. Once your libido kicks back in, you'll find yourself checking out others in the gym (on the street, in your office) even if your heart and brain aren't interested in following through.

I still wouldn't suggest you hit the local nightclubs but you are ready for a restaurant, café, bar or pub. You're not out there to meet anyone, just for the experience of going out single. Don't take it personally if no-one checks you out, chats you up or appears even remotely interested. You're still exuding 'poor me!' vibes, even if you don't realize it. Your self-esteem should be climbing back up, but don't test it. Asking out the new-and-most-lusted-after person in the office isn't a good idea. You'll take it as a rejection even if they turn out to be married with six kids.

By the end of the month, you begin to feel remotely normal. The word's out that you're single and everyone's inviting you to this party or that dinner. Your diary is nicely packed full of dates and you've got things to look forward to. You feel rightfully proud of yourself for having coped and think you're well and truly over them until – a song comes on the radio and suddenly it all comes flooding back. You're laughing with friends and *she* walks past – only it's not her at all, just some girl with the same haircut. You go to dinner with friends and your eyes slide down their bookcase and see a travel book on Bali and a memory of the two of you poring over that holiday brochure hits you smack between the eyes. It hurts *intensely* and you think, *Oh God, I'm kidding myself. I'm not better at all.* But you are because the pain does *fade* – even if you feel faded from the experience.

It's most unfair but you'll probably find all the memories of the two of you are good ones. Blame your brain. We idealize past relationships because our brains are programmed to throw up pleasant memories rather than painful ones. It's an instinct which usually works in our favour (to keep us as happy as possible) – but not in this case. Beat it by consciously dragging up a really unhappy, unpleasant memory about the two of you every time your brain throws up a good one. It puts things into perspective and helps ease the pain. Don't panic too much if you're still having the odd dreamy daydream about your ex months and months later. It's natural to think fondly of your last lover if you're a bit lonely single.

Two months later

You're laughing again. You're noticing things – like that great shirt or dress in the shop window (and the cute assistant standing at the counter). Life feels full of possibilities and after all those weeks of mooning around, you desperately want to *get on with it*.

It's around now that you suddenly feel the urge to meet someone new IMMEDIATELY! You still miss your ex but wonder if it's more the relationship you miss, than the person. By all means get out their and flirt your bottom off but do yourself (and them) a favour and keep any relationship you have on a casual basis for now. Give yourself time to grieve and heal and sort through all the baggage. The right time to start a fresh, new, serious relationship is when you honestly believe you understand what went wrong the last time and – even more importantly – feel confident of your judgement to pick someone who really will be good for you. Even then, take it slowly and keep both eyes *wide* open. Not just to protect yourself, but to see the new love of your life. Because if there's one advantage to breaking up, it's this: you get to go through that delicious falling-in-love stage, all over again!

If you lived together or were married

If you lived together or were married, the pain of separation is more intense, and you'll take longer to get over it. The above guide applies to you, but you need to multiply the time frame by about a thousand.

Live-in lovers don't get as much sympathy as marrieds who split, but if living together is a trial marriage, then splitting up is a mini divorce. And it's obviously going to hurt more if you lived together rather than simply went out. You shared the rent, the bathroom and the cat: you're not just losing the relationship, you're losing a life that you've built together. One of you has to move out, you have to decide who gets the fridge. His parents feel like your parents. Your big brother is now his best friend. You're used to sharing your life with someone, and it's difficult to close the gap when they're gone.

If you were married, it's even more heartbreaking. You've got the divorce to face. A whole house full of furniture to split up, bank accounts to divide. If you have children, you need to work out custody and visiting arrangements and accept the fact that, despite what's happened, you have to live with this person in your life for ever.

It's beyond the realms of this book to delve too deeply into the serious psychological fall-out of a divorce or major separation, and I would strongly suggest you see a counsellor to help you get through the first few months. At the very least, buy a few books which deal specifically with this topic and lean on your friends, specifically those who've been through what you have.

But even after the toughest break-up there is light at the end of the tunnel, and I've included a real-life story to prove it. Nick is a friend of mine whose 'happy' marriage came to a rude and distressing end two years ago. He seriously thought his life was over – and I can honestly say I've never seen anyone suffer quite as much over a break-up as Nick did. The reason I want you to hear his story is because he *did* come out the other side. And how. Nick's still single but judging by the bevy of (I'm not kidding here) truly amazing women vying for his attention at a dinner party recently, he won't be for long. He wasn't just smiling – I thought his face would split.

Later, I asked him privately, 'Better now?'

He nodded and said, 'Actually, better than when I thought I was happily married. I feel brand new.'

Have faith in yourself. If Nick, 38, can do it, so can you. Here's his story.

I lost my virginity to Andrea and she did me. We got married when I was 17 and for twenty years I thought I had the perfect life. Andrea's extremely attractive and I loved her utterly and totally. She wasn't concerned about looks, herself. She didn't care when my hairline started doing the old receding thing – not that I was ever up to her standard anyway. I'm sure people used to look at us and think, *What's she doing with him?* It's not like I'm rich or anything, but she was the model wife. She didn't look at other men, didn't flirt.

We both worked odd hours and sex wasn't a big deal for us. My sex drive isn't high and I just figured hers wasn't either. People said to me after the divorce, 'Didn't you realize something was up when you weren't having sex?' but I honestly didn't. We had enough to bear two children, who are a gift from God. They are my life, and if it wasn't for the boys I would have killed myself.

My parents live on a property and I'd often pack the kids in the car and stay a few nights there to give Andrea a break. She worked most weekends anyway. On one occasion, I told her I'd be home on the Monday but decided to come home early. I can't remember why, though I know it wasn't for sinister reasons, like not trusting her. After 20 great years with no signs of unhappiness or straying, you forget about all that stuff.

I remember it was exactly 11 am on the Sunday when I let myself and the kids into the house, because I looked at my watch and thought, *We'll have to be quiet because she'll be asleep from working a night shift.* The kids were outside running around and I came in through the lounge and went straight to the bedroom. The door was closed. I opened it and from then on it was like my mind registered everything in flashes.

The first thing I saw was a man's jacket thrown across the bedside table. Then I saw two people having intercourse on our bed. The man turned around slightly but I didn't know him. My first thought was, *Oh my God. Someone's broken in and been using the place to have sex in.* Then I saw her hair, all spread out on the pillow like it always is. At that point, she saw me and screamed, 'Jesus Christ!' They froze and stayed like that for what seemed like minutes: this guy's penis still inside my wife. I don't think any of us knew what to do.

I heard the boys racing up the stairs and opened my mouth to shout 'No! Stop!' but nothing came out. They stopped in the doorway but didn't go in, so they could see legs but not much else. They looked at my face and sensed something was wrong, though they didn't know what. I moved instinctively toward them and one of my sons said, 'What are you doing, Mummy?' and then he came and held my hand and my other son hid behind my legs. I remember holding their hands and leading them down the stairs, then ringing my best mate, Stuart. Then I put my head in my hands and just sat there.

I don't know how the guy got out but he managed to escape without running into me or the kids. Andrea took control of the situation. The kids were packed off to the neighbours, my mate arrived and she sat there with the two of us. I'm dead certain Stuart would rather have been anywhere else in the world than sitting between two people whose marriage has just crumbled, but we needed him. So he stayed.

Andrea told me the guy was someone she'd picked up and they had casual sex once in a while. He wasn't the first one. Turned out she'd been having sex affairs for around ten years. Why? It had nothing to do with her love for me, she said. She just needed good sex, and I wasn't interested and this way, she got what she wanted, I wasn't hurt and everyone was happy. Until she got found out.

Some husbands, I guess, would have forgiven Andrea. Maybe turned a blind eye or tried everything they could to turn her on and make sex great. I couldn't. I left for a while and sat for hours, in a motel room out of town. I was very calm and logical. I knew what I wanted – access to the kids. And I knew she'd give it to me because the courts wouldn't look favourably on her as a fit mother. Now, we have joint custody so the kids spend equal time at her home and mine.

The pain of all this was unbelievable. My sister pushed me into the dating scene and I felt like a complete idiot because I got married so young, I didn't know how to do all that singles stuff. I don't want another serious relationship right now, but I would like to have the life I had with Andrea. I loved being married and I would love to have another child, one I could have full-time, and to feel whole and happy again. I'm gun-shy, and all the women I've met know it and steer clear, but I can feel my confidence returning, and if I met the right girl and trusted her, I know I'd try again.

Ⓜ FOR HIM: WHY YOU'RE HURTING MORE THAN SHE IS

Mick and Sylvia split up six months ago. She's dropped from a size 16 to a size 12, sports a sexy, new short haircut and has just been promoted. 'I'd love to meet for dinner,' she bubbles over the phone. 'But it'll have to be in a few weeks because I'm just sooooo busy.'

Mick's also lost weight – in all the wrong places. He's got all the time in the world to meet for coffee because business 'just isn't happening'. He turns up in a crumpled black T-shirt with matching bags under his eyes and confesses (quite unnecessarily) that he's not sleeping. 'I just can't get over this. I can't stop thinking about her,' he says desperately.

It's an all-too-common scenario. Don't believe the romance novels: women aren't the love slaves. Psychologists have discovered that, while men still fall in love less often than women, when they fall, they fall harder, quicker – and out of love slower. And while a tougher, smarter breed of women cope better with split-ups, the new-age man, just starting to appreciate the joys of committed relationships, is finding it more difficult to let go. Why? Here's five good reasons.

1. Women have better coping strategies

A typical female reaction to a painful break-up is to hotfoot it to her best friend's house and spend the next three weeks (or three months) talking about her ex and her feelings to anyone that will listen. Women are more emotionally expressive and healthily in touch with their soft underbellies. By letting out our grief and sadness, we get the pain out of our systems and are able to move on quickly.

Men, God love you, bottle things up. Your reaction to a split with a treasured girlfriend is to mask the pain. You'll either a) not think about it and throw yourself into work in an attempt to reaffirm your own worth; or b) not think about it and start sleeping around for the same reasons; or c) not think about it, get drunk and stay out until 3 am, running yourself into the ground. In other words, you'll do just about *anything* rather than confront the pain and deal with it.

Men don't analyse, they just hope like hell time will make the pain go away. 'How do men cope when they're dumped?' says Andrew, a friend of mine. 'We don't. We go off the rails and have real trouble holding it all together. Work deteriorates and everything starts breaking down. All you want to do is go down the pub and get mindlessly pissed.'

Ironically, the more you're seen about town with replacement bimbettes on your arm, the more you're probably hurting. It doesn't mean you don't care – in fact, quite the opposite. When people lose someone they love, they're overcome by feelings of worthlessness. Women cope by getting their act together, proving their worth that way. For some men, it's simply easier to sleep around. *If I can pull the chicky-babes, I must be okay.* This is also why you become self-abusive. You're feeling unloved and unworthy, so you treat yourself accordingly, swallowing spirits and party drugs as fast as you can score them. What you really *should* be doing is quite the opposite: you should be looking after yourself more. Replace the love you've lost with another: your own.

2. You can't talk to your friends the same way she does to hers

'I simply can't imagine rocking up to a mate's house, sobbing my eyes out and saying, "I'm hurting," ' says Peter, 28. 'I've got balls. Guys don't do that. You just don't cry – it's a male thing.'

While female relationships are based on talking, especially about our feelings, men's relationships are based on doing: things like playing sport, joking around, having a beer. While some men do have substantial conversations with their friends, many don't. Talking about their pain or their problems just isn't acceptable: they feel stupid, weak and pathetic if they broach personal topics. As a result, men are more emotionally independent than women and are used to being self-reliant. Fabulous, until you hit a rough spot.

The female support system is infinitely more helpful at a time like this. We accept and value expression of emotion. We're good at advising and take it as a compliment if we're asked to help someone through a rough time. It's different for a guy. Even if your male friends *are* concerned about you, they often wouldn't have a clue what to say to fix it. According to Andrew, the only time he even comes close to talking in detail about personal matters is 'if you're really drunk. But then, if I was that drunk, I'd probably be more inclined to turn up at her place. Men are the stronger sex. We're not supposed to hurt.'

Darcy, 24, a journalist, says his male friends had three pieces of advice when he split with his girlfriend. 'Go out and bonk someone as quickly as possible, throw yourself into work and there's plenty of other girls out there. I don't think men like talking about it because it reopens the wound of *their* old break-ups. The most intimate thing I got was, "Mate, I got over Kate."'

But while it might not be okay to blab or blubber to a male friend, platonic girlfriends are sometimes a different story. She could well be your saving grace. 'If you want to talk about anything, you ring a female friend,' says Mike, 21, a student, echoing a sentiment expressed by lots of men I spoke to. 'For some reason, it's okay to get advice from a female. They even seem to *like* doing that sort of stuff!'

> Men carry the scars of divorce long after the relationship collapses – and it's all their wife's fault. Most men blame their wives not just for the problems which caused the split, but for the divorce as well (they did it because 'that was what *she* wanted').

3. You didn't see it coming

Women see the writing on the wall when it's in tiny, tiny letters. You wouldn't notice if she wrote, 'You're about to be dumped,' on the bathroom mirror. With your shaving cream. It's the right-brain, left-brain thing. The left side of our brain is the 'thinking' part (logic and facts); the right side works with 'feelings' (emotion, intuition, expression). Usually men are more left-brain dominated and women right-brain. So you're not as in tune with the touchy-feely side that would warn you she was about to leave.

She thinks she's given you lots of really obvious messages she's not happy, but you often miss them all. She's tried to solve the problems, resentment builds up and she gets so angry, she can't wait to get out of there. You didn't even notice there was a problem and are left thinking, *Hang on a minute, I thought we had a great relationship. What's happening?* Says Darcy, 'When Jenny moved out, I was left thinking, *God! If only I'd not gone out drinking with the boys. I should have bought her flowers more. I should have helped her with the dishes.* That's why I thought there was still hope. She might have tried her hardest but I hadn't.'

4. You lose mutual friends

While women lean heavily on good friends after a break, men often do quite the opposite. They tend to drop 'couple' friends in favour of single males who'll go out and party with them. Sometimes you'll avoid good friends of your ex because it's too painful to hear how well she's faring without you. The end result: you're lonely and dwell on the past. Brendon, 24, a personal trainer, says, 'The last thing I felt like doing was have these sad dinner parties with our old friends and talk about how tragic it was that we'd split up. Seeing them made me miss her even more, and her female friends always think that unless you're sobbing into the entree, you don't care about her – then they tell *her* that! Men are just better at covering up. We're used to hiding our feelings, so it's easy for us to pretend we're over it when all we've really done is put a Band-Aid on top of a sore that's festering away nicely underneath.'

Scott, a 26-year-old manager, agrees. 'She keeps all the friends because she's been crying on their shoulders,' he says. 'By the time you're over the party stage and ready to calm down again, they're annoyed because you haven't seen them or she's turned them against you. It's always the guy who has to get out there and build a whole new social circle.'

Women often look better after a break-up. They reappraise their image and develop a toughness that's attractive to men. Feeling great and looking fabulous, they're more confident and their social life blooms. If he's still moping about depressed, she does quite the opposite. Says Brendon, 'My girlfriend transformed herself after I left. It was quite remarkable: she'd gone from a shy wallflower to this incredibly confident girl who everyone wanted at their party. No-one asked me anywhere – probably because when they did, I stood in a corner and felt sorry for myself or behaved like a total moron by getting too drunk.'

5. You don't clear out the closet for next time

A crucial part of getting over someone is getting rid of – or at least putting away – remnants of the relationship. It's all part of letting go. If her old hairbrush is still in the bathroom, you may get stuck and *never* let go.

If your next girlfriend finds herself walking into a shrine of your ex, she will not be happy. You might defend the pictures on the wall by saying your ex is a friend, but it's obvious to her that you're looking for a new relationship to mask the pain of the last one. She also knows it's quite common for men to fantasize about sorely missed exes, masturbate while looking at her picture, imagine you're making love to her when you're with someone else. Call it women's intuition, but if that's what's happening, you won't get away with it.

Often, it's only when you meet someone new, someone you can trust, that you finally *do* deal with all the pain the break-up caused. 'You have to let go of the hurt at some point – and more often than not, it's your next girlfriend that cops it,' says my friend Michael. He says he realized he had to get rid of emotional mementos when a girl he liked heaps innocently put on a CD that made him desperately miss his old girlfriend. 'I couldn't believe it – I burst into tears!' he said. 'She sat with me and listened as all the pain came spilling out. Then she got up, took the CD and put it outside in the rubbish bin. It was a real out-with-the-old-in-the-new gesture. At first I felt angry and panicky that it was gone, then I finally felt myself letting go. I felt free for the first time in years.'

Revenge: ex-*tremely* stupid!

The best revenge is living well. *No it isn't*, you're thinking. The best revenge would be taking a sharp knife and making deep, satisfying scratches all over the gleaming paintwork of his brand new car. Or cutting off one arm of each of his suits with scissors.

WHY NOW? YOU CAN'T POSSIBLY DUMP ME – IT'S CHRISTMAS!

'I opened my eyes and thought, *Hey! It's Christmas,* says Fiona. 'I kissed my boyfriend on the mouth and thought, *Maybe he'll choose today to ask me to marry him.* We swapped presents (mine was perfume – which should have warned me) and went to his parents' house for lunch. Afterward, he asked me to come and sit by the pool with him. My heart did a flitter-flutter and I beamed at his parents who gave me sad little smiles. They knew what I was thinking, and they also knew what their son was about to do. He told me it was over the minute we sat down.

'I asked him, "Why now? We're expected at my parents' in an hour."

'And he said, "I know and that's what made me realize I can't live this lie. I can't face going to your parents' house and having your family ask when we're going get married, so I had to tell you now." '

I personally know three people who've been dumped on Christmas Day. I know another two who were dumped on their partner's birthday (*after* the present, I might add). Add about a dozen who've become suddenly single during their thirtieth or fortieth year and at least three couples who didn't make it to midnight on New Year's Eve. That's just in my circle of friends.

You don't need to be Einstein to figure out something's going on here. But why is it that people seem to have particularly bad timing and dump their partners at certain stages, ages and dates in their lives?

The answer is simple. Birthdays, anniversaries, Christmas and New Year's Eve force us to think about where our lives are going – and where we've been. Clever people appraise their progress constantly; others get so caught up in the daily rituals of living, that's *all* they do. They go through life on autopilot. For people like this, significant dates are like a wake-up call. They finally reflect on what happened the ➢

year before and decide they can't bear another one like the last. It's the equivalent of someone screaming at them through a loudspeaker, 'For God's sake. You've been unhappy for ages. DO SOMETHING ABOUT IT!' So they do. Right there and then.

Turning 21, 30, 40, 50 – any milestone birthday – is also a time of introspection. We all have a life plan, things we want to have achieved by a certain age, even if we don't religiously stick by it or are particularly conscious of conforming to a timetable. And out of all our goals, marriage and children are by far the most likely to have a deadline attached to them. It's sensible for starters, because women have a fertility cut-off point. If you're a female about to hit 38, want children and your partner won't even consider moving in (let alone marriage or kids), your birthday present to yourself might be to get rid of him. Give yourself the chance to meet someone who does want to start a family. Time waits for no man and, unfortunately for us, it doesn't wait for women either. Other life events also affect relationships. If your best friend gets married, it forces you to think about it. Realizing you could never get up there and say the sickness and health thing to *your* partner, can make you realize the relationship's going nowhere. The birth of a baby, death of a parent or someone close to you all have the same effect. They make us examine our lives and our relationships, and if you don't like what you see, there seems little point in continuing.

Or maybe poisoning those outdoor pot plants she loves so bloody much. Better still, the cat. That'll wipe the smile off her smug, arrogant face!

Damn right it would. I can't deny the temptation to hit the person who hurt you straight where it hurts them is appealing. Let *them* feel pain for a change. Let *them* see how it feels to have your heart ripped out. For at least a minute, you'd feel like justice has been done.

But here are five good reasons why revenge *won't* make you feel better in the long run:

1. They might retaliate by doing something even worse.
2. They might report you to the police, sue you or even get you thrown in prison.
3. They might tell everyone what you did (including your mother).
4. They'll have the satisfaction of knowing you're still hung up on them.
5. They might feel sorry for you.

> 'I sent hate mail to his boss, to his mother, to his friends and anyone else I could think of. I blabbed every secret he'd ever told me, repeated every bad thing he'd ever said about them. A mutual friend called me to say she'd read one of the letters and wanted nothing more to do with me. "No wonder he left you," she said.'
> Angela, 23, shop assistant

What do you honestly think would give you the most satisfaction one month from now? Running into your ex at a party and a) being abused in front of all the other guests, and their new girlfriend/boyfriend for behaving like a psychopath, or b) not even noticing they're there because you're too busy snogging *your* new partner. As they're gazing at you in shock, a total stranger interrupts to tell you how drop-dead stunning you look. And a friend shouts across the room, 'Hey Susie! Congratulations on that promotion!'

I rest my case.

THE DREADED EX: YOURS – AND THEIRS

I adore just about all my exes. Come to think of it, pretty well all my male friends *are* exes. Ask me to tell you the benefits of having an ex-lover as a friend and you seriously can't shut me up. About the only time I do is when I've first started going out with someone new. Strangely enough, not all men initially applaud my talent at being able to recycle old boyfriends as friends. Researching this chapter, I now know why.

Exes are a *huge* problem for many people. Either you've got one you can't stop obsessing about or an ex is hassling you. Or your partner's got an ex they're not quite over or one who's hassling them. Either way, it's

bad news. Exes can stop you moving forward and cause havoc for new relationships. If you need evidence of this, look no further than *Ally McBeal*. The entire TV show is based around the relationship between Ally and her ex, who also happens to work with her and also happens to be married to another co-worker (and of course she's blonde with long legs. Don't you just love TV?).

Just about every episode of Ally has some sort of ex-angst scene in it, and anyone watching instantly splits into enemy camps, depending on whose side they're on. If you've got an ex you're still in love with, you're desperate for Ally and Chisel-jaw to get together again. If you're on the opposite side and hooked up with someone who's got an ex of their own still hovering, you're praying like hell it doesn't happen (and you think Ally looks like a stick insect and who'd fancy her anyway?). Who knows what will have happened by the time you're reading this, but one thing's for certain: even if the show's disappeared, problems with exes won't have.

The final section of this chapter is for anyone who's stuck on an ex or convinced their partner is. Plus there's some answers to the age-old question: do relationships ever work second time round?

ARE THEY REALLY OVER THEM?

He loved her. He lived with her for two years and she helped mould him into what he is today. His mother sometimes calls you by her name. The recipe he drags out to make you Spaghetti Bolognese is in her handwriting. Turns out she bought the jacket you (used to) love on him. You find little 'I love you' notes under piles of old magazines.

It's not a nice feeling knowing your partner once loved someone else. Let's face it: if we could unwrap our lovers brand new and untouched, always be the first one to rip off the cellophane, we would. Unfortunately, unless you're planning on dating 12-year-olds, it's usually not possible to find someone who's never had another partner (one you'd want to go out with anyway). So, while none of us are thrilled about exes, we recognize they're an (albeit unpleasant) part of life that we have to learn to deal with.

Some exes don't worry us at all. If our partner dumped them, they usually arouse little more than curiosity and self-comparison. Then there are the ones who left our partners broken-hearted. And *they're* the exes that inspire an all-consuming, vicious jealousy. It takes a strong person to ignore the 'Wonder if they still love them? Wonder if they'd take them back if they rang right now?' questions. After first hearing the story of the ex-that-broke-their-heart, most of us feel paranoid and convinced they *are* still secretly yearning for them.

How to tell for sure? There are danger signs and you're wise to watch for them. Because if your partner hasn't let go of their ex, they're not ready for a serious relationship with you.

The break-up was sudden and they weren't prepared

'I think Mike was still in shock when I first met him,' says Jenny, a 23-year-old student. 'We went out for three months but it was like dating an empty shell. He was about to propose to his old girlfriend, wasn't aware of any problems, but came home one evening to find she'd cleared her things out. She gutted him so effectively there was nothing left for anyone else.'

Most of us assume the length of time our partner and their ex were together is the most important issue. But while it's relevant, it's far more crucial to find out if they were emotionally prepared for the split. If they had no idea it was coming, they're probably having a tougher time dealing with it. In other words, it doesn't matter if they were going out six weeks or six years, if they genuinely cared, it's still traumatic to have that rudely taken away from them.

When relationships fizzle out slowly, people have time to cope with the idea of being alone. They get used to the thought of not being a couple, and often deal with the loss before the relationship actually ends. It's when one person's blissfully in love and the other's planning to move out that there are problems. Trust is shattered, they doubt their judgement – and there are no prizes for guessing who usually cops the emotional fall-out. Their *next* partner.

Find out what type of relationship the two of them had. If the couple took on a 'we-ness' and did everything together, fasten your seatbelt: you're in for a rocky ride. If they both retained a level of independence and didn't live in each other's pockets, you're in a far better position. Unless, of course, they were their first 'true love'. We have all sorts of naive expectations the first time someone tugs on our heart strings. We think, *This is for life*, then, *How can I ever love someone else when they were my soulmate?* It's far more emotional, first time round.

The reason for the split seems trivial

Justin and Sarah were together for five years, had planned on buying a flat and both parents were eagerly awaiting 'an announcement'. She dumped him because the cute guy at work paid her more attention. Justin told his new girlfriend, Fiona, that he'd just been promoted and perhaps wasn't as doting as usual. 'And I know she'd never sleep with this guy.'

Nikki's new lover had only been single two weeks. He'd had a massive row with his long-term girlfriend over something silly and hadn't spoken to her since. Both Fiona and Nikki felt the same: they were in their boyfriend's bed but it was the ex that was still in his head. And guess what? They were right. Both went back.

If you can possibly help it, steer clear of anyone who's just split, and make sure enough time has passed so it looks permanent. It could well be just a fight. Also, be on guard for signs of 'rebound'. Are they genuinely interested in you or just want someone around?

It's like they never left

'It was almost as if he'd never left,' says Carl, still bruised after a short but intense affair with a newly single girl. 'The ticket butts to that special concert were still pinned on the notice-board. There were photos of him everywhere, all lovingly framed. There was even a shot of the two of them wrapped around each other next to the bed.'

You feel like an intruder because you are. The ex isn't out of their life until they've removed the evidence. (A brighter alternative is that they meant so little, they haven't even noticed their stuff is still around. But it's a long shot.) The same way mothers who've lost a child will sometimes leave their bedrooms untouched, turning them into shrines, some people do the same with their exes. Now if their ex did die, fine. Leaving photos around is all part of the grieving process. But if they're sitting around surrounded by paraphernalia from an ex who's very much alive and left three months earlier, it's not a great sign. It means they're loath to let go, don't want to erase them from their life and secretly hope they'll walk back in one day. Do yourself a favour and walk out.

> **Nasty is as nasty does. People who say nasty things about others risk it rubbing off on themselves. Researchers say when we accuse others of something negative, the person we're talking to is just as likely to think the same of us as they are of the person we're bitching about.**

Having said that, take into account their emotional maturity. If they're well over them and it was a nice part of their life that they remember fondly, the *odd* photo is quite healthy. It could also be a way of keeping a severely dinted ego intact. Sort of an 'I used to be loved' statement. But if they not only have pics of the latest ex stuck on the fridge but all their other exes as well, you're in a twilight zone. If each of their exes still has a piece of their heart, how much is left for you?

They talk about them constantly – even if it's to criticize

Anne suggested tuning in to an old *Seinfeld* repeat. 'Sally used to love this show,' Peter said with a sigh.

She came back from the hairdressers with a new, short cut. 'That looks terrific,' he said. 'When Sally cut her hair off, she said it was much easier to look after.'

Peter chose to eat at 'their' restaurant, played soppy CDs that were obviously significant and told Anne Sally's opinion on everything. 'I couldn't have cared less if Sally was the first female to set foot on the moon. In the end, I couldn't stand it.'

Equally nauseating and twice as dangerous is the person who takes great delight in constantly saying, 'It's so nice to be with someone who doesn't get jealous/criticize my driving/ loves my clothes. John/Jane was such a bastard/bitch.' You think, *If you're so happy to be rid of them, why do you still care what they thought of you?*

Constant ex chitter-chatter is by far the worst sign they're nowhere near over them. Be really, really, *really* careful, because this person's emotionally stuck. The odd relapse into a fond reminisce or an occasional bitchy comment is healthy. But talking about them all the time isn't. They're trapped. (If everything they have to say is negative, you're on even dodgier ground. The old cliché is true – there really is a thin line between love and hate.) It's a fact: some people marry, have children and drop dead at 80 still mourning the loss of the love of their life. You'll never be number one.

They still see each other as 'friends' – and drop everything the minute they call

On the surface, it all looked incredibly adult and mature. 'Sure we've split up,' Terry told Patricia, 'but why should I stop loving her as a friend? Why should I throw away all those years together?'

'How could I argue with that?' says Patricia. 'I not only accepted it, I admired him for it.' Until she noticed how he'd rush over to fix any (and every) problem his ex had, lower his voice on the phone if she called while Patricia was there, turn his back on her. 'I wasn't sure if I was being paranoid or immature, but when it didn't let up after months, I left.'

Let's be honest here: there aren't too many people who've been in intense relationships who can move easily and *immediately* into friendship. The dumped person's motivations are questionable (they're hoping they'll realize the huge mistake they made leaving) and so are the dumper's. Lots of people keep their exes on a string: they don't want them but they don't want you to have them either. If they're friends and only been split a month or so, be careful. Guilt is another factor. If your partner dumped them, they're more open to manipulation. Playing rescuer as a 'friend' makes them feel better.

When you run into their ex, your partner either ignores you or is over-affectionate

Mike walked into a party, and guess who was standing in the kitchen looking unfairly good-looking? His girlfriend's ex. She dropped his hand like it was red hot, blushed, then dived into the fridge to get herself a drink. She asked her ex if he'd like one – and forgot to ask Mike.

Lyn's boyfriend had the opposite reaction when they ran into his old girlfriend at a barbecue. 'This is the guy who doesn't usually even hold my hand, but the minute she appeared he started nuzzling my ear right under her nose. He practically sat on my lap and insisted on telling everyone – loudly – the intimate details of the weekend away we'd just had.'

Either reaction isn't ideal. If they're ignoring you, they still think there's a chance, and are pretending you mean nothing to appear single and available. If they're all over you, they're rubbing salt into the wound and trying to make them jealous by saying, 'See? I can get someone else to love me!' Both mean they're still caught back there.

Having said that, be a little sensitive. It's normal for anyone to be embarrassed and ill at ease when they run into an ex. It's even okay to be a little more affectionate than usual in an attempt to allay your fears. If they were the ones to break it off and are less loving, they might simply be being respectful by not blatantly showing they've fallen for someone else. It's extreme, out-of-character behaviour that's the warning sign.

They sometimes seem sad and far away, spend a lot of time alone and often don't want to see you

'We'd be in a restaurant and suddenly he'd go quiet,' said Kate. 'He was always gazing off into the distance looking as though his heart was about to break. Sometimes, he'd confess that he was thinking of her. I felt incredibly sorry for him, but still felt

ripped off that I was with someone who couldn't get another
girl out of his mind.'

If they're still mooning
around, they're still in the
depression cycle of the grieving
process. Be understanding for a
while but if they don't improve
after a few weeks, book them in to
see a good counsellor. As I said

> 'Three weeks after we
> broke up, I talked him
> into giving it another try.
> I felt stupid and
> desperate and
> embarrassed about
> begging him. It wasn't
> worth the humiliation.'
>
> Jayne, 36, consultant

earlier, some people *never* get over their exes. If they won't get
help, disappear. They probably won't even notice you're gone.

They won't commit past Saturday night, even though you've been together a few months

This one's a little tricky. While their ex may well be the reason
they're not keen to get involved again (they want them back), it
could also be the whole experience has left them a little commitment shy. Alternatively (and this is *not* what you want to hear),
they might love to settle down but just not with you.

Catherine found this out the hard way. 'I hung in there for
years with Alex, all the time thinking once he trusted me and
got his ex out of his system, he'd come around to the idea of
living together. He didn't. Instead, he dumped me, met another
girl two weeks later and moved in and married her within a
year.'

Use your judgement as you would with any other partner
on this one: be assertive about your own needs and make it clear
whatever it is you're looking for. Then make up your mind
whether you're willing to wait. If you are, decide on a length of
time you think is reasonable, mark the date in your diary and
stick to it, or you really are wasting your time. It doesn't matter
if they're the love of your life – it's irrelevant if they don't feel

the same. (You might also like to read the section on commitment phobia in Chapter 3, page 156.)

Should you give it another try? What to do when the dumper dares to come crawling back

'Hi, uummm, it's me,' they say on the phone. 'Please don't hang up. I'm calling because I'm sorry. I have to see you. I think I made a horrible mistake . . .' Your heart practically bursts through your chest. You feel sick and elated simultaneously. This is the call you didn't dare hope for. The call your friends said wouldn't happen. The call that somehow makes the tears, the debilitating misery you've experienced now seem unimportant. They want to come back, they *do* love you. Life, once more, will be perfect.

Or will it? Before you tape together the ripped-up photos and cancel that holiday to Europe, before you even agree to see them, sit down and do some serious thinking. Second-time-round love affairs are risky business and, more often than not, that 'one last try' simply breaks your heart one more time. Is it really worth the heartache?

Beware the first flush

It's your (second) first date. He comes over for dinner.

'Wow, that looks great,' he says, snuggling up behind you as you cook his favourite meal. 'And so do you.'

After a glass of wine, he tells you he had to change hairdressers because she wore your perfume and it upset him too much. You confess to six Saturday nights in succession spent sobbing on your bed. He swears he doesn't know what possessed him to let you go and promises he won't go out with the boys so often. You say, 'No, don't be ridiculous. I was being silly. Of course you should see your friends.' All round, it's the perfect evening.

The initial euphoria of being reunited is heady stuff – and by all means, enjoy it, because it won't be long before reality rudely intrudes. Within a couple of weeks, you'll probably start falling back into old patterns. He remembers how argumentative you were; you discover he still spends every Tuesday night and Sundays with his mother. You're at make and break point – again.

Why? Because problems don't disappear just because you've had time apart. If your 'let's get back together again' talk consists of simply telling each other how miserable you were apart, the relationship is destined to fail for the very same reasons you broke up in the first place. Unless you have a good idea of what led to the break-up and have some realistic solutions to the problems, *it's not going to work*.

> 'My girlfriend got pregnant accidentally and wanted to keep the baby. We were so young, I talked her into having an abortion but she never forgave me. I didn't see her for years then, one day, looked her up on a whim. She thanked me for being sensible, I told her maybe it would have been the best thing that happened to me. We've been together two years now – and she's trying to get pregnant.'
>
> David, 26, manager

When it's worth a second try

- **The circumstances have changed – or the person has.** As with any relationship, new or recycled, there are no guarantees it will work. But you can make a sensible assessment of your chances of success by looking at the reasons why you split in the first place. If you separated because of outside stresses – their job demanded too much time, they had family issues to sort out, someone close to them died and they lost perspective – it's worth going back if the situation has now been resolved. Stress affects people's ability to think clearly and make good decisions. If they've sorted out whatever was stopping them committing to you, it could have a chance of succeeding.

- **You think you can trust them again.** It's a key issue. Even if they didn't leave you for someone else, they still walked out and left you hurting. Can you trust them to stick around the next time you hit a rough spot? What would she do if you got sick and were bedridden for months? What would he do if you got accidentally pregnant? Will they stick around for the hard stuff?

- **You're sure you haven't idealized the past.** Are you 100 per cent certain you want to try again? Look realistically at your old relationship. Was it truly as wonderful as you remember? We all have a marvellous capacity to forget pain and idealize our losses.

- **They're willing to talk through your problems and put in the hard work.** Arriving on your doorstep saying sorry is great, but unless they'll sit down and talk about why you split, forget it. 'It's enough that I'm here,' is not acceptable. The past needs to be resolved and there needs to be a genuine attempt to change the behaviour, attitudes or situations that caused the breakdown. Sit down together, talk about why you split up and how to avoid it happening again. You should both have clearly thought out logical solutions to avoiding a repeat performance and be happy to make the changes they require.

- **Give it a test run before you get too involved.** If you can test their commitment to change, do it. You broke it off because he was insanely jealous? Deliberately put him in a situation that previously would have caused fireworks. She was an outrageous flirt? Take her to a party and let her loose.

- **What are your chances of making it long term?** A good, long-lasting relationship isn't about romance. It's about having shared goals and values, agreeing on parenting, how to handle money, communicating well, resolving arguments quickly – even splitting up the household chores. It's not enough to lust after and love someone – you have to like them as well. Once the in-love stage passes, getting on day to day is crucially important.

- **Ask your family and friends for their advice.** Take into account any hang-ups and jealousy but listen to what other people have to say. If your best friend, parents and everyone at work reacts to your joyful news with, 'You can't possibly be serious. That bastard/bitch nearly destroyed you last time,' rethink – everything! If you're taking back someone who treated you badly, skip the romantic reunion dinner for a session with a good counsellor.

- **You need to go back to move forward.** Sometimes, letting an ex come back one more time, even if you *don't* think it will work, is a good idea. If you're haunted by 'what ifs', give it one last go. That way you can finally convince yourself that you did give it all you had and it still didn't work. It's called 'reality testing': going back to check you really have done the right thing.

- **You're certain you can protect number one.** You genuinely believe things will be different. They seem like a changed person and you're prepared to take the risk. Terrific! By all means give it a go – but give it time before you give them your heart. Keep an objective eye on things and proceed with caution. Look after number one – yourself! Be flexible and positive but be careful, and don't drag it out. If they haven't changed or the changes don't last, break up quickly and for good. This is one situation when 'third time lucky' doesn't apply.

How to make it work

- **Accept the relationship won't be as it was.** The old relationship is over. You need to make a new one together.
- **Treat each other with respect** – if you can't forgive, don't go back.
- **Don't talk about what happened while you were apart.** Don't tell them if you went out with someone else unless it was significant. Don't ask them who they dated. Remove any lingering signs – cards, notes, diary dates, clothes – and ask them to do the same. Call up anyone you're seeing casually and tell them you're back with your ex and all you can now offer is friendship.
- **Act as a team.** Think in terms of 'we' rather than 'I'. Make sure they do the same.
- **Agree on a time limit.** If you're both not happy after a specified period of time, it's over.

> 'I went out with a girl for three months and ended it because it was getting too serious. Two months later, I found I missed her friendship, rang her up and we got back together. Within a month, I wanted to leave again. A friend of mine once said: never go back and repeat your favourite holiday, you'll always be disappointed. He was right.'
>
> Tom, 27, fitness consultant

When you should forget it – and them

- **You forced them into giving it another go.** If you've threatened suicide or pleaded and cajoled until they've given in, your chances of success are close to zero. Hold a gun to someone's head and you're asking for trouble. You can't force them into loving you.
- **They treated you badly.** If they were cruel – mentally, physically or emotionally abusive – don't even think about it.

- **They try to sleep with you the first night you get back together.** They're horny, not sorry.
- **You're lonely and there's no-one else around.** Please.
- **They've just been dumped themselves.** Everyone decides their ex wasn't that bad when they've been dumped. They're coming back for a confidence boost and will be off again the minute they feel secure.
- **The problem was commitment.** If you were ready to settle down and they weren't, tread cautiously. It can work – but then again, it often doesn't. In some cases, a break is just what's needed to sort your ex's feelings out – they're miserable without you and can finally take the leap. Or maybe they've just grown up and finally accepted that no relationship is perfect and the things that irritated them aren't that important. Some people have a life experience that finally convinces them to settle down. Others find the appeal of nightclubs and pubs finally wearing thin and realize their wants and values in life are deeper than what they thought. In all of the above scenarios, there's a chance it might work. But be careful. Some exes return simply for regular sex. Others come back for security. The singles scene wasn't quite what they imagined, they got knocked back once too often and they'll leave you again the minute someone interesting shows interest in them.
- **They say they're willing to change but you suspect it's all talk.** People will say anything

Do you hate your ex with a passion or count him as one of your best friends? Surprisingly, neither matters when it comes to your ability to get over the break-up: it's how often you think about them that's the key. Intense but infrequent bursts of hatred are better for you emotionally than constant, cosy daydreams and trips down memory lane.

to get what they want and if they know you well, they'll know how to win you over. Promises to change are just words – it's their behaviour that's important. By all means listen but watch as well. If their behaviour doesn't back up what they're promising, get out of there.

Can you ever be friends with an ex?

'Let's be friends.' Let's be honest: it's the oldest cliché in the world. Few people mean it but we're all guilty of saying it in those last dying throes of a relationship. When you can't pledge undying love, friendship seems the next best thing, slipping in nicely after the 'I'm sorry, but I don't want to go out any more' speech. Never mind that you'll be crossing the street to avoid them from now on. Saying you'll stay friends leaves both of you feeling warm, fuzzy and terribly adult.

But then there are times when you really *do* mean it. Okay, so you aren't working out as a couple but the thought of never seeing them again? It's unbearable. You say, 'Let's be friends,' and actually call them the day after the split to check they're okay. You leave it at phone calls for a few months, then when you think they've got you out of their system as a lover, meet for coffee. It's all a little strange to start with but kind of nice. Love changes into caring and before you know it, your boyfriend has turned into a best friend.

Ask anyone who's ever had one: friendships with exes are special. There's a comfortableness and familiarity male and female friends only ever achieve when they've got sex out of the way. If you're sick, he's the only one you'll allow to see you with unwashed hair and pink, fluffy slippers because *he's* seen it all before. You're a bit snappy? No need to explain: he's suffered through enough of your PMT episodes to recognize the symptoms 20 paces away. She understands how significant losing that promotion was because she knows your dreams. It's her shoulder you'll cry on because you don't need to explain yourself. You can touch and hug each other without fear of it being taken the wrong way, so when your new lover dumps you at 3 am, it's their doorstep you turn up on and their body you snuggle up to that night, feeling comforted but not obligated sexually. New lovers may hate them, your parents may never understand but, just because you don't love someone any more, doesn't mean you don't still love them.

Of course exes can be friends! But there are two golden rules you must abide by. Friendships with exes only work if you a) give each other time to make the transition from lovers to friends, and b) the split was pretty mutual. In other words, neither of you is still in love with the other or has a hidden agenda of wanting to take it further.

Another word of warning: be wary of using exes as substitute boyfriends or girlfriends. If you're such good friends you rarely venture out without the other, your chances of meeting someone new are slim. Everyone who knows the two of you will assume you've still got something going and strangers always assume any male/female combo is a couple. Then there's the sex thing.

Sex with an ex is awfully tempting when you're both single, climbing the walls for it and – the clincher – you've done it before. Sometimes it works. I went through a period where I didn't want a relationship but still wanted regular sex. I told an ex, he said he was in the same boat and it seemed silly not to paddle together for a while. We did exactly that for a few months and managed to remain friends at the end of it. But I know plenty who drowned the friendship in the process. Falling into bed with a comfortably familiar body often seems like the perfect solution, but just make sure it's not going to reignite any hopes you're unaware of. If they're still holding a candle for you (or you for them), you're not just fanning the flame by bonking them, you're pouring oil on it.

JUGGLING AN EX AND YOUR NEW LOVER

- **Let them meet each other early on.** If it really is just friendship – on both sides – your partner will see first hand and won't be threatened.

- **Include them.** Not every time but enough. If you want to see an ex alone (which is natural – after all, you want their opinion on your new lover!) do it during your lunch hour or on week nights. Not date nights.

- **Don't take trips down memory lane if your partner's there.** This is the one area everyone slips up on: the tendency to slip into the 'wasn't that weekend fabulous', 'didn't we have a good time' stuff. Even if it is all over and you do just appear to be friends, it's not fair. That's called rubbing your partner's nose in it.

If you're on the other side

- **Get the full story on what happened between them.** Listen carefully and use your judgement. Check the 'Are they really over them?' section above (page 488).

- **Ask to meet them.** If it truly is just friendship and your partner's serious about you, the ex will be over the moon they've found someone to make them happy. If they're off-hand or unpleasant to you, they're still hoping for a reunion or worried you'll hurt them. If you're genuinely in love, allay their fears. If they're still chilly after that, assume it's the former.

- **If you're convinced the ex is still in love with your partner, even though they're over them, let them know.** Tell your partner the reasons why. Explain why it makes you feel uncomfortable. Suggest they call or see the ex to make it very clear it is all over, they've moved on and are now involved with you.

- **If they want to see each other minus you, ask for reassurance.** Get your partner to call you when he or she gets home. It's normal to feel a little paranoid to ➢

begin with, even if you're convinced there's nothing going on.

- **If the ex is an ex-wife or husband and they have children together, accept reality or leave: this ex is not going away.** If your partner and their ex-spouse are adult and sensible, they'll try damn hard to get on for the sake of their children. It is not your place, or your right, to interfere with or jeopardize any friendship they have. If you honestly think there's a chance they'll reunite, get out of there now for your sake and theirs. You will get hurt. When kids are involved, pretty well all parents will give it a go even if there's a mere shred of hope. They do it for the sake of the children. If you don't think either of them want to get back together but you just can't stand the thought of them together without you, again, leave. I don't care how much it hurts, you're being selfish and immature. If it makes their kids feel better if he or she turns up alone to the odd family event, put up with it. If you can't stand the heat, get out of the kitchen. Do you want to be responsible for making a small child, who's already hurting like hell, utterly heartbroken because Daddy couldn't come to his birthday party because his new girlfriend wouldn't let him? Shame on you!

I don't want them but I don't want anyone else to have them either

Naughty. Very naughty – though, I have to admit, I also suffer the odd, irrational, jealous pang when a significant ex finds someone they're serious about. It's natural. After all, they once held *your* hand like that, looked at *you* with that soppy expression on their face. It used to be you brushing the hair out of his eyes and holding on to his arm and – oh, for God's sake, if she got any closer, she'd be in his pocket. I mean, she's all over the guy! How does he stand it?

Most of us become illogical about much-loved (maybe even still loved a little bit) former boy or girlfriends. If we're single, it's a blow to our ego that they dared to find someone else before we did. Even if we dumped them and are shacking up with Christie Brinkley or Matt Damon, the idea of an ex liking (let alone loving) anyone more than us is unthinkable! Seeing them happily in love with someone else is like giving your friend a dress you never wear, then seeing them in it and wishing you had it back.

If you dumped them and remain on good terms, it's nicely reassuring to know they're still single. Exes are a love safety net: if all else fails (that is, you don't find someone better), you can always go back to them. But the minute they match up seriously with someone else, they're off the market. Out of bounds. If they're *really* serious (like you're avoiding the mail in case there's a wedding invitation), it's even more of a shake-up. You can't *ever* get back together. Neither of you is going to turn around and say you made a horrible mistake. You can't turn up on their doorstep whenever you feel like a cuddle and/or an ego boost. You have to find a new standby for 'and partner' functions. It feels so final because it is.

If you're like most people, the first thing you'll do when you get home after seeing the happy couple (*Grrrr!*), is rummage through your drawers to find the old love letters and cards. *We were good together,* you think, flicking through photo albums and dreamily idealizing every good time you ever had. If you're realistic and mature, you'll wake up the next day and realize you feel a bit funny simply because the door is closing on a nice part of your life.

Or you'll feel like renting *My Best Friend's Wedding* – to find out where Julia Roberts went wrong, so *you* can get it right. Instead, why not try these suggestions.

How to snap out of it

- **Give yourself time to get used to it.** It will seem weird at first but chances are the feeling will pass. Inject some realism. If your ex arrived on your doorstep, right now, saying they'll ditch their new partner if you'll marry them, would you honestly be able to say yes and know you'd be together at 80?

- **Make an effort to get on with their partner.** The more you like them, the easier it will be to accept – and the more chance you've got of maintaining a friendship with your ex. Don't turn it into a war or you'll find yourself desperate to get your ex back, just to show their partner a thing or two. Do you really want to be responsible for breaking their heart just to score points?

- **Don't interfere.** Even if the shock of seeing them together has made you realize you do love your ex after all, tread carefully. Wait two weeks before doing anything, to make sure your feelings are genuine. If you still feel the same way (*sure* you do?), call your ex, say you want to see them privately and confess you still love them. If they feel the same way and decide to break it off with their current partner, fine (just pray you still want them a few months on). If they say, 'Sorry but I really do love X,' be an adult and accept it. You had your chance and blew it, or you've been hanging out for someone who never did want you. Don't sabotage their relationship just because you can't have one with them.

If they left you

- **Accept that you will feel humiliated when they meet someone new.** Everyone knew how upset you were when you split, how it took you months to get over them. Now, here they are making goo-goo eyes at someone else and all your friends know you wish it was you. They'll probably make things worse by being sympathetic (they haven't forgotten), but they mean well. Have a few lines prepared ('Oh, I got over Brad ages ago,' or, 'Oh well, that's life') for nosy acquaintances and save the cut-to-the-quick feelings for close friends.

> 'I once went out with a model. Everywhere we went, guys eyed her up and my ego dived. I slept with an ex to boost my self-esteem, she found out and it was all over. The irony is, I think she really did love me.'
> Nathan, 20, student

- **Read 'The get-over-it-guide' (page 456) and do some of the exercises designed to get your ex out of your system.** If you're stuck, read the section below.
- **If it hurts too much, avoid events and places where you'll bump into them.** Good friends will understand why you don't want to come to their party; feign sickness with others. Wait a month or so until you've had the chance to get used to the idea, then face the two of them. Take a good friend with you for support.

Help! I'm stuck

It depends on the length of the relationship and the level of commitment as to how long it'll take you to truly get over a break-up. After all, if you were married for ten years, you're obviously going to take longer to heal than someone who went out with their ex for a few months.

But if your friends and family are starting to look worried, the pain is still intense and unbearable and it's been a few months, you might need to see a counsellor. A few counselling sessions really can help you see things more clearly. Call the British Psychological Society and ask for a list of qualified therapists in your area. They will help you work through the pain and get on with your life.

Alternatively, these are some reasons why you might not be able to move forward.

The relationship drifted apart for no apparent reason
If you're not quite sure what caused the break-up, you can't help but keep dwelling on it. Apart from not being able to learn from your mistakes, curiosity alone can drive you crazy.

Solve it by: If you're the sort that can handle feeling vulnerable, contact your ex (if you know where to find them). Explain you're having trouble getting over them because you don't have a clue why you split. Ask them to tell you, straight out, without sparing your feelings, what it was that caused them to leave. Take it on the chin, analyse it for a week, then drop it. If you can't, again, see a counsellor. If you're too embarrassed to do this or your ex moved to Saudi Arabia to escape you (and funnily enough, didn't leave a forwarding address), ask a close friend who you trust to give you their opinion, *without sparing your feelings*. If they won't or can't help you, go straight to the nearest counsellor's office. Perhaps they can make sense of it all.

The break-up was your fault and could have been prevented
The relationship was going wonderfully well and you had a one-night stand and got caught, or you didn't give them enough time because of work pressures, or the timing was wrong for you. You can't stop thinking, *If only I'd done this or that.*

Solve it by: Giving it a second go, if you can. If you honestly think it could work if you changed your behaviour, call your ex and ask for another chance. Explain the reason why it didn't work last time for you and your reasons for thinking it might now. If you cheated, chances are they'll hang up in your ear. If it was something forgivable, they still might hang up in your ear (their new lover is listening). Or they'll agree to try again. Whatever happens, you'll get rid of that 'if only I tried harder' feeling. Even if they knock you back, you've given it your best shot *now* and that's all you can do. You can't turn back time.

Reminders are everywhere

You're still living in the house you bought together. They're still best friends with your best friends and you run into them constantly. Even worse, you work together.

Solve it by: Removing the reminders. If it seriously is ruining your life, it's worth changing jobs, selling the house, even changing cities if you have to. Drastic measures, I agree, but necessary if it finally gets you over them and into a fresh, new life.

You can't stop spying on them

You know it's ridiculous but you find yourself parked outside their flat, watching the window. You walk three kilometres at lunch time to watch them eat a sandwich in the park. Every time you see them, the pain hits you again.

Solve it by: Keeping a diary. Write in it before you're tempted to play Sherlock and when you get back again. One of three things will have happened: a) you've seen something that's upset you (that is, they've found someone else); b) they caught you and you feel like a complete idiot; or c) nothing happened and you just feel empty and lonely. Record all these feelings and when you're tempted again, use the old smoker's trick of putting it off for five minutes. Spend that five minutes reading about how awful you felt after the last episode.

Resisting the rebound

Replacing an ex with another warm body will make you feel temporarily better. You've got someone to go to the movies with, a human hot-water bottle, your self-esteem gets a boost and it *will* take your mind off your ex. And that's essentially the problem. Jumping straight into a new relationship means you won't heal from the last one. Even if you are an unemployed psychologist, no-one can sort out the hurts from an old relationship while simultaneously giving a new relationship the energy it takes.

Another point to consider is judgement. When you're hurting and desperate for someone to love, even the elderly pensioner who walks their dog in the park looks good. You throw yourself even more enthusiastically into this relationship than you did the last one because you're even more desperate for this one to work. Invariably, the person you chose turns out to be so wrong for you it's not funny. You're forced to dump them (never fun) or they dump you (even less). So anything other than *casual* relationships are out, and you're only allowed those when you're starting to feel remotely normal and follow these rules:

- **Only have casual sex if you're the type that can handle it.** In other words, if you're going to wake up feeling guilty, don't do it. If you're the sort of person who can't help but turn anything sexual into a 'proper' relationship, don't go there.

- **Make it plain to the person you're seeing that you're there for a good time, not a long time.** If you think there might be potential, tell them you're still getting over an ex and want to take it really slowly. Tell them you don't quite trust your feelings yet – so neither should they.

You're ready to take it further when . . .

- You're absolutely certain you're not going to make your next partner pay for the crimes of your last.
- You stop comparing all new partners to your ex.
- You're prepared to take it slowly.
- You're confident in your judgement. By now you've had a few dates with Mr or Ms Wrong but got out of there the minute you saw the danger signs.
- You realize not all men or women are like your ex. Just because they did the wrong thing, it doesn't mean others will. You're able to trust a little.
- You can watch a romantic movie without wanting to hurl your popcorn at the screen.
- You don't *need* to change the radio station when 'your song' comes on (even if you want to).
- You run into your ex and forget to tell your friends about it.
- You run into your ex and think, *That's weird. They don't look like how I remembered them at all.*

You're nowhere near ready for a relationship if . . .

- You still run out of coffee shops because you think you saw your ex walk past.
- You have spare copies of your song stashed away just in case CDs actually can wear out.
- The labels of tinned food in your pantry are all neatly aligned, you've reorganized the cutlery drawer three times this month and mopped under the fridge twice.
- Your ex has a security guard posted at his front door.
- You care so little about your appearance, you bought five of everything, all in the same colour, so wear the same outfit every day.
- You still drink yourself silly every weekend.

- You're so cynical about love, your best friend didn't even invite you to their wedding.
- The last time you saw your ex, they were pushing a pram but you still haven't given up hope.
- You don't find this list funny at all, just intensely painful. (*Please*, book yourself in to see a counsellor. It really will help.)

And the Rest

Still haven't found the answer to *your* relationship dilemma? This could be where you'll find it

• •

This chapter covers a broad spectrum of subjects ranging from long-distance love affairs and office romance to moody partners and what to do if you fall in love with your lover's best friend. It's a round-up of all the questions people frequently ask me that I haven't already covered in previous chapters (including the one on how to get past that 'say they hear me when I go to the loo' thing).

Does sex via the Net count as cheating? I did it once out of curiosity and didn't think much about it at the time. But now I feel guilty and wonder if I should tell my boyfriend.
Yes, it does count as cheating (how would you feel if you walked in on him typing, 'Now I'm sliding my tongue down your . . .' with one hand and doing whatever else with the other?). But, given the choice, I think most of us would prefer to know our partner's one-night stand was via the computer rather than in

the flesh. As for confessing, what's the point? If it was a one-off, the potential punishment doesn't fit the crime. You stand to lose him and what for? One night playing around on the Internet. Don't confess but don't make a habit of it, either.

My boyfriend wants me to do kinky things in bed. I'm not sure.

'Kinky' is a very subjective term because what's kinky to one is standard sexual behaviour for another. So you need to establish whether what your boyfriend's suggesting is worth trying once (and you're being a little uptight) or if it's way out there and best left as a fantasy. If you can't check with a good friend, look up a sex book. Is it listed as something most couples give a whirl now and again or under deviant behaviours? If it's under 'deviant' or includes other people, I'd be wary. Ditto if it involves physical pain (and just a quick word on anal sex: if you're going to try it, read a sex book first. There's a right and wrong way to approach it).

If his request seems reasonable, look at your attitude to sex generally. Think back to any comments past lovers have made and conversations you've had about sex with your girl-friends. Do they seem much more laid-back about it than you are? Far more sexually adventurous? Maybe it's time to push yourself out of your comfort zone. If your relationship with your boyfriend is good, you trust him and know he'd stop if you didn't like it, why not try it once and see how you feel?

If you decide not to give it a go, come up with something else new that appeals to both of you. That way he won't feel cheated and you're working together to keep sex fresh and exciting (which is, of course, why he wants to try something different in the first place).

We've got a motto in our office that sex in another country doesn't count. In other words, if there's absolutely no way your partner will find out, what's wrong with it?

Here's a true story that'll chill you to the bone: a girlfriend of mine had a three-night fling during a work trip to LA. About six months later, she got a call at work to say a 'surprise' visitor was waiting for her in reception.

'Hi!' her LA lover said. 'I remembered where you worked and thought I'd drop in.'

Jesus! she thought and quickly shuffled him off into a corner.

Thinking she was being intimate, he squeezed her bottom and grinned wickedly, 'Any chance of a very long lunch? I haven't stopped thinking about your body since the conference. God, the sex was good!'

From behind her a very familiar voice said, 'I think it's all over, Cassandra.' Her boyfriend had walked through the door that very second to see if she wanted to grab a coffee. Three-year relationship over.

Quite apart from surprise visits, sleeping with someone else counts as betrayal, whether you do it at home or overseas. Yes, it's tempting. Yes, lots of people do give in under those circumstances and if you're determined to do it, there's a lot *less* risk of being caught. But it's *never* guaranteed you won't be. Weigh up if you're prepared to lose what you have at home and if the answer's no, don't do it.

My partner wants me to talk dirty to him during sex. I've got no real objections to it but don't know quite what to say.

Years ago, the same thing happened to me. The mood was hot and heavy, we were in the middle of a passionate kiss when suddenly my boyfriend said, 'Talk dirty to me.' I looked at him blankly. Like you, I didn't have any objections but all I could think to say was, 'Give it to me, big boy,' and I sure as hell couldn't say that without laughing. It is hard not to come across like a poorly paid extra from a porn film.

The percentage of men who say they'd be willing to take a male Pill if they were available: 66 per cent. The percentage of women who'd trust him to do it: 45 per cent.

It's probably best to tackle it this way. Start by simply making noise during sex – groan, moan, say, 'Ummmmm.' The next time, try, 'God, that feels so nice,' or, 'I can't tell you what this is doing to me.' Once you've broken the silence, the rest is easy. Try giving him a running commentary of every sexy thought that's going through your head: how much of a turn-on this or that is, how you get hot by being able to make him excited, what you'd like him to do to you, what you're going to do to him . . .

Use fantasy as a springboard. Say you had a sexy dream last night (make one up), then tell him about it while you're having sex. The more detailed and explicit the better, but even, 'You took my clothes off and we made love on a beach,' is better than nothing. Match the pace of the dream or fantasy to your love-making. As the fantasy climaxes, so do you.

He wants you to use four-letter words? Even if you're the type that says 'sugar' and 'gosh' outside the bedroom, would it really kill you to let loose in it? Being 'naughty' by using language you wouldn't dream of usually is all part of the fun and the turn-on. It's also a healthy way to exorcise the good-girls-don't-enjoy-sex hang-up and he'll love seeing your wanton side.

My flatmate sleeps in the room next to me and when she has sex with her boyfriend, I can hear them clearly. At first, it annoyed me, but now I find I'm getting aroused. Is this normal?

Watching or listening to other couples make whoopie is called voyeurism. It's way up there in most people's fantasies and plenty would get turned on in your situation. While we regularly watch couples roll around on television, it's rare to see or hear a *real* couple have sex. Throw in the turn-on appeal of it being forbidden (your flatmate would throttle you if she found out!) and I'm not surprised you're finding it hard to sleep some nights. Don't embarrass your flatmate by confessing, but don't feel guilty about it either.

I adore my boyfriend of two years but can't stop fantasizing about sex with his friends and other guys. Does this mean I've fallen out of love with him?

No – though it could mean you're a tad bored with your sex life. What's more likely is that you've simply got a healthily high libido and a vivid imagination. People often feel guilty if they fantasize about someone else while making love to their partner, but it's more common than you think and, in my view, totally acceptable. I wouldn't tell or even hint to your boyfriend you're mentally lusting after his friends, but it's a far cry from being unfaithful in reality. Fantasies are a way to add spice and variety without the moral dilemmas and complications of an affair. Indulge guilt-free.

When I was about ten years old, I masturbated by rubbing myself against my dog. I've only just recently remembered and now feel disgusted with myself, like I'm some sort of weirdo.

Relax! At ten years old, you'd just discovered a previously unknown pleasure zone: your genitals. This is the age when lots of girls discover helping Mummy do the washing is an oddly pleasurable experience when you're sitting on the machine and it's on spin cycle. You're also not the first young girl who's got very friendly with Fido, the family dog. If something felt good, you did it: it's an instinctual automatic response and nothing to be ashamed of. Sure, it's probably not the sort of confession you'll ever drag out at a dinner party, but you've got no reason at all to feel guilty.

During a particularly hot sex session, my boyfriend took some erotic photos of me. I've now dumped him, but have since found out he's showing the pics to whoever wants a look. What should I do?

If you ever let a guy take sexy polaroids of you again, rip them all into tiny pieces the minute the sheets have settled. All too often, they do turn up in your mother's letterbox. What your boyfriend's doing is outrageous, but it's probably because he's hurting and, instead of feeling sad, has switched into revenge mode (how better to totally humiliate you than with some intimate pictures?). Call him immediately and arrange to meet at his house. Once there, explain that you didn't mean to hurt him, his actions are totally out of line and ask him to destroy the pictures, *now*, in front of you. If he refuses, tell him you'll be taking legal action and follow it up with a threatening letter from a lawyer. It's probably not worth suing over, but the letter won't cost much and it will convince him you're serious.

I've been seeing a guy for a month or so and want to plan a weekend away for his birthday. The only thing is, I don't want to sleep with him yet and suspect he'll think sex is part of his present.

You bet he will! If you've already hinted at it, he's already imagining the champagne on ice, you sprawled on the bed and the do-not-disturb sign superglued to the doorknob. Most people, male or female, presume sex is on the menu if you're sharing a hotel room. If it's not, you need to spell it out *very clearly* beforehand. (Even then, he'll be optimistic and you'll spend all weekend trying to fob him off.) There are plenty of other ways to make the guy feel special without making it awkward for the two of you. Save the weekend away for when you are having sex, truly comfortable with each other and able to make the most of that lovely, big hotel bed.

I love my boyfriend, but there's a problem with our sex life. He's never given me oral sex and refuses to even consider the idea. He thinks it's unhygienic and kinky.

Puhleeze! Are you dating a boy scout or is your boyfriend just incredibly naive? While lots of guys are a little squeamish about hygiene (instantly cured by having a shower together first), your boyfriend's unwillingness to give it the old college try and his perception of oral sex as 'kinky' speak volumes. I suspect his upbringing, cultural or religious values have left him with the male equivalent of the good-girls-don't syndrome. This means he secretly thinks sex is 'dirty' and 'bad' and he's too inhibited to relax and enjoy it.

Ideally, your boyfriend should visit a sex therapist to work through his inhibitions. Alternatively, buy him a good sex book as a present which talks about how natural and essential oral sex is for a satisfying sex life. Also point out, many women *only* orgasm through oral sex. If he won't consider either of these suggestions, trade him in on a more modern model or resign yourself to a sex life that'll be about as exciting as watching *Last of the Summer Wine* repeats.

I suspect all my partner wants from me is sex, even though we've been going out a few months. How do I find out for sure and let them know I want more than that?

Do they only want to see you when they're positive sex is on the agenda? Are they only interested in you when you're naked? Is 'Your place or mine' the only whole sentence they utter? Then, they're only in it for the sex. But if they're simply ravishing you as often as possible, it could be they're stuck at the bonkarama stage of your relationship while you're ready to move onto the lovey-dovey bit. Why not suggest a few dates that obviously won't end up in the bedroom: a picnic in a public place, going shopping together or seeing a movie (all minus the detours back home). If they refuse or grumble, ask them outright what the story is. Can they see a future between you or is it purely no-strings sex? If they say it's more than that, ask if they'd like to make the relationship monogamous. It's a fair question after a few months and guaranteed to have them sweating if they're not in it for the long haul.

My boyfriend's got loads of female friends. Can men and women really just be good friends or has one usually got a hidden agenda?

You're friends with your brother, aren't you? What about male colleagues, and your girlfriends' boyfriends or husbands? Of course platonic friendships are possible, and thank God they are.

The world would be a very boring place if we had to screen out 50 per cent of the people in it. What you're really asking is: if my boyfriend's friends are attractive, single and available, should I be worried?

First up, you're not the only one to be threatened by your partner's opposite-sex friends. Usually, it's easier if they were already friends *before* you met. That way you know if there was anything between them, they could have acted on it but they've chosen not to. As for people your partner meets *after* the two of you are an item, it's pretty normal to think, *Would they be together if I wasn't around?*

Is stress stopping you from falling in love? Don't laugh – it could be. US researchers found relaxed female prairie mice were ready to commit for life within six hours of being 'introduced' to a new partner. Relaxed male mice spent a whole day deciding whether or not to stay. Subject the mice to stress and the scenario reverses: the male mice latched on fast and held on tight, the females dithered and took their time. Just how the researchers measured commitment in mice is rather intriguing, but since they've always mirrored human behaviour, it's another reason to stop either of you being workaholics!

Get over it by asking your partner to introduce you. If the friendship is genuine, she'll make every effort to acknowledge your special place in his heart and respect your relationship. If you think there's sexual tension between them, ask him afterward. Say you noticed an attraction and feel a bit threatened by it. Do you have anything to worry about? If he doesn't seem interested but it's quite obvious she wants more, it's still in your interest to be charming and nice. It's one thing trying to break up a relationship when you don't know the other person, quite another if you've met and like them. Ask him to have a chat to set her straight or see her together until she wakes up to herself. Otherwise, drop it. Even if his friends are Kate, Claudia and Cindy, he should be capable of keeping them at arm's length if he's serious about you.

My partner's prone to be moody. I'm getting a bit tired of not knowing what to expect.

Are we talking anger or sadness here? Is it real depression or a tendency to see storm clouds where you'll see a rainbow? If they sink into depressions on a regular basis, they're excessive, uncontrollable and all out of proportion to the circumstances – or seemingly *unlinked* to any event – get them to see a doctor. True depression can sometimes be cured by drugs or therapy. If we're talking the odd bad mood, just get them to steer clear of you while they're in it.

More a case of them waking up ferocious and always flying off the handle over little things? Good luck! It's not much fun feeling your stomach turn over when you walk in the door because you're not sure what's greeting you on the other side. If anger, bitterness, sadness or an all-consuming rage is constantly simmering beneath the surface, you'll spend the relationship walking on eggshells. You'll also cop most of the anger, being the person who's closest to them, and will no doubt be told it's all your fault. Moody people rarely blame themselves and after a while, you start to think it *is* your fault. Add to that being the one who's left to smooth the feathers they've ruffled (the waiter they were rude to, your family or friends) and you can see why it's like living with an adult-size sulky two-year-old.

Why would you even bother? Many moody people are extremely attractive. Their highs are higher than the average persons and the sex is fabulous because it's equally as intense. Some women hook up with moody men because it appeals to their instinct to fix things and rescue people. Whatever, if you're rearranging your life to cheer your partner up, stop now and/or get out. Ditto if you're constantly apologizing and making excuses for their bad behaviour, searching for reasons why you can't make them happy or think it's your fault they're not.

Sit down with your partner when they're in a good mood and explain that life's not much fun on your side. Ask them to think about why they're so moody and whether there's anything they can do to even their temperament. Make it clear you're not to be used as a punching bag and don't want a partner who's always down in the dumps or angry at the world. If they recognize it's a problem and work hard at trying to change, meet them halfway.

My boyfriend cries at the drop of a hat. I know I should be patting him on the back for being 'man' enough to express his feelings but I'm starting to think he's a big drip.

You've absolutely got to give him full marks for courage: a man being moved to tears in front of anyone was unheard of a few years ago. Now men in public positions could be accused of turning *on* the tears to win sympathy.

Crying gets a huge tick of approval by psychologists. It means you're emotionally healthy enough to react sensitively to other people and events, and when you shed a tear, you shed stress-induced toxins. A good cry releases tension and feelings of sadness or anger: it's good for you! Having said that, there is something off-putting about having a partner who's always blubbering on your shoulder. Your boyfriend could simply be prone to tears (like others are to blushing) and well adjusted enough to not worry about it. It could be a ploy for attention, to make you understand how important an issue is for him. Or he's under intense pressure, stressed to the max and frustrated and using crying as a means of release. Ask him in a light-hearted way why he cries all the time, and see what he says. If it makes you feel uncomfortable, don't acknowledge the tears and continue talking as though nothing's happened. The more reward he gets for crying ('There, there'), the more he'll do it.

Why is it all the successful women I know are all-round nice people and all the successful guys I know are all-round arrogant bastards? Why doesn't wealth and power go to our head as much as his?

You've made a rather sweeping generalization but I do think you have a point. Very wealthy, powerful men often do exude an air of arrogance that's missing from their female counterparts. It's got a lot to do with expectations of each sex and the fact that women are better at playing different roles and switching between them.

Women who make it big in business straddle two totally different worlds. By day, we work in a corporate atmosphere where male qualities like ruthlessness and decisiveness are valued. At night, we return to friends, lovers and family who expect traditional female qualities like caring and support. We get to play both parts so switch easily from one to another when required. The all-round nice women you've met socially might be ball-breaking bitches in the office, then revert back to being 'themselves' outside of work.

Men tend to behave the same wherever they are, whatever role they're playing. The same qualities valued in business – the ability to be controlling, dictatorial and make hard decisions that sometimes hurt others – are valued in men generally. It's changing: most women now prefer a guy who's sensitive and caring, but plenty like 'a man who's a man', who'll take control and take over. If he's never had a girlfriend who's encouraged his vulnerable side, why wouldn't he stick with what seems to work?

As for ego, again, it's all to do with traditional expectations of the sexes. Men are *supposed* to be good at business, his self-esteem is strongly linked to his job and he's expected to boast about it. Women get their self-esteem from lots of different areas (namely relationships) plus we're more self-deprecating. If a woman scores a top job, she'll put it down to good luck rather than talent. If she misses out, she'll put it down to lack of ability. It also doesn't pay for us to be too cocksure (wonder where that term came from!). Friends, family and partners often feel threatened by a successful female, so you can see why she's conscious of not sounding too smart, too strong or too *male* when she's with them. Some career women are submissive, vulnerable and *over*-eager to please in their private lives to stop people feeling intimidated.

Why do my partners dress like dags the minute they're comfortable with me?

In the beginning, you'd rather cut your big toe off than let your partner see you looking less than perfect. As the relationship progresses and you feel more secure that it's no longer totally based on looks, it's natural to get less 'dressed up' to see each other. Slop-around clothes are a lot more comfortable and it's an effort to look great all the time. But while not washing their hair for three days and pulling on egg-stained T-shirts once or twice a week is a healthy sign they're comfortable with you, never, ever making an effort means they've slipped into 'I've got them, now I don't need to work at it' mode. Pull them up on it. Say, 'Call me strange, darling, but that pink and purple sweatshirt and lime green trackpants don't make me climb the walls with lust. It's nice we feel comfortable enough to slob around together but I think we should make the effort to look nice some of the time.' When they do, compliment them. Let them know you appreciate it when they go to a bit of trouble and they'll do it more often.

I was left alone at my girlfriend's place recently and couldn't resist having a snoop through her things. I found lots of phone numbers of guys I don't know and also some letters from an ex saying he still loves her. I don't know when they were written and can't confront her because she'll know I was snooping.

Dead right – and that's one of the reasons why spying rarely pays off. Rifling through your partner's wallet for suspicious phone numbers or condoms, rummaging through drawers in search of old love letters, checking out their address book to see who's listed – we've all done it at some stage with someone. If we're unsure of a partner's faithfulness, it seems the obvious way to find out without confronting them. The problem is, even innocent things take on ominous overtones when you can't ask for an explanation. For all you know, the phone numbers are work contacts, good friends or guys she met six years ago and never rang. The letters from the ex also mean nothing. They're *his* perspective on the relationship, not hers, and could be wishful thinking. Unless you admit you checked up on her, you're now plagued with fears that could be groundless.

But the most obvious question is: why were you snooping in the first place? You obviously don't trust her and aren't confident of her feelings for you. The only way to solve this is to talk to her, not sneak around behind her back. Spell out your needs, how you expect her to behave and your hopes for the future together. Be honest and keep going even if she looks uncomfortable. At the end, look her straight in the eye and ask if she wants the same thing. Put on the spot, most people give themselves away. Watch her face and body language: they're far better indicators of her feelings for you. If you're still itching to go through her handbag the minute she leaves the room after that, read the section on jealousy in Chapter 7, page 326, or book in to see a good counsellor.

I'm 32, a lawyer, and people tell me I'm very attractive. I get on well with men and chat easily, but no-one ever seems to ask me out. My male friends say it's because men find brains, looks and personality all in one too threatening. They say the fact that I earn a six-figure salary and drive a flash car makes it worse. Are they kidding me or is this true?

I suspect there are more than a few people out there wishing desperately they had your problems, but I'm not surprised you have troubles getting men to make the first move. Your friends aren't having you on, lots of men would feel inferior if their achievements don't match up to yours, and I bet plenty assume you only date millionaires or models. Joe Average wouldn't think he had a chance in hell.

The next time you meet a guy you like, make it painfully clear you fancy him – better still, *you* ask *him* out. Leave the Ferrari in the garage, steer the conversation away from careers and concentrate on getting to know him. Men should be proud to go out with such a successful, gorgeous woman, but the male ego can be pathetically fragile. Whipping out the gold Amex card and offering to settle the bill on the first date will depress him more than his home team losing the grand final. So tone it down – but not too much. After all, you worked hard for your success, you shouldn't be ashamed of it. There are plenty of secure, confident guys out there who find brains and ambition a turn-on and respect your achievements. When you find one, *you* grab *him*.

Sure, you spoil each other rotten on birthdays, but you'll last longer if you celebrate lots of milestones. Keep a record of significant dates and mark each as an anniversary. It keeps you focused on the positives.

I'm engaged but my fiancé refuses to marry me unless I take his surname. He says I should be proud to, but I don't see why I should give up my individuality. I've offered to hyphenate our names but that's not good enough for him either.

You're arguing about much more than a name change, and I'd take a good look at your relationship and expectations of marriage before setting a wedding date. Taking his name is becoming less and less common these days. Your fiancé sounds conservative and traditional, and I bet he has set ideas on how a 'wife' should behave as well. You obviously want to maintain your independence and probably see marriage as more of a partnership.

It's not a fab sign of future happiness when you're prepared to compromise by hyphenating your surname and he's not. Will all your future arguments be solved by him getting his way? You've got a lifetime of decisions to make together which are far more important than surnames. The bottom line is *all* should be made as *joint* decisions with each of you prepared to meet in the middle. If he won't now, he won't later.

My boyfriend has just asked me to marry him, but it doesn't feel special because he was married once before years ago. I can't help feeling second best to his first wife: after all, he loved her first and if she hadn't left him, he'd still be with her.

This is an extremely immature reaction to a marriage proposal, and if you're over the age of 18, I have two words of advice for you: grow up! Your boyfriend is showing both courage and optimism by giving marriage another go. There are plenty of other dumped divorcees out there who are so disillusioned and hurt by the experience, they'll never marry again. You should feel immensely complimented and very special indeed. If he split years ago, he's not doing it on the rebound but just trusts and loves you enough to put his heart on the line again. It doesn't matter who left who or who he loved first. All that matters is you're the person he loves *now*. Buy him the biggest bunch of flowers you can afford (men are even more chuffed by flowers than we are because they rarely get them) and say you feel like the luckiest person in the world.

My girlfriend's too good-looking. Wherever we go, guys stare at her. I don't think I'm unattractive, but I'm certainly not in her league. She says she loves me for who I am inside and out, but it still worries me.

While we all drool over the beautiful people in the world, it takes a confident person to date one. Having to constantly fend off hovering hordes every time you come back from the loo isn't fun – but it's how *she* reacts to them that's important. If she's smugly lapping up the attention, she's not worth the dents in your ego. But if she makes it perfectly clear she's spoken for, you can't really blame her for being born gorgeous. Regardless of looks, she's chosen you (from many) to go out with. That makes you pretty damn special – so start believing it yourself.

I've just found out my boyfriend slept with a prostitute three years before he met me. He said he did it on a whim when he was drunk and used a condom, but I can't stop thinking about it. Why would he need to do that when he's young and attractive?

Because it was risqué and therefore appealing to a drunk, sexually curious, hormone-driven young man. Paying for sex wasn't the issue, the experience was. He did this way before he met you and I'd say it was a one-off (he obviously has no intention of repeating it or he wouldn't have confessed). Sure, the idea isn't very appealing, but neither is the thought of him sleeping with anyone else but you. Don't ask for details and let it go. He's not the first good-looking guy to be lured by a sex worker and he won't be the last. Judge him not on his past but how he treats you now – with honesty.

My boyfriend's been invited on a stag's weekend, and I'm convinced it's going to break us up. There will be women involved, and I feel I can't trust him under these circumstances. What should I do?

Personally, I think both stags' and hens' nights are silly, sexist, outdated traditions which cause more problems than they're worth. They were originally conceived when married couples didn't go out without each other, but today's couples are different. Nevertheless, old habits die hard, so girlfriends and boyfriends of anyone invited along to these dubious celebrations continue to feel paranoid. In some cases, it's justified. Too much booze, peer pressure and 'available' talent is a fine formula for infidelity. But it doesn't have to be.

If your boyfriend is mature and respects you, he's not going to be tempted even if he is on his 25th beer and being nudged along by his mates. Instead of protesting, try reverse psychology. Send him along with your blessing. Resist the urge to deliver a long list of don't dos, kiss him goodbye and say, 'Enjoy yourself. I trust you.' If he loves you, he won't so much as *look* at another female without feeling guilty. Don't ask for post-party details, refuse to listen to rumour and innuendo and whatever you do, don't look at the photos.

Men always seem to dump me after three dates. It's like the minute I sleep with them, it's all over. How can I stop this happening?

Very easily. Don't sleep with a guy until you're sure he wants more than just casual sex. How will you know? The guy who's dating just for sex won't hang around past date four if you don't deliver. If he's still interested after date six, it's likely (though never guaranteed) he's interested in more.

Check with a friend to make sure you're not giving off vibes you don't want to and attracting the wrong type of guy. Stop searching the room for Mr Right and, instead, laugh and have fun talking to anyone you find interesting, not just potentials. That way, you'll be less likely to attract men who see you as easy prey. There's absolutely nothing wrong with sex for sex's sake but it is true: some men will discount you as long-term material if you have sex too soon. We all know people who've ended up marrying a person they slept with on the first night because it felt right and they both knew it. But they really are exceptions to the rule. Play prude for a little while and see what happens.

My boyfriend swears he loves me, but he can't remember the first time we met, which was in a bar. I can recall what he was wearing, what his first words to me were and lots more. Is this a bad sign?

No. You probably remember more detail because you were open to falling in love (perhaps even looking for it) when you met him. It's a bit of a female thing as well. Because we tend to seek out long-term relationships more so than casual sex, we pay a lot more attention first up, wondering if this guy is going to be special. So there's no need to worry if he can't remember much (he was probably half-sloshed at the time). Ask him to describe the first time he realized he really liked you instead. If he recalls that experience in glowing terms, consider yourself special. Has he pledged monogamy? Talked about the future together? Does he treat you with respect and love? All these are far better indicators that he's planning to stick around.

I'm about to go away for a holiday with my boyfriend, but I'm paranoid about sharing the loo. How do I keep my dignity but also let nature take its course? I find it all so horribly embarrassing.

A girlfriend of mine has it down to a fine art. First, she quickly lines the loo bowl with wads of paper, does her business, then flushes at that exact moment (I think you know the moment I mean) so there's lots of background noise. Then she lights a match to disguise any after-odour. Laugh all you like but she's dead serious. Her other tip: send him out for emergency supplies whenever you feel the urge. Perhaps a more sensible option is to confess your fears. Say, 'Look, I have to go to the loo and I'd be mortified if you heard me. Can you wait outside or turn the telly up loud?' Chances are he'll not only burst out laughing but be tremendously relieved (in more ways than one) that you've brought the subject up. Men get funny about things like that too.

At the grand old age of 30, my partner has discovered God. I'm an atheist and so were they. They've changed overnight into a person I don't know and can't relate to. What should I do?

I guess the obvious question is: what prompted the conversion? People often turn to religion if they've been seriously ill or someone close to them has died. If this is the case, it could be a passing phase rather than true, long-lasting belief. Regardless, it sounds very much like you've both grown in different directions and have stopped communicating. Sit down and ask them why they converted. What's religion providing that was missing before? Explain that while they have every right to worship whatever god they choose, it doesn't mean you want or have to. You don't share the same belief, and they shouldn't try to convert you.

Also point out they have a responsibility to the marriage as well as their church. Be honest. Tell them they're not the person you married and you're concerned it's disrupting a relationship you enjoyed. If you can agree to disagree about the subject (they don't preach and you're happy to sleep in or nip off to a coffee shop while they go to church), it's workable. If they're so devout you can't enjoy things you did previously, you're in trouble. Then it could be time for some couples counselling.

What's the deal on splitting expenses when you're not living together but your partner's spending a lot of time at your house? I'm going through things like loo paper and toothpaste twice as quickly and starting to feel a bit resentful about it.
Be upfront. Say, 'Darling, I've run out of loo paper/milk/ tissues again. I seem to be going through them twice as fast these days! Could you pick up the things on this list while you're out?' If they're intuitive, they'll get the hint and foot the bill as well as start chipping in for essentials you both share. If they ask for cash when presenting you with the groceries, say, 'Oh. I figured since you're also using these things it's fair that you pay for them occasionally.' If they're strapped for cash, trade other things like back massages, housework or washing the car.

I'm single, 40, and desperately want children. I'm seriously considering a sperm donor and bringing up the child on my own. What do you think?

A married-with-young-baby friend of mine happened to call while I was writing this,

The taller your boyfriend, the more likely he is to offer to pay for you. The Wall Street Journal *found men over 187 centimetres earn an average of 12.5 per cent more than men under 183 centimetres. Shorter men aren't ungenerous, they're just not as rich!*

so I put the question to her. 'Jesus!' she said. 'I wanted this child *and* I've got a supportive partner and it's still a bloody nightmare!' So that's the advice straight from the horse's mouth: forget it.

From the perspective of someone who's never had a child and also considered doing it solo (namely me and note the consider*ed*), you still need to think through an awful lot of issues. Coping with a baby is difficult when you've got a partner to thrust the child onto at the end of the day. Raising a child alone means double the work: you've got no physical *or* emotional back-up. Are you able to support the child and yourself? Do you have friends and family to help you? Are you strong enough and mature emotionally to cope with motherhood? What if your child resents being brought up without a father? What if a future partner resents you having a child? If you're prepared to put your life on hold for ten years, work like a dog and cope with the inevitable criticism, maybe it is the right thing to do. Do me a favour: for the next two weeks, imagine your life the way you would have to live it if you had a small baby to look after. If you're still keen after that, it deserves serious consideration.

My mother hates my long-term boyfriend and refuses to have him in the house. She's difficult to get along with at the best of times and won't even discuss him. He never complains, but I think it's atrocious he's not invited to family get-togethers.

I'm not surprised he never complains. While you're dutifully scooping up your peas and broccoli and justifying why you had to wear *that*, he's got his feet up, watching telly and having a fine time. Assuming your boyfriend wasn't rude or obnoxious when Mum first met him, there's probably no basis for her dislike other than he's not the guy *she* would have picked for you. So unless you want to trade him in on a drippy shorts-with-long-socks-and-sandals boy, you'll never win. Tell your boyfriend Mommy Dearest is being difficult (as usual), make the most of the relationship you do have with her and grin and bear it. But this doesn't stop you getting together with the rest of your family. Why not hold a family 'do' at your place and invite Mum as well? She may realize how petty she's being if everyone else accepts but her.

I broke up with my ex-wife years ago, but my family remained friends with her. I was the one who left and initially I encouraged them to keep in contact, but I feel a bit peeved it's continued this long.

I'm not surprised. You're probably wondering if you made a mistake leaving such a nice person, which she obviously is if they want to be friends with her. Or maybe you're a bit put out because she's obviously over you if she can maintain contact with your family (it'd hurt too much otherwise). It's not on if your family is dangling your ex in front of you in the hope you'll reconcile or making it uncomfortable for your new partners. But if they're simply friends with her, get a life! It shows your family are warm people who love your ex for her, not because she was your wife. You're the one with the problem, not them.

I'm thirtysomething but still feel like I did in my twenties. It seems like there's *years* before I have to 'grow up' and settle down. Am I being immature?

You manage your own company but rent *Spice Girls: The Movie*. You've bought your own flat but rollerblade in the park on Saturdays. In other words, you've accepted the responsibilities of adulthood and are doing fine thanks very much but still aren't quite ready to turn into Mum or Dad? No, you're not being immature, you're just typical of your generation.

Plenty of 38-year-olds feel more like 28. Our diet, health and exercise regimes are better than our parents' were, so it stands to reason we'll look and feel younger. There's only one reason to rush the emotional ageing process and play house: you're female and want to have kids. While our fertile years are also being stretched, the elastic will ping at some point.

I've just fallen pregnant to my boyfriend of two years. It's really bad timing but, on the other hand, we are intending to stay together long term. We're not quite sure what to do.

I can point out the pros and cons but this is something you two have to solve together. First up, have either of you got any fertility problems? If you have problems conceiving further along the track, you might well regret having had a termination.

These are some other things to think about: What was the

gut reaction of each of you when you found out – dread or secret delight? Are you financially able to support a child and give it the best possible chance in life? Can one of you afford to take time off from work? Will you resent the child later if your career suffers? Are you emotionally mature enough to be good parents? Have you got a good support network of friends and family to help you through? Would you prefer a few more years just the two of you before becoming the three of you? Is your relationship strong enough to withstand the pressures of parenthood? Talk to friends with small children and read the section on parenting, page 298. That'll give you a good idea of what you're letting yourselves in for. Deliberately push the romantic illusions to the back of your minds and make the decision of whether to proceed with your heads. Listen to others but don't be pressured by parents or friends. Whatever you decide, one thing's obvious. You need to get or switch to reliable contraception so you're not faced with the agonizing dilemma again.

My partner and I argue all the time, even though we love each other passionately. Friends of ours never argue and they're constantly telling us our relationship is in dire straits. Are they right?

No. It's probably more dangerous to have no arguments than lots of them. Your friends are either apathetic about each other (not really caring if they've heard or understood) or terrified of rocking the boat in case one buggers off. No two people think the same all of the time, no matter how compatible they are. In their case, one partner or both is agreeing for the sake of keeping the peace.

As for you two volatile creatures, I think you hit the nail on the head when you said you loved each other passionately. Passion is a strong emotion, and if you're both intense, dramatic people you might well be picking fights because you enjoy the drama of a good brawl (or the make-up sex). It could also be because you crave a closeness the other couple don't. There's more to argue about if you yearn for total understanding from your partner. If you're both enjoying the relationship and the arguments don't worry you, ignore your friends' comments. If they are causing a problem, read Chapter 6 on more efficient ways to solve conflict.

I'm always getting dumped by women who tell me I'm too nice. They seem very interested initially, then cool off after a few weeks, even though I've done all the right things and sent flowers. What's wrong with treating women well, and why don't they like it?

If I had a pound for every time a guy asked me this question I'd be bashing out this book from a villa in Tuscany rather than a two-bedroom apartment in Sydney, so here's the lowdown. If you ask a girl out who you've just met and she says, 'You're really nice but I'd rather be friends,' it means, 'I don't fancy you' (though she might well want to be friends). If she says yes to the first few dates *then* delivers the 'you're too nice' speech, it means she did fancy you but now you're too much of a sure thing.

You're being *too* agreeable, spoiling her *too* much, telling her you're mad about her *too* soon. If, after three dates, she feels she's got you wrapped around her little finger, it's all been too easy. In essence, you've removed the challenge. She doesn't have to call her girlfriends after every date and analyse if this or that means you like her, because she already knows. Your heart's not just on your sleeve, you presented it to her along with a bottle of her favourite perfume on date three.

Flowers and chocolates *every* date, rushing ahead to open *every* door, telling us we look beautiful *every* five minutes, paying for us *all* the time, hanging off our *every* word, even when we're speaking absolute drivel: it's all just too much. All of these things are much appreciated when they're unexpected, delivered at the right moment and we're not bombarded with them, but we want to *earn* your love, not have it handed to us *simply because we're female*.

Which leads me to my main point: when men say 'treating a woman nicely' they usually do mean doing all the traditional things like opening doors and giving flowers and chocolates. Quite frankly, if it's excessive we start to feel like we're in an Audrey Hepburn film. It's all a bit old-fashioned and reminds us of the days when women didn't have the vote. If he's so traditional in these areas, we think, *Maybe he doesn't really consider me an equal.* We feel we're being treated almost exclusively as a *female* rather than a *person*, and it makes our liberated eyes water. The fact is, we don't want you to agree with us all the time; we like spirited arguments and being challenged on our views. We want you to think of us as strong and capable (which we are), not helpless and reliant (which we're not). The message we want you to give us is: I'll treat you like a princess if you deserve it, but I'm not a pushover and I don't put up with shit.

Don't stop the gifts and chivalrous gestures, just tone it all down. Make her feel special as a *person*, as well as a woman. Send flowers because she scored an account or got that promotion, not just because 'she's beautiful'. Ease up on the 'your eyes look beautiful in the candlelight' and instead ask her about her family, her job, her passions, her ambitions. Talk about your own, and don't automatically include her in any discussions of future travel or career plans. Let her think, *Oh no! He wants to live in Paris. I wonder if we're going out whether he'll ask me to come with him.* Don't censor your conversations because 'women don't like talking about things like that'. If she expresses an opinion that's inaccurate or one you don't agree with, challenge her on it. The idea is to have her thinking she's lucky to have you rather than knowing you think you're lucky to have her.

Why do women only ever want to be my friend? I've got a million female friends but none of them ever fancy me.

Read the answer to the above question. It could be because you're doing the too-nice thing. Also take a good look at yourself in the mirror. How's your dress sense? Are you making the most of your looks? If you don't like what you see, get one of those female friends whose taste you admire to go shopping with you for clothes (and maybe get a good haircut while you're there).

If neither of these apply to you, it's probably because you've got the opposite problem to the guy before: you jump straight into 'friend' mode with women rather than playing the me-Tarzan-you-Jane flirting game. On the bright side, women obviously feel comfortable around you so your communication skills are probably good, you're open and honest about your feelings and you're a great listener. I bet your girlfriends tend to treat you like one of the girls: tell you their 'boy' problems and ask advice on how to handle men. Sounding awfully familiar? Okay: here's what to do.

The next time you meet a girl you want more than just friendship with, don't suggest doing a 'friend' thing like coffee or hanging out at the beach together. Ask her on a real 'date' so it's crystal clear she knows you fancy her. The whole take-her-out-to-a-nice-restaurant bit, complete with picking her up, dropping her home and a quick snog at the front door afterward. Hold her hand walking to and from the restaurant. Most men I know who have your problem, do it the other way around: they try to be friends first, then ask the girl out. This doesn't work because she's already put you in the friend basket, and if you're a good friend, she may say no to a date because if you break up she stands to lose your friendship. Get it? She likes you too much to risk that.

So if you want to be her boyfriend, act like one right from the word go. If she's not interested, then you can add her to your harem of buddies with boobs.

Why do women do that come-here-go-away thing?

God, we're difficult creatures, aren't we? Two reasons are usually responsible for come-here-go-away behaviour (one minute we're all over you and want you all over us, the next totally disinterested or want 'space'). First, she's not sure if she really likes you or not but wants you to like her until she makes up her mind. Here's how it works: you go out and have a so-so time and she thinks, *Nuh*, so next time you call she's cool.

You get the message and don't call her for a few days and she thinks, *Have I done the right thing? He was kinda nice. Maybe I'll give it one more go. Say I never meet anyone better? Say he finds someone else and I'm all alone?* so she picks up the phone and calls you to say, 'I've missed you. Why didn't you call?'

The second reason is she's testing you and you're failing a few. You're all snuggled up watching a video and she says, 'Don't you think Kim Basinger's the sexiest thing you've ever seen?' You nod enthusiastically. Silence. You continue watching the movie and forget all about the conversation. She's privately thinking, *Bastard!* (The correct answer was, 'Yes, she is sexy. But you're sexier.')

Within ten minutes she's shuffled herself, inch by inch, to the opposite end of the couch. 'What's wrong?' you ask, confused.

'Nothing,' she says. You get a cool kiss on the cheek and sent on your way.

The next day she thinks it through, talks to her girlfriends and decides she was being silly and you don't need punishing after all. That night she greets you with a lip-smacker and a 'Hi gorgeous!'

Yet another reason (I don't blame you if you've given up trying to fathom this one already) is that we, like you, want different things at different times. If we're feeling soppy, we want you closer than cling-wrap. If we're feeling independent and in that 'I am woman hear me roar' mood, we want space or maybe intense, urgent conversation. Because women can read mood changes quicker than the menu at McDonald's, we assume you can do the same and instantly know *when* we feel like *what*. Most men aren't great at deciphering body language so spend most of the time in the land of utter confusion. Says a fed-up male friend of mine, 'Women change the goal posts all the time. One minute they want you all over them, the next they don't. If you don't chase after them when they want, you're a bastard. If you don't leave them alone when they want that, you're too clingy.'

There's only one way to deal with the come-here-go-away girl: confront her and make her open up. Say, 'I'm a bit confused here. One minute we're getting on well, the next you don't seem interested at all. What's going on? Can we talk about this?'

I've got my eye on the ex of a friend. What's the protocol?

Handle this one with utmost care. Sure, you have every right to date whoever you want and they're not going out any more but, however illogically, most of us still claim ownership of exes long after we've broken up.

If the ex is an ex of a good friend, approach them before you start moving in. Be honest. Say, 'Jessica, are you and Rob well and truly over? Because I really like him myself.' If Jessica gives the correct answer ('We're just friends. But be warned – he snores'), your problems are solved. Still, be a little tactful. Jessica isn't to be used as a sounding board for your relationship, and anything either party says (or has said) about the other remains confidential.

If her answer isn't what you expected ('I can't believe you'd move in on Rob! How could you!') you're then left with two choices: forget Rob or be prepared to put your friendship on the line. If he really is the one for you and you think it'll last past a few dates, it may be worth it. If she can see it's true love, with time, she'll probably soften up. If it's more a lust thing, find someone else.

I fancy someone at work. Who's off limits in the office?

Ever sat next to a drop-dead gorgeous guy on a plane, swapped life stories, kissed while waiting for your luggage and gone on to live happily ever after? Neither have I. Ever met someone you fancied at or through work? Join the club. It stands to reason you're likely to meet a potential partner in the place you spend most of your time. But when is it safe to proceed and when should you resist temptation for fear of ruining your career and reputation? Here's a few hints.

Forget it and them if:
- **They can help you get ahead.** If it's your boss or someone in an influential position who signs reviews or authorizes pay rises or promotions, steer clear. If it's genuine, one of you will have to move on.
- **They're related to your boss.** Dump them later at your own risk.
- **They're married.** If you want sneaky, dishonest and disrespectful instantly added to your work résumé, go right ahead.

- **You're the boss, they work in the mailroom/They're 12 years younger than you.** Another instant authority stripper: you'll be seen as a slave of your libido (everyone will assume it's sex, which it usually is) and lacking good judgement. (I'm not saying any of these reactions are justified, just filling you in.)
- **You're the fifth person they've been out with in the office.** Even if they do have a smile so bright they could light up a small town during a blackout, resist. You'll instantly alienate the other four exes (who've possibly cried on your shoulder) and again, people will doubt your judgement. He's a cad/she's a cow, why can't you see it?

You've got the green light if:
- **They're on a similiar status level to you or work in a department that's not connected with yours.** A co-worker in the true sense.
- **None of the 'forget it' reasons apply.**
- **It really is true love.** We're all romantics at heart. Even if the odds are against you and feathers are ruffled initially, if time proves it was love not lust that brought you together you might even decide to ask the whole work team to the wedding.

I've fallen in love with my partner's friend. What now?

Ouch! This rates extremely high on the 'You Bastard, God. This Just Isn't Fair' scale. Whether it's serious between you and your partner or you've only been out twice, it's still an uncomfortable predicament to be in. For starters, read the 'Help! I'm in love with two people' question on page 549 and do the suggested exercise. This will ensure your feelings for the friend are real and you're not walking out on something that could be saved. Then refer to the section following which applies to you.

It's not that serious between you and your partner

Sure it's not a case of the grass being greener on the other side (that is, you'd fancy your partner if you were dating the friend)? When you say 'in love' do you mean love or lust? If it's lust, give it a few weeks: those wicked desires might well disappear when you start to see the 'real' them (that is, picking their nose when they think no-one's looking). If you honestly have fallen for them, the first thing to do is break off your existing relationship, because dating someone to get to someone else isn't nice. Explain, quite truthfully, that you don't think it's going to work out long term and *don't* suggest staying friends, it'll make it even more difficult long term if something does transpire.

Before you do this, make sure you have some way of contacting the friend independently, but don't tell them they're the reason you're splitting up. (They're not, and if you've done the suggested exercise, you'll have already established that.) A week or so after the break-up, call the friend to say you're no longer seeing so-and-so but would like to keep in contact with them. Make it pretty clear you'd like more than just coffee, then leave your phone number and the ball in their court. If the feeling is mutual, they'll make a date instantly or call to ask you out within a few days. If they don't, they're either not attracted to you or your ex is upset and their loyalty to them is stronger than their feelings for you. If you do end up getting together and it looks like continuing, it's courteous though not essential for you to ring your ex and tell them what's going on. Not to ask for permission, but to assure them the relationship started *after* you split.

If it's very serious between you and your partner (you've been going out for years or you're living together or married)

A psychiatrist once told me, 'When making a crucial decision, stay at the point of confusion for as long as possible.' Why? The longer you're frantically tossing up this side and that side, the more pros and cons you'll think of and the better decision you'll make. I can hear you groan from here: this is exactly what you *don't* want to hear. You're already feeling stressed, guilty and so upset by it all, you want the world to stop spinning so you can get off.

But he's got a point. This is not a decision to be made overnight. It requires a lot of time and thought, because if you leave your partner for a good friend of theirs, the fallout will be *enormous* and the guilt difficult to bear. You're robbing them of a long-term lover *and* possibly the person they would have turned to to help them through it, simultaneously. They're being betrayed on two levels at once. By removing both support systems, you're not just pulling the rug out from under them, you're polishing the floor so it's nice and slippery. They can't help but fall flat on their face.

Even if you didn't so much as kiss the friend before confessing, your partner will imagine you've been having an affair, right under their nose, the entire time. Bonking in your bed. They'll feel stupid and totally lacking in judgement. Why didn't they see it coming? They'll think back to all the heart-to-hearts they had about you to the friend and about the friend to you and think, *They must have been laughing at me.* Their life will feel like one big lie. They'll find it extremely difficult to trust again, both friends and partners, and probably need six months in therapy.

That's what you have to accept. I'm not saying all this is your fault (*no-one* deliberately falls for a friend), but this is what's going to be thrown in your face once you confess, by your partner and people who love your partner who will hate you for causing them this much pain. It would want to be worth it, so don't let anyone pressure you into making a decision until you're ready.

The only way you and the friend will get through all this is if you both feel so strongly for each other you honestly can't imagine living happily without the other. So make sure you're 150 per cent certain it isn't lust or idealized romanticism that'll fall flat the minute it's out in the open. Do the five-step plan to choosing between two lovers (see the next question) several times over, several days apart. You need to be absolutely sure you won't regret leaving your partner if it doesn't work out with their friend.

Both of you assume the worst: they'll lose their friendship with your partner *for good*; you'll lose your partner *for good*. Be prepared for friends and family to judge you. Some will stand by you, knowing you didn't set out to hurt anyone, and that there was no point in you staying when love had left. Others will call you names, slam the door in your face and never, ever see you again. All your friends will have to choose between you and your long-term partner: you stand to lose 50 per cent of them. If you're very, very lucky, and handle it extremely diplomatically, they might well forgive you in the future. But in the meantime, you'll be the 'bad person'. The one who caused the whole damn mess.

You know all this and have given it time but remain utterly convinced it's the right thing to do? Set the wheels in motion. Sit down with the friend and decide when you're going to break the news and where you're both going to live. Is it better to live separately for a little while? Organize accommodation discreetly and start thinking through practical matters: who's going to keep the house, the cat and (God help you) the children. In fairness to your partner, it's reasonable for you to be the one to move out initially, even if a later settlement does award you the home you own together.

If you have a good relationship with your family and trust them to keep quiet, consider warning them before you deliver the bombshell. Close friends may also need to know, though it goes without saying that if you have any doubt whatsoever they'll deliver the news to your partner before you can, keep quiet.

As for what to say on D-Day, there's no alternative but the truth. Tell your partner you need to talk, sit them down and say, 'I'm so sorry. This isn't working out for me and hasn't for a long time. I don't know what happened (if you do, say what) but I don't love you any more and haven't for a while. I stayed hoping it would work out but in the meantime, I fell in love with someone else. You will possibly never forgive me for this but it's X. No, we haven't been having an affair but (however long ago) we had a talk and both realized we felt the same way. I am not leaving you for X, I'm leaving because it's over between us. But I do intend to pursue a relationship with X and I think you should know that.'

Their reaction could be any one of a number of things. The talk will probably end with both of you crying hysterically and one leaving. When that happens, make arrangements (as best you can) to ensure your partner isn't alone. Ring a close friend of theirs or relative of your partner who you know will be supportive of them. Fill them in quickly, put up with whatever abuse they fling at you and tell them you're worried about them and think they need support.

The first place your partner will go after finding out will probably be the friend's place. Personally, I'd make sure I wasn't there: this is between the two of them. It goes without saying you'll have warned them when you're about to confess, and it's a good idea if they also have some sort of pre-prepared speech ready. Not that your partner will take in much of what either of you say – they're in shock – but it may sink in afterward.

What happens now? You'll both spend the next few months

feeling guilty, being abused by everyone from the drycleaner to your parents and worrying yourself sick about your partner. The friend will blame him or herself for causing all this. You will blame yourself. Friends will sort themselves into for-her and for-him camps. You'll start the painful process of splitting up mutual possessions. But, *if you honestly have done the right thing*, you'll also feel relief. No more hiding, it's out in the open and while your new relationship will be strained – you're constantly saying to each other, 'I'm so happy to finally be with you but Christ, this isn't easy is it?' – the sheer pleasure of being with the person you love will help ease the pain.

Help! I'm in love with two people and can't choose between them.

> **Drag this one out as a bit of trivia at your next dinner party. This is what palm readers claim you can tell about your partner by looking at their hands.**
> - *Will they be faithful? Check out the lines on the side of their hand, below their little finger. One deep groove signifies commitment; the more grooves the more easily tempted they are.*
> - *Have they got a high or low libido? If their ring finger's longer than their index, they have a high sex drive.*
> - *Are they a giver or a taker? If you can see light through the gaps at the bottom of their fingers when they're closed together, they're giving. If no light shines through, they're more selfish.*
> - *Will they be fun in bed? If the tip of their thumb tips back, they're impulsive and fun. If it's straight, so are they.*

We tend to think we're immune to falling in love with more than one person, but it's definitely possible to love two people at the same time. The human heart is a wonderfully generous organ (yes, it's not the only one) and if you're a warm, open person who adores meeting new people, you could fall in love with ten people at once if you let yourself! We've all got the potential. What stops us is commitment to the relationship we're already in and time and energy. It's hard enough making one relationship work let alone ten of them simultaneously!

Usually, if someone says they're torn between two lovers they're choosing between an established relationship and a new one. There you are, quite contentedly sailing along with a partner until *Wham!* out of the blue someone appears who makes your heart thump out of your chest and liquefies your loins. Then you're faced with a huge dilemma: which one should you choose? The tried-and-true or new and infinitely more exciting? Most long-term relationships go through boring patches and, if you meet someone rather tempting smack bang in the middle of one, that's when there's trouble.

What's even more confusing is it's impossible to compare old love with new love. One part of you is massively enjoying that glorious, mad, falling-in-love feeling. But you can't really enjoy it because you look at your existing partner and the guilt kicks in, deflating the euphoria like someone just stuck a pin in a balloon.

Love feels very different at different stages in relationships. The new person is on best behaviour. They're showering you with compliments and giving you 100 per cent attention – which is what your old love did in the beginning, too, remember! You're meeting the new one on the sly which makes it even more exciting and, of course, they're forbidden – which instantly makes you want them more. While we might love our old love, if you've been together a while, it's more a comfortable sort of feeling. New love is like being on a rollercoaster, laughing hysterically and screaming from the top of your lungs. It's rather like comparing a pair of worn-in, comfy slippers to the brand new snakeskin stilettos you bought last week. You might break your neck in the stilettos but you can't wait to try them on and strut your stuff.

How to make sense of it all? Try the following five-step plan.

Step 1: give yourself breathing space

Stop seeing the person you've met most recently and put everything you've got into trying to make it work with the person you've been with the longest. Why? Because the biggest mistake you could possibly make is to leave a good relationship – one that could have been saved with a bit of work – for someone who turns out not to be quite as fabulous as you thought. Break up with your old lover because there's no hope for the two of you, not because of someone else. I swear you'll regret it otherwise. Most relationships seem promising in the first month or two but few make it past that.

Step 2: decide what you really want from a relationship

Do the relationship and partner wish lists in Chapter 1. Also think about whether you really want a long-term serious relationship. Perhaps this new person is simply a symptom: you'd prefer to be single and date casually than be settled down right now. Take a good, long look at these lists before moving onto step 3.

Step 3: look objectively at the relationship you've been in the longest

On one side of the page, write down all the things you like about the relationship. On the other, write down all the things you don't like. Beside each *don't like* point, tick those things you think you could change if you both worked hard on the relationship. Put a cross beside those you don't think will alter, no matter what both of you do. For instance, 'Doesn't get on with my friends' is something you could sort out (even if it means seeing them without them), so that gets a tick. Go back up to the start of the 'don't like' side and start again, this time rating each point out of ten on how important it is to you. (One is not important, ten is extremely important.) 'Find them unattractive' might rate a ten, 'Not getting on with friends' a four.

When finished, this list represents the state of your relationship and what hope there is of saving it. If the 'don't like' side also has mostly crosses and tens, it means there's a lot you're unhappy with, it's all important to you and largely unfixable. If that's the case, it probably is time to move on.

If it's the opposite: the 'do like' side has lots of points and the 'don't like' side lots of ticks and low numbers, stay where you are, at least temporarily. There's plenty left to work with, your gripes aren't that important to you and your attraction to the new person is probably because you're in a rut with your old lover.

Step 4: focus on the new person
List the things you like about them, then areas you suspect might cause problems. If you're honest with yourself, your gut instinct should give you a few clues. Write down ten reasons why you think a relationship with this person would be better than the one you've already got. Are they logical, sensible, long-term reasons, or do they look flimsy to you, even in this deliriously optimistic stage?

Step 5: trust your gut reaction
In most cases, the lists will point you pretty obviously in one direction or another. What's equally as important is your reaction to the decision they're telling you to make. Say the odds are definitely in favour of staying with your old lover. Does the thought of it fill you with joy – or dread? It's not going to work if, in your heart, you don't want it to. You haven't put your finger on the reason yet, but it's there all right.

It's pretty obvious you should leave your lover and give it a go with the new person but that makes you terrified? You're probably scared to take a risk because you're frightened you'll end up alone (read Chapter 1). And don't forget there is a third option: don't choose either of them. Stay single for a while until you're really sure where your heart lies.

I'm bored with my partner but not sure if it's just a rough patch. How do you know when to hang in there and when to move on when your relationship goes stale?

For most of human history, the question of whether to leave a long-term relationship was almost irrelevant. Marriage was seen as an unbreakable contract, and it was often impossible economically for women to survive solo. Divorce was unsavoury, so most people made their bed and lay in it, even if on the very edge.

Today, it's not only acceptable to leave spouses or live-in lovers, you're viewed as a bit of a loser if you stay in a relationship that's not going amazingly well. Which is just as unrealistic as the old formula. No-one's happy all the time. *All* relationships go through bad patches and down stages. So it doesn't necessarily mean it's over or will never get better if you're more interested in polishing the chandelier than swinging from it.

If you've entered the so-so zone – your relationship's not bad enough to leave but 'if this is the future they can stick it' – it might well be an indication you really aren't as compatible as you thought. But it could be you've both simply settled into Dullsville: you do nothing but routine things together, you do fun things apart and you rarely make love. If this sounds horribly familiar, give each other a swift kick up the bum and *instantly plan six fun things you can do together this week. Continue doing this for a month.* If you're still not enjoying each other's company four weeks later while lounging around that fabulous five-star resort, yes, you're in trouble. It sounds like an overly simple solution to the problem, but according to most of the couples counsellors I know, if the relationship can be saved, that saves it in 70 per cent of cases. Make the relationship No 1 importance in your lives for a little while (if not permanently), instead of placing it behind family, friends and career.

Think about reasons *other* than the relationship that could be responsible for you feeling this way. Are you both under extreme pressure from work? What's your past relationship history? The reason why many of us hover in relationship limbo-land is that we doubt our judgement. Perhaps previously you've left when others would have stayed, or stayed when others would have left. If this does apply to you, my advice would be to do the opposite to what you usually do. If you're the sort of person to up and leave at the first hint of trouble, stay – at least for a while longer. You might be pleasantly surprised to discover relationships *can* recover from hiccups and grow stronger. If you have a tendency to drag relationships out until they're hanging by a thread, it's probably wise to get out. Here are some other things to think about.

The leave or stay checklist

1. **Don't base your decision exclusively on retracing the history of your relationship.** Your memories are biased by what you're feeling at the moment. If you're feeling pessimistic about your partner, says US psychologist William Doherty, you'll put a negative slant on things. Say you met at school and married young. What you previously thought was romantic, you'll now see as impulsive and foolish. This memory bias means you'll colour the relationship history when repeating it to friends and family, which of course means the advice *they'll* dole out is inaccurate. They might tell you to pull the plug on what's essentially a good relationship or, if you've painted a rosy picture, stay

in a bad one. Recognize that you're probably rewriting history and take this into account.

2. **How willing are you and your partner to work at making the relationship better?** People often abandon relationships that could be saved with a bit of work. It's all part of our throwaway lifestyle: if something's broken, don't fix it, buy a new one instead. How much energy and effort have you both already put into trying to make the relationship good? If the answer's hardly any or none at all, stay where you are. You haven't even tried yet!

   If you've spent months trying to fix things but your partner's made no effort at all, even though they're aware you're not happy, it's a different story. Ask yourself, 'If I stopped working at this, would it fall to bits?' Try it for two weeks and find out. You *both* have to be prepared to work on the problem and come up with viable solutions.

3. **How long have you been stuck at this point?** Think of your relationship like an old LP record. Even in good relationships, the needle won't move smoothly through the grooves; it'll skip now and then, and you need to give it a thump to stop it getting stuck in scratches. If you're thinking of leaving, it probably feels like the needle's been stuck in a groove, playing the same few notes over and over and over again (possibly sung by Barry Manilow) for ever. The question is: how long has it been stuck there? A few weeks, months or years? Are you feeling mild irritation or intense annoyance? If you've been together a long time and it's been so-so for three months, hang around. Give the relationship the equivalent of a thump by planning a few weekends away together. Eat, drink and be merry. If you're both already working hard on it and have felt disillusioned for more than a year, that's the time to consider moving on or therapy. Ask yourself, 'If I had to repeat the last six

months of this relationship over and over until I died, would it make me happy?'

4. **Are you staying because you can't bear to give up on all that hard work?** If you've been together for years, it can seem like such a waste to throw it all in and start again. If that's the *only* reason you're staying, get out. Cut your losses and leave now, so you're not wasting even more time.

5. **What if you leave and don't find someone else?** If you find yourself asking this question and it's the *only* thing that's stopping you packing your bags, again, you're definitely hanging around for the wrong reasons. It's normal to ask yourself, 'Will I find someone better eventually?' It's not healthy to cling onto something that's over just because you can't bear the thought of watching telly alone. (Get a flatmate or a cat.)

6. **Have you outgrown the relationship?** Two years ago, you might have been compatible, but different life events sometimes force us in different directions. Ask yourself, 'Are we such different people now we really don't have anything in common? Or could we bridge the gap by talking more and letting each other in on our lives?'

7. **Have you been influenced by other people?** If your girlfriend and your family have spent the last year constantly running down your lover, it's natural to start thinking they're right. Separate what *you* think from what *others* think you should do.

8. **Make two lists.** The first: what do you have to gain by staying? Emotionally, your lover might make you feel secure and loved, be a great shoulder to cry on, dispense terrific advice, give great orgasms. Practically, they might pay half the mortgage or rent, give you a better lifestyle than you'd have alone. Write down all the good things your lover brings to your life. Ask, 'Am I in it just for

the ——?' Sex? Something to do on the weekend? Be honest with your reasons for staying. The second list is: what do you have to gain by leaving? Repeat the exercise from the opposite perspective: write down all the advantages of leaving. More time to spend on you? The chance to meet someone you're truly compatible with? The freedom to travel? You never have to sleep with them ever again? List all the pluses for flying the coop.

9. **Are you being honest with yourself?** Look at the lists again. Do your reasons for wanting to stay or split seem good reasons? Imagine meeting a stranger on a bus and telling them objectively why you left. Will they look at you and say, 'How sad! It sounded like you could have made it,' or, 'That's sad, but you've probably done the right thing.'

10. **Do you need more information?** You may decide you would like to stay with your partner but want to travel solo for six months. It's worth asking rather than assuming they'd say no.

11. **Does your decision feel right?** If you've decided to leave, do you feel a bit excited about the future, like once the painful part of telling them is over, you'll feel a massive relief? If you've decided to stay, do you feel a renewed commitment to your partner? Are you looking forward to the relationship becoming all you've wanted it to be?

It's time to go when:

- You only share one or two things in common: a hobby, sex, the dog.
- You're doing all the work to solve the relationship's problems.
- They're unwilling to change or compromise. They don't think you have any problems even though you've confessed you're not happy.

- Your partner treats you badly.
- Your partner takes you for granted or you're so bored you can barely work up the enthusiasm to kiss them goodbye before leaving for work.
- You love them but don't like them much. It sounds bizarre, but love isn't a reason to stay. You can love your partner on one level but still not be suited long term. If you've been with the person a long time, of course you still care desperately about them and have lots of shared history and good times. But if your head tells you you're not only both moving in entirely different directions but very happy about where you're headed, it's time to kiss each other tenderly and change the relationship to friendship.

I've just met the perfect person on holiday. How do I know if it's just a fling or the real thing?

Sun-soaked days, moonlit nights and nothing to think about but which cocktail to order and whether to have a snooze now or after you go for a dip. Is it any wonder holiday romances seem so special? The most savvy of us lose perspective on relationships on hols because we've switched into vacation mode. City cynics turn into hopeless romantics, our brains turn off and our libido switches to high. Which is why we take holidays in the first place! Everyone's in expansive, generous moods and treating themselves to whatever they want. Fancy chocolate for breakfast? Why not? You're on holiday! Wondering what the great-looking girl or guy would look like with the lycra peeled off? You're on holiday! What's stopping you finding out?

Okay, so you told everyone back home all you wanted was time to read your book and chill out. But something odd happens on day three: swarms of attractive people appear. Your eyes start drifting from the book in front of you and, *'OhmiGod! Did you see that?'* You get chatting which turns into a drink then dinner and, before you know it, you're acting like boyfriend and girlfriend because the relationship *has* to play on fast-forward because you're on limited time. Unlike your relationships back home, there's no arguments with your holiday lover. What have you got to argue about? Against the fairytale backdrop, the relationship feels so perfect – why, it seems positively *criminal* not to continue it. Just as it now seems perfectly plausible (in fact, you can't understand why you didn't think of it before) to suggest to your boss that the new staff uniform be a sarong, it seems ridiculous to break up just because you live in different cities. Then – *thump!* – you go back to your real life and the illusion usually fades. Holidays put us into a time warp. People behave differently and we see them differently. The guy who buries his toes in the sand in Fiji and says, 'What do we care what time it is?' is the same guy who goes ballistic when you leave a coffee stain on the bench when you come to visit. The good-looking babe who snuggled up by your side in that ski lodge stares at you in horror when you turn up, full of hope and optimism, at her front door two weeks later. It hits you that she wouldn't look twice if you tap-danced naked in front of her in a bar back home. You just happened to be the best on offer at the resort.

I'm being pessimistic? Yes, I am – for good reason. Most holiday flings don't survive when you pluck two people out of an idyllic surrounding and plonk them into the lives they live day to day. Believe me, it was just a fling if:

- Every time you saw each other, you had sex.
- You're not the only one they'd slept with at the resort.
- They weren't really interested in hearing about your life back home – or telling you about theirs.
- They told you they loved you on the second night. Instant declarations mean they're immature or after something (sex for instance?).
- Your gut instinct screamed, 'Beware!' when you first met

them. You thought he was too smooth/she was too full on initially, but they talked you out of it. Initial instincts are often correct.

- You live in different countries. You'll be lucky to last unless one of you travels a lot for business. Even lovers who've lived in each other's pockets for years have problems when forced to live miles apart.
- You remained on best behaviour. The more 'normal' you were with each other, the better.
- The timing's wrong. If one of you took a holiday to get over a broken heart, forget it. That's rebound.
- You tried to make arrangements for back home but they seemed uncomfortable. If you live in the same city, it's natural to say, 'I'd really like to see you when we get home. How's Saturday night for you?' If they made excuses, don't bother waiting by the phone. If they started talking excitedly about which restaurant to go to, they're as keen as you are.

You're convinced you had the real thing? Basically, my advice would be this: if you live far away from each other but have the cash or career to swing regular trips, it's worth giving it a go. Talk on a phone a few times, plan a *brief* visit and see if you're still as keen. If it's unlikely either of you can visit, swap phone numbers and addresses and look them up if ever you're in town.

If you live in the same city, it's far easier. You'll either sit across from each other and marvel at how strong the cocktails must have been or feel a little uncomfortable initially, then move into a 'normal' relationship.

Do long-distance love affairs ever work out?

Sometimes it's a holiday fling that developed into more. Other times you were already an item, then one of you had to move cities for work reasons. Whichever, long-distance relationships are becoming more and more common. Gone are the days when we settled for the girl or boy next door. We travel more – both through work and personally – and want more from relationships, so it stands to reason we don't automatically discount someone just because they live miles away or in another country.

But building and sustaining a relationship is difficult enough when you're five minutes away – doing it via the phone or e-mail is near impossible. You've got a lot more chance of making it if you have lived in the same city for a period of time before being forced to live apart. At least you know it does work when you are together permanently. Hardest of all is the relationship that's always been long distance.

Why? Long-distance love affairs intensify and magnify everything. You're living in a fairytale world. It's all so romantic and passionate. Every second together is so precious you'll spend weeks planning one evening together. You have no idea how you'll relate in the real world because you're never with each other long enough to get past the best-behaviour part and live in it. It's for this reason you need to examine your motivation for wanting a long-distance lover in the first place. Is it because they're so special you'll try anything to make it work? Or are you a little scared of intimacy and this is a handy excuse for not getting too close?

There are other things to think about if you're considering one. Can you afford a long-distance love affair? They're expensive: all those phone calls and air tickets add up. Can you cope with always having to say goodbye? Jealousy can be a problem, loneliness almost always is. When the rest of your friends head home in nicely matched twosomes, you come home to an empty flat and a TV dinner, wondering it *they're* curled up with someone else. If you have an argument over the phone, you can't kiss and make up. Last but definitely not least: what about sex? Phone sex helps, so do raunchy letters, but it's still not the same as having a flesh-and-blood body in your bed.

Have I put you off yet? If you're still determined after absorbing all that, then maybe you do have a chance. And there is an up side. When you want a night in with a trashy video or a night out with the girls or guys, there's no questions asked. If you're super-busy with work or don't really want a full-time relationship right now, this is for you. Another plus if you do end up living together: once the thrill of being together permanently wears off, you'll probably find you're healthily independent. Unlike clingy couples who do everything together and end up bored, you know you can amuse yourself, so you keep the excitement level high by doing lots with your lives.

Inclined to give it a go? There's one thing a long-distance relationship *must* have in order for it to work: a light at the end of the tunnel. If neither of you can conceive of ever being able to live in the same place, honestly, what's the point? This may mean one of you has to sacrifice friends, family, a career to make it possible. Are you liable to end up feeling resentful?

Also, you need bucketloads of trust and you'll only get this through effective communication. Work out a way to have lots of regular contact. Ideally, you'd contact each other at least once every two days. Little details are as important as big ones: fill each other in on the small things that happen to you, not just the big issues. You both need constant reminders you're on their mind as much as they're on yours. E-mail's reasonably cheap and don't forget the good old post and fax machine. The phone's not the only means of communication.

Try hard *not* to spend every second of every visit doing 'romantic' things. In other words, try to live as you would if you were living together: use the time to find out if you really would be compatible long term. If you get on better when you're apart than when you're together, you're in love with the idea of each other rather than who you really are.

Dear Diary

Four lives, four relationships: how does yours stack up?

∙∙

In my previous book, *Hot Sex: How to Do It*, I asked six people to keep sex diaries for one month. Some took a bit of convincing (like, how detailed are we talking here? Are you sure my boyfriend won't recognize it's me?) but everyone I approached agreed. (Hell, once word got out, I was knocking back volunteers!) Not so with the relationship diaries.

Singles refused: 'Say I don't meet anyone? I'd look like such a loser.' One married man refused: 'I think if I was forced to write it all down, I'd have to leave.' The same girl who'd provided me with a highly explicit sex diary refused point blank to even consider committing her feelings about relationships to paper. 'No way. That's too *personal*,' she said. 'Sex is sex. Love is private. I don't care if people know I had bad sex but say my boyfriend cheated on me? I'd feel humiliated if everyone knew how devastated I really was.' I agree with her. Revealing feelings *is* more intimate, and if a relationship is suffering, it is painful to record.

Finally, I found four people who I felt represented a broad

cross-section of relationships and their different stages. Jason was having real problems with his girlfriend of six years. Jodie, a career girl, was happily cruising along and convinced she not only wouldn't meet anyone, she didn't want to. 'If you're happy for me to talk about relationships generally, fine. But I'm telling you now, it'll be more about past relationships than current ones.' (Amazing what can happen in six months, isn't it?) I chose Carla, married and trying to 'make babies', because she represents a very traditional model of marriage. And then there's Brad. Brad, well . . . let's just say (hope?) he represents a small minority of single men (though if you read between the lines, he's actually not as bad as he likes to think). I'll give him this: he's certainly honest.

Each person was asked to keep a diary for six months. They were permitted to use false names for themselves and others but not allowed to alter or exaggerate any details of their lives. They could write about their current relationships, any significant past relationships or their views on relationships in general. Each diary is recorded in their own words.

Jason

Jason, 32, is a journalist who lives in Melbourne. He wrote his diary at the tail-end of a six-year relationship and is currently (by choice) single.

The beginning

I can't just present you with a diary for the last six months because I need to go back to the beginning to make sense of it all. The whole thing was like something out of *The Celestine Prophecy*. Like, we were never in control, just two people being blown along and together by other forces. It was through a string of coincidences that we met and they lent a fairytale feel to the relationship. I think that's what made me lose perspective on what was really happening. Whenever things went wrong and I was tempted to chuck it in, I'd think, *Believe in fate. This is meant to last for ever.* I'm such a strong believer that people meet for a reason, I found that one of the toughest things to accept in the end. It was like, 'Why did God go to so much trouble to put us together if it wasn't meant to be for ever?' Idealistic, naive, stupid: maybe I was all of those things. Even by writing this down, I realize that the coincidences weren't *that* amazing, but at the time they seemed unbelievable. Such is the benefit of hindsight.

I was travelling around America with a friend when I first saw Christine on a train. She was totally absorbed in a novel. We spoke briefly, the usual stuff like where we were headed and so on. I found out she lived in Boston and was travelling with a girlfriend. That was the extent of it. The next day, we all ran into each other again, walking around the tourist traps. A few hours later, my friend and I walked in to have lunch at a café and there was Christine and her friend. We all said the 'we've got to stop meeting like this' stuff and ended up going for a drink. Christine mentioned she was having a party when she got back to Boston and invited us. We said, 'Great! It's where we're headed but we have to meet up with some other people and unless you want ten of us . . .' But (due to *another* string of coincidences) the rest of the crew didn't turn up. We had nothing else planned so we rang Christine when we got to Boston and said, 'Hey, about that party . . .'

At that point nothing was happening. I didn't fancy her – if anything I fancied her friend – but we got on well. I was staying in a backpackers' place in town and we saw lots of each other. She was shy but interesting and for two nights we stayed up all night talking. On the second, without any warning at all, she kissed me. It was exactly on midnight. I had no romantic feelings for her whatsoever before then, but when she leant over and her lips touched mine it was like *Bing!* I said, 'Why did you do that?' and she said, 'Because it's been exactly a year since I broke up with a guy who almost ruined me. I survived to meet someone like you.' It was such a heavy, vulnerable statement yet I knew she wasn't attaching any strings to it: it was more an acknowledgement of the moment. I admired her courage so much then; now I realize there was something odd about it. She didn't know how I felt about her but she jumped right in there. Later, when it was safe for her to do so, she couldn't.

We made love that night and she cried when she climaxed. At the time I was blown away but now I see it was the beginning of things to come. The wall went up – or maybe it never came down – because she never, ever told me why having an orgasm made her cry and while at the time I thought it was a happy cry, in reality it was bitter and sad and messed up.

She went back to work, I continued travelling. I met someone else in the meantime and forgot about Christine for a little while. Then the new girl had to leave for a few days and I had the choice of waiting for her to come back and seeing her a second time or calling Christine again. I decided to wait for the girl, but again, something happened that meant she couldn't meet me. So I called Christine instead and it turned out she had two weeks' holiday, so we met in San Francisco. I remember we were in a jazz bar and I was at the counter, buying drinks. I watched her, sitting there, looking self-conscious and gorgeous and innocent and so much like a little child that I fell in love with her. (Her? Or who I thought she was?) When the two weeks were up, I went home with her and didn't leave for a year and a half.

The middle
It's weird when I look back. I thought I was so in love with Christine the whole six years yet friends remind me of conversations when I confessed I didn't think it was going to work. But I had nothing to judge it against. I'd slept with my fair share of women but she was the first to claim my heart. She was the first girl I lived with, the first one I said 'I love you' to. I had such a sugary, romantic idea of love. I used to think that once you were in love, truly in love, that was it. I'd see people split up and think, *Ahh! Well, they weren't in love after all.* Now I know it doesn't mean they weren't, they just fell out of it. It should last for ever, but it doesn't always.

Again, in hindsight, there were clues I'd never really known her. She'd have nightmares, *real* nightmares, and wake up screaming in the middle of the night. But she'd never tell me what they were about. Ironically, she thought she was very open with her feelings and used to give me a hard time about not being expressive enough. It was like she put up boundaries, not realizing that she had. I didn't know it at the time but I think maybe my subconscious figured it out and that was why I didn't show her what was in my heart. It often felt like she was there with me in the flesh but her soul and spirit were somewhere else. Some bad place. There were times when we'd have a discussion and her interpretation of it was so completely different to mine, I'd question my hearing and my sanity. Maybe she drifted off to the same place during arguments.

I had to return to Australia and it seemed natural for her to come with me. She lined up work and then I was amongst my friends again. I started looking at other people's relationships and they seemed a lot more grounded than ours was. The couples would talk, laugh, rib each other and smile and you could see they *liked* each other. Christine and I, I think we loved each other but I'm not entirely sure we liked each other as lovers. We liked each other as friends, but as lovers? I don't know. Yet for the first two or three years, I'd see her across a crowded room and know there wasn't anyone else. I'd think, *We're meant to be together.* No matter who was there she was always the one I wanted to wake up next to the next morning. Every morning. For ever. There was that feeling, then there were the nagging doubts. One or the other: never both simultaneously.

I feel I grew from a boy to man when I was with Christine. I felt confused as to how much she was responsible for and how much I would have achieved on my own. I really wanted to stay with the person I'd travelled that journey with. She was a witness to an integral part of my life.

The (long, drawn-out) end

I was in love but who was I in love with? I knew what Christine had for breakfast, I knew that if she crinkled her nose she was thinking hard about something. I knew where to put my tongue to bring her to orgasm, I knew what writers she admired, what movies she hated. But she was still a mystery to me – and not in a good way. More a really frustrating, 'hey, if we're going to get closer, you have to let me in' sort of way. I tried so hard to make her feel safe enough but it didn't happen. And so the blinkers clanged to the floor and in that crowded room there were suddenly other attractive people. She might still be the one I wanted to wake up with but she wasn't necessarily the one I wanted to go to bed with.

I finally put my finger on it: the passion was missing. She'd never truly let go with me sexually. She didn't get passionate about life like I did. I wondered if she found me sexually attractive at all. I went to the gym. I built muscle. 'Do you realize why I go to the gym?' I asked her once. She shrugged. 'Because I want you to look at me and want me.' I can't remember what she said, it was probably something really nice, but it wasn't the right answer, because she didn't understand. Sex trickled from sporadic to nothing. We talked a lot about doing things to improve our sex life. We tried this and that but it didn't work because it was me trying this and that, she never really did.

I worried that maybe she wanted marriage and kids and that was responsible for the coldness, because I hadn't asked. But whenever it came up, she gave the impression she wasn't ready. She'd say airily to friends, 'Oh. I'm not ready for *that*. I'm not sure I ever will be.' Yet, after we split, she told a close friend that's what she really wanted. She wouldn't talk about long term. That would mean one of us choosing to leave our country permanently. We were both tense but still in love. If I had to say what emotion I felt most at that point it was confusion.

There was a girl I worked with who I knew I would have asked out if I hadn't been with Christine. I really liked her. I tried to avoid liking her. One night after work, we went out to dinner. I knew I was putting myself in a dangerous situation but I wanted to prove to myself I could get through it: my love for Christine would be protection. The other part of me knew why I was really there. I wanted to feel someone melt in my arms and kiss me like they meant it. We had dinner, we went back to her place and played CDs. Nothing happened. I kissed her goodbye at the front door and walked to my car then thought, *No!* and went back and she was still standing there, watching me, and we went inside and it was so bloody amazing to hold someone and know they wanted to hold me and touch me and make love to me as much as I did them. I savoured the feeling but broke it off before anything of consequence happened. I got in the car and had a half-hour drive ahead of me and I knew the minute I got home I was going to tell Christine what happened. Sure enough, she was in bed, awake. Every other time I'd gone out with friends, she was asleep when I got home. I told her and she said she knew. She'd picked up the vibes. Did she? Or was it another metal door clanging down, the key thrown away for ever?

It all basically disintegrated from there, but I honestly don't think it was because of that kiss. The separation was happening way before that happened. I wanted to go on holidays together, she didn't. We agreed to separate for two weeks and live life as single people. Implied in that was if we met someone else, we'd act on it. See if we *could* make love to them. See how it felt, how it made us feel about each other. At least, that's what I *thought* we agreed on. It was yet another of those conversations where I thought we said one thing and she thought another. As it turned out, I did meet someone when I was away. I thought she was special. Alison made me think there was someone else out there for me, that Christine wasn't the only one.

I came home and Christine and I tried again. After six weeks, she asked if I'd slept with anyone while I was away. I told her the truth: we'd agreed to be honest about whatever happened. But all of a sudden, I was a bastard. I'd betrayed her. The conversation we'd had hadn't occurred as far as she was concerned. Again, I wondered if it was me, stupid me, me who couldn't even listen properly. About one week later Christine went home to the States to see her family and we decided it was time to pack up shop and split permanently. She'd found somewhere else to live, I was going to move out of the flat we shared.

You know what? I didn't care less at that point. I'd had enough. The first thing I did was call Alison and invite her down for the weekend. Again, coincidence.

'You won't believe this,' she said. 'My boss just told me I have to take holidays – I've got way too many owing. I can come down for two weeks.'

Two weeks was a lot different than a weekend. I freaked out. It had all started to hit me: Christine and I had split. I picked Alison up at the airport. She didn't look the way I remembered. I took her out and she started touching me and I could feel myself flinching. I hated myself for that. It wasn't Alison's fault: she was emotionally fragile too, she'd had lots of bad stuff happen to her. If she'd come for a weekend, it would have been fine. But two weeks was way too much for me. Bad karma.

Alison left after three days and that was when I had what

felt like an emotional breakdown. I collapsed emotionally. I felt no connection with anything or anyone. I'm a social person, but for two weeks I didn't contact any friends. I felt like someone had scooped out my insides and forgotten to stuff me with straw. I felt completely hollow. It was a non-emotion. I could get through the day but I couldn't reach out to people.

It passed and I moved in with friends. The emptiness translated into a 'let's bonk the world' feeling. I had one one-night stand with someone but it wasn't great. Then Christine came back and we started seeing each other as friends. We didn't know what else to do, so it seemed logical. There was talk of getting back together. I remember crying with her and wanting to be with her. She wrote me a letter and I still don't know if it said it was over or to give her time. I had no idea what she was feeling. I asked her if she loved me and she said, 'How can you ask that of me?' And I felt bad, like I shouldn't ask. I kept wondering what was wrong with me. Why was I so inappropriate all the time? That's one thing I won't tolerate in my next relationship: when you're in love with someone, you do have a right to answers.

The bottom line though was I thought she *did* still love me. I thought all this aloofness was a test that I was meant to pass. All I had to do was change and get to the point when I was ready to say, 'No-one else but you, Christine,' for ever. I even read fucking John Gray: Mars and Venus. Even before reading the book, I thought it was a wank. But I thought maybe that's what she wants: a guy like that. I reached the point where I thought: I'll never meet anyone better than her. I'm willing to put up with what she doesn't give me and take what she does. I was ready to take the leap: marry her and have kids.

I planned to tell her on New Year's Eve. We were at a friend's place. She was predictably cool, which started me wondering if there was someone else. So I asked. I said, 'Look, is there someone else?' and she looked at me and said, 'I don't think I want to be with you,' and it was like she ripped my heart out and threw it against the wall. And before I started crying, I said to her, 'I wanted to marry you. I thought you were the one. I thought we were going to have children together. I thought we were going to have that perfect life. I always thought once I was ready for that with you, you'd be ready for me.'

She looked sad but her eyes were like a stranger's eyes. I found out later there was someone else. Who knows how long for.

I went home that night, lay in my bed in the new flat we were meant to start a new life in and looked at the four walls. I cried like a babbling idiot. I had to work the weekend and couldn't get out of it. So I'd cry all the way there in the car, wipe my eyes, do the job, get in the car and cry all the way home. I woke up crying, I went to sleep crying. I cried like that for a month and even after that it didn't let up completely. Ironically, I quite enjoyed it in a bizarre sort of way. It was the opposite to how I'd felt before. Before I felt nothing; now I felt everything.

But I still wanted her back. For four to five months I wanted her back. I've only *not* wanted her back for the last month or so. My fear used to be that I'd find someone else and start to feel something for them and *then* she'd come back and I'd let her and all the crap would start over again. Now I know, that won't happen. I saw her the other day with mutual friends and for the first time, I felt nothing but pity for her. I think maybe something really bad happened to Christine and until she deals with it, no-one will get close. She's with another guy, the guy she was seeing while I thought she was still connected to me, and I wonder if their relationship is different to the one we had. For his sake, I hope so.

Jodie

Jodie is 36, single and works in an advertising agency. She's divorced, has lots of short-term relationships and, although she's not ready to settle down again, finds the tick of her biological clock quite alarming.

Month one

Everything is just brilliant right now. I secured a major, major client for the agency and I'm flavour of the month. Whoever said success breeds success was right. Before, I'd work so hard on clients and not get anywhere. I'd take them to lunch, do that whole wining and dining thing and then they'd book one piddly page in a cheap newspaper and complain if it didn't double their business overnight. This isn't the only major account I've won but times have been tough lately and I could feel myself slipping down a rung or two on the career ladder, the younger executives biting at my heels. Now I'm back on top: enthusiastic, motivated and want more, more, more business.

I know this diary is meant to focus on relationships but they're so low on my priority list at the moment. I don't have time, I've only got so much energy and I want to devote all that to my career. By the time I'm 40, I want to own my own ad agency, so I'm spending most weekends working: reading, making plans and organizing my finances. All I want to do on Friday and Saturday nights is flop in front of the telly with a trashy video. Only one problem: I'm as horny as hell. Power, winning, feeling so alive, it makes me want to have fierce, passionate sex. I've got a male friend who I sleep with now and then in situations like these but I don't really want to call him because he's now involved with someone. I guess it's just me and the trusty vibrator.

Month two
This month started with a bang – literally. I rang my male friend and turns out it's not serious with this new girl, so we spent a whole day shacked up, shagging. Afterward wasn't so hot, though. I think maybe he felt bad about cheating on his girlfriend, which makes me think it probably is serious, he just couldn't resist a bit on the side. That makes me feel cynical about men and myself. Are men capable of being faithful? What if I was involved with some guy: would he say no to no-strings sex? And what does this say about me: what sort of woman am I to steal someone's boyfriend, even if just for a day? I keep reading that women find it difficult to have sex with men they're not in love with, yet I can quite easily. To me, there's two different sorts of sex: sex for fun and sex you have when you're in love with someone. They're totally different. I wouldn't dream of having sex for fun if I was involved with someone and loved them, but what's wrong with satisfying yourself in the meantime? I can rationalize it but still: what was meant to be fun ended up being tinged with guilt.

That nasty feeling continued, not helped by the fact that I turned 36 on the 20th. Bloody wonderful – now I'm the wrong side of 35. Stupidly, I passed up the offer of dinner with friends for dinner with my family. My sister was there, also single at 32, and Mum went to town. 'What's wrong with you?/Why can't you find a nice man and settle down?/Steve was such a nice man, I can't understand why you divorced him.' I wanted to say, 'Well, Mum, it's this simple. I found out he'd had a two-year affair with the office slut. God knows why, but it upset me since I was trying to get pregnant at the time.' Mum has no idea why I left: most people don't. I kept quiet, not out of respect for him, but for myself. I was embarrassed that I didn't suspect, just kept on loving him. I felt like a fool and still do.

Turning 36 also dragged up that whole kids dilemma again. I know I've supposedly got years to think about children. I've seen girlfriends churn out their first at 40-plus but it makes me nervous, this constant ticking. Say I've got fertility problems? Say I have an early menopause? Each month I inspect my tampons and worry because there seems to be less and less blood. I asked my gynaecologist whether that meant time was running out and he said it didn't. But I'm not sure I believe him. It feels like someone's set the timer and I have to find someone I want to spend the rest of my life with really soon. And I'm not ready yet. I don't know if I'll be ready before I turn 40: there's so much to focus on career-wise. If I was a man, I'd set the agency up first, get it running smoothly, then find someone, spend a few years getting to know them, then have kids. But I can't do that because I'm female and I'd be closer to 50 by the time that's all happened. I love being a woman but it makes me angry that I can't control my own body.

Month three

Fabulous! Just brilliant! Just when I'm starting to crawl out of this mini-depression and enjoy being single again, my ex-husband knocks on the door with flowers. He forgot my birthday. No, he didn't forget, he was just so busy with work and wanted to see me when he could give full, 100 per cent attention to me blah blah blah. Like, save it for someone who gives a damn. Save it for someone who believes you. I hate him and it hurts that he can still muster up such a powerful emotion in me. I lie in bed some nights, imagining him with her, and it's still so painful. The pain's lessened but it hasn't gone away, and seeing him brings it all back, sharply into focus again.

I slept with my friend again and this time it made me feel

better. He's broken up with his girlfriend so it wasn't serious after all. I like Alan – he's warm and funny and makes me laugh at myself. He knows all about my ex and helped put that into perspective.

An agency client asked me out today at a work function. He's a client of a workmate of mine and he's actually really nice. I think he'll do well once his business has a few years behind it. But it's agency policy not to date clients, even if he's not my personal client. I told him and he laughed and threatened to transfer his business to another agency unless I said yes to dinner. I laughed and changed the subject and he didn't push it. Still, it was a nice ego boost and made me forget about exes and babies for a few hours.

Month four

So much for my deliberately cultivated office image as the hard career woman who only lives for work (to get ahead in this firm, you can't afford to act female). The agency manager called me in with the biggest smirk on his face and thrust a letter at me. It was from Martin, the client who'd asked me out. Martin wrote to ask official permission to ask me to dinner, wanting assurance that it wouldn't affect my position within the firm. His argument was that since I didn't work directly on his account, the policy of not dating clients shouldn't apply. It was wittily worded, struck just the right tone and couldn't possibly offend. I was ridiculously pleased but still my stomach turned over. My boss is moody and unpredictable: some days, he'd find this funny, others he wouldn't. Turned out to be my lucky day.

'Do you want to go out with this guy?' he asked.

'I guess so,' I said, rather nervously.

'Then I think it's best you do.'

He swore he wouldn't tell anyone, but I knew it'd be around the agency within an hour (and it was). My boss rang Martin and gave him the go-ahead. Then Martin rang me, suitably nervous. We arranged to have dinner that Saturday (a date night!).

Getting ready I felt all girly and silly, like I was 18 and going to the prom. Three girlfriends rang to wish me luck which instead made me feel annoyed and righteous. Like, did I look desperate? I was hardly hard up for dates.

'It's just because he wrote that letter,' said my best friend. 'It's like we all want something to come of it because of it.'

Well, it didn't. Dinner was nice but I think the expectation was too much. We'd lost that easy flirting we'd had at the function and it was all stiff and horrible. He said he'd call but I don't think he will.

He called the next day. Early. Like I was still in bed. 'Jodie, it's Martin. I'm calling to say what a bloody disaster last night was and to see if you've got enough of a sense of humour to see the funny side or whether you never want to see me again.'

I saw the funny side so we went out for lunch, drank and laughed ourselves silly and ended up back at my place. The booze helped but it seemed totally natural to climb into bed (underwear on) and watch the late-night movie snuggled up. He made no moves on me, I made none on him. It was possibly the nicest night I've had in years. It worried me plus I was late for work. I'd forgotten why I didn't want a relationship: it's because it always ends up interfering with my career.

Month five

I so much wanted my diary to be that of a fast-paced career girl without any romance in it at all. I wanted it to show women don't need men. Like, we really like you, but you're not essential, you know! We can live quite happily without you. And that's still true: the best years of my life have been the single ones. But now Martin and I are very definitely a couple and I'm enjoying that as well. He's the first guy I've gone out with that doesn't mind that I'm so work-obsessed. He accepts I don't want to see him every night and that I work most weekends. He's not a hindrance to my career, he's a help. I find I'm using him as a sounding board for my ideas and he's as excited about me starting up on my own as I am. The sex is great but I think good sex is easy to find. It's the partnership thing I'm most impressed with.

I'm more vulnerable with him than I have been in the past. One night I got drunk and told him all my fears about the child thing: worried that if I have kids, I'll hate the effect they have on my life, worried that if I don't, I'll regret it later. The next morning, I was so embarrassed. But instead of making me feel exposed, he said he felt the same things. He's 45 and though he doesn't have a time limit on his fertility, wonders about all that too. Don't panic: we've only been going out a month and aren't going to do anything rash. But I think when you've had a few long-term relationships under your belt, you recognize early on which are going to be special and skip through those initial stages more quickly. This is one of the special ones.

Month six

Work's going well, my relationship's going well. Life's settled in a nice, easy, contentedness which I've never experienced before. I have no idea whether Martin and I will be together by the time this book is published. I'd like to think so but won't fall in a heap if we're not either. We've had our fair share of arguments (bloody feisty ones, too!) but more than our fair share of good times. The best thing about it is, for once, I feel I'm getting the best of both worlds. My career is enhanced by my relationship because Martin's so supportive; my relationship is enhanced by my career because I'm smart enough to help him with his too. I guess what you can take from my story is this: it is possible to have both.

Author's note: Jodie and Martin are still going strong.

Carla

Carla is 25 and was born in Italy. She went to Australia when she was ten years old and married a year ago. She is currently trying to fall pregnant.

Month one

I am, perhaps, a typical Italian girl who's grown up in Australia. I've adopted Australian ways but retained things from my own culture that I truly believe in. I love my parents and my husband and I spend most weekends at their home. My husband's parents live in Italy but we call them on weekends so we're close to them also, just in a different way. My parents' opinion of me is very important, even though I'm now married. They strongly influence me, but in a good way. I respect them and I respect their advice and opinions. I ask them, 'What should I do about this or that?' and nearly always follow their advice. My Australian girlfriends don't understand this. They think it's weak, that I should grow up and distance myself, make my own decisions. I think, *Why not benefit from their wisdom? They love me, they've been through what I'm now going through and I know they won't lead me astray*. I consider this sensible. But I have a different value system to my friends. They believe they are different to their parents, that a generation between them means they can't understand. I don't believe this is true, but I accept their views and don't criticize. I wish they would accept mine as readily.

My Australian friends think I married too young. My Italian friends and family believe I married late. Such is the curse of being a little of one, a little of another. I think I married at the right time. My Australian friends think my husband Marco is chauvinistic. My Italian friends think he is too Australian. He's like me: a little of both. He is warm and supportive, but likes a woman to be a woman. I put on make-up and dress up so I look pretty when he walks in the door after work. He appreciates it and compliments me. I like this, I don't find it demeaning or unliberated.

I consider myself as liberated as my friends: if my husband beat me or cheated or treated me badly, I would leave. But my husband and I still believe it's the woman who should be the one to look after the home and cook the meals and have babies and look after them too. I try to make my friends understand that I'm not being forced into this role, I want it. I like it. It makes me very happy and him too. So what's the problem?

Month two

I am trying to fall pregnant. We stopped using contraception two months ago but nothing has happened yet. My mother is already looking anxious but she has no reason to be. I've read good books on pregnancy and know it takes longer, and neither Marco or I are interested in turning sex into something we have to do at a certain time. We're just having sex like we normally do and waiting to see. Sex is different because we're now trying to make a baby. Marco is more affectionate and tender during it. Afterward, he cuddles me and says, 'There! That made a baby!' I love him. He's like a man and a boy all in the same person. At home, he's affectionate and playful. At work, he's boss and people are a little scared of him. He's got a temper and can't understand that Australians aren't as volatile as we are and take his temper very seriously. If Marco and I argue, we shout and throw things and slam doors but ten minutes later, it's forgotten. I'm used to it but my friends aren't. Once, a girlfriend was here when Marco came storming in and she practically hid under the table when he shouted at me. But it was nothing. He was upset because the fridge was empty and I hadn't been shopping. There was nothing for him to eat and he was hungry, that's all. My friend told me his behaviour was unacceptable. That if the fridge was empty, *he* should go out and do the shopping rather than shout at me about it. But it's my job to make sure he has things to eat. His to make money for us. I'd shout at him if he didn't do his job; it's fair he shouts at me when I don't do mine. Besides, it only lasted five minutes.

The same friend is worried that when I have a child, my husband won't help me. She means changing nappies and helping with housework. I don't need or want help with that. What I want Marco to do is play with the baby and give it lots of love and attention. I know he'll do that and I think that's more important.

Month three

My best Australian girlfriend is sick. She has glandular fever which means she can't work or look after herself. Her family live interstate and I'm worried about her. She doesn't have a husband and I don't understand why her parents don't come to look after her. She says it's because they've both got careers and can't afford the time away. I find that hard to relate to. If Marco's parents, who live in Italy, found out he was sick and he didn't have me, his mother would come over immediately. I asked Marco if she could stay with us until she gets better (she's the girlfriend who thinks he bullies me). He knows she doesn't like him but said fine. So I offered but she refused. I guess I'll just help by taking her food.

Marco and I have sex lots but still nothing. What started as a 'let's wait and see and not stress' thing, has turned into pressure. My mother asks me every day if anything has happened; my father keeps telling me not to worry – I'm Italian! Of course I'll be able to have children! I wish maybe I hadn't told my parents we're trying. But they kept asking and asking when we would have children and I thought this would stop them nagging me. It hasn't. It's made it worse.

Month four

Still no baby. I went to my gynaecologist who suggested Marco and I get some simple fertility tests done. Marco won't hear of it. I know why. He couldn't bear it if there was something wrong with him. He wouldn't be a 'real man' if there was something wrong with his sperm. For once, I agree with my girlfriends that he's carrying the macho thing too far. Another part of me worries that there's something wrong with me. If I couldn't provide Marco with children, I would be devastated. I know he loves me but I know he also wants a family. A friend of mine, her husband left her when he found out she couldn't bear children. She understood but now can't find another husband. All men want children. I would feel like such a failure as a woman and a wife if I couldn't give Marco a son.

Month five

My period was late. I told Marco and he immediately rang our families to announce I was pregnant. I wasn't. My period was two days late, that was all. It really upset me. I told Marco he was a stupid pig for doing that. I made him ring everyone back and went to the bedroom and cried and cried. He came in afterward and said he was sorry and we both cried together. I asked him, 'What if we can't have babies? Will you still want to be married to me?' He told me I was crazy, that he wanted children badly but would never choose them over me. I told him I was frightened there was something wrong with me and he said he was worried there was something wrong with him. I asked him again if he'd come with me to get fertility tests done and this time he agreed.

We got the tests done yesterday and now wait, impatiently, for the results. Marco is quiet and anxious. We didn't tell our parents we'd had the tests because we didn't want to worry them.

Month six

Celebration! Both Marco and I are given the all clear! We're both normal and healthy and all we need now to make babies is patience. We are both so happy and the relief is enormous. In a sense though, I'm glad we had problems and I didn't fall pregnant straight away. Our marriage is better for what happened. I feel closer to Marco, knowing that he must truly love me to want to stay with me even if I couldn't have babies. There's a tenderness and togetherness that wasn't there before. We are now relaxed and making love happily again. My parents still nag, nag, nag, but it's okay now. I don't mind because I think it will happen soon.

Author's note: Carla is now two months pregnant.

Brad

Brad, 28, works in his family's business. He is single and enjoying living in a city of 'desperate thirtysomethings'.

Month one

My life is pretty routine. It has to be because I work 6.30 am till 6.30 pm, six days a week. Monday nights I spend getting over the weekend, Tuesday nights I play sport and have a few beers with the boys afterward. Wednesday nights, who knows, Thursday maybe I'll see my semi-girlfriend. Friday night is boys' night. No girls allowed. We get on the piss, perve, play pool, tell lies, tell jokes, have a punt. Saturday night and Sunday day is girlfriend time, usually spent seeing her friends who bore me stupid because all they do is talk about work. Sunday night I'll go drinking again. The boys always get priority.

I wrote 'semi-girlfriend' because my girlfriend's a headcase. Headcases always seem to find me, I attract them. This one can't handle her grog and she rings me three, four times a day at work. She'll say, 'I love you . . .' and it's like, 'Look, can this wait? I'm busy here . . .' Every time we go out, she gets a few drinks into her and then she's off. I don't mind a woman with a temper – it shows she's got guts and soul – but Jesus!

Month two

The boys and I moved flats last weekend. As we were unloading our stuff, this old biddy from the unit next door said, 'I hope you're quiet. We've had a lot of rowdy people up there in No 9.' Like, yeah right, lady, we'll try to be quiet. The first night, I had a blue with my girlfriend down at the pub. She lost it again and I told her to wake up to herself, leave me alone and don't come near me. Half an hour later, I'm at home, watching TV and I hear her outside, yelling obscenities at me at the top of her voice. I'm like, 'The neighbours are going to *love* this.' I got her inside, made her sleep on the couch and told her not to come near me. This is the kind of girl who'd get up in the middle of the night and slash your penis off. I'm not joking, she's seriously weird. She's a psycho. But I woke up later that night to find her mouth wrapped around my penis telling me how much she loved me. A great way to wake up, but it's over.

She wanted to be friends and I thought: why would I want a woman as a friend? What have guys got in common with women, really? I'm 28, I play sport, I punt. What would we talk about if we weren't screwing? I've got my mates, why bother? Don't get me wrong, I love women. I grew up in a household of women: my Mum, my sister and my Nan. I'm good friends with all of them – I just don't need any more female company.

Month three

I've been in love once, when I was 18. Her name was Nicole. When I met her, she was going out with someone else and so was I, so we'd see each other on the sly, whenever we could. She'd come over every Friday night while my other girlfriend was at work. I'd go to sleep with one girlfriend, wake up with the other: Nicole would come over and leave through the night, then Trish would come home so I'd wake up with her. It was forbidden, which made it better.

Nicole had 'it': everybody's got someone who does it for them. She had the body, she was great in bed, she was funny. She was also selfish and a bitch, but I'm selfish and an arsehole so we got on well. We were a good couple. We'd walk in somewhere and kick arse all night. We went out secretly for four years, then moved in together for a year. I loved her but I found out she'd been screwing someone else. She did the sly on me. I lost it because it fucking hurt. I was doing it tough money-wise, so we decided to keep living together until the lease ran out. That was hard. It was bad.

I haven't been in love since then but I say it. Girls say, 'I love you,' a month into the relationship. I'll say, 'I love you,' back. I do love them in a way, but not the way they mean it. I never lie to people but to women? That's different. I have no qualms about it. I just say whatever it takes to get whatever I want. I told you, I'm an arsehole.

I was an idealist, now I'm a pragmatist. I look at other people rock through relationships and I think, *I don't need this. I've got enough hassles with work, let alone a relationship.* I guess a part of me is scared of getting hurt, but I think it's more to do with not meeting the right girl. All I want to do with my life is meet a really nice girl, have kids, have fun. Who's my ideal girl? I like women with brains, but they're smart enough to steer clear of me. She can't be stupid though. She's got to be a good sort, she's got to be good in bed. If she's not good in bed, there's no point to it really. She's got to be independent. She's got to like sport. She's got to get on with my friends and family. And she's got to let me have at least three nights a week out with the boys. If I met a girl like that there's no way I'd cheat. Not at all. Not if I was totally in love with the chick.

Month four

I'm seeing a girl who's a good sort but all she does is keep up this constant, inane chatter about her career. She's a model/actress/dental nurse. Another nutter – and so dumb!

She rang me one night – for the sixth time that day – while I was cooking dinner and it was really giving me the shits so I hung up on her, or at least thought I did. The phone in the lounge room was off the hook and she stayed on the line because she could hear everything we were saying. I'm saying to my flatmates, 'That stupid bird. She's driving me mental. If she wasn't a dental nurse, I wouldn't even talk to her. I just want my teeth done for free.' Then we started talking about one of her friends who we all want to screw and what we'd do if we could get our hands on her. About 20 minutes into the conversation I hear, 'I can hear you,' from the phone receiver. I hung it up immediately and thought of what to do next. I decided to pretend we'd done it deliberately. Like, we knew she could hear us and were trying to stir her. She fell for it. Like I said: dumb.

Month five

There was another girl I liked. She was lovely but not a good sort at all. Once, on Valentine's Day, she booked us into a really nice hotel as a surprise, spoilt me the whole weekend and paid for the lot. That was the nicest thing a woman's ever done for me. No girl's ever paid for me when we go out for dinner. I always pay if I'm earning more. If she earnt more, we'd go halves. But I'd never expect her to pay for me. It doesn't sound like it but I do treat women nicely when I like them. Flowers now and then. Take her out to dinner all the time. Go to the movies. Hold her hand.

But it's too much fun being single right now because this is a city of desperate thirtysomethings. Desperate unless she's a good sort, of course, then she'll get the pick of the room. I like older women, though. They know what they want, they don't giggle every five seconds. They're good in bed, comfortable in bed. It doesn't worry me if a woman's older than me. I don't think many guys are hung up on age these days. It's 1999: women can have babies when they're 43. Age is irrelevant.

Women should know that if they're a good sort, men find them unattainable. Which is silly because if you've got the gift of the gab, you can get them all. I don't usually approach women, I wait for them to approach me. One of my mates, he's always saying to girls, 'Hi. Want a fuck?' Nine times out of ten, he'll get slapped across the face. But the other time, he'll drag something. Some of the girls I've seen come out of his bedroom are horrendous. Another friend walks around all night looking at the good sorts, then at 3 am he'd say, 'I've got to find a pig.' Because he knows, the uglier the girl, the more likely she is to put out that night. I don't do one-night stands, I don't like them. I've had about five in my whole life.

Good sorts are different. But you don't have to be good-looking to be one. It's about sex appeal. You can have a very ordinary girl who's got sex appeal, *oozes* it, and she's gorgeous. It's the way she holds herself, the way she walks, the way she'll give some other guy the brush, the way she looks at you.

Month six

I can't meet a nice girl with my lifestyle. I work 70 hours a week. When I'm not working, I'm either playing sport, watching sport, drinking or carrying on like a yahoo. There aren't too many women around here who'd put up with that.

But I'm not chauvinist. Relationships now aren't like what our parents had. They're more like a business partnership. You can't expect a woman to come home from working all day and cook the meal, and do all your washing – it doesn't work like that these days. Most men my age know how to do all that shit anyway. Plenty are better cooks than women. I love cooking. I'll come home, cook for the boys, put the washing on. But I never iron. If I have to go somewhere and we're going out with her friends, the chick has to iron whatever I'm going to wear.

We still have roles, though. It's still the guy who has to put the garbage out, the guy who has to kill the spiders, the guy who has to go around and hassle the neighbour. The girl still buys the furniture and pictures to hang and makes the place look nice. Blokes aren't interested in that stuff. But if my woman was earning more than me and we had kids, I'd stay home and look after them. No drama at all. I'd love it. Kids are easy. I think they're great. Every guy wants kids, you've got to have someone to carry on the name. And speaking of names, why don't women take the man's name any more? I'd take it as an insult if a girl didn't take my name in marriage. We can't give up everything. We've given up being the breadwinner. We've given up coming home to dinner on the table. At least take the guy's name, for God's sake.

I don't know if I'll find the relationship I want. I'll probably end up marrying some scrubber, we'll have two or three kids then three or four years later, we'll get divorced. Just like my parents. I hope I'm wrong but it worries me I'm going to be right.

Index